THE MEMORY EFFECT

THE MEMORY EFFECT

The Remediation of Memory in Literature and Film

Russell J.A. Kilbourn
Eleanor Ty, *editors*

WILFRID LAURIER
UNIVERSITY PRESS

This book has been published with the help of a grant from the Canadian Federation for the Humanities and Social Sciences, through the Awards to Scholarly Publications Program, using funds provided by the Social Sciences and Humanities Research Council of Canada. Wilfrid Laurier University Press acknowledges the support of the Canada Council for the Arts for our publishing program. We acknowledge the financial support of the Government of Canada through the Canada Book Fund for our publishing activities. Funding provided by the Government of Ontario and the Ontario Arts Council. This work was supported by the Research Support Fund.

LIBRARY AND ARCHIVES CANADA CATALOGUING IN PUBLICATION

Title: The memory effect : the remediation of memory in literature and film / Russell J.A. Kilbourn, Eleanor Ty, editors.
Names: Kilbourn, Russell J. A. (Russell James Angus), 1964- editor. | Ty, Eleanor Rose, 1958- editor.
Description: Paperback reprint. Originally published 2013. | Essays based on the international conference, "Memory, Mediation, Remediation: Memory in Literature and Film," held at Wilfrid Laurier University, Waterloo, in April 2011. | Includes bibliographical references and index.
Identifiers: Canadiana 20240358570 | ISBN 9781771126694 (softcover)
Subjects: LCSH: Memory in literature—Congresses. | LCSH: Memory in motion pictures—Congresses. | LCSH: Collective memory—Congresses. | LCSH: Mass media and culture—Congresses. Classification: LCC P94 .M46 2024 | DDC 791.43/653—dc23

Cover design by Heng Wee Tan. Cover image: *Ancestry* (mixed media on paper), by Gloria Kagawa, reproduced courtesy of the artist. Visit www.gloriakagawa.com. Text design by James Leahy.

© 2013 Wilfrid Laurier University Press
Waterloo, Ontario, Canada
www.wlupress.wlu.ca

Every reasonable effort has been made to acquire permission for copyrighted material used in this text, and to acknowledge all such indebtedness accurately. Any errors and omissions called to the publisher's attention will be corrected in future printings.

No part of this publication may be reproduced, stored in a retrieval system, or transmitted, in any form or by any means, without the prior written consent of the publisher or a licence from the Canadian Copyright Licensing Agency (Access Copyright). For an Access Copyright licence, visit http://www.accesscopyright.ca or call toll free to 1-800-893-5777.

Contents

Acknowledgements vii

Part I: Memory Studies: Theories, Changes, and Challenges

1 Developments in Memory Studies and Twentieth- and Twenty-First-Century Literature and Film 3
Russell J.A. Kilbourn and Eleanor Ty

2 "Joy in Repetition"; or, The Significance of Seriality in Processes of Memory and (Re-)Mediation 37
Sabine Sielke

3 Hirsch, Sebald, and the Uses and Limits of Postmemory 51
Kathy Behrendt

Part II: Literature and the Power of Cultural Memory/ Memorializing

4 British Propaganda and the Construction of Female Mourning in the First World War 71
Sarah Henstra

5 "Rhetorical Metatarsals": Bone Memory in Dionne Brand's *Ossuaries* 93
Tanis MacDonald

6 Mediation and Remediation in Carlos Fuentes's *The Old Gringo* 107
John Dean

Part III: Recuperating Lives: Memory and Life Writing

7 Resisting Holocaust Memory: Recuperating a Compromised Life 125
Marlene Kadar

8 "In Auschwitz There Is a Great House": The Location of Memory and Identity in the Roma *Porrajmos* (Devouring) or Holocaust 143
Sheelagh Russell-Brown

9 Autobiography and the Validation of Memory: Neil M. Gunn's *The Atom of Delight* 161
K.J. Keir

Part IV: Cinematic Remediations: Memory and History

10 *La Jetée* and *12 Monkeys*: Memory and History at Odds 175
Amresh Sinha

11 The Traces of "A Half-Remembered Dream": Christopher Nolan's *Inception* (2010), Wong Kar-wai's *2046* (2004), and the Memory Film 195
Anders Bergstrom

12 "You must remember this …": Watching *Casablanca* with Marc Augé 211
Graeme Gilloch

13 The Cinema of Simulation: Hyper-Histories and (Un)Popular Memory in *The Good German* (2006) and *Inglourious Basterds* (2009) 225
Stefan Sereda

Part V: Multimedia Interventions: Television, Video, and Collective Memory

14 The *Heritage Minutes*: Nostalgia, Nationalism, and Canadian Collective Memory 249
Erin Peters

15 Disaster and Trauma in *Rescue Me*, *Saving Grace*, and *Treme*: Commercial Television's Contributions to Ideas about Memorials 267
John McCullough

16 Creative Re-enactment in the Films and Videos of Omer Fast 287
Kate Warren

Works Cited 307
About the Contributors 335
Index 339

Acknowledgements

We would like to thank our families, friends, and colleagues for their encouragement and support over the past couple of years, and particularly through the research, writing, and editing of these essays. We would also like to thank the editorial staff at Wilfrid Laurier University Press for their invaluable assistance and support.

The editors are grateful for the financial contribution of the Social Sciences and Humanities Research Council of Canada, which awarded us with a Knowledge Mobilization grant, enabling us to hold "Memory, Mediation, Remediation: An International Conference on Memory in Literature and Film" at Wilfrid Laurier University from 28 to 30 April 2011 (conference reviewed in *Memory Studies* 5.4 [October 2012]: 497–9). We are also very grateful for support from Laurier's Office of Development and Alumni Relations; the Centennial Celebrations Committee; the Office of the Dean of Arts; and the Department of English and Film Studies.

Alexis Motuz provided invaluable assistance with editing and the collation of bibliographical references. Victoria Kennedy was the student administrator and conference organizer par excellence. We are also grateful for the help of these students at the conference: Kaitlin Tremblay, Anders Bergstrom, Stefan Sereda, Kevin Hatch, James Hrivnak, Stephanie Butler, T.A. Pattinson, Nadia Suihong Van, Nike Abbott, and Sylvia Terzian.

Part I

MEMORY STUDIES: THEORIES, CHANGES, AND CHALLENGES

1

Developments in Memory Studies and Twentieth- and Twenty-First-Century Literature and Film

Russell J.A. Kilbourn and Eleanor Ty

Introduction

This collection[1] came about in response to the following question: How do changing ideas of memory affect how we think about *texts*, whether literary, filmic, or in some other medium? By framing an approach to memory informed by post-structuralist theories of the subject, language, and representation, we assert that memory, like history, is understood to be a discursive construct. This position, which in the twenty-first century sounds outdated, remains in our view the most radical and therefore the most valuable in terms of the insight it allows into the ontology and epistemology of memory today, insofar as this is *not* an understanding of memory as discursive-textual construct in a second-order sense, as in classical or early modern conceptions of an "art of memory" distinct from memory as a "natural" faculty or capacity of the mind. Classical theorists such as Cicero saw memory as a rhetorical category, and artificial memory therefore as something to be *learned* through the mental construction of a memory palace inside one's head. This pre-modern model is predicated upon the two longest-standing metaphors of memory as storage place and as system of inscription (see, e.g., Yates, Carruthers, Frow), by which relatively complex assemblages of information can be deposited, recollected, reordered, and reproduced at will. Centuries of cultural and technological—not to speak of cognitive and neurological—development have resulted in a world in which it is now possible to walk around with a USB key or "flash drive" in one's pocket or briefcase, containing as much information as the Library of Congress—enough data, in short, to consume several lifetimes of learning or of practical application. For most of us today this is what memory is, in a first-order sense, or rather in a sense that transcends any "natural"-technical binary: an external, prosthetic storage tool, operating on its own or as part of another machine (camera, laptop, cellphone, tablet, e-reader), entirely distinct from the "natural" human sensorium, the physically embodied mental "self," yet already indispensible, a crucial component in what is emerging as a wholly new kind of cyber- or post-human interface, yielding never-before-possible subjectivities and modalities of identity. This, at least, is the utopian scenario; a more cynical view sees in this tendency the colonization of memory as an always already artificial technology, but where, in a symptomatically postmodern irony, the loss of the distinction between "natural" and technically enhanced memory is to be nostalgically mourned. We would not be the first to point out that for many people today the "natural" memory is employed primarily in the second-order task of storing and retrieving (or not) the knowledge of how to retrieve the mind-bogglingly vast quantities of information now available via various digital media platforms.

Memory Studies Today: Humanities and Cultural Research

As we began writing this introduction, German scholar Astrid Erll's book, *Memory in Culture*, appeared. The first three sections of Erll's succinct introduction address the key questions "Why 'memory'?," "Why now?" and "What is meant by 'memory'?"

"Why" and "what" indeed. It is fast becoming a commonplace to point out that memory today is a hot topic, as it has been for some time. As Erll, among many others, observes, a preoccupation with memory suffuses contemporary culture, in the form of an ever-increasing calendar of national, ethnic, and religious commemorations, especially (for Americans) in the wake of 11 September 2001. Memory has a prominent place in a variety of cultural discourses, populist and official, fictive and documentarist, right wing and left (Erll 1). Indeed, memory is precisely one of those modes, nodes, or nexuses where otherwise disparate or contradictory discourses intersect. Therefore we include here a "brief history of memory," focusing on the major developments in theories of memory in modernity, always in relation to shifts in the ways in which memory has been conceived and represented in literature and film in the twentieth century—shifts that have proven to be as prescient as they are symptomatic.

What we call here for shorthand "modern memory" has deeply premodern, indeed ancient, roots. But if we are to focus on theories of memory connected to modern notions of self or consciousness in the arts and sciences—where the interpenetration of these two realms or discourses marks the condition of possibility of the modern—then we have to begin with the major Romantic theories of memory, most famously perhaps Wordsworth's theory of poetic composition born out of "emotion recollected in tranquility," a far more complex notion than is often recognized. We include poets and novelists in this lineage alongside philosophers and theorists precisely because of this volume's expansive, interdisciplinary focus. If there is one precept standing behind our general approach to memory, it is that whatever "truth" of memory we might discern can only be located in the interstices, the interfaces between and among discourses, disciplines, areas and realms of thought, whether scientific, humanist, deconstructive, or other. That said, there are two main strands of memory theory for twentieth-century modernity: the Marxist-psychoanalytic and the Nietzschean-deconstructive. For the purposes of brevity we will focus here on the interrelations of a representative handful of the main theorists of memory emerging from one (or sometimes both) of these traditions: Henri Bergson, Marcel Proust, and Sigmund Freud. While there are many other contenders (such as Walter Benjamin; see Amresh Sinha's essay in this volume), these three (all men)—a philosopher, a novelist, and the "father" of psychoanalysis—represent the most influential thinking about memory as it manifests in a distinctively modern context. On this basis we will take a few pages to elaborate upon what are for this volume a few of the most pertinent questions and issues around memory theory in relation to the theme or problem of subjectivity in a post-cinematic era, in which film and literature persist as significant cultural modalities.

Together with more contemporary authors, such as Vladimir Nabokov and W.G. Sebald (see below), Marcel Proust stands as a bona fide theorist of memory, despite his decision to explore these questions through fictional narrative discourse. The opening chapter of the monumental *In Search of Lost Time* (1913–23) presents one of the key theories of modern memory. Here Proust distinguishes between "'the memory of the intellect,' or what he called voluntary memory, and involuntary memory, which exists 'beyond the reach of the intellect,' but can enter consciousness as a result of a contingent sensuous association" (Bennett, Grossberg, and Morris 215). In the famous passage from *Swann's Way*, the narrator-protagonist recounts the experience of recognizing the operation of "involuntary memory": "Undoubtedly what is thus palpitating in the depths of my being must be the image, the visual memory which, being linked to this taste [of lime tea and petite madeleine], is trying to follow it into my conscious mind. And suddenly the memory revealed itself. The taste was that of the little piece of madeleine which on Sunday mornings ... my Aunt Leonie used to give me" (53–54). The sensory and sensuous flavour of tea and cake heralds what Proust calls "the vast structure of recollection" (54). For Proust, as for Bergson, memory is immaterial: the memory as such is not contained "within" the cake or its flavour; the madeleine is the precipitant or prompter of what for Proust is memory's complete and authentic unfolding. "Through involuntary memory, the past is brought into the present and the passage of clock time is suspended in an awareness of the duration of inner psychological time. With pure memory the totality of our past is continually pressing forward so as to insert the largest possible part of itself into the present action" (Ward 11). In one of modernity's greatest refutations of memory's failure, the authentic (visual) memory is "resurrected" through consumption of the cake, which prompts recollection of the past in its authentic wholeness. This is memory's "redemptive" potential: as Jeffrey Pence puts it, the capacity to "make good" real or imagined losses (243). Proust's "involuntary memory," unlike Freud's notion of repression, is able to release its contents to a conscious (and pleasurable) purview via the intercession of the precipitating factor that, in another context, Russell Kilbourn has labelled the "madeleine object."[2]

Henri Bergson's significance for modern theories and practices of memory comes largely through Proust's extraordinarily influential novel. Anticipating Proust's famous distinction between voluntary and involuntary memory, Bergson gives us a phenomenological focus on memory (and therefore time) that is experienced subjectively in the nexus of body and mind, or consciousness, reflectively and affectively organized, not so much in actual empirical-cognitive as in fictive-textual terms. Bergson theorizes two kinds of memory: (1) "instinctual recognition," or habit-memory, and (2) what he calls "attentive recollection" (in an anticipation of Proust's voluntary memory). "Unlike habit ... [attentive] recollection involves an active effort of mind" (Martin-Jones 51).[3] According to Bergson, "the memories which we acquire voluntarily by repetition are rare and exceptional. On the contrary, the recording, by memory, of facts and images unique in their kind takes place at every moment of duration" (Bergson 1988, 83). This ongoing recording of memory-images, accumulating within the body, enabling us to function in our world, is of particular interest to us here. To fully appreciate the import of Bergson's ideas for contemporary film studies, for example, it is necessary to take a brief detour through Gilles Deleuze's two-volume work on cinema. In *Cinema I* Deleuze in effect adapts the two types of Bergsonian memory (instinctual recognition versus attentive recollection) to elaborate what he calls the movement-image, the approach to filmic narration one finds in the classical Hollywood style and whose apotheosis is in the contemporary action genre, where the subject's continuous movement through space, instantiated in montage, dominates form and theme alike (see Kilbourn 2010). In his explication of Deleuze in the context of national identity and narrative time, David Martin-Jones shows how Bergson's dynamically spatial conception of time can be used to better understand a film such as Hitchcock's *Vertigo* (1958). Martin-Jones invokes Bergson's "cone of time" (fig. I.1) which figures time in a dynamic and linear manner, the subject a point positioned on the plane of the present, the past radiating back or away from this point, in an ever-larger cone comprised of a potentially infinite number of planes of the past; slices of past time, constellated by memory-images, any of which the subject may recall, depending upon his bodily attitude at any given moment. Deleuze translates this notion into the quasi-literary construct of a fork—or forks—in time. Martin-Jones links this structure to Hitchcock's famous vertigo shot (fig. I.2) as a visual-cinematic realization of this model (of memory) in illusory 3D.

This shot, the result of a simultaneous forward zoom/reverse track, results in a visually dynamic, destabilizing, strikingly graphic externalization of the protagonist's interior subjective state—as if he were looking back down the cone of time and feeling memory's vertiginous pull. Viewed, as it is filmed, horizontally, the vertigo shot of course "reads" vertically, and is contrasted in the film, as Martin-Jones observes, with the swirling horizontality of the complementary shot of Scottie and Judy in the hotel room scene, after her transformation back into Madeleine (Martin-Jones 55–56), the film's doubled structure redoubled microcosmically in this key 360-degree shot (fig. I.3), which is also a flashback.[4]

In Martin-Jones's reading, these two special-effect shots parallel the two types of image in Deleuze (Martin-Jones 58): the time-image and the movement-image, respectively. With respect to memory (in Bergson's terms) these are incompatible: reflective memory is the property of the time-image, and thus art film style, while unreflective habit-memory is the property of the movement-image, and thus classical style.[5] What is curious about *Vertigo* in this view is the manner in which Hitchcock combines the

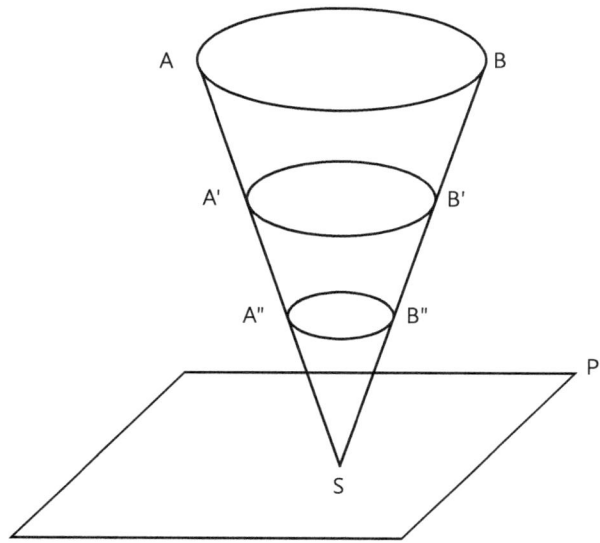

Figure I.1 Bergson's "cone of time" (*Matter and Memory*, 1895)

unreflective action of the movement image (when Scottie is able to act, as it were without thinking, as when he saves Madeleine from drowning in San Francisco Bay), with the reflective perception of the time-image, in which time and the past make themselves visible, in which memory comes into operation, and in which Scottie therefore falls into passive victimhood, succumbing to vertigo. Thus we see how *Vertigo* merges a kind of "art film" sensibility with Hitchcock's recognized mastery of classical style, in a sort of allegory of what Deleuze calls the crisis of the movement-image "as it neared the realization of its own completion" (Martin-Jones 58), registering the emergence of the time-image in postwar art cinema.[6]

In order to underline the significance of this Deleuzian–Bergsonian approach to understanding the representation and significance of memory in film narrative, especially in the more popular cinema that is the ongoing legacy of the "movement-image" in its increasing *intensification* (to borrow David Bordwell's term), we would point out that the principles Martin-Jones identifies in *Vertigo* are also found at work in many contemporary films. We will cite one example, the opening scene of *The Bourne*

Fig. I.2 The "Vertigo shot" (image courtesy of the Kobal Collection)

Ultimatum (2007, Paul Greengrass), the third instalment of the "Jason Bourne" series. As the titular hero breaks into a pharmacy to procure painkillers for a bullet wound, he experiences a kind of mnemic hallucination, rendered as a subjective flashback initiated by a close-up of a tap dripping into a bloody sink. This elides over a cut with the obviously traumatic memory of his initiation a few years before into Treadstone, the CIA's

Fig. I.3 The 360-degree shot (image courtesy of the Kobal Collection)

top-secret anti-terrorist program. Among other things this sequence forcefully and economically illustrates the same point Martin-Jones makes with the example of the 360-degree flashback shot in *Vertigo*: just as Scotty, as he kisses Madeleine, cannot help but find himself again in the Mission stable setting, because that was where they first kissed (Martin-Jones 56), when Bourne finds himself bent over a bloodied sink, tap a-drip, he is visited by memory-images that come flashing back, out of the recent past, triggered not just by specific objects, sights, or sounds around him but by his very bodily position or attitude: Bergson's unreflective habit memory in action. This is the film's founding conceit: suffering from amnesia, Bourne discovers an unconscious "body-memory" of deadly skills well before he recovers his former identity. Thus Bourne himself, embodied by the actor Matt Damon, becomes another memory-image for the viewer, struggling in a directly analogous manner, not with PTSD *per se* but with its traumatic symptoms: the memory-images that in some cases flash up so quickly as to be indiscernible in a casual viewing.[7] At the same time one needs to be aware that such paradigmatic instances of contemporary popular cultural identities are problematic not least in their ongoing hypostatization of an ex-nominative masculine subject distinguished by an absence of "marked" identity attributes: whiteness, heterosexuality, and so on.

The other feature of contemporary theories of memory to which the Bourne film draws attention in an instructive way is an apparent contradiction between Cathy Caruth's highly influential writings on trauma and PTSD, and current memory science. Recent memory studies can be represented here in the following passage from José Van Dijck's analysis of *Eternal Sunshine of the Spotless Mind*: "memories effectively are rewritten each time they are activated; instead of recalling a memory that has been stored some time ago, the brain is forging it all over again in a new associative context. Every memory, therefore, is a new memory because it is shaped (or reconsolidated) by the changes that have happened to our brain since the memory last occurred to us" (Van Dijck 32). In contrast to this is Caruth's contention that "to be traumatized is precisely to be possessed by an image or event"—that is, an *image* of the event, a memory-image. Therefore, "the returning traumatic [image] ... cannot be understood in terms of any wish or unconscious meaning, but is, purely and inexplicably, *the literal return of the event against the will of the one it inhabits*" (Caruth "From Trauma and Experience" 200; my emphasis). And it is this literality, moreover, "that possesses the receiver and resists psychoanalytic interpretation and cure" (201). Contemporary psychoanalytic theory is thus at odds with memory science on the question of the relative stability or fixity of the memory-image—not to speak of the question of the primacy of the memory as image over the role played by other sensory data in a given memory's full dimensionality. The point to be derived from the Bourne example, however, is that popular cultural representations of memory at work—whether traumatic or otherwise—tend to privilege the visual representation of memory as static, repeatable quantity and quality. It is only when one moves beyond the bounds of overtly commercial cultural fare that one finds exceptions to this rule.

A different perspective on contemporary trauma theory emphasizes the distinction between "traumatic memory" and "narrative memory": the former "merely and unconsciously *repeats* the past," whereas the latter "*narrates the past as past*" (Leys 105), the "goal of therapy [being] to convert traumatic memory into narrative memory by getting the patient to recount his or her history ... so that it can be integrated into [her/his] life story" (105). Thus overcoming trauma entails turning trauma's "static" images into words, a process that underpins the kind of work on life writing, autobiography, and so on, that is reflected in this volume. We contend that literary approaches to (understanding) real-world trauma prove more valuable than their more clinical models. To be able to recount one's trauma as a story, in other words, means to be on the way to being healthy again. Whether or not this is always true is one thing, but it remains the case in this model that the skills required to analyze and interpret a narrative text are the same as those necessary to diagnose and if not cure then understand another person's traumatic experience. Such a seeming reduction of subjectivity to textuality (not to speak of the pathologization of the act of narrative fabulation) is in fact a renewed recognition of the very old idea, dating back to St. Augustine at least, that, while it is impossible to know the mind of another, it is possible to read and understand a text that s/he writes in order to communicate or represent her/himself.

Among the literate of late antiquity, verbal texts mediated between a nascent subjective interiority and the radical, absolute exteriority of divinity (transcendent otherness) in relation to which the self was constituted. It is therefore necessary in a contemporary context to attempt an articulation of the Augustinian idea of mediating the self–other relation through texts with something like the Deleuzian notion that cinema as thinking (or as "philosophy") is itself an "epistemology" (see Kovács 40–44). Rather than go so far as to propose another Deleuzian reading of film, we are aligning ourselves with the tradition from Augustine to contemporary social constructivism which holds that one cannot know the mind of the other except through texts. Indeed, in the most radical view, there is no mind, only text, just as there is no memory without media. To quote Astrid Erll again: "the medium is the memory" (115).

In this context it is necessary to acknowledge the other, major critique mounted against Caruth's highly influential work on trauma for literary studies, exemplified in Ruth Leys's more clinically rigorous trauma theory, which rejects the notion, implicit in Caruth's post-structuralist-inflected approach, that traumatic memories may constitute transferable content between one subject and another, regardless of actual experience. According to Leys, Caruth tends to "dilute and generalize the notion of trauma: in her account the experience (or nonexperience) of trauma is characterized as something that can be shared by victims and nonvictims alike, and the unbearable sufferings of the survivor as a pathos that can and must be appropriated by others" (Leys 305). This is an extremely important observation in the context of Humanities memory theories predicated on the potential of fictional narrative to communicate something of another's experience, regardless of the presence or absence of a common life-world; indeed, this effect is arguably all the stronger when the reader or viewer shares nothing with the writer or filmmaker but an interest in fathoming otherness in some degree. Having made this point, it is also necessary to observe that this is the most problematic aspect of influential theories of artificial memory, from Alison Landsberg's "prosthetic memory" to Marianne Hirsch's notion of "post-memory"—in other words, theories that allow for or even demand the taking upon oneself of the other's memories and therefore her/his experiences, be they painful and traumatic or otherwise.

Sigmund Freud's contribution to contemporary understandings of memory is complicated and widespread, for he, like Plato long before, considers memory in different texts in various aspects, always (unlike Plato) with the question of the individual (paradigmatically masculine) psyche foremost in his consideration. And also, as with Plato, Freud offers more than one "theory" of memory. For Freud, memory is a key component of identity, perhaps even the fundamental one, lurking behind such crucial notions as repression, neurosis, and trauma. The fact is that there would be no lingering symptoms of the Oedipal crisis—and its resulting subjectivity—without memory there in the first place to provide the conditions for its own failure. In other words, the emergence of modern consciousness is predicated on the *prior* presence of memory—a modern valuation of memory that owes itself, ironically, to the thoroughly premodern mediations of St. Augustine, in his *Confessions* (without which Heidegger's monograph *The Concept of Time* would not exist).

Freud's impact is particularly detectable in the cultural sphere, even though he has long ceased to be taken seriously by the scientific community. In Hollywood, a "vulgar Freudianism" has permeated the screenplays of innumerable feature films—a fact exemplified, once again, in Hitchcock; this gave rise in the 1970s to the feminist-psychoanalytic critique of the pervasive "male gaze" in films of the classical Hollywood period of the 1930s to 1950s. Well before, in the heyday of Freud's influence, in the modernist period in European literature in the 1920s and 1930s, writers such as Virginia Woolf and James Joyce sought to capture and record the very processes of thought and memory in what still stand as radical experiments in narrative. The catchphrase "stream of consciousness," however, tends to occlude their real achievement, which was to demonstrate in a very exciting and creative manner the degree to which what we take to be memory is not merely represented or reproduced, but mediated and re-mediated, constituted in and through cultural objects, especially texts. It is now possible to see, however, that, as the twentieth century progressed, and even at the height of the modernist period, the dominance of narrative in textual form—pre-eminently the novel—began to wane against the emergence of a variety of other media forms, beginning with photographic images, which prepared the ground for the advent of the fiction film as the dominant narrative mode for much of the previous century. This is not simply the story of one medium supplanting another, however, but one that questions the much more complex relations of exchange and remediative influence between and among literature, cinema, and other cultural modalities. Therefore persistent concerns about the integrity or authenticity of specific media or art forms appear all the more strange, as the roots of what we now call intertextuality or intermediality extend well back beyond any putatively late or postmodern moment, meaning that formal and thematic interpenetration, hybridization, and even corruption have been the order of the day throughout the modern period, despite the persistent resistance of reactionary and Romantic views.

In the postwar period, concerns about authenticity in the culture were extended to the question of identity, both personal-individual and social-collective. Having emerged from the Civil Rights era, such concerns had crystallized by the mid-1960s around the axes of gender, sexuality, and race, with the women's and gay liberation movements laying the ground respectively for third-wave feminism and the contemporary queer movement, and with black power issuing forth in a variety of (seemingly contradictory) cultural forms, from the Black Panthers to hip hop. This rapid and profound social and cultural change resulted in a renewed emphasis on the individual and the emergence of what came to be known in the 1980s as identity politics. Thus the post-1968 period was the first in human history in which individual identity came to be seen as a political issue, alongside abiding concerns with national identity, which itself was given new impetus in the post-colonial period after the Second World War, when many former colonies gained independence, beginning with India in 1947. While "identity politics" as a term may be historical, its associated concerns, such as those of nationhood, persist with renewed urgency in today's globalized world.

The concept of collective memory, first popularized by Maurice Halbwachs in France in 1950, speaks directly to this utterly modern tendency to conflate the personal-individual and the social-political, not to mention the equally typical tendency to blur the heretofore distinct borders between memory and history. For Halbwachs, collective memory meaningfully bridges these gaps, standing as it does behind contemporary theories of artificial memory, a term (re-)coined by Steven Rose in the early 1990s to oppose to a so-called "natural" memory. Halbwachs emphasizes the irreducibly *social* character of modern collective memory. This theory differs fundamentally from more pervasive psychological (i.e., Freudian) models of memory in its insistence on the "completion" or fulfillment of individual memory in the memories of others. As John Storey puts it, "what is provisional in our own memories is confirmed by the memories of others. [...] We often remember with others what we did not ourselves experience firsthand" (Storey 101–2). This broader valuation of memory as a fundamentally social or cultural phenomenon opened the door to a variety of subsequent theories: Alison Landsberg's "prosthetic memory," Marianne Hirsch's "post-memory," Aleida and Jan Assmann's "communicative" and "cultural memory," and so on (see below). For Halbwachs, "collective memory is embodied in mnemonic artifacts, forms of commemoration such as ... shrines, statues, war memorials ... what French historian Pierre Nora calls 'sites of memory' [*lieux de memoire*]" (qtd. in Storey 104). Storey adds to Halbwachs's list of mnemonic artifacts what he calls "the 'memory industries,' therefore that part of the culture industries concerned with articulating the past" (104). This includes "heritage sites and museums ... but we should also include the mass media (including cinema). [...] The memory industries, like the culture industries of which they form a part, produce representations ('cultural memorials'), with which we are invited to think, feel and recognize the past. But these representations do not embody memory as such, they embody the *materials* for memory; they provide the materials from which "collective memory" can be made" (104, emphasis mine).

In the 1970s and 1980s, concern with identity politics was linked to the restoring of specific ethnic groups' "stories" set against official History. Stories about what happened to Japanese Americans and Japanese Canadians during the Second World War, such as Joy Kogawa's *Obasan*, broke the silence about Japanese internment and relocation. Toni Morrison's *Beloved* urged readers of any ethnicity to "rememory" the sixty million and more African slaves estimated to have died in the Atlantic slave trade (Morrison 215). Hollywood war films during this period posed questions such as "What really happened in Vietnam?"—that conflict through this period acting as a kind of screen onto which any number of diverse social and political anxieties were projected. Although a scattered few films dealing with the Holocaust had been made since the 1950s, the Holocaust industry did not really kick in until the Vietnam revisionist war film was well established—as if audiences (at least in America) would only deal with the bigger, more general, historical calamity once they had already worked through what was presented as a uniquely American political-military debacle. Holocaust studies, it goes without saying, is a whole field in itself, one of the generative contexts rather than a subset of memory studies. But it is possible to see how this relation is being overturned, as memory studies spreads and slowly swallows up its precedents. This would include autobiographical studies, which has arisen alongside of other generative contexts for memory studies, including false memory, trauma, repression, and so forth. Today, as we move beyond the postmodern, post-colonial, and post-human(ist), it becomes easier to see the degree to which "memory has displaced class, race, and gender as the signature category of our generation."[8]

One contemporary writer who brings together in his *oeuvre* a number of the foregoing valences of memory is the German W.G. Sebald, whose relation to the Holocaust, and to the field of Holocaust literature, is predicated on a kind of post-memory in Hirsch's sense of memory-content mediated through photographs (and other technologies) appropriated by a subject who is neither a survivor nor a victim of the Holocaust, nor even Jewish. In one of the first collections commemorating Sebald, who died in 2001, Martin Swales describes his prose output as "a matchless set of reflections ... on the narratively mediated demands of postmemory" (83); in this way, Swales has helped initiate the study of Sebald as a writer of "postmemorial" fiction whose status in the subgenre of Holocaust literature is still debated.[9] According to Stewart Martin, "Sebald is perhaps less a 'holocaust writer' than a writer of destruction, or, to use some of his own words, a writer of the natural history of destruction who takes the whole passage of European history as his subject matter" (18). Sebald's prose works both reflect on and exemplify the cultural and political status of the novel in what is now the post-cinematic age—the tail end of modernity, during which, to quote Jeffrey Pence, "cinema carried the burden of memory" (Grainge 237). Kathy Berendt's essay in this volume interrogates the question of Sebald's status as post-memorial writer.

At the inauguration of the University of Warwick Centre for Memory Studies in 2009, sociologist and memory scholar Andrew Hoskins[10] noted that the current "memory boom" over the past few decades had been due to several factors, including these: the supplanting of some kind of objective "History" by more subjective notions of "memory," including "collective" memory; an increased interest in Holocaust studies; the emergence of trauma studies; and the emergence, especially in the wake of the 9/11 terrorist attacks, of a culture of commemoration/remembrance/memorialization ("Launch"). To this list we would add the following (echoing Astrid Erll): the coining and dissemination of concepts such as "post-memory" and "prosthetic" memory; a renewed interest in archives and archival studies, especially in the wake of Jacques Derrida's *Archive Fever* (1998); "cultural" and "transcultural" memory; a renewed interest in nostalgia in the wake of 1990s postmodernist theory; renewed interest in oral history/ies, testimony witnessing, and autobiography or, as it is as often known, "life writing"; the 1990s wave of "false memory syndrome"; an interest in "Heritage," coupled with the historical re-enactment movement (see Sturken); post-colonial revisionism; truth and reconciliation commissions in South Africa and Bosnia; and, of course, 9/11 itself, which, according to Hoskins, became within a couple of months of its occurrence the most documented event in history.

At the same time, memory is now at the centre of a thriving academic industry, under the collective banner of "memory studies." One need only page through any issue of the journal *Memory Studies* (founded in 2008) to get a clear idea of the state of memory studies in the social sciences today. Here, the harder sciences—cognitive science, behaviouralism, clinical psychology, even neuroscience—get mentioned often enough to give one the impression that memory today is primarily the property of scientists who study real people in real places and situations. Hoskins identifies cultural studies, history, psychology, and sociology as the traditional disciplinary pillars of memory studies ("Launch"). If one construes cultural and communication studies as manifestations of the social sciences, then the study of the role of media, mediation, and mediatization, of remediation and now premediation, still returns one eventually from text, image, or media-event to the real in its mundane (but no less urgent) sense, to social reality, especially in its ethical and political implications. We will return to this point below.

According to Erll, "[o]ver the course of the last two decades, memory as an interdisciplinary phenomenon has become a key concept of academic discourse across established fields. However 'memory' is not owned by any one ... discipline. Instead, sociology, philosophy and history, archaeology and religious studies, literary and art history, media studies, psychology and the neurosciences are all involved in exploring the connection between culture and memory" (Erll 1–2). It is upon this latter qualifier—"culture"—that we want to focus in what follows, in order to illuminate the territory in which this collection stakes its specific claim, and in which the value of its contribution to memory studies is best measured. As the title of Erll's book indicates, her concern—as with much of the current scholarship—is with what Aleda and Jan Assmann have termed "cultural memory" as a necessary updating of the (now superseded) notion of "collective memory," most famously formulated by Maurice Halbwachs (see above). The Assmanns usefully distinguish between two forms of collective memory: cultural memory and communicative memory. Communicative memory is "based on forms of everyday interaction and communication"; cultural memory "is more institutionalized and rests on rituals and media" (Erll 28).

One can readily detect here in Erll's account of cultural *vis-à-vis* communicative memory the impact of cultural studies, even as it transforms and fragments into various subdisciplines. This is especially clear in the emphasis in contemporary memory studies on contemporary culture generally and specific contemporary cultural objects in particular, most notably newer media forms and technologies that are reshaping our perceptions and understanding of life, the world, history, and ourselves, in the very moment of this writing. And ironically, it is precisely this attention—or rather, this preoccupation—with the present moment, the now, that characterizes memory studies today, making it symptomatic of cultural study more generally. The nature of mediation—and mediality—has evolved since the 1990s, the most significant change coming in its temporal relation to its subject matter. Now it is no longer the past or present but the future that is not simply mediated or remediated but *premediated*. In order to understand what memory means today, it is necessary to briefly consider these concepts, especially in terms of their centrality to contemporary cultural production and its critical reception.

Remediation and Premediation

First, a word about remediation: much of the terrain covered historically by the concept of adaptation has been usurped by the newer, more encompassing term *remediation*.[11] In the context of cultural communication, remediation, as the word suggests, implies at once mediation and its repetition: the reproduction of one medium in another (Bolter and Grusin 3–15). German theorist Astrid Erll ties film as a modality of cultural memory to media theory more broadly, putting it in the context of remediation and intermediality. Erll reads remediation, in particular, as a concept of memory studies, as the "ongoing transcription of a 'memory matter' into different media" (141). Remediation is to new media what adaptation was to an older paradigm epitomized by popular, intertextually determined literary or cinematic narratives that underpin social and individual identities. Remediation accounts revealingly for the double logic of (post-)modern memory: to repeat, reproduce, and repurpose and to do so invisibly, without drawing attention to these processes, in order to uphold the Romantic myths of originality and creative authority so valued by late capitalist society. Erll ties film as a modality of cultural memory to media theory, putting it in the context of remediation and intermediality, reading remediation as itself a theory of memory. Thus remediation—along with related theories of intermediality and premediation—stands as a helpful new concept for understanding the operation of cultural memory across media, whether new or established.

Jay Bolter and Richard Grusin identify remediation's contradictory or even paradoxical "double logic" of immediacy combined with hypermediacy. Contemporary culture, they argue, is characterized by a drive to transparency and *immediacy*—the basis of, for instance, Hollywood realism, which is itself based in narrative and stylistic continuity—over against an often spectacular self-reflexivity or *hypermediacy*, where the means of cultural production are laid bare within the image or text or narrative itself. "Both new and old media [invoke] the twin logics of immediacy and hypermediacy in their efforts to remake themselves and each other. [...] [The] two seemingly contradictory logics not only coexist in digital media today but are mutually dependent" (Bolter and Grusin 5–6).

According to Erll, "[t]he most impressive popular versions of the past can be encountered in the cinema of cultural memory—which produces and disseminates what I call 'memory films.' These films fall into two broad categories. Movies such as *Blade Runner* (1982), *Total Recall* (1990) and *Memento* (2000) address concepts of memory, and problematize and imaginatively realize acts of individual and collective remembering. They are thus memory-*reflexive* films" (Erll 137). Memory-reflexive films foreground hypermediacy over immediacy. "*Apocalypse Now* (1978), *Schindler's List* (1993) or *Saving Private Ryan* (1998), on the other hand," Erll continues, "tell us little or nothing about the workings of memory, but they have led to the powerful global dissemination of images of the past. These are memory-*productive* films" (137). Such memory-productive films also demonstrate the privileging of immediate transparency, or realism, over hypermediate reflexivity.

According to Richard Grusin, premediation, unlike run-of-the-mill prediction, gambles on being wrong: it mediates possible negative future scenarios in order to "protect us from the kind of negative surprises that might await us in an unmediated world" (127). In other words, premediation keeps us in a kind of purgatorial present indexed to an apocalyptic future that we hope never arrives, a state of perpetual anticipation whose function is cathartic insofar as its predictive potential always fails. Grusin's concept underscores the central themes of a media-saturated post-9/11 world determined by the logic that Derrida famously labelled *toujour déjà*: the future anterior tense in which most of us supposedly eke out our wirelessly connected, socially mediated, hyper-securitized lives. This is a view of the contemporary world in which the twenty-first-century mass media at once produce and mitigate the "shock of the new" that is endemic to twentieth-century artistic modernism and still a central pop cultural myth.

Although by this name it is a firmly post-9/11 phenomenon, it is both ironic and appropriate that Grusin's theory of premediation should be reminiscent of other, older ideas about how culture continually produces versions of reality that variously prepare us for, protect us from, or conceal outright the social reality just ahead in what we fondly call the future. Premediation calls attention to the way mediated moments of the past frame our understanding of future experience (Erll 142). We do not intend it as a criticism to say that there is something "unoriginal" about premediation, despite Grusin's repeated claims to the contrary; in part, he is justified in arguing for its twenty-first-century currency, tied as the concept is to contemporary technologies of cultural mediation and remediation, most prominently the Internet and other manifestations of the new media that now pervade everyone's life to some degree. To put it another way: to accuse premediation of being "unoriginal" is to miss the point that its "unoriginality" is precisely the point. For, according to Grusin, in the post-9/11 period, the United States strove to ensure "that the American public never again experienced *live* a large-scale catastrophic event that had not already been premediated" (12; my emphasis). In other words, premediation means that an *actual* catastrophe like 9/11 is replaced in the media by a "real-time" simulacrum of itself—a scenario premediated, ironically, by Don DeLillo in 1985's *White Noise*—the intention being that, should the American public of necessity undergo another such catastrophe, at least it will not be one, like 9/11, that was mediated, and continues to be remediated, but was so woefully un-premediated.

What Grusin calls "premediated time" (33) is really another name for the perpetual present of consumption, no matter how much he talks about the necessity of remediating the *future* after 9/11. For if the future signifies at all for the average person in the present, it is on an affective level, and not as a distinct temporality as it were visible from the present, as in certain sci-fi scenarios. And, after all, such filmic and televisual visions of possible futures are on a conceptual level ultimately extensions of the present, while, ontologically, like all photographically based images, they are uncanny emanations of the past. All this talk of the future or futures is highly misleading, however, since once the future arrives it is always already present. In this sense Grusin's critique of Baudrillard becomes a distraction, as the question of the "real" versus simulacra becomes moot when the object is the future as such (and not just its representations): the future *as such* has no empirical existence; therefore it is not 'real" except as something that can be imagined, predicted, or feared—that is, as image or representation whose reference is always ultimately the past. If anything, premediation is entirely dependent on Baudrillard, as an extension of the concept of simulacrum as a term beyond the binary of real versus unreal, model versus copy, or referent versus image. Grusin seems to forget that the ultimate thrust of Baudrillard's theory is the disappearance of the real not as something to be nostalgically mourned, but as something forever rewritten in our new relationship to events via their representation in the media—their "mediatization."[12]

Ironically, perhaps, premediation, rather than being the pre-emptive anticipation of possible futures, is in fact a theory of *memory*, insofar as it describes a process whereby the subject, confronted by the future, recognizes it as something always already seen and therefore, in a certain sense, known—like the visions of possible futures seen by the "precogs" in Steven Spielberg's *Minority Report* (2002), filmic scenarios visually no different from the home movie flashbacks contained on mini-disks in the film's carefully researched future world. The premediated future is thus stripped of its unknowability, its otherness, reduced to a version of the same, the present, which is all we ever really have anyway. What premediation represents, then, is the further erosion and impoverishment of the imagination as an organ of creativity, balanced by the final consolidation of memory as prosthetic technology whose form, content, and function are entirely determined by forces outside of and often wholly at odds with the best interests of the individual subject.

What seems to be a more practical and less front-loaded approach to a similar constellation of phenomena is found in Andrew Hoskins's notion of "digital network memory," which more directly connects contemporary transformations of cultural prosthetic memory with the digital media forms, both hard and soft—most notably the Internet itself—that stand at the centre of such radical change (Hoskins calls the Internet a "temporally dynamic networked archival infrastructure" [98]). For Hoskins, "contemporary memory is principally constituted neither through revival nor through the representation of some content of the past in the present. Rather, it is embedded in and distributed through our socio-technical practices" (92). This is what is meant by "an emergent digital network memory" wherein "communications in themselves dynamically add to, alter, and erase, a kind of living archival memory" (92). Here and in all his work Hoskins addresses the very current manifestation of what Russell Kilbourn traces elsewhere in a somewhat deeper historical perspective: the rapid technologization and de-ontologization of memory in the twentieth century and beyond (Kilbourn 6). This means that memory's ostensive ductility and fluidity get fixed in place by technical media, most significantly cinema—a process that has been going on since the invention of writing but that is amplified many times over with the intercession of photographically based media. The other useful thing about Hoskins's approach to these questions is that it does not muddy the analytical waters by worrying about "affect," which Grusin foregrounds in his theory of premediation.

José van Dijck advances a more effective treatment of the intersection of memory, embodiment, and materiality in *Mediated Memories in the Digital Age* (2007), part of Stanford University Press's tellingly named series "Cultural Memory in the Present." Van Dijck's book is one of the best recent studies of memory in the digital age, not least because of its handling of the vexed question of the emotional dimension of memory and the intersection of body, mind, and material object in her theory of the irreducibly mediated nature of modern memory. What is odd about this and other recent theories of memory, however, is that, like Grusin's premediation, they can begin to sound more like theories of present tense experience (Hoskins 94): "the increasingly digital networking of memory not only functions in a continuous present but is also a distinctive shaper of a new mediatized age of memory" (96)—a point that must always be balanced against the observation that "humans have historically co-evolved with technology, distributing their cognitive and other functions across an increasingly complex network of technical artifacts" (Grusin, qtd. in Hoskins 95).

A recent editorial in *The Guardian Weekly* (19–25 January 2012) offered the latest evidence of this effect in the next generation of "smart" personal electronics and household appliances linked through new software applications: not just computers, tablets, televisions, and game consoles but washers and refrigerators that will collect and relay reams of information about consumer-users—data that could be used in all sorts of ways, commercial or otherwise, pending tighter regulatory controls. But our interest in this latest symptomatic expression of a techno-corporate infrastructure capable of collecting far more data than any individual could ever possibly use or want to use is not with regard to privacy, surveillance, identity theft, or biometrically based niche marketing, but rather in terms of the sense in which this inconceivably vast quantity of information about ourselves constitutes merely the latest and most egregious example of a new kind of collective prosthetic memory, a massive archive of the minutiae of twenty-first-century life, recorded in something like "real time," stored on servers or in the ether or up in the clouds—a kind of enormous virtual simulacrum of the contemporary world.[13] We can recognize in this a very strange and perhaps unprecedented form of artificial memory, at least in terms of scale and in terms moreover of what it says about our changing understanding of privacy, individual identity, and subjective interiority, not to speak of the irony of a shared social memory that lacks all but the most cursory and highly mediated historical depth.

It is difficult to miss the irony, indeed the paradox, in the observation that memory studies by and large concerns itself with a conception of memory (not to speak of "history") that is grounded in, predicated upon, a certain understanding and valuation of the *present*—and in a contingent sense, the future—as the most significant temporal construct. Following Pam Cook, we privilege the term memory here over history (or over other categories, such as nostalgia)[14] because it seems to still bear the connotations of subjectivity, individuality, the personal or private, and so on, over against history, with its persistent—popular cultural—connotations of objectivity, collectivity, public and social. And it is precisely the human "sciences," the humanities and social sciences, liberal arts, and so on, in which not simply the one pole or the other (memory "versus" history) but the tenuous relation between them historically has been most successfully and usefully explored. For it is hardly possible for the "hard sciences" to consider such imprecise and frangible terrain: the space in which we observe individual identity mediated by and through material objects—signs, images, texts, commodities—as well as all the discourses in and by means of which power and knowledge circulate, are perpetuated or subverted. In other words, to restate what is by now an axiom of contemporary cultural-humanistic studies, individual identity constitutes itself or gets constituted by means of the irreducibly social dimension of cultural mediation; there is no "I" without the other, just as there is no "other" without its representations or approximations in the culture. To invoke Derrida's hoary formulation: there is nothing outside the text, for memory signifies and has value for us today—whether we mean memory as content or as process—in a very real sense as text, intertext, and intermediality.

The Archival Subject of Modernity

Andrew Hoskins pays considerable attention in his recent work to the status of the archive as model and metaphor for memory in the digital era: "archives as they have become increasingly networked have become a key [stratum] of our technological unconscious, transcending the social and the technological," properly speaking (97). But constitutive of modern memory more broadly construed is what Jacques Derrida in *Archive Fever* calls a "prosthesis of the inside" (19) as a way of talking about "the sense that memory [in modernity] ceases to be a pure matter of consciousness, and comes to reside in the *materiality* of our social or psychic life" (Long 113; my emphasis). "There is no archive without a *place* of consignation," writes Derrida, "without a technique of *repetition*, and without a certain *exteriority*. No archive without outside" (11). Place or space, repetition, and exteriority: these are the three, perhaps irreducible, material conditions of modern memory (see Sabine Sielke's essay in this volume). For Derrida, therefore, "the theory of psychoanalysis ... becomes a theory of the archive and not only a theory of memory" (19). The subject today *is* archival, to use Jonathan Long's phrase, just as the subject, once constructed, becomes the foundation, the "substrate," of the archive as "compensatory" structure (26–27).[15] This chiasm has an absence at its heart: "we must also remember," writes Derrida, "that repetition itself ... the repetition compulsion, remains, according to Freud, indissociable from the death drive. And thus from destruction" (11–12). One implication of this (to adapt Derrida's observation) is that the archive contains within itself the seeds of its own destruction, which for the archival subject means not memory but forgetting, not anamnesis but amnesia. Structured according to the logic of the (Derridean, Levinasian) *trace*, this memory does not remain within the opposition established by Plato; it encompasses, as writing does for Derrida, *mneme* and *hypomnesis* alike.[16] In this sense (to adapt Derrida's famous formulation once again), *there is nothing outside of memory*—but this is a very particular form of memory. Most significantly, the relation between self and other in memory becomes paradigmatic of the self–other relation as formulated in dialogic terms. In other words (to reiterate), in terms of late- or post-modern subjectivity, memory here looks toward the extra-subjective and therefore the possibility of the post-subjective: a memory, if not utterly free of the individual subject, is then at least not limited to or determined by that subject. This is a best-case scenario. As Derrida puts it: *"There is no archive without ... a certain exteriority. No archive without outside"* (11). In José van Dijck's view, all memory is embodied, but, thanks to technological mediation, this takes a more complex form than a traditional metaphysics allows: "Mediated memories ... can be located neither strictly in the brain nor wholly outside in (material) culture but exist in both concurrently, for they are manifestations of a complex interaction between brain, material objects, and the cultural matrix from which they arise" (Van Dijck 28). The relentless and ineluctable technologization, exteriorization, and virtualization of memory is mitigated by this model of memory as intersubjective, dialogical, social exchange. The possibility of an ethics of memory—and of a *more ethical form of memory*—is embodied precisely in our engagement with the texts and other cultural objects by which we are surrounded, and without which life—even one determined by economic imperatives—remains strangely unthinkable.

Memory Effects

Of all the categories in the human and social sciences, perhaps only subjectivity compares with memory in the number of discourses in which it signifies: psychoanalytic, narratological, art historical, philosophical. Unlike subjectivity, however, memory cuts across social and collective paradigms as well. Andrew Hoskins's list (above) of topics and questions that are now subsumed under the rubric of "memory studies" is indicative not only of the field's constitutive diversity, but also, in a second-order sense, of the broad inter- or multi- or trans-disciplinary nature of this field. To repeat: memory studies is irreducibly interdisciplinary. According to an editorial in one of the first issues of the eponymous journal: '[t]he field of memory studies mobilizes scholarship driven by problem or topic, rather than by singular method or tradition. Yet divergence in backgrounds and assumptions must be highlighted and deliberately negotiated, not wished away. Only by encouraging the open, careful contesting of concepts can we exploit the strengths of the daunting range of disciplines—from neurobiology to narrative theory, from the developmental to the postcolonial, the computational to the cross-cultural, and on and on—which can all drive the collective and various enterprises involved" (1:2, 5–6). With anthologies emerging every few months,[17] a dedicated journal (*Memory Studies*: first issue 2008), and academic programs,[18] memory studies is already well established as one of the most urgent contemporary interdisciplinary fields. This is where the present volume can be seen to stand apart: in its focus on the two fields of film and literature, on the one hand, and in its methodological approach, which is grounded in the concepts or processes of memory, mediation, and remediation, on the other. More specifically, this volume seeks to consider memory self-reflexively, in a context informed by contemporary intermedial adaptation or remediation theory (Bolter and Grusin; Stam; Hutcheon, etc.). In other words, it seeks an engagement with not merely the representation and redefining of memory (and history, and nostalgia, etc.) in both literary and filmic texts, but also with the question of the degree to which either individual or social memory gets constituted, legitimized, "naturalized," replicated, and reproduced through narrative or visual media forms. In short, this volume seeks to explore literature and/or cinema as themselves veritable modes of memory, in the shape of allusion, adaptation, remediation, translation, intertextuality, and appropriation.

This seemingly limited focus on filmic and/or literary texts, within this particular approach, has strategic value in terms of a perceived need for certain branches of humanistic study, certain academic disciplines, departments, or faculties, to stake out their own territory within this burgeoning field, for particular reasons. In short, this volume seeks in part to demonstrate the full implications of this interdisciplinarity: that "memory" as an object of study is never the property of any single discipline or discourse, and that, if anything, literary and film scholars have a certain advantage over medical and social scientists, psychologists, historians, and so on. This advantage inheres precisely in the extent to which the scholarship being done today on literature and film is pre-eminently interested in texts, representation, mediation, language, style—in short, *form*—as well as narrative, subjectivity, identity, and other concerns.

This is not about "taking ownership" of something as amorphous and as inclusive as memory studies (not to speak of memory *in itself*, whatever that means); rather, it is about drawing attention to the fact that many of the discoveries about memory claimed by the medical or social sciences find their counterpart—if not their anticipation—in the work of authors and filmmakers, that is, "cultural producers," and of critics and theorists alike.

Critical Readings

In keeping with recent developments in memory studies, the essays in this book highlight the ways in which memory is a discursive and constantly shifting process rather than a stable set of retrievable recollections. Our contributors look at a range of texts—literature, film, television, art, and culture from the United States, Canada, Britain, Hong Kong, Mexico, France, Germany—to explore the limits of current theories of memory; the links between memory and identity; the ways in which memory is used as resistance in life writing, and in nation building; the way personal memory can contest histories; and the politics of memorializing. We begin with two essays that challenge current theories in memory studies. Sabine Sielke's "'Joy in Repetition,' or The Significance of Seriality in Processes of Memory and (Re-)Mediation" attempts to bridge the gap between cultural studies and the cognitive sciences by reconceptualizing memory and mediation as seriality. Sielke argues compellingly that "seriality informs and affects processes of individual and cultural memory" and that memory is a series of "repetition[s] with variation," as Gertrude Stein noted. In this original essay that draws from the theories of Charles Darwin, Gilles Deleuze, Walter Benjamin, Niklas Luhmann, and others, Sielke raises the question of how we can account for the effects of remediation through technologies of reproduction—film, television, and new media—in the works of Emily Dickinson, Henry James, and Gertrude Stein. She makes an innovative and original argument about looking at memory and forgetting together as "serial operations" and as forms of "recontextualization."

Kathy Behrendt's "Hirsch, Sebald, and the Virtues and Limits of Postmemory" examines the importance of Marianne Hirsch's theory of "postmemory," the notion that children whose parents were victims of or witnesses to trauma are deeply affected even though they have no first-hand experiences of these traumas. In her essay, Behrendt uses the example of W.G. Sebald, whose work has been classified by Hirsch and others as "postmemorial," to point out some of the ethical dangers and limitations of "Hirsch's emphasis on empathic access to the past experiences of the victims of trauma." Behrendt raises critical questions about memory and personal identity, asking, for example, if a subject can have a "memory-like relation to the experience of another." The essay urges us to re-examine the central role of the witness, of testimony, the value of historical accuracy, and to distinguish between types of narrative perspectives when we participate in collective remembering.

The second section of our book features three essays that use literary texts as the primary example of the way memory and memorializing function in three very different cultural and historical contexts. Sarah Henstra's "British Propaganda and the Construction of Female Mourning in the First World War" examines women's writing during the First World War against the backdrop of patriotic discourses that encouraged maternal sacrifice and heroism. Henstra's research recovers dimensions of public memory and remembrance practices that have not been highlighted by traditional narratives of the Great War. She examines the use of women's mourning and loss in iconographic images of the period, and the disjunction between women's private feelings and the messages from the state, and links them to the larger questions of conventions of memorializing. Reading the works of feminist pacifists like Helena Swanwick, Mary Sargant Florence, C.K. Ogden, and Catherine Marshall, Henstra argues that these authors "built in significant changes to the state-sanctioned interpretive framework in order to defamiliarize world politics and to encourage women to see militarism differently" from men. Through their writings and speeches, "female *grief*" is "transformed rhetorically into a set of female *grievances* that demand recognition and recompense ... female mourning presses past sentimentality into political action." Henstra draws from literary, trauma, ethical, affect, and emotions theory to present a sophisticated reading of the ongoing peace efforts by these women.

Tanis MacDonald's "'Rhetorical Metatarsals': Bone Memory in Dionne Brand's *Ossuaries*" argues that poetry, the "least commoditized art," can challenge public forgetting and, at the same time, articulate the pain of colonial history experienced by African diasporic people. MacDonald notes that in Canadian literature, "the metaphor of scattered and dishonoured bones ... and the recollection (both metaphorical and literal) of [these] bones" is a device used by oppressed groups, such as First Nations, Asian, and Black Canadian authors, to reclaim and materialize their history. Similar to Toni Morrison's aim in *Beloved*, Brand's project explores the legacy of the Atlantic slave trade and the "problem of living with a history of the body that is both unlocatable and omnipresent." MacDonald discusses the ways in which these "irreparable gaps in kinship and family narratives" can be partially resolved with the help of art, especially by moving lyric and political poetry such as Brand's.

John Dean in "Mediation and Remediation in Carlos Fuentes's *The Old Gringo*" reminds us that history entails both a forgetting and a validation of selected memories. Using Linda Hutcheon's theories as a starting point, Dean explains that Fuentes remediates history "by weaving historical events into consciously fictive reconstructions to expose the fictive nature of history." For Dean, the remediation of memory not only shapes early-twentieth-century politics and creates official history, but also contributes to constructions of Self and Other that characterize the relationship between the United States and Mexico. Using postmodern devices such as the incorporation of historical figures, the performance of history, and the juxtaposition of real and fictive events, Fuentes reveals the ways in which imperialism hinged on the "American collective memory of mobility and cultural expansion as divine rights." Dean's essay insightfully reads Fuentes's use of the tropes of seeing and mirrors to demonstrate the way official history can be re-envisioned.

The essays in the third section of the book examine the implications of memory and life writing in various forms. In "Resisting Holocaust Memory: Recuperating a Compromised Life" Marlene Kadar records her extraordinary journey of tracking the life of a former concentration camp guard "whose story is constructed from a/b (autobiographical) fragments, news media sources, and more recently, historical and legal documentation." Kadar's essay wants us to "trouble the contradictions" in our remembrance of someone with an unsavoury life, but whose life still is a human one. As she contends, "there is repressed material in the stories we tell ourselves about evildoers and the enemy among us, about their difference from us, about our national purity and/or safe borders, and about humanity." In this self-reflexive and fascinating essay, Kadar uncovers how immigration officers, archives, and different interpretations of the law mediated the life of Hermine Braunsteiner, known later as the "old mare" from Ravensbrück, who worked in two women's concentration camps during the Holocaust. After more than a decade of searching for this elusive subject, Kadar makes a number of startling and perceptive observations about the process of tracing a life that resists remembrance and how that life challenges our assumptions about the moral nature of women.

Another essay on the Holocaust focuses on a group of people whose stories have not been well-documented in history. Sheelagh Russell-Brown's "'In Auschwitz There Is a Great House': The Location of Memory and Identity in the Roma *Porrajmos* (Devouring) or Holocaust" explores the "rememory" of those "Roma" or Gypsy people who lost their lives under the Nazis. By 1945 "approximately four-fifths of Europe's Roma were dead as a result of National Socialist policies," and few of those who survived break "with the Roma tradition of silence to recount their experiences of Auschwitz," except through song. Russell-Brown presents a number of possible reasons for the absence of communal memory about Roma losses, including their otherness, their lack of legitimacy in society, their lack of a social environment and shared history for such commemorations, and their sense of shame from their experiences in the camps. Since the early 1980s, however, Romany activists have begun to reshape their "memory and identity politics" by writing autobiographies and by performing their songs. These works recuperate and construct genealogies, calling attention to the culture's "traumas as well as its victories."

In "Autobiography and the Validation of Memory: Neil M. Gunn's *The Atom of Delight*," Kenneth Keir argues that "autobiography, more than any other literary genre, calls attention to problems regarding the function of memory in literature, the status we assign to memory in a text." While a number of postmodern scholars highlight the roles of cultural mediation, discourse, and representation in autobiographies, Keir notes that these approaches do not resolve the "problem of mnemonic unpredictability." Using Scottish writer Neil Gunn's fictional autobiography as a case study, Keir raises a number of textual issues about self-memorialization and fiction and the porous boundary between history and art. An autobiography that marks the transition from a modernist to a postmodernist aesthetic, *Atom of Delight* demonstrates the ways in which memory in autobiographical texts is mediated by history, philosophy, and the understanding of genres, such as the spiritual autobiography. Finally, Keir explores Gunn's notion of the "second self" as an example of the otherness of memory.

In the fourth section of this book are four essays that discuss the representation of memory in film. Amresh Sinha's "*La Jetée* and *12 Monkeys*: Memory and History at Odds" explores the intriguing links among time, repetition, and memory in Chris Marker's 1962 short film, which consists mainly of photographic stills, and in Terry Gilliam's 1995 film, which was inspired by Marker's. While both films are about time travelling, Sinha argues that the earlier film is actually more radical than Gilliam's because it refuses to be bound by chronology. Reading the film as a critique of the "mythological foundations" of history's institutional character, Sinha remarks that in *La Jetée*, "memory is anterior to consciousness." The essay adroitly compares the two films, using insights from Benjamin's theses of history, Barthes's theories of the photograph, and trauma theory to discuss voluntary and involuntary memory and to engage with the difficult question of how filmic texts translate the difference between memory and history.

Anders Bergstrom examines the ways in which two twenty-first-century films continue to play with notions of time, identity, and memory. In 'The Traces of 'A Half-Remembered Dream': Christopher Nolan's *Inception* (2010), Wong Kar-wai's *2046* (2004), and the Memory Film,' Bergstrom argues that "by visualizing philosophies of memory on the screen," these films demonstrate the manner in which "cinema has shaped and continues to shape our conception of how memory operates." He points out that the differences between the genres of the two films—Nolan's being a popular action and heist film and Wong's a transnational art film—account for the differences between their treatments of time and space, dream and memory. Reading their complex uses of diegetic layers, nostalgia, elements of science fiction, repetition, and the imagery of mirrors and trains, Bergstrom concludes that both films deserve a place in the lineage of what is now called the memory film.

Graeme Gilloch's "'You must remember this …': Watching *Casablanca* with Marc Augé" looks at French anthropologist Marc Augé's *Casablanca* (2007, translated in 2009 as *Casablanca: Movies and Memory*), exploring Augé's concern with the relationship between cinema and memory. Gilloch emphasizes that it is the whole experience of going to the cinema that is important, the "ritualistic aspect" of visiting the little cinemas that once flourished on the Left Bank. For Augé, "the form of the cinematic medium itself—the concatenation of film images, their sequencing and editing, their staging as montage—is in some way analogous to the work of memory." In particular, *Casablanca*'s themes of "escape, exile, fear, waiting, and displacement resulting from the Occupation of 1940 mesh with Augé's memories of this traumatic historical moment." Gilloch reads the film as a melodrama of remembering and forgetting, focusing on the use of music, the flashback, self-sacrificial love, and the intertextual link to Goethe's novella, *Die Wahlverwandtschaften*.

Stefan Sereda's "The Cinema of Simulation: Hyper-Histories and (Un)Popular Memory in *The Good German* (2006) and *Inglourious Basterds* (2009)" looks at "a genre of films that intentionally favours an understanding of history as always-already mediated and therefore malleable." Diverging from Baudrillard's and Jameson's pronouncements about the disappearance of history and politics in the films of late capitalist modernity, Sereda notes that this "*cinema of simulation* fashions novel aesthetic arrangements through which to engage with history for contemporary ethico-political purposes." This genre, emerging in the 1970s and after, "speaks to a history that is indebted to popular media artefacts," and views history as a discursive construction. Sereda examines the influence on the twenty-first-century cinema of simulation of a number of Hollywood Renaissance nostalgia films, such as *American Graffiti* and *Chinatown*, as well as Woody Allen's mockumentary *Zelig*. Films like Steven Soderbergh's *The Good German* and Quentin Tarantino's *Inglourious Basterds* blend historical fact with fiction, presenting "hyper-histories that combine historical records with dramatization, fabrications, and media artefacts from and about the periods being depicted" to establish political commentary that can challenge or reinforce hegemonic political discourses in the contemporary moment.

In the last section of our book, three essays examine the ways in which television and videos contribute to our collective memory. In "The *Heritage Minutes*: Nostalgia, Nationalism, and Canadian Collective Memory," Erin Peters studies *The Heritage Minutes*, a series of short advertisements that dramatized episodes in Canadian history to enhance Canadians' understanding of history and to reinforce Canadian identity. As Peters notes, "this memory project was considered to be not only … entertaining, but … crucial for the survival and prosperity of the nation." In the late 1970s and 1980s, Pierre Trudeau's multicultural policies "changed the way Canadians were asked to see themselves, from bilingual and bicultural to multilingual and multicultural." While these policies allowed diversity, they also led to a more fragmented sense of Canada itself. Peters notes that it was the task of the *Heritage Minutes* to "identify a set of common connotations of Canadianism" that would "allow individuals to see themselves" in history and with a sense of nostalgia. Peters looks at a number of the contentious issues handled by the *Minutes*, such as the relationship between English and French Canadians, regionalism and geography. She notes that in attempting to build a collective national memory, the *Minutes* became "pieces of Canadian cultural memory themselves."

John McCullough's "Disaster and Trauma in *Rescue Me, Saving Grace*, and *Treme*: Commercial Television's Contributions to Ideas about Memorials" looks at three television series that deal with the aftermath of three recent events in the United States that killed many people and were highly mediated: the bombing of the Alfred P. Murrah federal building in Oklahoma City in 1995; the attacks on the World Trade Center in 2001; and the devastation caused by Hurricane Katrina in 2005. McCullough notes that these three series have the common goal of memorializing through a broad range of aesthetic strategies typically associated with the serial television form and "quality TV." He looks at the particular memorial spaces produced by television, "the way that it designs intervals, creating rhythms and textured spaces filled with data and affect, or, more provocatively, history and memory." Seriality, fantasy, technology, and populist conventions are all part of the process of working through trauma in television, creating powerful and often contradictory affective experiences for viewers.

Finally, Kate Warren's "Creative Re-enactment in the Films and Videos of Omer Fast" considers the cultural and historical phenomenon of re-enactment, its defining characteristics, and its role in the remediation of cultural memory using the gallery-based installations of Israeli-born artist Omer Fast. Fast is drawn to "those whose memories, experiences, and personal narratives have been contested and compromised by processes of representation and remediation." His *Spielberg's List* (2003), based on *Schindler's List* (1993), for example, demonstrates the way that the memories and experiences of the Holocaust have been compromised and complicated by Spielberg's film. The extras who participated in Spielberg's film were placed in emotionally charged environments that actualized the confusion between the "real" and the representation. Fast observes that they had "*real* experiences, of a very *unreal* situation." Warren notes that "[s]trategies of re-enactment straddle and pose challenges to our society's obsession with memory on the one hand—or, as Huyssen describes it, the 'hypertrophy of memory' (3)—while on the other hand confronting historiographical concerns about how history is written." Re-enactments are "often highly affective experiences, where boundaries and distinctions between past, present, and future become blurred and porous." By editing his interviews with people who work or participate in re-enactments and by creative assemblages, Fast produces videos and installations that reveal the difficulty of distinguishing the "past and present, memory and fantasy, real and fiction" for the participants. Warren contends that this confusion that begins at the individual level extends ultimately to the "broader historicization of events" in contemporary culture. This and the other essays in the volume reveal the richness and variety of scholarship being done in literature, film, and other media forms in the field of memory studies.

NOTES

1 The result of a major international conference, "Memory, Mediation, Remediation: Memory in Literature and Film," held at Wilfrid Laurier University, Waterloo, in April 2011.

2 See Kilbourn 14.
3 According to José Van Dijck's reading of Bergson: "'to picture is not to remember,' meaning that the present summons action whereas the past is essentially powerless; recollection images are never re-livings of past experiences, but they are actions of the contemporary brain through which past sensations are evoked and filtered" (30).
4 According to David Bordwell the ubiquity of this shot type today originated here in Hitchcock's *Vertigo*, where it was established as a motif for dynamically isolating the turning point in the protagonist's life (Bordwell 2006, 144).
5 See Kilbourn 16–18.
6 We refer to the modernist art cinema's characteristic disruption of logical causality, its intentional ambiguities, self-reflexive realism, and anti-Oedipal subjectivities. See, for example, Bordwell, "The Art Cinema as a Mode of Film Practice."
7 See the analysis of this scene and of this film in Kilbourn 136–40.
8 Jay Winter (Yale University), review of Aleida Assmann, *Cultural Memory and Western Civilization*.
9 Originated by Hirsch: "[p]ostmemory can be defined as the highly mediated memories of those who did not witness the traumatic event but who have inherited, by way of a cultural affiliation or familial legacy (even though that traumatic inheritance may be one of silence and the failure of witnessing), memories so affective they feel as though they have originated in the postmemorial generation" (Crownshaw "On Reading Sebald Criticism" 20).
10 Andrew Hoskins is founding editor-in-chief of the Sage journal *Memory Studies,* founding co-editor of the Sage journal *Media, War, and Conflict*, co-editor of the Palgrave Macmillan book series *Memory Studies*, and co-editor of the Routledge book series *Media, War, and Security*.
11 Not to be confused with *environmental* remediation, which, as Wikipedia tells us, "deals with the removal of pollution or contaminants from environmental media such as soil, groundwater, sediment, or surface water for the general protection of human health and the environment or from a brownfield site intended for redevelopment" (Wikipedia).
12 "Mediatization in part refers to the impact of the media upon processes of social change so that everyday life is increasingly embedded in the mediascape" (Garde-Hansen et al. 24).
13 Cf. Google corporation's recently instituted changes to its so-called "privacy policy," wherein the corporate giant as of March 2012 collects and stores for unknown future uses an unthinkably vast quantity of information about each individual user, based on her/his search choices.
14 Pam Cook places these three terms on a continuum, with history and nostalgia at either end and memory in the middle, as mediator; see Cook (*Screening the Past* 4).
15 In his monograph on W.G. Sebald, Long identifies the "archival subject" of modernity: one who "compensate[s] for his lack of memory by substituting the archive for interiority" (Long 2008, 162).

16 See Derrida 1996, 11.
17 For example, Rossington and Whitehead; Erll and Rigney; Radstone and Schwarz; etc.
18 For example, Newcastle University's M.A. in "Writing, Memory, Culture"; the new Centre for the Study of Cultural Memory at the University of London; Nottingham University's recently inaugurated Centre for Memory Studies; and the University of Warwick Centre for Memory Studies. We may now add to this list the recently inaugurated Wilfrid Laurier University Centre for Memory and Testimonial Studies.

2

"Joy in Repetition"; or, The Significance of Seriality in Processes of Memory and (Re-)Mediation

Sabine Sielke

In the humanities and the social sciences, common wisdom regarding how memory works is being challenged from two different directions. Recent scholarship in cultural and media studies has suggested, quite convincingly, that "the medium is the memory" (Brody) and is making ever finer distinctions as to how (re-)mediations are affecting and transforming our experience of the increasingly visual cultures we engage in, more or less all day long. The cognitive sciences, for their part, have "renaturalized" concepts such as consciousness and mind; researchers, employing methodologies that raise little concern about issues of mediation, insist that perception, experience, agency, and memory are first of all physical matters. Indeed, neurobiologists admit that even neuroaesthetics—that is, the study of what happens when we experience art[1]—is far from certain what difference it makes, in terms of brain activity, whether we recognize, for example, a face on a screen or in an interpersonal exchange. In other words, in terms of methods, memory research in the cognitive sciences and memory studies as a central issue on the current cultural studies agenda are moving in opposite directions. Furthermore, the prestige of the sciences in general and of the cognitive sciences in particular tends to undermine as it challenges the meticulous work being done in cultural studies. So if memory is indeed a key concept in the ongoing transformation of scientific cultures, how can our readings of cultural practices figure in processes of both mediation and cognition and still hold? And given their fundamental differences, how do concepts of memory in cultural studies and those in the cognitive sciences relate to each other?

My essay explores these questions in a two-part argument that by its nature remains open-ended. In the first part, I show how the fundamental differences in methodology I have just delineated pose severe limits and crucial challenges for transdisciplinary research in memory studies, an enterprise that has gained much currency and popular esteem in recent years. In fact, once we arrive at the crossroads where cultural studies and the cognitive sciences meet, we may be surprised at the amount of miscommunication that occurs in conversations across disciplinary lines. We should not be: after all, the research objects that are central to the cognitive sciences and cultural studies relate as apples and pears do—they are alike (in that they seem to focus on the same field of inquiry called "memory") but also different (since their conceptions of memory mean different things calling for different methods). This is a clear case of repetition with variation—or seriality. At the same time, I map some of the potential crossroads that bind memory research in the cognitive sciences to conceptions of memory as (re-)mediation projected in cultural studies—crossroads I explore in a larger project on memory, mediation, and seriality from which the argument I make here has evolved. In the second part of this essay, I show how memory, whether we approach it in terms of (re-)mediation or as a cognitive process, can be conceptualized by way of seriality, as repetition with variation—or insistence, as Gertrude Stein put it—and how in this way we can reconceive of how conceptions of memory in cultural studies and cognition research relate to each other.

I call on Stein here because she is a central figure when it comes to memory (and, much more importantly, to forgetting) and seriality—a term that remains, as I argue below, undertheorized and, yes, somewhat nebulous. Objects or phenomena appear serial when they are arranged as or come in a succession or sequence; they are joined by recurring elements whose very interrelations—causality, temporality, logic, or pattern—are part of an ongoing debate, regarding which I will offer some suggestions below. Stein, famously portrayed by Picasso in 1906, is of interest for my (admittedly somewhat generalized) reflections on seriality because she transferred the principle by which seriality works to her own literary practice,[2] as in her 1912 portrait of Picasso, which aimed at capturing the rhythm of a person by engaging in a processual kind of writing:

This one was one who was working. This one was one being one having something being coming out of him. This one was one going on having something come out of him. This one was one going on working. This one was one whom some were following. This one was one who was working. (335)

And this is how Stein accounts for her own way of working:

I was doing what the cinema was doing, I was making a continuous succession of the statement of what that person was until I had not many things but one thing. [...] I of course did not think of it in terms of the cinema, in fact I doubt whether at that time I had ever seen a cinema but, and I cannot repeat this too often any one is of one's period and this our period was undoubtedly the period of the cinema and series production. And each of us in our own way are bound to express what the world in which we are living is doing. ("Portraits and Repetition" 176–77)

What does it mean, though, to rethink memory and mediation by way of seriality? I came to understand seriality as a structural principle, although structure is not the right term, for it presupposes a centre, which serial formations lack. Thus better perhaps one could say that I use seriality as another perspective on how things and subjects relate to one another, and I explain what this means in a series of claims I make in the second half of this essay. As we acknowledge the significance of seriality, we come to see why certain media formats, including film and TV series, have been particularly successful, why memory and forgetting closely interrelate, and why all of this has more relevance for our concern with the future than for our respect of the past. As we account for the importance of serial processes, we also register, of course, that there is—to quote from a multiply covered tune by African American singer, songwriter, musician, and actor Prince—"joy in repetition."[3]

I. At the Crossroads of Cultural Studies and the Cognitive Sciences; or, Disciplining Memory

As an American studies scholar engaged with memory processes and their cultural mediation, I have become particularly interested in the interfaces between concepts of memory in cultural studies, on the one hand, and memory research in the cognitive sciences, on the other. Part of that interest is due to my background in biology, which in recent years has motivated me to explore the crossroads between cultural studies and the sciences that are crucial to my current research. The central question I raise in this context is what cultural studies would look like if, instead of engaging in hermeneutics, we focused on how we, as subjects, actually perceive and cognize cultural practices. Using three central concepts of current cultural analysis—memory, mediation, and seriality—and the work of three canonical American authors—Emily Dickinson (1830–86), Henry James (1843–1916), and Gertrude Stein (1874–1946)—the larger project from which this essay emerges interfaces methods and research questions of literary/cultural studies with those of the cognitive sciences and explores the potential of such transdisciplinary dialogue to enrich our sense of cultural practice and subjectivity.

Why choose the works of these particular writers? Dickinson, James, and Stein are of particular interest for a project on memory and (re-)mediation because they mark paradigmatic moments in an interdependent history of cognition and media ecology that allows us to historicize the concepts of cognition, memory, mediation, and seriality. In Dickinson's poetics, for instance, (loss of) consciousness and (the limits of) perception are central issues and the frequent displacement of the concept of mind by the term "brain" acknowledges that her writing develops alongside neurophysiological insights into the workings of cognition. Moreover, she was writing at a time when a substantial "reorganization of vision" (Christ and Jordan xix) was on its way, and her poems invite explorations of memory and seriality[4]—an invitation that Dickinson scholarship has not taken up so far. Instead, the standard reading of Dickinson is that she was a precursor of a modernism that has been conceived mainly as a series of ruptures of aesthetic conventions and digressions from tradition; this sort of reading, then, focuses on the poet's single-minded forms and philosophies. And this is despite the fact that, as the author of almost 1,800 poems, she wrote lyric texts in series, so to speak, featuring "supposed person[s]" (as she called them in a letter of July 1862, vol. 1, 268) who become familiar figures to us as we read on; that her later poems update earlier texts; that dashes leave most of her poems open-ended and render them cliffhangers; that her fascicles may perhaps even be seen in analogy to the seasons of contemporary TV series; and that we may see new dimensions of her work once we think about her in terms of intertextuality and intermediality and recognize the significance of patterns of "repetition and difference" (Deleuze) in her verses' textures instead of retaining residual notions of the autonomy of works of poetic art. Once we tap into aspects of sequence and seriality in her poems, we resituate her in a narrative about the emergence of (post)modernism and its cultural effects that ceases to build on notions of originality that even modernists found dubious. In other words: acknowledging seriality is first of all a shift in critical perspective.

Stein's poetry and prose welcome the impact of "cinema and series production" on the human mind ("Portraits and Repetition" 177) and unfold the relations between phenomena of seriality and (the neccessity of) forgetting. My research, though, is not based in the literary texts of Dickinson, James, and Stein; rather, it explores how we "cognize" their serial remediations in contemporary culture and *how* and *what* we in fact perceive and "remember" of these figures in the process. For instance, the legacy of Dickinson, who shunned publicity during her lifetime, has become subject to a thriving "Dickinson industry," driven in part by a continuous desire to refashion our sense of who she was. A large portion of that "industry" is dedicated to remediating and thus recycling the poet's writing in multiple ways, making her significance both more sustainable and a matter of flux and constant (re-)construction. There are a number of (mystery) novels and plays that revolve around the poet, the "mysteries" of her secluded life, and the radiance of her poetry; these include William Luce's one-woman, two-act drama *The Belle of Amherst* (1976), as well as fiction such as Jerome Charyn's *The Secret Life of Emily Dickinson: A Novel* (2010) and Joyce Carol Oates's "EDickinsonRepliLuxe," featured in *Wild Nights: Stories about the Last Days of Poe, Dickinson, Twain, James, and Hemingway* (2008), whose title pays tribute to Dickinson's poem "Wild Nights—Wild Nights!" (Fr269). We can also consult films and TV productions on Dickinson; but closer to home, so to speak, is the transposition of poetry into music that acknowledges both the medium's—historical and aesthetic—proximity and Dickinson's predilection for the hymn stanza. Dickinson's unconventional texts, both poems and letters, have inspired many musicians and composers, including Elliott Carter, Douglas Coupland, and Leon Kirchner, to mention just a few prominent names. "Quiet, introspective Emily Dickinson" has become, as Valentine Cunningham puts it, "the darling of modern composers" and "is reckoned to be the poet most set to music ever" (17)—and music here means hip hop and rap as much as classical composition. In addition, Dickinson frequently reappears in visual media, including painting, sculpture, and digital art as well as cartoons and video games.

Similarly, James's fiction, which experimented with point of view and gradually moved narrative perspective into the consciousness of his protagonists, is preoccupied with modes of perception, explicitly engages media history, and mistrusts the emergent "scopic regimes" (Martin Jay) of modernity, yet projects perception and memory as highly inter- and trans-medial faculties; his novels, prefaces, and essays are replete with references to other arts, including painting and architecture. What difference does it make, I wonder, if, instead of engaging the authors' literary texts, we encounter the poet in a cartoon or make an image of Dickinson our avatar in a video game? And what happens in our brains when we experience James's art of portraiture[5] transposed onto the screen, as in Jane Campion's 1996 cinematic adaptation of his *The Portrait of a Lady*? As with the perception of all texts and images, the cognitive engagement with portraiture involves the blending of mental capabilities. A visual portrait inspires narratives, while fictions and poems of portraiture paint images in our minds (narratology has engaged the cognitive sciences and the concept of "mental images" to help explain these processes). This is one reason why, for James, different arts could easily serve as analogies for one another and architecture and painting could serve as recurrent tropes for the art of fiction—an art that he clearly privileged over the technologies of photography. Still, as Werner Wolf has argued, the written portrait engages the reader's visual perception in less direct ways and guides him or her by staging modes of perception (23). Moreover, portraiture in James's novels, for instance, may render facial features, bodily postures, and social status, yet it capitalizes on insights into a protagonist's mindscape that open vistas that require their own devices in the visual arts, devices that, however, foster speculation rather than certainties. Since facial recognition is crucial in James's fiction, what happens when we fail to recognize Isabel Archer in Nicole Kidman, who stars in Campion's version of James's novel? How does a re-encounter with Stein in a BMW ad, on a T-shirt, or in a *Simpsons* cartoon register in our mindscape? And what impacts do such remediations have upon memory processes, transforming our sense of ourselves and of the world we inhabit?

Since the medium is (still) the message and new technologies keep extending our bodies, remediation does make a significant difference to the ways we perceive the world around us. Yet questions like these obviously overstrain the analytical scope of literary and cultural studies; so far, we have only begun asking what effect reading literary texts—an activity to which we assign so much cultural value and importance—has on our cognitive faculties. My current research aims at exploring how far we can come in answering such questions and explains why it is important to raise them. The study's (larger-than-life) objective is to interrogate how the evolution of media technologies has affected our position as subjects. Evidently, this is a million-dollar question that can only be approached in tiny steps. What issues relevant to current memory research in cultural studies can, in fact, be interrogated at the crossroads with the cognitive sciences, and vice versa? One such crossroad is marked, I would suggest, by the interrelation between the polymedial genre of portraiture and the phenomenon of face recognition that constitutes the highest capability of the human visual system. My analysis interfaces the art of the portrait, in (James's and Stein's) literary texts as well as in film and photography, with the faculty of face recognition; at the same time, it interrogates a crucial dimension of subject constitution—intersubjectivity—and the ways in which the face of another person (de-)stabilizes our own position. How do theories of cognition account for the effects of cultural mediation? They hardly do, in fact, which is why transdisciplinary dialogues remain crucially important. And in what ways can cultural analysis and cognition research be mutually instrumental—for example, for an updated sense of a subject that is also, if not first of all, a "cognizing subject" (Varela, Thompson, and Rosch xvii)? In other words, what does it mean if literary/cultural studies and the cognitive sciences mutually recognize each other? And what's seriality got to do with it?

Interrogating phenomena of (re-)mediation in cultural practices—practices that transform literature into film, painting, cartoon, or advertisement—I raise the question of how seriality informs and affects processes of individual and cultural memory. My (preliminary) answer is that seriality allows us to relate these processes, which, despite the tendency to blur the difference between individual and cultural memory, remain two fundamentally distinct modes of remembering. My thesis is that we can conceptualize memory—whether we approach it in terms of (re-)mediation or as cognitive processes—by way of seriality, repetition with variation, or insistence. We can also capture the relations among various disciplinary approaches to memory—approaches that cannot be spliced or collapsed into one another—in terms of seriality, or as repetition and difference. Seriality, I suggest, can be employed as a perspective that frames the ways in which both our brains (or physiologic processes of cognition) *and* biological and cultural evolution work (and this, I admit, is a grand claim that I hope will become more transparent as I move along). At the same time, I want to be perfectly clear that I use seriality not as a *sine qua non* concept but rather a methodological choice that involves a considerable shift in what remain dominant perspectives on matters of memory, mediation, and remediation.

II. The Significance of Seriality for Memory Research: Eight Theses on the Principle of the Series

Seriality is a driving motor of modernity and modernisms; it informs technologies of reproduction, from the printing press to digital cultures, just as much as it does modes of rhetoric such as irony, parody, and mimicry; it is a central operation in literary texts (and in some genres in particular, such as poetry), the trade mark of many artists' work (Claude Monet comes to mind as much as Andy Warhol, of course, and Elaine Sturtevant); and it is—most evidently, perhaps—central to photography, cinema, and the television format. Yet seriality remains an undertheorized concept (see thesis 1, below), notwithstanding its significance in the literary *and* critical practice of Stein; in the work of Walter Benjamin and Umberto Eco; in the debate on mimicry that Luce Irigaray, Homi Bhabha, and Judith Butler have engaged in; and, most importantly for me, in Deleuze's theory of repetition and difference. Much work remains to be done to develop a theoretical and methodological framework out of a proliferating practice and aesthetics of serial forms; and in this regard, Deleuze's work on repetition and difference is a good if not the best place to start—in part because it echoes Stein's belief that "[t]here is a world of difference and in it there is essentially no remembering" ("Portraits and Repetition" 183). In other words, Stein and Deleuze both hold that there is no such thing as repetition. Or as Stein put it: "It is very like a frog hopping he cannot ever hop exactly the same distance or the same way of hopping at every hop. A bird's singing is perhaps the nearest thing to repetition but if you listen they too vary their insistence" ("Portraits and Repetition" 167).

Making a case for Deleuze's sense of repetition as an operation not of sameness, but of singularity and variability (as opposed to generalization) we are in for a fundamental shift of perspective that, based on the re-cognition of a previously disregarded and if not aesthetic than certainly cultural procedure, involves a shift in (more precisely, an abstention from) ethics as well. More precisely, seriality leans toward "indifference," not in the sense of lacking difference, but as an attitude of disinterestedness (see thesis 2 below). Seriality, if we follow Deleuze, is a category that allows us to capture a kind of relation that is not based on either identity or difference. Instead, seriality circumnavigates these terms, which have dominated cultural studies for too long and which tend to freeze what is actually an ongoing process of subjectivity. In this way, seriality also calls into question common notions of representation—a rather contested term in both cultural studies and the cognitive sciences. Accounting for the relation between subjects and things in an "indifferent" or "disinterested" way, seriality thus turns its back on a dominant mode of our research agenda, one that is preoccupied with matters of identity politics and practices. Along those lines, we may also note that the series—in the sense of a string, chain, or succession that works recursively, not linearly—constitutes a very different kind of operation than the network that has become our privileged way of conceptualizing (social) relations with a trope overdetermined by ethical discourses; I will come back to this matter shortly.

Most significantly therefore (and this is thesis 4 below), I employ seriality as the key term for a fundamental shift in perspective that has been on its way for some time now. In fact, what we are witnessing is not so much a drift toward cultural practices that favour seriality, but rather a gradual transformation of viewpoint, resulting from serial practices such as film and TV: modernism taught us to privilege formal modes of the "experimental" and aesthetic gestures of "mak[ing] it new"—modes that in the context of American cultures appear and reappear in series; strategies of technological reproduction (including processes of mediation, remediation, and appropriation) have now moved to the forefront of our attention. And this, I deem, is largely due to the success of new and newer media—especially computer and Internet technologies that have come to structure a considerable degree of knowledge production in the sciences as well as in everyday cultures. In this context, Deleuze's work on repetition and difference can function as the basis for an extended sense of seriality that acknowledges, for instance, the significance of serial processes for memory studies, both in cultural studies and in the cognitive sciences. At the same time, we need to accept that seriality does not—indeed cannot—account for processes of memory themselves; it merely shifts our ways of accounting for such processes. No concept can capture processes, be they cultural or cognitive, in an immediate or direct manner—and generally speaking, the humanities and parts of the social sciences are more willing than the sciences to admit such matters of mediation

Still, we can take things a step further. Seriality is of particular interest here because among the insights of memory research in the cognitive sciences are that, first, both memory and forgetting can be understood as serial operations; second, memory depends on forgetting; and, third, processes of memory serve the present and future more than the past—in other words, we "remember forward"[6] rather than backward (see theses 4 and 5 below). Memory cultures attempt to come to terms with the past, whereas the cognitive sciences have come to consider memory as a strategy that deals with the present in order to enable the future (Welzer "Kriege" 46). In this process, forgetting is crucial since our ability to remember depends on our ability to forget.[7] Accordingly, acts of remembering dissolve previously stable memory traces more than they consolidate information. Remembering in fact *weakens* memory, puts it at risk by irritating reconsolidation processes. "Reinstalling memory traces," Wolf Singer underlines, "is closer to perceiving than to reproducing the original content of memory" ("Erinnern" 56, translation mine). Memory is no longer conceived of as storage and retrieval of learning processes and information, but as a form of continuous rewriting, updating, forgetting, re-membering, and re-cognizing in new contexts. Memory itself thus works as "repetition with variation," as continued transformation of what we are already familiar with, in the course of a process whose main accomplishment is forgetting and keeping the future in mind rather than pondering with the past.

There is one thing here that may strike us as contradictory. The insights into the serial mutability of memory are in line with the trope of the computer—a trope that, owing to the impact of the information-processing approach, reigned as the master trope for communication and information systems, the development of living organisms, and the work of the human mind for over fifty years, and that moreover is closely aligned with concepts of seriality. By the 1990s, that paradigm had made way for the parallel distributed processing approach (also called connectionism or the neural networks approach),[8] which displaced the serial conception of memory with notions of "simultaneous processing" (Mountcastle 31), synchronicity, connectivity, and reversibility. When no longer conceived of as retrieval from a database, memory becomes an act of patterned construction and recontextualization whereby what is being remembered is related to, integrated in, and reconstructed by what we already know—that is, by the connections or synapses already established in our brains.

Neuroscientists today privilege connectionism over serial models, acknowledging that cognitive processes involve more than one area of the brain simultaneously. Thus, on the one hand, the concept of seriality is called into question as the trope of the computer and the classical paradigm that conceived of "brains as serial computing machines" gets displaced by the trope of the network (Engel and König 157, my translation). On the other hand, computer technologies persist as a dominant figure in memory discourse. And the very transformation of the tropes of mind—from mind as computer, to mind as neural network,[9] to mind as brain—can itself be seen as a serial process. Thus seriality underlines that the displacement of the computer metaphor by that of the network does not follow a cogent causality but rather the seriality of (dominant) technologies.

A closer comparison between the principle of the series and the trope of the network illuminates what's actually at stake here (see thesis 6 below): while the net maps a territory, connecting different points in space, the series drives a recursive (as opposed to progressive) temporal extension that builds on forgetting. While the net is associated with the ethics of inclusive connection ("everything is connected"), the series operates a non-directional evolution that is subject to sudden leaps of change and free of value judgments (although its "openness" may itself be read as a value, of course). As a form of echo making and mimicry, seriality nonetheless informs intersubjective processes, despite its "social" indifference (or "disinterest"). Numerous recent studies in experimental social psychology present human mimicry—an oftentimes unconscious tendency of humans to imitate the behaviour of their *vis-à-vis*—as a fundamental cultural technique of social cohesion as well as a method to win over and manipulate an opponent.[10]

Of ultimate significance for a project that accounts for memory as a process of both cognition and (re-)mediation is that seriality is a central operational mechanism of mass media and constitutive of their function (see thesis 7 below), whose "main accomplishment," according to Niklas Luhmann, is "forgetting" (180, translation mine).[11] Even if we resist following Luhmann all the way, we may easily concur that there is no memory without mass mediation and without the serial operations of forgetting that mass media inspire— indeed, rely on—in order to reproduce their own systems and mechanisms—mechanisms that continuously transform information into non-information so that newness or irritation can be generated over and over again. Or as Luhmann writes in *Die Realität der Massenmedien*: "Memory is not to be understood as storage for past conditions or events. This is not what media and other cognitive systems can be burdened with. [...] Instead memory constructs repetition, redundancy, with continuous openness for current matter, with constantly renewed irritability" (76, my translation). Luhmann does not use the term seriality, yet it seems implicit in his theory of mass media, whose tirelessly impellent arrangement of society he compares to the workings of the brain. But when he suggests that media function "in an endogenously restless way like a brain" (98), he is driving an analogy that *need not* be read in terms of the likeness of two self-reproductive systems. As he applies the term self-reproduction to both technologies and bodies, he is not necessarily suggesting that this is how brains and media "truly" operate; rather, this alignment hints that we can reconceptualize the relation of culture and cognition, media and memory, in terms of repetition and difference, or, seriality.

Yet this serial sense of how media and mind/brain relate also reminds us—and this is my last thesis (see thesis 8 below)—first, that seriality is the principle of evolution, the theory of which fundamentally shifted our sense of what it means to be a human subject; and, second, that Darwin's sense of the evolutionary process co-evolved, as Philipp Sarasin has argued convincingly, with the modern medium of film. Unlike many of his colleagues, who were preoccupied with biological classification, Darwin considered the concept of species debatable, because as parts of an ongoing and to a certain degree contingent process, all individual species are temporary, transitory phenomena (cf. Sarasin 36–50). In fact, it was Darwin's genius to read the series of individual life forms he encountered as he travelled south as a development or movement. Sarasin speaks of "a hallucinatory experience" in this context (51) and makes the interesting argument that Darwin's insight coincided with contemporaneous optical inventions that took advantage of the afterimage effect and with the emergence of images that move in time (53). Focusing on the big (moving) picture, Darwin was able to see that *Homo sapiens* was not the offspring of divine creation, but evolved within the animal kingdom. This synchronicity of media history and evolutionary theory allows us to rethink the relation between (cultural) evolution and our understanding of the human subject as a serial phenomenon and intersubject while also highlighting the importance of temporality—not in the sense of progress, though, but as consistent recursion.

"Now actively repeat at all, now actively repeat at all, now actively repeat at all," Gertrude Stein "insisted" in "If I Told Him: A Completed Portrait of Picasso" (1923), an update of the earlier portrait of the artist, part of which I quoted above (464). Thus in closing, I would like to—"insistently"—propose the following claims to underline the significance of seriality in processes of memory and (re-)mediation:

1   Seriality is a dominant motor of modernity and modernisms; it informs technologies of reproduction from the printing press to the cinema to digital cultures. Yet seriality remains undertheorized so far; it

needs more systematic work, taking off from cultural practices as well as from the suggestive work of Gertrude Stein and Gilles Deleuze.

2. Seriality as a concept of "indifference" allows us to frame relations (in the sense of "proximity" and "kinship") that are not based on either identity or difference; it thus challenges central terms of cultural analyses that fail to account for process and "experience."

3. The increasing relevance of seriality in cultural studies and media research marks a fundamental change in perspective that constitutes a revision of modernism and its paradigmatic aesthetics, forms, and functions and that challenges our tendency to think of history as succession of eras or epochs.

4. Since memory is no longer conceived of as the storage and retrieval of learning processes and information, but rather as a form of continuous rewriting, updating, forgetting, re-membering, and re-cognizing, memory and forgetting—in both cultural practice and cognition—can be understood as serial operations.

5. Seriality accounts for the fact that processes of memory serve the present and future, not the past, that we "remember forward" rather than backwards.

6. The "indifference" of the series works in contrast to the "ethics" of the network: its emphasis on process privileges constellations of time over configurations of space and favours recursion over connectivity. The series juxtaposes the strong trope of the network by a metonymic dynamism of echo, mimicry, and adaptation. In the realm of the series, sociality and communication are no longer primarily ethically motivated; they follow no linear path and possibly move in leaps.

7. Seriality is a central operational mechanism of mass media and is constitutive of their function.

8. As the principle of evolution that co-emerged with the modern medium of film, seriality allows us to rethink the relation between (cultural) evolution and our understanding of the human subject.

PS: To be continued …

NOTES

1. A prominent example is the work of neurobiologist Semir Zeki; see also Cupchik.
2. On the "literary invention of the series" in Stein's work see, for instance, Haselstein.

3   Prince, "Joy in Repetition," *Graffiti Bridge* (1990), 4:53 min. Two (among many more) cover versions are Dayna Kurtz, "Joy in Repetition," *Beautiful Yesterday* (2004), 4:46 min.; and My Brightest Diamond, "Joy in Repetition," Live, Le Ciel, Grenoble, February 2007, 6:38 min.
4   See Sielke, "Dickinson and Seriality," unpublished manuscript and paper presented at "The Emily Dickinson International Society (EDIS) Discussion Institute" on "The Role of Narrative in the Poetry of Emily Dickinson," EDIS Annual Meeting, 1 to 3 August 2008, Amherst.
5   James repeatedly used the trope of the portrait to align the "art of fiction" with painting.
6   I make reference here to the exhibition of Aboriginal art after 1960, titled "Remembering Forward," that took place at Museum Ludwig, Cologne, in the spring of 2011. See http://www.museenkoeln.de/museum-ludwig/default.asp?s=3178.
7   This also holds true for literary practice as I have shown in the context of my work on constructions of subjectivity in the writings of the American poet Adrienne Rich; see especially the chapter "'Living Memory' and 'the Power to Forget'" in Sielke, *Fashioning the Female Subject*, 201–17.
8   The "magnitude" of the number of connections that link brain structures, particularly those between areas of the cerebral cortex, is considered "[a] new fact about large-scale brain anatomy" (Mountcastle 12).
9   On the trope of the network, see Schäfer-Wünsche. The prominence of the term network is underscored by the fact that it is currently displacing the trope of the (family) tree in evolutionary biology, which suggests a degree of linearity for the evolutionary process and can no longer account for the complexity of kinship relations as they developed in the course of evolution.
10 See van Baaren et al.; Chartrand und van Baaren.
11 I deliberately use my own translation of Luhmann and do not rely on the English version *The Reality of the Mass Media: Cultural Memory in the Present*, trans. Kathleen Cross (Stanford: Stanford UP, 2000), which tends to become unnecessarily opaque at times.

3

Hirsch, Sebald, and the Uses and Limits of Postmemory

Kathy Behrendt

Marianne Hirsch coined the term "postmemory" to encompass a subject of enduring interest—namely, the fraught position of the generation that follows a period of collective trauma. Her specific focus in her initial work on postmemory was on the relationships that children have with parents who were victims or witnesses of such trauma. Hirsch is explicit about her personal connection to the subject: she is a child of parents who escaped the Holocaust, and she grew up in a climate in which the after-effects of trauma and victimization manifested themselves in countless ways.

Hirsch developed her conception of postmemory in a series of works, and that conception has, over time, proven to be quite malleable. In one sense, the term simply refers to the ways in which members of the generation following a catastrophe (although Hirsch also includes members of the "1.5" generation—child survivors of catastrophe) are aware of and connect to their elders' past suffering. Often, though, the term includes not only that awareness but also the often publicly available imaginative and/or aesthetic responses (sometimes called "postmemory work") of members of this generation to the trauma their family endured. For the most part, my concern is with this latter sense of postmemory. Although postmemory is malleable, it has several more or less constant features: the experiences of the victim are transmitted to the descendant through narrative and sometimes through images (photographs being especially important to Hirsch); the post-rememberer strongly identifies with the victim while remaining aware of the distance between them; postmemories are powerful and are invested with emotion; the post-rememberer connects to the past through imagination and creativity; and, finally, post-rememberers are not passive recipients of memories, but place themselves in the morally imperative role of witness, entrusted with preserving the past they have inherited and transmitting it to others. How best to convey the memories they are bequeathed remains a source of constant scrutiny, both by the post-rememberer and by the interested wider audience.[1]

A prime example of postmemory work, for Hirsch, is Art Spiegelman's complex biographical and autobiographical graphic novel *Maus*, which recounts Spiegelman's father's life before Auschwitz and his time as a prisoner there. This is interspersed with the author's present-day dealings with his aging and irascible father, as they meet in order that the son can record these oft-told tales of family struggle and persecution. The work is as much about his father's past suffering as it is about Spiegelman's own inherited guilt, angst, and ambivalence as the one surviving son (another did not live) of death camp survivors. As the numbers of living primary victims of that particular catastrophe wane, interest in the generation following them continues to grow, and their situation becomes a subject of interest in its own right, replete as it is with its own pain. Insofar as members of the next generation are compelled to ensure that their parents' experiences are not forgotten, the pain is supplemented by a deep sense of responsibility. Hirsch is only one among many writers who recognize the special position of the post-trauma generation, and the notion of postmemory is her attempt to provide a conceptual framework able to illuminate their situation and guide their endeavours.

In what follows, I explore the virtues and shortcomings of Hirsch's conception of postmemory. To draw out the virtues, I will tap recent developments in the philosophy of memory. Having done that, I will argue that by expanding her conception of postmemory to include works that lack those virtues, Hirsch risks diluting them. Her recent move to classify author W.G. Sebald's work as postmemorial is a case in point. Finally, and again through appeal to Sebald, I will issue cautionary words about postmemory in general and about the ethical dangers and limitations inherent in Hirsch's emphasis on empathic access to the past experiences of the victims of trauma.

I

Hirsch's concept of postmemory intersects with several areas of emerging interest in the philosophy of memory. Gone from memory theory is the hegemony of the "archival" model of human memory, whereby past experiences are fixed entities contained in some interior metaphorical storage closet so that memory's success is judged solely in terms of how little damage we do to these items when retrieving them. Many memory theorists now contend that change and reconstruction are inevitable aspects of memory.[2] Some argue that *good* remembering is not static; rather, it can alter when our evaluation of the past alters (Campbell §2.3). In a related development, memory is no longer being treated as necessarily private and interior. It can also be public, often taking place "through action, narrative, and other modes of representation in public spaces" (Campbell 362). Memory's capacity to evolve according to the ever-changing present context does not necessarily entail distortion. Memory is always selective; we cannot represent every possible detail of a past experience, but must pick and choose among them—and these choices may be good or bad. Thus, "good" memories select details of the past that are significant and relevant from the standpoint of the present—what we know, understand, and feel about that past situation *now*. Sue Campbell calls this *accuracy*: selecting, sometimes from among an abundance of details, those elements that we now take to be salient in light of our current knowledge and intentions *vis-à-vis* the remembered content, and doing so in a way that strikes the appropriate emotional tone (Campbell §§3.2 and 3.3).[3]

Postmemory is in keeping with these revised conceptions of memory and has great potential to exemplify Campbell's virtue of "accuracy." Postmemory seeks to do justice to ancestral memories—to get them right by capturing the emotional content of those experiences and by isolating those elements that will convey what we *presently* understand to be the devastating extent of what was suffered in the past. This is often done for the purpose of enhancing others' understanding of those events. Additionally, postmemory is often conducted in a public forum through creative and imaginative expression, with a vigilant attentiveness to what might be, at any given cultural moment, the most appropriate aesthetic means of preserving and conveying the past (an art installation, a graphic novel, etc.).

Tied to the aforementioned developments in memory theory is a separate recent move to acknowledge a moral dimension to memory.[4] Talk of an ethics of memory is increasing, alongside examination of the moral implications of bearing witness to the past. Often, such witnessing is achieved through the institutions and conventions surrounding "collective memory," be these museums, memorials, truth and reconciliation committees, or efforts to preserve a threatened Aboriginal culture. Clearly, Hirsch's concept has resonance here too, and she explicitly holds up postmemory as a model for "an *ethical* relation to the oppressed or persecuted other" ("Surviving Images" 10). Insofar as the post-rememberer has been assigned the role of witness, she is—often in publicly available forums—fulfilling an ethical imperative in receiving, preserving, and passing on what was known, felt, and experienced. Hence, the work of postmemory is never merely aesthetic, notwithstanding its creative aspects; it also entails a duty to sustain the integrity of the original experience—something not necessarily demanded of a purely artistic endeavour.

Accuracy on the one hand, and the fulfillment of the moral imperative to bear witness on the other, are two of postmemory's virtues. And both are tied to the broader possibilities of memory as a tool for advancing emotional and intellectual flourishing (i.e., instead of memory being a mere repository of past experience). Hirsch's more recent (and broader) elucidation of postmemory, however, threatens to dilute the concept's strengths.

II

While there are some philosophical models underpinning postmemory, there are also problems with the concept. Two significant strands of criticism have emerged. The first of these we might call "the Butler objection," after Joseph Butler, who famously argued that—contrary to what John Locke supposedly implied in his groundbreaking writing on personal identity—memory *presupposes* personal identity.[5] If a subject at a later time remembers having had a certain experience at an earlier time, it is because the experiencing and the remembering subject are one and the same. It is *because* the experience is his that he can have memory-consciousness of it; it does not become his by virtue of his having such consciousness (and therefore the memory relation does not *create* but merely *presupposes* personal identity, *pace* Locke). While Butler's point has since been disputed as a claim about what is possible with respect to memory,[6] it remains relatively uncontroversial that, contingently speaking, his account captures how things do in fact go in real life; we are built such that we can remember our own experiences and no one else's, and identity between a subject at an earlier time and a subject at a later one coincides with any memory-like relation between them. Hirsch does not appear to be in the business of disputing received views about the empirical facts of memory (or personal identity), so wherein lies her entitlement to claim that one person can have a memory-like relation to the experience of another? In particular, how can she go so far as to claim that the experiences bequeathed to the post-rememberer are "so powerful, so monumental, as to constitute memories in their own right" for the post-rememberer ("Surviving Images" 9)? Gary Weissman nicely captures the tenor of the Butler objection when he writes that "no degree of power and monumentality can transform one person's lived memories into another's" (17).[7]

Hirsch is well aware of this line of criticism and has confronted it directly in a recent paper. She absolves herself of committing a basic empirical error about memory by making clear that, as far as she is concerned, we cannot have *literal* memories of another's experiences ("The Generation of Postmemory" 109). But in attempting to address the objection at hand, she walks straight into the sights of another criticism—one that often gets conflated with the Butler objection but deserves separate consideration. Hirsch maintains her rhetorical entitlement to the term "memory" on the grounds that postmemory *seems* like memory in crucial respects—specifically, "it approximates memory in its affective force" ("The Generation of Postmemory" 109). Thus, *affect* is the key point of resemblance between a victim's experience and a post-rememberer's connection to it, and this affective resemblance is, as said, achieved through imaginative means. Imaginative and affect-laden identification with the victim is a mark of postmemory, and lest there be any doubt about what this looks like in practice, Hirsch makes it clear: "It is a question of adopting the traumatic experiences [...] of others as experiences one might oneself have had, and of ascribing them into one's own life story" ("Surviving Images" 10). In short, it is a question of empathy—of imagining what it is like to be another, or at the least, imagining how things would be for oneself if one were in another's circumstance. It is Hirsch's continuing commitment to this aspect of postmemory that feeds into the second strand of criticism—namely, the appropriation objection.

According to the appropriation objection, we are, with postmemory, dealing with something akin to counter-transference on the part of the post-rememberer, wherein "empathy [...] shades into overidentification" and the focus is primarily on the self, not the victim (Franklin *A Thousand Darknesses* 224–25). When the post-rememberer adopts the victim's experience as her own, there is nothing to bar her from "coloniz[ing] victims' memories and identities" (Crownshaw 216). What fuels the criticisms here is not the Butleresque concern that Hirsch is simply mistaken about the proper ascription of memories to subjects of experience. Rather, it is the intimation that the post-rememberer can herself live through anything resembling what the victims lived through, feel what they felt, or forge and possess her own traumatic experiences, with the victim as facilitator of this exercise. These intimations, more so than any tendency toward an overly liberal or literal use of the term "memory," are what I take to be the true target of the appropriation objection.

Insofar as empathy is a key component of postmemory, I do not think Hirsch ever fully escapes the appropriation objection. Although perhaps we can somewhat alleviate the sense that the act of postmemory is essentially self-regarding by recalling that it is the child of the victim-parent who is the post-rememberer, indeed, a child who grew up immersed in manifestations of the victim's trauma—not just publicly available information, but deeply personal family stories, images, and psychosomatic symptoms. A sympathetic reading would allow for a degree of entitlement to identification here, consonant with the nature and extent of the relation between the rememberer and the post-rememberer. If Hirsch's personal connections to the memories she preserves and conveys are a potential safeguard against the appropriation objection, however, why then does she expand her concept of postmemory to include people who don't have familial ties to survivors of the trauma? On the expanded depiction of the postmemory generation, anyone with an affiliative connection to, or even just an interest in, the traumatic event is potentially welcome into the fold of postmemory.[8] In addition—and as is more my concern—what qualifies as postmemory work is also altered and expanded beyond the narrower bounds I discussed at the outset.

Hirsch's expanded conception of postmemory, if left unqualified, seems to allow the concept to be applied with equal facility to not just the children of Holocaust survivors, but also the authors of fraudulent Holocaust memoirs.[9] The warning that postmemory work may absorb "unregulated fantasy" into its ranks has been issued before (see Long *W.G. Sebald* 118). Leaving this criticism aside, I will, for present purposes, focus on just one recent entry into Hirsch's enlarged cast of post-rememberers—the German author W.G. Sebald. I will argue that he does not qualify as someone engaged in "cultural postmemory work," as Hirsch would have it ("The Generation of Postmemory" 117). This is ultimately tied to the manner in which he escapes accusations of appropriation by eschewing imaginative empathy. Moreover, there are also particular features that are conspicuously absent in his work, which distances it from the milieu of the postmemorial.

III

Sebald is certainly engaged with the general phenomenon I mentioned at the outset: the position of the generation that comes after a catastrophic event. This, along with his harvesting of real-life anecdotes, archival data, and especially photographs from that past, is no doubt what endears him to Hirsch. But at the same time, Sebald's status as a member of a postmemory generation is complicated by the fact that his heritage does not directly tie him to the victims; he was born in Germany at the end of the Second World War, to a father who was a captain in the German army. Moreover, Sebald was raised in an environment wherein, by his own account, little was said or spoken about that time (see Jaggi). Only when he had distanced himself, both spatially and temporally, far from his national and family origins, did he even begin to explore that past through creative means.[10]

Hirsch claims to be able to cope with these discrepancies between Sebald and more "conventional" post-rememberers, such as Art Spiegelman ("The Generation of Postmemory"). My concern, though, is less with the clear disparities between Sebald and the children of victims, and more with the differences between the creative products of their separate pasts. Sebald's work is not in keeping with much of what I have identified as philosophically prescient about postmemory. In particular, his works touch on the Holocaust in a way that is often antithetical to the qualities of witness and accuracy—qualities that, as discussed, are exemplified in Hirsch's conception of postmemory. These points can be drawn out through consideration of the title character of *Austerlitz* (the book Hirsch focuses on), Max Ferber of *The Emigrants*, the narrators of both works, and consideration of the various ways in which none of them qualifies as a post-rememberer. Hirsch focuses on *Austerlitz*, although much of her analysis would apply in equal measure to *The Emigrants*, in particular the section on Max Ferber, which has much in common with the story of Austerlitz (especially the acutely felt loss of the mother and the relation of the characters to the narrator.) I include them both for interest's sake, but whether taken together or separately, the stories of these two characters reinforce the absence of many key features of witness and accuracy in Sebald.

Both Austerlitz (an art historian) and Ferber (an artist) were sent to Britain as children and are descendants of Jewish parents left behind in mainland Europe, who were subsequently killed or lost in the Holocaust. Both convey accounts of their lives, and of the lives—as much as is known—of their parents, to an unnamed narrator over a series of conversations that take place over a long span of time. As in all of Sebald's "prose fiction,"[11] certain clues lead or mislead us to note a striking resemblance between the anonymous narrator and Sebald himself, but the genre-transgressing nature of the works impedes a fixed and determinate identification.

Detailed discussion of what it means to be a witness is relatively new in the philosophy of memory, but some plausible criteria have been proposed by Jeffrey Blustein.[12] A witness must, at the very least, have epistemic authority if she is to be credible; she must know whereof she speaks, and those to whom she testifies must be aware of, or able to obtain, these epistemic credentials. Conversely, a good deal of the irremediable misfortune of Austerlitz's and Ferber's situations arises from the fact that neither of them knows in any detail what happened to their parents; they can only surmise. The limit of their knowledge circumscribes their potential as effective witnesses; if one purpose of witnessing is to render salient to the audience what was salient for the sufferer, then neither Austerlitz nor Ferber is in a position to do this.

Another arguable feature of the witness is agency—witnessing being an active and deliberate undertaking for a perceived purpose. Hirsch herself extols the "anchors of agency and responsibility" in postmemorial aesthetic treatments of the Holocaust (*Family Frames* 264). Yet Austerlitz and Ferber are so often presented to us as passive vessels for the past, as not in control of the effect it has on them, and as all the more vulnerable because of this. For both these characters, the past often manifests itself in involuntary or unconscious ways, such as through the vivid dreams they relate to the narrator, the possibly hysterical symptoms they display (Ferber's increasing agoraphobia and memory gaps concerning a recent visit to Lake Geneva, and Austerlitz's anxiety attacks and incidences of cognitive and emotional paralyses), and their tendency toward obsessive-compulsive behaviour (Austerlitz's endless night walks around London, and the artist Ferber's scraped down and restarted paintings). Similarly, both characters exhibit visceral responses to places that bear some relation to their family's past (both return to locales from their childhood and experience anxiety and despair) and have inexplicable affinities to certain other places that connect more obliquely with that past (the outskirts of Manchester, for Ferber, with its bleak post-industrial vistas dotted with warehouses and chimneys; Liverpool Street Station in London, for Austerlitz, later discovered to be the site of his arrival in Britain on the *Kindertransport*).

In addition to Austerlitz and Ferber's lack of agential freedom, there is another related feature of agency that is conspicuously absent for them—namely, the conscious and deliberate. Even if we consider the above examples of manifestations of the past to be forms of memory, none of them amounts to a form of testimony, because testimony cannot be largely unconscious or "unwitting" (Blustein 315).[13] While Blustein's demand for conscious control over the content of one's testimony is a more controversial feature of witnessing, there is a strong case to be made for it in connection to the aforementioned epistemic feature. We cannot align unconscious testimony with the epistemic authority required of bearing witness; one cannot bear witness to a truth that is largely inaccessible or obscured to oneself. A degree of insight into the source of one's memory-activity is needed in order to bear witness, otherwise one lacks competence and authority to speak to others of such matters (Blustein 316). The notion of unconscious or unwitting testimony also threatens the all-important ethical element of testimony at stake here, by raising the unpalatable prospect that something of such normative significance may be accidental.

Certainly lack of insight and self-understanding dominate the lives of characters like Ferber and Austerlitz, which is why they remain in a perpetual state of remorse, each engaged in his obsessive pursuits. It may also explain why they both commit acts that are anathema to postmemory witnessing: they relinquish rather than safeguard what little they have in the way of material connection to their family's past. Austerlitz gives over his collection of photos to the narrator; and in a quite literal abandonment of any pretense of standing as a conduit for his mother's past experience, Ferber gives up not just photographs but also his mother's manuscript memoirs.

Thus, Ferber and Austerlitz fail with respect to the broader purpose of postmemory: to bear effective witness. I also believe, however, that they fail at the level of the second of the two aforementioned virtues of postmemory: *accuracy*.

IV

"Accuracy," recall, means in part the selection of salient elements from the details the past presents us. Yet at key points in Sebald's texts where accuracy would seem to be most required, it is significantly absent. Sometimes this is due to a want of detail (Austerlitz's retrograde amnesia being a clear case in point), sometimes due to an excess, as Austerlitz is also frequently overwhelmed by the details of the past, in various guises. He pores over the Nazi film footage of Theresienstadt in slow motion, searching every frame for evidence of his mother, who was interred there. Likewise, he searches the monolithic new Bibliothèque Nationale in Paris for information about his father, but bureaucratic and architectural obstacles prevent him from finding anything meaningful among the vast archives. Crucial details also escape Ferber. He repeatedly tries to paint from memory the man with the butterfly net, who saved him from possible suicide on an occasion when he revisited a key locale from his childhood, but he cannot ever capture the face of his rescuer. Nor can Ferber remember the parting words of his final encounter with his parents—instead he recalls trivial details, such as the make and model number of the airplane he flew out on.

Although he is comparatively exempt, accuracy eludes even the narrator himself at times. The narrator of *The Emigrants*, much as he would like to, cannot give the names of the three women in the photograph from the Łódź ghetto, which he describes at the end of the chapter on Max Ferber. He toys with the possibility of three Hebraic names before withdrawing that speculation and, instead, naming the women after the three fates of Roman mythology—Nona, Decuma, and Morta. We have a key artifact of postmemory here—a photograph—but no one is left who can extract what should be of primary significance—namely, the identity of the subjects. They are plunged instead into the realm of myth, and so again accuracy is lacking: what ought to be salient is inaccessible (and the destructive power of the artifact—a recurring motif in Sebald—is compounded).[14] This functions, among other things, as a salutary warning to the reader of the narrator's own limitations in getting to the heart of matter on our behalf.

In sum, recurring elements of Hirsch's postmemory include witness and accuracy, and Sebald's characters display little evidence of speaking to these qualities. This is not to say that Sebald's work is lacking qualities it would have benefited from; rather, he is engaged in a different project, and one best not subsumed under the umbrella of postmemory work. Hirsch is cognizant that Sebald brings new and complicated issues to bear on her conception of postmemory. She is aware of the ambivalence and complexity of a work like *Austerlitz*, and she tries to incorporate such features into a more complex and problematized conception of postmemory ("The Generation of Postmemory"),but this effort is not fully successful. This is not because there is a single, fixed set of possibilities for what can constitute postmemory work; what may qualify will evolve according to the needs of the time, as noted (see my section I; and Hirsch, "The Generation of Postmemory" 117–19). Rather, it is because there are certain key recurring aspects of postmemory that are less expendable insofar as they help define what is valuable within the concept.

The concept of postmemory began largely as an attempt to capture the relation of children of survivors to their parents' memories, through emotional engagement and empathy. The means for this is creative imagination, and the goal is to preserve remembered events. If we expand postmemory to include cases like Austerlitz and Max Ferber's stories, where some or all of these elements are absent or suppressed, we obscure what is of value in both Hirsch and Sebald.

V

One response to all this would be to argue that although some of Sebald's characters fail to qualify as post-rememberers in any unproblematic sense, his narrator largely succeeds. After all, with respect to his candidacy as witness, the narrator's epistemic and agential credentials are all apparently intact. Although he may, at times, be limited in his ability to be accurate (in Campbell's sense) in what he conveys, he is not pathologically so; the suffering and misfortune of those for whom he speaks are relayed with great detail and sensitivity and resonate with our current understanding and expectations of such people. Perhaps I have simply misidentified the possible location of any alleged postmemory relation in Sebald. Hirsch, too, focuses on the character of Austerlitz, although she does credit the narrator with being an affiliative post-rememberer ("The Generation of Postmemory" 119).

I think it is also not advisable to treat Sebald's narrator as a post-rememberer, for reasons that concern a crucial difference between Hirsch and Sebald—namely, the role of empathy.[15] Among all the central qualities of postmemory, this is clearly an important one for Hirsch, as well as the most problematic. Hirsch's emphasis on imagination and emotional channelling as the primary means of engaging with another's past, and her talk of "identification with the victim" and adoption of their experiences as "experiences one might oneself have had" ("Surviving Images" 10) are, as mentioned, what open the door to accusations of appropriation. I had suggested that we might alleviate this criticism on Hirsch's behalf by allowing post-rememberers special dispensation as close relatives of the rememberers in question. This of course does not help make the case for bringing Sebald's German, gentile, mere acquaintance of a narrator into the fold of post-rememberers. But there is something beyond these relatively superficial disparities between Sebald's narrator and Hirsch that, I believe, separates the narrator from a narrowly conceived post-rememberer. The central issue here is not any putative entitlement to empathic access to another's past experience, but the very idea of empathy itself as a means of ethical engagement with another. I want to draw on one final, recent philosophical discussion in order to illuminate what may be worrying about the appeal to empathy, and also to reinforce the disparity between Hirsch and Sebald in this regard. In doing this, I will cast a more critical gaze over the postmemory endeavour in general.

Peter Goldie, in "Dramatic Irony, Narrative, and the External Perspective," discusses the attempt to imagine the mental life of others—their thoughts and feelings—from the inside, from their perspective. He calls this "perspective-shifting" and warns that it is an overrated and even dangerous means of ethical engagement with others (Goldie 78). For one, perspective shifting rests on the assumption that either there are no substantial differences between myself and the other, or, if there are, that they can be readily overcome. Even occasional perspective shifting runs the risk of "egoistic drift" (Goldie borrows the term from Martin Hoffman): I shift my perspective to someone else's and in the course of imagining how things were for them, I naturally bring to mind a similar situation I myself once endured, and the attempt to empathize "ends up as something rather self-indulgent" (Goldie 80). *Sympathy*, by contrast, requires an external perspective, according to Goldie: "In thinking of the other person as another, our sympathy does not mirror his suffering: it is an ethical response to his suffering; we feel *for* him," and, "in contrast with perspective-shifting, we are free to think of him in all his particularities, appreciating his perspective on the world as ineliminably his, and perhaps as radically unlike our own" (82).

Apart from this appreciation of the other as another unique and autonomous being, there are further normative benefits to maintaining an external perspective. We refrain from putting ourselves in another's position, partly in order to defray egoistic drift and so to focus on the other's situation and not our own, as is appropriate in a situation where it is the other person's suffering that is meant to be the focus of ethical attention. This also, crucially, allows us to bring to bear our own perspective in evaluating the other—something we could not do if we simply allowed our perspective to be displaced by that of the other (Goldie 82). As it happens, Hirsch herself at times alludes to the situation (although not the full dangers) of losing one's own perspective within the postmemory act: "Postmemory's connection to the past is thus not [...] mediated by recall but by imaginative investment, projection, and creation. To grow up with such overwhelming inherited memories, to be dominated by narratives that preceded one's birth or one's consciousness, is to risk having one's own stories and experiences displaced, even evacuated, by those of a previous generation" ("The Generation of Postmemory" 107). If Goldie is correct, then there are serious repercussions to such a displacement: one loses one's own evaluative perspective on the situation and has nothing to offer in response to the reported trauma other than simply to reflect back to the sufferer his own pain. While this may not always be avoidable (and in the case of close relatives in certain environments, may be inevitable), it is not to be commended or endorsed as "an *ethical* relation to the oppressed or persecuted other" (Hirsch "Surviving Images" 10).

Finally, perspective shifting is limited because it is dependent on imagination, and imagination is limited, especially when it comes to exceptional and/or terrible events. The upshot of this is that when we are incapable of successfully imagining certain things, the demands of the perspective-shifting enterprise lead us to a place of mere incomprehension (Goldie 83). The potential for mistaken, confused, inadequate, or egregiously inaccurate imaginings is rife in such situations. By contrast, the external perspective leaves room for understanding based on an appreciation of how very different that person is to us and of the unique circumstances she was in. Understanding of the other, far from being undermined, is reinforced when we admit to the impossibility or inadequacy of imaginatively adopting her perspective.

If the trauma is not remembered, or only partial information on it is available, or if the one who comes after is not capable for whatever reason of confronting or absorbing any such details, then postmemorial perspective shifting and empathy is simply not an option. Ferber and Austerlitz cannot shift their perspective to that of their parents' suffering; they know too little about it. That is in part the source of *their* suffering. Sebald's narrator is in a somewhat different position, having a broader and, in some respects, more informed perspective on the past sufferings of others.[16] But note that Sebald's narrator makes no pretense of adopting the position of the people whose stories he recounts. Their speech is always indirect; he reports what they say and makes no presumptions about how things are for them beyond the accounts that they themselves, or those who speak about them, supply. In one oft-cited instance early on in *The Emigrants*, he briefly attempts to encroach on the interior territory of one of his characters, Paul Bereyter, only immediately to withdraw on seemingly moral grounds. Having tried briefly to picture Bereyter's final moments prior to his suicide from that character's own point of view, the narrator desists in going further, explaining that "such endeavours to imagine his life and death did not [...] bring me any closer to Paul, except at best for brief emotional moments of the kind that seemed presumptuous to me. It is in order to avoid this sort of wrongful trespass that I have written down what I know of Paul Bereyter" (29). In this way, the narrator establishes that an external perspective is not merely the means he happens to have chosen for conveying the story of another, but is the very basis for sustaining an appropriate moral stance towards that person. In these respects, the narrator is a model of the external perspective and its virtues.

The mechanizations of the external perspective are in turn mirrored in the experience of the reader of Sebald, who must constantly negotiate the intricacies of the embedded narratives, and who can never get entirely lost in one voice or perspective if she is to appreciate the layers of dramatic irony at play—something that itself demands an external stance. Goldie compares the benefits of taking the external view in real life to the significance of dramatic irony in the reading of great literature, and he himself uses the example of a text with embedded narration (in this case, Willa Cather's *My Ántonia*). For dramatic irony to function in a novel with multiple layers of narration, the reader must keep in mind and evaluate all the different perspectives of the narrative. While there are many examples of embedded narratives in literature, Sebald is notorious for the extent to which he deploys this technique, sometimes leaving us with four or more layers of narration (such as the narrator's report of Austerlitz's account of his former nanny's conversation with Austerlitz's mother). Our ability to appreciate, or even comprehend, the complexities of an embedded narrative would be lost if we consistently shifted our perspective to that of the voice at the bottom-most layer; we would fail to appreciate the significance of the fact that what is being conveyed reaches us through the filter of multiple, differing points of view. These skills of a good reader extend to real-life engagement with autobiography, or diaries, or history. We do not take everything at face value, but must consider the sources when evaluating the content, and comprehend and respect the differing points of view at play.

Perhaps the external stance is heightened in Sebald because of the author's own acute awareness of his particular vulnerability to accusations of overidentification and appropriation. About this, we can only speculate.[17] I do not, in any case, think that Hirsch's closer ties to the victim-rememberers she empathizes with exempt her from any lessons to be learned from Goldie's critique of empathy—lessons that are clearly meant to apply across the board. Insofar as Hirsch expresses occasional ambivalence about the powers of postmemory, Goldie's discussion helps articulate and reinforce that there is indeed serious cause for concern. Meanwhile, Sebald's works, if anything, stand as a countervailing influence to the displacing powers of postmemory's perspective shifting.

VI

A.S. Byatt once said of Sebald that he "connects with immense pain, only to say you can't connect; he tries to make you imagine things that he then delicately says are unimaginable" (cited in Franklin *A Thousand Darknesses* 186). That is almost right: I do think Sebald allows us quite unequivocally to connect with immense pain—not, however, from the often unimaginable position of the victims of it, but rather from the stance of those who are excluded from imagining it: descendants who were bequeathed no memories or who simply could not cope if they were, or the compassionate observer who documents their plight. Hirsch speaks of postmemory as "defined through an identification with the victim or witness or trauma, [and] modulated by the unbridgeable distance that separates the participant from the one born after" ("Surviving Images" 10). While so much of what is important for her is the impulse to identify with the victim, it is that unbridgeable distance that is the defining feature of Sebald's work. This is not surprising, given that it is the absence of memory that is so often at the heart of his stories.

Hirsch's concept of postmemory is of most value when it is restricted to cases in which there is close and relatively unfettered access to the victim's past on behalf of the post-rememberer. It is in such instances that the virtue of accuracy has the most potential to display itself, and the qualities required to carry out the moral imperative to bear witness are more likely to be in place. Even then, as Goldie argues and Sebald illustrates, there are risks and limitations involved in any form of empathic engagement with the past of another.

NOTES

1 These features are extracted from discussions in the following works by Hirsch: *Family Frames*; "Projected Memory"; "Surviving Images"; and "The Generation of Postmemory."
2 See Campbell; Hacking; Neisser and Fivush; and Schachter.
3 Campbell's discussion of accuracy in turn borrows heavily from Adam Morton's work on emotional accuracy. I will continue to use the term "accuracy" in her technical sense as outlined; it therefore is not intended to convey what

the term sometimes might be taken to imply with respect to memory—for example, an abundance of detail and/or a reduction to the concept of truth; see Campbell §3.2.
4 Though books in philosophy on this topic remain rare. See Margalit; Blustein.
5 Butler first appendix; Locke bk. 2 ch. 27.
6 See Parfit's controversial quasi-memory hypothesis, §§80–81.
7 Ruth Franklin is even less tolerant than Weissman of Hirsch and others' deployment of the "buzzword ... 'memory,' in all its forms" (see *A Thousand Darknesses* 223–24).
8 At her most expansive, Hirsch expresses the inclination to welcome, ideally, anyone who has visited the U.S. Holocaust Memorial Museum in Washington into the throng (*Family Frames* 249). Though see Weissman 17–18 for something approaching a defence of this.
9 Such as the notorious case of the apparently sincere but evidently deluded Binjamin Wilkomirski (his book *Fragments* being an example, if ever there was one, of the concerted effort by a relative outsider to ascribe the traumatic experiences of others into his own life story; see Lappin; Eskin). For a (somewhat oblique) attempt to exclude cases of mere delusion and fantasy from the category of postmemory on Hirsch's behalf, see Long ("History, Narrative, and Photography").
10 See Anderson for a compelling discussion of why Sebald's national and political identity and personal background render him an unlikely candidate for inclusion in the "postmemory circle" (142). I don't pursue this line of argument, so well covered by Anderson, but it is compatible with and a supplement to the various theoretical-philosophical differences I identify between Sebald and Hirsch's more narrowly construed conception of postmemory.
11 Sebald's own tentative term for his style of narrative, which defies easy categorization; see Wachtel 37.
12 I will draw from Blustein's criteria as given in Chapter 6.
13 See Felman 15–16 for a discussion of Freud's notion of unconscious testimony. There is some (possibly deliberate) equivocation on Felman's part in that she also speaks of manifestations of the unconscious as *evidence* for conscious, cognitive testimony (by the analyst if not the analysand). Of course, hysterical symptoms and other manifestations of the unconscious, like physical scars, may stand as evidence for testimony, and perhaps indispensable evidence at that. My claim, following Blustein (315–16) is simply that they are not in and of themselves testimony in any sense that has notable epistemic and ethical constraints—constraints that Hirsch herself would endorse.
14 See Franklin "Rings of Smoke" 142 for a different and more critical reading of this passage. I believe that when we cease reading Sebald as attempting the "work of memory" (Franklin 142) or postmemory, Franklin's criticisms fall by the wayside.
15 Long considers Sebald's narrator a Hirschean post-rememberer; see his "History, Narrative, and Photography" and *W.G. Sebald*. My criticisms in this

section apply broadly to his analysis as well, although space prohibits the detailed consideration his claims deserve.

16 This is at least true in the case of Austerlitz up until a certain point, since Austerlitz by his own admission deliberately avoided or repressed all information about the Second World War and the Holocaust well into adulthood. See Behrendt for an account of the special problems and issues surrounding this situation.

17 Though, again, see Anderson for a discussion that touches on this.

Part II

LITERATURE AND THE POWER OF
CULTURAL MEMORY/MEMORIALIZING

4

British Propaganda and the Construction of Female Mourning in the First World War

Sarah Henstra

During the First World War, official remembrance activities in Britain and the Commonwealth often centred around the figure of the deceased soldier's bereaved female relative. In the postwar years, women made up the majority of a population left reeling by death and destruction on a scale that exceeded the consolatory capacity of traditional mourning and memorial activities. What to make of the century's first catastrophic losses was a question answered vociferously by state propagandists, but the insufficiency of such answers has left a lasting gap in Great War history, literature, and scholarship. Alessia Ricciardi goes so far as to claim that the "triumphalism" of the dominant culture in this period destroyed the possibility of any public, ethical dimension of memory: "The failure of the twentieth century to develop a hermeneutics of loss in this sense results in a problematic philosophical and ethical condition that I define as being beyond mourning" (4). The effort to place female relatives of dead soldiers "beyond mourning" by referring their grief to a lexicon of sentimentality and sacrifice both constrained and enabled women's commemorative practices during the war. Memorial modes in women's First World War writings thus developed a complex and ambivalent orientation toward loss: they manifested a deep awareness of individual responsibility and complicity in these "state-sanctioned" deaths, along with necessarily defensive postures against mainstream media and even fellow feminists calling for support of the war effort. Many women writers and speech makers of this period, grieving and aggrieved over individual and collective loss, succeeded in reworking the propagandistic constraints. In particular, writings by feminist-pacifists like C.K. Ogden and Catherine Marshall re-envisioned female mourning and remembrance to include the building of an affective community of mourners, the experience of abiding with grief, the call to witness, and the extension of responsibility beyond national lines. My interest in exploring women's routes to successful mourning in a culture of wartime propaganda, and in investigating those remembrance practices that went against the grain, is part of a wider, ongoing project of recovering passed-over dimensions of First World War public memory and remembrance practice, a project that many scholars in recent decades have undertaken.

Contemporary literary and cultural memories of the Great War centre on the experience of the white male soldier on the Western Front. The familiar elements of this dominant story include the experience of disillusionment, fragmentation, and breakdown under fire; the theme of a "lost generation"—the best men of a generation sacrificed, dead, or traumatized; the breakdown of class barriers; the revelation of a new way of seeing; and the birth of modernism. As Sharon Ouditt notes, though, these stories as well as the "reimagined" First World War narratives by contemporary novelists are driven by "a lost memory": "[they] circle around the void, sometimes reproducing the emptiness at the center, sometimes filling the void with meaning as an act of reparation and interpretation" ("Myths, Memories and Monuments" 258). For Ouditt, the retrospective picture of the First World War remains incomplete and fragmented in part because women's stories have been omitted from the established myth (259).

During the war, women were barred from first-hand experience of the "forbidden zone" except as volunteer nurses, a job described by American nurse Ellen N. La Motte as a traumatic encounter with the "Backwash of War." The introduction to La Motte's memoir of that name describes this "backwash" as follows: "It is very ugly. There are many little lives foaming up in the backwash. They are loosened by the sweeping current, and float to the surface, detached from their environment, and one glimpses them, weak, hideous, repellent. After the war, they will consolidate again into the condition called Peace" (3). The difficulty of fitting such experiences—meetings with anonymous, transient people, struggles to piece together maimed and broken bodies—into the master-narrative of individual heroism and national pride meant that many women's wartime stories were relegated to the margins before they were even written down. For the most part, however, women in wartime suffered due to the absence and loss of loved ones. According to Joan W. Scott, "Examinations of women's experiences in war, especially those based on oral histories, are remarkable for their emphasis on death and deprivation. They contrast dramatically with the official emphasis on heroism and valor aimed at mobilizing national support" (28). Sylvia Pankhurst, for example, recounts how ubiquitously loss was experienced from day to day on the home front: "Yet the talk in the cottages was not of Victory, but of grief and bereavement, scarcity and high prices ... Those who had relatives in the Channel seaports told heart-rending tales of the grievous return of vast numbers of wounded" (369). Rather than perceiving women's grief as separate from or secondary to the trench experience, we can extend the image of war's "backwash" through Pankhurst's account to describe how women's grief was structured and continuously modulated by a dynamic relationship to the battlefront. Whether through the hearsay statistics washing up on the Channel shores or through the news of deaths circulating in newspapers and letters, female relatives' experiences of loss and bereavement were both cumulative and nearly synchronous with those of the soldiers.

Popular myths of First World War history include the notion that, just as class distinctions broke down among soldiers at the front, the collective experiences of loss at home drew British women together into a classless "community of mourners" that later helped establish modern social institutions. Indeed, the idea that grief might erase class boundaries was actively encouraged by the Cabinet Memorial Services Committee in its criteria for seating at postwar remembrance services in 1920: "first consideration would be given to those [bereaved mothers and widows] who were entitled to it: it would be a bold and dramatic stroke, because you might find the Duchess next the charwoman; and it might even have its effect, however small and imperceptible, upon the industrial situation" (qtd. in Grayzel 230). However, this prevailing idea overlooks the ways in which wartime bereavement *divided* women and made collective mourning impossible. The terrible, continual climb in casualties created not only grief but also rising expectations of further loss. Anticipation produced a continual state of anxiety for women on the home front, as a girl's letter to the *Times* transcribed by Vera Brittain in a letter makes clear: "she must watch and wait in a long agony of uncertainty, not knowing the hour of her mourning, but knowing well that already it may have struck" (qtd. in Acton 63). If mourning is typically regarded as the expression of grief, and grief as the emotional response to bereavement, the chronology of this linear formulation becomes snarled in cases of anticipatory mourning. The "long agony" without certain knowledge or emotional closure meant that the boundaries around potential communities of mourners were continually shifting, and women who had not yet received bad news could neither identify with such a community nor safely exempt themselves from its sorrows.

In the United States, the first organized feminist response to the war was a women's antiwar parade held in New York City on 29 August 1914, less than a month after the war began and before the United States became involved. Dressed in mourning garb, more than 1,500 women marched in silence except for the beat of muffled drums (Alonso 57). This early public action powerfully dramatized the trauma of anticipatory mourning incurred by women in wartime. However, Joyce Berkman emphasizes how rapidly most feminist-pacifists both in Britain and in the United States "exchanged their peace politics for patriotism" (147). Berkman puzzles over the reasons for this sharp wartime division among feminists, noting that the fault lines developed even within individual families: "Sylvia and Adela Pankhurst adopted a passionate pro-peace position, while Christabel and the mother of all three, Emmeline, were no less ardently pro-war" (149). Suffragists in particular disagreed over their civic responsibilities, some joining pacifist causes but most arguing, like Millicent Fawcett in the suffragist periodical *Common Cause*, that "we have another duty now ... LET US SHOW OURSELVES WORTHY OF CITIZENSHIP, WHETHER OUR CLAIM BE RECOGNIZED OR NOT" (qtd. in Wiltsher 27). The varieties of individual responses to loss created lasting divisions in feminist organizations. Trauma theorist Kai Erikson argues that "fault lines" like these come to characterize any community that has experienced catastrophic losses, supplying a "prevailing mood" and dominating the community's "sense of self" (237). Alienation becomes a part of collective grief, and grief becomes a shared experience without being a unifying one. Divided by their varying relationships to loss and their varying perspectives on how to respond to it, bereaved women in the First World War could not easily refer their grief to a mourning community or seek consolation in shared experience.

Female mourning was also the target, and the object, of sustained propaganda campaigns urging support for the troops. The public messaging coalesced around two related representations of femininity and its role in the war effort. The first representation, epitomized in the popular iconography of the Voluntary Aid Detachment (VAD) nurse, figured woman as balm to the afflicted soldier. For example, a 1918 American Red Cross campaign illustration by Alonzo Foringer that was also widely circulated in England featured a *pietà*-like illustration depicting a heroic nurse/mother figure cradling the body of a tiny, wounded soldier on a stretcher (fig. 4.1). Another image represented woman as object of chivalry, waving her knights off to battle (fig. 4.2). Both images attached to femininity qualities of redemptive martyrdom, passivity, and sacrifice. Media discourse elaborated and circulated variants on these images until they became synonymous with patriotism. Visual images are typically credited with possessing, in Karen Sandlos's words, the "grammar of indisputable knowledge." According to Sandlos, images are capable of "branding" political debates in ways that generate particular identifications and commitments (79). I will therefore discuss in some detail how the "grammar" of these two closely linked images laid out the terms for dealing with grief in the context of the First World War's heavy losses.

Foringer's illustration invokes Mary, the *Mater Dolorosa*, as archetype of female mourning. The *pietà* configuration transforms the nurses, in relation to their soldier-patients, from peers into mothers who cradle and comfort as well as heal—but who also, if they are like Mary, readily relinquish, sacrifice, and mourn their "sons" for a greater cause. Valorizing the nurse-figure through her monumental size, her voluminous robes, her bare toes (in the manner of Greek statues), and her sorrowful gaze to the heavens certainly ascribes both dignity and agency to women's role. In direct proportion, the male soldier-figure is so emasculated and infantilized—minuscule, laid out in horizontal inaction, blindfolded—that it seems to suggest that heroism is an either/or proposition when it comes to gender. Margaret R. Higonnet's essay "The Double Helix," seeking to describe the how men and women moved within gendered power structures during the First World War, argues that while the war "inverted the relationship of men, trapped and sacrificed in the trenches, to women, on the homefront," it also maintained and reinforced gender differences (42).

Painting the Red Cross nurse in Christian colours is, of course, not unique to this illustration, and many nurses' memoirs express the gendered discomfort, and occasional elation, at being more powerful than their male patients. Vera Brittain narrates an operating-table scene from her VAD nursing days in which she hallucinates that it is her dead beloved Roland under the knife, "with His beautiful eyes closed and his sturdy limbs all helpless; it was from Roland's wound that I saw the blood pour out in a scarlet stream" (*Chronicle* 322). In this grief-driven fantasy, as

Figure 4.1 "The Greatest Mother in the World: Red Cross Recruitment Campaign" (A.E. Foringer, July 1918. Library and Archives Canada / National Archives of Canada fonds/e-010754261)

Santanu Das points out, the capitalization of the masculine adjective suggests a Christian interpretation that has conferred a godlike martyrdom upon Roland (250), and, I would add, a corresponding Mary-like importance upon Vera. Das argues that for First World War nurses motivated by "the supreme fantasy of *service*," both comfort and meaning could be derived from "reading" the bodies of the dying soldiers through the central trope of "the young male body on the Cross, the wound in that body, the pain in that wound" (251).

Figure 4.2 "Women of Britain Say—'Go!': Parliamentary Recruiting Committee, London" (E.V. Kealey, May 1915. Hill, Siffken & Co., London. Library of Congress, Prints & Photographs Division, First World War Posters LC-USZC4-10915)

In addition to serving as balm to the soldiers' suffering, women were called upon, in propagandist imagery, to encourage their male loved ones to enlist. The "Women of Britain Say—'Go!'" illustration depicts two women standing at a window waving off a regiment of soldiers. The shorter woman's arms encircle the taller one's shoulders, while a small boy tugs on the shorter woman's shawl. Who are these "everywomen" with their gazes determinedly on the departing men, should a husband look back? The shorter woman's darker complexion, and her hair and clothing, suggest a difference in class from her yellow-clad, blond companion; perhaps they are intended to embody that ideal of class-irrelevance in the face of shared grief. However, the fact that the women are indoors suggests that they comprise a single household, in which case it is more likely that the shorter woman is a servant and/or nurse, physically supporting her beloved mistress through this moment of domestic crisis. Details aside, in this formulation of wartime femininity, kinship bonds are subordinated and sacrificed to national needs, and women's role is both to enact this sacrifice gladly and to actualize the need for it; that is, in their passivity and dependency women embody the moral ideals being fought for at the front. Through the reproduction and circulation of images like this, women were, as Ouditt puts it, "persuaded to adopt the role of repository of spiritual values" (*Fighting Forces* 5).

The language of sacrifice to the national cause became ubiquitous in framing women's bereavement. Mothers, in particular, were seen as "giving up" their boys and thereby actively contributing to the war effort. A letter to the editor of the *Morning Post*, infamous since Robert Graves transcribed it in *Goodbye to All That* as an example of the "foreign language" that British civilians seemed to him to be speaking during the war (271), captures the popular understanding of the flag-waving maternal role: "We women pass on the human ammunition of 'only sons' to fill up the gaps, so that when the 'common soldier' looks back before going 'over the top' he may see the women of the British race on his heels, reliable, dependent, uncomplaining'" (qtd. in Graves 273). Another exemplary account appeared in the December 1915 issue of *Everywoman's World*, a Canadian periodical with a circulation of 67,000. In an article titled "I AM A PROUD MOTHER THIS CHRISTMAS And I Will Tell You The Reason Why," a Mrs. E.A. Hughes described how her initial shock at receiving the telegram of her son's death passed quickly into pride and rejoicing:

> I did not see the crown; the cross was omnipresent, Gethsemane was where I walked. But that has gone. I am a proud mother this Christmas. For I gave Canada and the Empire a Christmas present. I gave them my chiefest possession. I yielded what was more than aught else in the world to me. I sacrificed the life of my boy. (qtd. in Evans 86)

The ready lexicon of patriotic sacrifice offered a number of routes to consolation for grieving women. First, it proposed a meaning for their loss, a scripted explanation that, however poorly it addressed their suffering, was better than perceiving the loss as senseless. If the lens of hindsight exposes propaganda as pernicious mistruth or demeaning sentimentalization, or if we've since unearthed the dissenting voices whose grief was exacerbated by state disavowals, the fact remains that for most women during the First World War, the choice was between the framework of sacrifice or no framework at all. Similarly, women like Mrs. Hughes were invited to speak publicly in the voice of the sacrificial mother; expressing sorrow in this voice would have been more conducive to mourning than not being able to express anything. Also, these soldiers' mothers won for themselves a productive agency through the vocabulary of "human ammunition." This vocabulary extended and exaggerated the work that women had undertaken to raise children. The boys were "all they have to give," as though they had contributed to society in no other manner; indeed, they were the only reason the boys had made it to the age of enlistment (and, just as in Foringer's *pietà*, the agency conferred on the female seemed to have come at direct cost to the male). This narrowly focused view of women's productive labour nonetheless offered an alternative to the crippling helplessness and passivity involved in waiting for news, imagining loved ones in mortal danger, and being unable to influence their fate. Avowing one's loss as a state sacrifice—in other words, *dis*avowing one's loss *as a loss*—became a way of being publicly honoured for one's war work rather than remaining consigned to silence and invisibility.

The slim payoffs for grieving women offered by the propagandist models of female mourning described above—and, more significantly, the fact that women grasped at these models despite the pervasive despair they experienced privately—demonstrates how tightly grief was regulated and controlled in wartime. While women's voices didn't officially "matter," the state's intense interest in women's negative feelings and the strict foreclosure on any expression of them suggests that the management of emotion was crucial to the war effort. Indeed, the sublimation of female grief into national spirit achieved by the discourses of pity and sacrifice made this grief available for further positive messaging: the sorrows of idealized mothers, widows, sisters, and daughters became the justification for further aggression against the enemy that had caused their pain. The presence of so many suffering Marys offering their sons for the Cross could not but sanctify the war effort.

In official commemorations both during and after the war, this carefully framed understanding of female bereavement took a central role.

Permission was given to British mothers to wear the medals awarded posthumously to their sons. In Australia, mothers were issued a badge that bore one star for each son or brother who had died. Canada launched a Silver Cross award for war mothers that is distributed to this day; and since 1939, the Canadian Legion has chosen one Silver Cross mother to lay a wreath on the War Memorial in Ottawa on behalf of all the war-bereaved mothers of the country. The United States, too, boasts a very active Gold Star Mothers Memorial Association. Decorating women like soldiers who have distinguished themselves in battle visually collapses two identities into one. She authored his contribution; now he lives on through her. We will return to the way mothers are subsumed into their sons through this commemorative practice, but for now it is important to note how the public recognition of loss, and the public responsibility to be faithful to that loss, was laid upon women. As Susan R. Grayzel notes in the British context, "mourning mothers, by thus publicly representing the experience of bereavement due to war, were meant to be *visibly* giving notice of their patriotism" (228). To comply with the normative discourse was to gain access to public recognition and thereby to some consolation for loss. Only later, when it became apparent that being publicly honoured did not mean being protected from financial and social neglect (e.g., due to sluggish or insufficient pension payouts), did many war-bereaved women feel that "their pain had been denied in being re-named as glory and honour" (Damousi 27).

If propagandist prescriptions for mourning meant a near-total foreclosure on grief—or at least a swift conversion of grief into patriotic resignation—how did bereaved women in the First World War mourn otherwise? Until recently, even feminist critics have deprecated women's mourning-related literature of the period. Nosheen Khan, for example, points to the prevalence of sentimental and propagandistic themes in women's First World War poetry and argues that those themes "[serve] to exorcise a personal sense of loss" through conformity to the traditional "light out of darkness movement characteristic of all elegiac writing" (146). In part, such assessments testify to the difficulty that women writers face, in a culture of propaganda and jingoism, to imagine an alternative route to mourning. Carol Acton, in examining the wartime correspondence between Vera Brittain at home and Roland Leighton at the front, observes that Brittain's patriotic attempt to share vicariously in his experience at the front was partly motivated by her desire to escape from a situation in which "men must work and women must weep" (Brittain qtd. in Acton 67). Brittain's negotiation of the mourning-woman role imposed on her involved a "retreat" from her pre-war assertiveness and ambition into the consolatory language of patriotism, duty, and sacrifice, even as Leighton's letters worked to disprove this language (Acton 69). The "insidious link" between grief and propaganda demonstrated by Acton to be too strong for even as independent-minded a writer as Brittain to break (80) helps account for women's complicity in war (61).

Of course, the difficulty of unearthing alternative approaches to mourning in First World War women's writing also underscores the lasting dominance of the soldier's-view narrative model in First World War scholarship. Through the sustained scholarly efforts of feminist historians like Margaret R. Higonnet and Sharon Ouditt, a "canon" of formerly sidelined women's wartime writings is finally, belatedly, emerging. However, the limits placed on public expressions of loss and grief are not solely the product of wartime meaning management. I have argued elsewhere that despite the wide variety of remembrance-related endeavours we may encounter, our cultural repertoire for making meaning from loss is always strictly circumscribed by generic and rhetorical conventions. The demand for consolation, in particular, is central to memorial practice, and all commemorative discourse that attempts to do something other than follow the shortest route to consolation risks becoming unseemly or even unintelligible (Henstra 4). Given these risks, it is important to recognize that if women's public expressions of grief in the First World War were to be heard and taken up by a community of listeners or readers, they first of all needed to fit into a recognizable lexicon of public discourse about loss. The remainder of this essay therefore examines not instances in which women escaped or avoided this lexicon altogether, but those women's texts that sought to mobilize the lexicon in new directions or against the state interests it was intended to serve. Could the "mourning mother" ever comprise a rhetorical standpoint from which women could petition for public sympathy and state attention while resisting the tendency to retrench or to acquiesce to old models of nationalistic revenge seeking? Could the logic of maternal sacrifice lead to an alternative set of conclusions about war?

In fact, a number of First World War writers very deliberately reworked the myth of the grieving mother in order to capitalize on its cultural currency. Feminist-pacifists like Helena Swanwick, Mary Sargant Florence, C.K. Ogden, and Catherine Marshall used the figure of the mother as a way of making their radical responses to wartime losses more palatable to the public and of facilitating readers' identification with their descriptions of women's experiences. At the same time, these writers and speechmakers built in significant changes to the state-sanctioned interpretive framework in order to defamiliarize world politics and to encourage women to see militarism differently from men. Ogden's *Militarism versus Feminism*, written with Mary Sargant Florence and published in 1915, argued that peace is, by nature, women's prerogative:

> For the times have changed, but the nature of woman cannot change, as some of her enemies have most truly declared. Woman, because to her has fallen the task of bringing into the world those human souls and bodies which in war are but food for cannon, is able to realize what man is not able. "For such a purpose," she might well say now that she has attained self-consciousness, "I will not bring more human life into the world." (63)

The clause "as some of her enemies have most truly declared" gestures to the adversarial political history from which this text is emerging, a history in which women's bid for a public voice was denied on the basis of arguments about "natural" gender roles. The authors here claim to accept these arguments ("most truly") while casting them into doubt by naming those who wield them "enemies" of women. This doubled rhetorical strategy—simultaneously accepting and refuting a dominant description of femininity—operates centrally in all the alternative remembrance discourses I am examining here. By riding the line between touting conservative models of the feminine and radically reimagining them, Ogden can thus defend himself against potential accusations of treason even while calling for defiance: "It will not seem treachery to a cause: it will not seem the coward's mean appeal; for it will be but the voice of Nature driven to rebellion by the horrors of violence and destruction" (63).

To call women's voices "the voice of Nature" is to invoke an essentialist view of gender inherited from the Victorian period. Feminists throughout the past century have debated the wisdom of relying on "separate sphere" gender ideology as a basis for any political agenda, even—or, perhaps, especially—a feminist one. For Janet Radcliffe Richards, the Victorian legacy that regards women as special repositories of Christian virtues means that contemporary peace movements attempting to distinguish themselves as feminist blur two incompatible kinds of feminism, the "women's values kind" and the "equal-rights kind" (213). Those who would make peace a women's issue inadvertently reinvoke traditional separate-sphere ideologies that undermine the demand for gender equality. On the other hand, Gayatari Chakravorty Spivak has used the term "positive essentialism" to describe those coalition-building discourses that bolster membership and action in a young, grassroots movement (205). Lauri Umansky similarly traces the development of a universalizing "mother right" in the 1970s designed to heal the internal fractures in feminism that developed along lines of race, class, and sexual orientation (111). Given the rifts that plagued the suffrage movement after the First World War began, it makes sense that women in search of an alternative mourning community reached for a discourse of femininity that had the capacity and cultural sway to heal the breach. And Sara Ruddick suggests that, rather than relying on notions of motherhood as a universal or "natural" identity as a basis for politics, women can and do "exploit their culture's symbols of femininity" (222–23). When women declare themselves "the mother of humanity" (as pacifist women did in the proceedings of the 1915 International Congress of Women), as the "motherhalf of the nation" or the "life force of the future," they invoke difference not in the image itself, which is still quasi-biological and essentialist, but in the rhetorical effects for whose purpose the image is exploited. Beneath the familiar alignment of maternity with nature, women are being exhorted to act directly against the grain of their prescribed wartime roles.

The first rhetorical shift in the way First World War mourning mothers are figured involves the assertion of women's epistemic privilege—that is, the experiential knowledge that women are seen to possess through mothering becomes the basis for a political voice. Dr. Anna Howard Shaw, in a speech to the U.S. Women's Peace Party in 1915, argued that losing the children they had mothered gave women special insight into war:

> And looking into the face of ... one dead man we see two dead, the man and the life of the woman who gave him birth; the life she wrought into his life! And looking into his dead face someone asks a woman, what does a woman know about war? What, what, friends in the face of a crime like that, what does man know about war? (qtd. in Ruddick 229)

As in the official remembrance ceremonies honouring mothers of the war dead, woman's identity is violently collapsed, in the argument above, into that of her dead son. However, the traditional rhetoric of sacrifice is here reworked to articulate an authoritative knowledge that demands public consideration. Olive Schreiner's *Women and Labour* (1911), a text extremely popular among British feminists before the war, had already described women's losses in war in economic terms: "There is no battlefield on earth ... which it has not cost the women of the race more in actual bloodshed and anguish to supply, than it has cost the men who lie there. We pay the first cost on all human life" (222). In 1916, Helena Swanwick extended the metaphor of women's reproductive/economic labour to read women's bereavement as a violation of her rights: "Every man killed or mangled in war has been carried for months in his mother's body and has been tended and nourished for years of his life by women. He is the work of women: they have rights in him and in what he has done with the life they have given and sustained" (*Woman and War* 2). Here women's maternal "labour" is translated into economic and political terms—men are her production, her vested interest, her rights—as a way of demanding a place at the table without wholly departing from the normative discourse of femininity.

The argument that a dead soldier is a woman's labour brought to ruin made something more of female grief than a bid for public sympathy. Indeed, putting the rhetoric of separate spheres to work for women meant demonstrating how war was infringing on "women's sphere" not just as a disappointment of her pacific values but as a violent material disruption of her domestic life. So Carrie Chapman Catt, in a 1915 letter to the *New York Times*, painted a much wider picture of women's wartime suffering:

> That is a case where man's business of war and women's business of conserving the race have clashed, and women are helpless to defend their own. Hundreds if not thousands of women have been forced to bear children by soldiers of their country's enemy all along the war zone. It becomes the terrible business of the mothers of the race to secure the right of a political protest in every nation. When war murders the husbands and sons of women, destroys their homes, desolates their country and makes them refugees and paupers, it becomes the undeniable business of women. (qtd. in Alonso 61)

Catt was here aligning the peace issue with the suffrage campaign; yet she would later declare the suffragists' support for American involvement in the war—a turnaround that exemplified the lack of any "natural" pacific mandate for women. What is important to notice in Catt's speech, however, is the way female *grief* is being transformed rhetorically into a set of female *grievances* that demand recognition and recompense. While in this formulation women's role is still "conserving the race," this role becomes a "business" rather than a biological imperative, and when war contravenes her interests, she has an obligation to protest. Female experience is thus moved from its traditional location in a purely physical and emotional realm to an arena of reasoning, discourse, and exchange; female mourning presses past sentimentality into political action.

In a particularly effective example of the "doubled rhetoric" I described earlier, even the official insignificance of women's voices in wartime is reframed as a route to a public audience. C. K. Ogden argues that men, not women, are the object of state censorship and control: "*She* may speak where *man* dare not. In the past she had no voice to raise: she was not conscious of her power. Today, if she will but realise it, the redemption of civilization rests with her, and perhaps with her alone. Woman has but to become conscious of her power, of her privilege" (60–61). Couching this call to action in the familiar vocabulary of "redemption" through feminine virtue does little to dilute its defiance of gender expectations: the state authorities' traditional disregard for women becomes an ironic safeguard against the charge of treason that would otherwise threaten any stance against the war. The leeway of being able to speak for peace is titled, in this essay, "Women's Prerogative." Her subordinate status offers the opportunity not for subordination—for those supporting roles she should be playing in wartime—but for self-assertion and the articulation of radical dissent. Of course, exploiting the potential in being ignored by state powers requires a level of ironic self-awareness to which most First World War women, struggling under the dual load of personal grief and public disavowal, lacked access. Envisioning such a woman, imagining such an alternative standpoint in relation to state discourses, is a crucial function for any text that seeks new meaning for women's encounters with loss. Catherine Marshall's essay "Women and War" describes the emergence of the same kind of self-consciousness sought by Ogden: "The mother-heart of womanhood has been stirred to its depths; and it is a womanhood whose sense of responsibility has been developed, whose mind has been educated, whose capacity for cooperation has been trained by the Women's Movement, with all that it has meant of awakening and enlightenment, and the widening of sympathy" (38). In this one sentence the personification of "womanhood" moves very quickly from traditional femininity with its universal "mother-heart" to a portrait of the activist-feminist (i.e., suffragist) ethos. These are performative moments that aim to create what they purport merely to describe: the possibility of an alternative mourning, wherein grief might transform women into informed and active citizens whose voices intervene effectively in the public sphere.

Part of becoming conscious in the face of loss involves a commitment to active witnessing and appraisal in place of sentimentality and sacrifice. "Let us look steadfastly at war and the consequences of war, with our women's eyes—our mothers' eyes—and tell the world what we see," declares Marshall (41). Like Ogden with his claim about "women's prerogative," Marshall suggests that the vision offered through "women's eyes" has a special clarity, an ability to reckon the value of human life that cuts through propaganda's lies. The disastrous death tolls of the trenches are thus revealed not as normal or inevitable but rather as the result of particular political structures and investments of power. Along with this gendered clarity, though, comes a responsibility not to accept consolation and comfort too quickly: "Shirking none of the pain and the horror, refusing to be blinded by glamour ... we must let the pity and the shame of it enter deep into our hearts" (41). To call on women's traditional capacity for feeling without invoking traditional schemes of containment and consolation is already radically to disrupt the norms. That Marshall actually *encourages* women to tarry with, and be moved by, negative emotions signals how far this author travels beyond the familiar landscape of wartime prescriptions for female grief. The experience of "pity and shame" with which Marshall wants her readers to abide lends to mourning an ethical dimension that anticipates contemporary feminist rehabilitations of melancholia as the refusal of linguistic compensation or consolation for loss. For example, Ewa Ziarek in "Kristeva and Levinas" states that "[t]he inability [in melancholia] to trade the loss of the other for the 'symbolic triumph' does not strike me as necessarily a disorder of the subject but as a powerful critique of the desire to master alterity through the order of representation" (73). Ziarek discerns in this critique an alignment with "the face-to-face encounter in the Levinasian ethics" (74). Marshall's injunction to refuse the "glamour" of military triumphalism similarly moves female mourning from conservative passivity toward an arena of ethical engagement.

Another aspect of witnessing as an innovation in women's mourning and remembrance emerges in the overcoming of national differences. "We all sorrow alike and together," declares a 1915 letter in *Jus Suffragii*: "My dearly loved eldest son who has been killed is but one among thousands ... It is my Hugh; it is their Jacques, their Fritz, their Nicholas. What does nationality matter! All mothers feel for each other in sorrow;

it binds them together in spite of all differences of nationality or rank or religion. The mother's heart is the same throughout the world" (qtd. in Ouditt *Fighting Forces* 142). Again here we see the two-pronged use of bereaving maternity: as expected, it produces sympathy that ideally binds women into a community of mourners—but this community is unexpectedly transnational and therefore flies in the face of patriotism. A more direct articulation of gender- over state-based loyalties occurs in Ogden: "'Women of all nations unite!'; that should be the new cry—not 'Woman has *no* country!' but 'Woman must have every country!'" (63). Mourning is given a new power to push woman not just beyond her proper "sphere"— that is, past the bounds of insular domesticity into public life—but past the very national borders that determine friend and foe in wartime. The encounter with grief thus generates for women a collective subjectivity outside of the terms dictated by the (patriarchal) state.

Also proposed here is a wider continuum of responsibility in mourning than the rubric of sacrifice would allow. The "mother's heart" that grieves the enemy's dead as well as her own extends the work of mourning to an imaginative identification with the "other" that would have been very difficult for women living in a culture saturated with propaganda's dehumanizing portrayals of this "other." Such a difficult notion of responsibility lies at the heart of what Sara Ruddick terms a "rationality of care"—a maternalist-feminist model of sociality that, Ruddick hopes, might stand up to militaristic state reasoning. Care "require[s] patient identification with different 'others' in their particularities," and Ruddick admits that "extensive sympathetic identification remains a fragile achievement for those whose lives have been shaped by passionate loyalties to their 'own'" (250). Reformulating maternal grief in this way made First World War women witnesses in two senses: they were able to speak from the experience of what they had seen and felt (loss for their sons), and they were able to bear witness to something unseen but fervently believed (that women behind enemy lines felt the same about *their* lost sons). These two facets of the witnessing role are described by Kelly Oliver as integral to the establishing of a viable subjectivity, a socio-political standpoint that is at once historically determined and enlivened by the possibility of affective connection with others (18). According to Oliver it is the sense of the "response-ability" potentially opened by the performance of bearing witness on the other—the capacity to respond to others' experience in a way that in turn opens response by others—that enables successful mourning, the "working-through rather than merely the repetition of trauma and violence" (18). By staying faithful to the experience of grief rather than foreclosing it through consolatory shortcuts, by extending responsibility beyond familial and national boundaries, these reformulations of maternal mourning sought a deeper and more ethical path to healing.

There are risks to deriving a collective subjectivity from the shared experience of grief, as several contemporary feminists have pointed out. Wendy Brown, for instance, is leery of the potential for "wound fetishism" in any political claim based on historical trauma or oppression, since identifying too insistently on a shared woundedness can prevent the possibility of a future that overcomes it (55). Lauren Berlant warns against reliance on "women's traditional identification with suffering on behalf of virtue in the family" (34). Narratives of trauma and suffering are situated on ethical high ground, on the (erroneous, in Berlant's opinion) assumption that to be virtuous requires feeling the pain of others and being transformed (both at the level of individual conscience and collective political conviction) by this experience (35). In response to such qualms, Sara Ahmed stresses the importance not of forgetting the pain that brings groups together and into political consciousness but of "learn[ing] to read and interpret that pain." For Ahmed the "work of translation" is what moves pain into a public domain and thereby transforms it (173). Catherine Marshall's encouragement to women to face their losses without shirking is directly followed by what she hopes will result from such a confrontation: "we must let the pity and shame of it enter deep into our hearts and rouse a passionate determination that these things shall never be again." Refusing easy consolation thus allows pain to *work* on women for transformative ends: "It is by this deliberate opening of our hearts to all the pain and suffering, this sharing in the sense of responsibility and sin, that even the simplest and humblest of us may attain the power and the wisdom to build up the new world of our dreams" (41). Rather than ontologizing pain as the basis for a shared identity or laying claim to virtue through suffering, Marshall exhorts women to undertake the work of translating their pain into a publicly engaged plan for the future.

While I have been referring to the strategy of First World War alternative engagements with the figure of the bereaved woman as "doubled rhetoric," I would here like to examine more specifically the use of irony as a key tool in feminist-pacifist texts of this period. Phrases like "food for cannon" and "human ammunition" suggest the importance of irony in resisting the dominant discourse of battlefield heroism. Indeed, the image of mothers forced to produce "cannon fodder" was used in both the founding document of the Women's Peace Party in the United States and in the initial call to the Hague Conference (Berkman 154). In her essay "The Great War and Female Elegy," Higonnet observes how ironic language becomes a central mode in female poets' self-conscious engagement with the consolatory mandate of their wartime roles. American poet Mary Borden's 1929 poem "Song of the Mud," for example, is an antipastoral in which the consolations of nature are replaced by the personified mud of the trenches, a rapacious, inhuman force that absorbs the body of the downed soldier and demonstrates his disposability (Higonnet "The Great War" 132). Genre expectations are similarly overturned in the mock obituary of Virginia Woolf's 1922 novel *Jacob's Room* (Ouditt *Fighting Forces* 176). Higonnet's introduction to a reprint of Borden's and Ellen N. La Motte's wartime writings emphasizes their "satiric" and "sardonic" vision of war. Recounting the reception history of these works, Higonnet notes that the ironic frankness that originally saw them banned in France and Britain had become the object of praise by the 1930s, when the expectations for First World War narrative had come to include these characteristics (xxvi). Dori Laub's assertion that certain traumatic events involve a "collapse of witnessing," wherein the force of the event is felt as a gap or absence of knowledge and memory, might be another way of accounting for the irony that characterizes women's literary remembrances of the war (qtd. in Caruth "Trauma and Experience" 7). Self-awareness for many women writers was possible only later on, in retrospect, so an ironic gap opens between the norms to which they adhered in wartime and the feelings they have looking back.

Ogden's comments about women's relative insignificance in wartime use irony to encode registers of anger and protest within seeming acquiescence to traditional expectations. If women refused to produce more human life as "food for cannon," we are told, "man would neither understand nor would he be greatly shocked. It matters not to him what women are saying or thinking, for women are but women" (Odgen 63). A similar bitterly ironic note is struck in the way mothers' wartime role is figured in a piece from the 28 July 1917 edition of *Four Lights*:

> Women must not feel that they cannot help in the Great War because they are accustomed to dealing with little things ... Women must not feel that because they work in the narrow confines of the home, they cannot help in the great work of destruction ... Accustom your children gradually to the sight of blood. And for yourself learn to kill a little every day. (4)

Irony is not intended to comfort or console, in these texts, but to shake benumbed readers out of their complacency and to express anger at the pernicious banality of propaganda. Jay Winter is thus correct in pointing out that ironic modes complicate remembrance practices: "Irony's cutting edge could express anger and despair, and did so in enduring ways; but it could not heal. Traditional modes of seeing the war, while at times less profound, provided a way of remembering which enabled the bereaved to live with their losses and perhaps to leave them behind" (29).

Rather than operating as a symptom of modernist fragmentation or general disillusionment, however, irony is aligned in many First World War feminist-pacifist texts with resilience and responsibility, a crucial doubling of consciousness that acknowledges language's contingency and its complicity with structures of institutional power. Particularly in women's writings, irony can be seen as a rhetorical mode that springs from recognition of the arbitrariness of the socially constructed self. Nancy Walker describes a split perspective in many women's novels arising from a "consciousness of the ironic difference between reality and their stories"; the narrative point of view is composed of two "selves," one enduring reality and one standing back to comment on the first (204). In the context of the First World War, feminist remembrance is necessarily ironic, because it confronts the grievous complicity of traditional femininity with militarism (maternal sacrifice as a contribution to the war effort), while at the same time being forced to participate in this complicity in order to say anything at all. Irony thus becomes a way of playing both sides of the field, of simultaneously employing and questioning patriarchal structures of power. As Winter notes, the "cutting edge" of such approaches to the figure of the grieving woman resists recuperative models of mourning insofar as it exposes, rather than forgets, pain and absence. As we have seen, however, this exposure becomes a critical alternative to the swift foreclosure of grieving prescribed by the discourse of sacrifice.

Rather than "coming to terms" with loss, then, alternative representations of female bereavement during the First World War regarded loss as a motivation for women to reach out to others in a manner that would be not just productive, but ethical. Cathy Caruth's work on trauma suggests a similarly positive potential in the inability to dispatch trauma through language: Kenneth Kidd explains that "for Caruth, the impossibility of sufficient response to and representation of trauma is itself traumatic and inaugurates an ethics of collective memory and cultural work" (167). While traumatic loss such as that incurred by female relatives of soldiers in the

First World War was crippling for individuals and divisive for communities, it also produced an ethical call to imagine life differently. This call, as articulated by writers like Ogden and Marshall against the strict wartime constraints on remembrance, comprises a minority discourse buried under "official" histories and literatures of the First World War. The work of unearthing it and assessing its implications has been taken up by subsequent generations, particularly in the context of inspiration and support for ongoing peace efforts by women. Ogden's 1915 *Militarism versus Feminism*, for example, was reprinted in 1987 along with Catherine Marshall's essays in a Virago edition edited by Margaret Kamester and Jo Vellacott. These editors' introduction reveals that the reprinting is itself an act of feminist remembrance explicitly designed to intervene in the rising threat of nuclear warfare:

> The spark kindled by them, by Catherine Marshall and by many others, though barely perceptible at times, has not been extinguished and remains to be fanned by their spiritual heirs in a world even more threatened by antagonism and disunity. Again and again the words of *Militarism versus Feminism*, written in urgent response to a tragic world situation, strike us in the 1980s with their topicality and their warning. May they not have been written in vain. (33–4)

One of my objectives here has been to reconsider our criteria for "successful" mourning and remembrance projects in light of what feminist texts—those written during the First World War, and those inspired by their foremothers' engagement with loss—say about affect, responsibility, transgenerational inheritance, and political engagement. The legacy of female mourning certainly involves imagining the future as much as reconciling with the past.

5

"Rhetorical Metatarsals": Bone Memory in Dionne Brand's *Ossuaries*

Tanis MacDonald

Men make their own history, but they do not make it just as they please; they do not make it under circumstances chosen by themselves, but under circumstances directly encountered, given and transmitted from the past. The tradition of all the dead generations weighs like a nightmare on the brain of the living.
—Karl Marx, *The Eighteenth Brumaire of Louis Bonaparte*

The bone / is an organ like any other
—Dionne Brand, *Ossuaries*

In her keynote address as the Ralph Gustafson Chair of Poetry at Malaspina College (now Vancouver Island University) in Nanaimo British Columbia, published under the title *A Perfect Kind of Speech*, Dionne Brand notes that she believes strongly in "poetry's job in tending to the wrecked and brutalized consciousness of oppressed peoples," and acknowledges that the "ubiquitous occupation of coloniality" has been her guiding subject matter since she began writing poetry as part of her social justice work in the 1970s (18–20). When Brand's tenth book of poetry, *Ossuaries*, was shortlisted for the Griffin Poetry Prize, Brand declared in an interview with journalist Michael Oliveira that "poetry is the least commoditized art … yet its reach is incredibly great" (2011). Poetry's reach in public culture and in public memory may be, as Henri Bergson suggests in *Matter and Memory* (1991), a call to "withdraw ourselves from the action of the moment" in order "to call up the past in the form of an image" (78). Although Bergson designates this action as "the will to dream," Brand's long-standing Marxist work would suggest that her poetry calls up the past in order to establish a dialectic between the ongoing nightmare of "all the dead generations" and the dream of a diasporic counter-public. Brand has long been admired in Canadian literature for the ferocity of her politics, the multi-genre output of her writing career, and the rhizomatic lyricism of her poetics, and *Ossuaries* is a book that Brand has been moving toward—politically and stylistically—for many years. When Brand was awarded the Griffin Prize for *Ossuaries* in late May 2011, she noted in her acceptance speech: "I made these ossuaries—these bone cabinets or bone boxes if you will where I wanted to put all of the toxicity of our society" ("Dionne" 2011). The result is a book that displays Brand's argumentative dexterity with ideology, with history, with governments, and with poetry itself as a genre that is not immune to hiding history's "presumptive cruelties […] in the lyric" ("ossuary XIII," 108). Thinking about poetry as "the least commoditized art" and recalling that poetry can perpetuate "presumptive cruelties" that have been folded into retellings of the history of the Middle Passage, Brand's double metaphor of the ossuary as a "bone box"—one that is both made of bones *and* made to hold bones—introduces a complex interrogation of memory.

In his work on the significance of forgetting as a spur to memory, John Frow notes that the storage bin or "cluster of boxes" has been an important major metaphor for memory in Western culture, and also that such a metaphor has its limitations, including "its inability to account for forgetting other than as a fault or as decay or as a random failure of access. It is a model of memory to which forgetting is incidental" (226–27). Brand's argument pivots on how public forgetting may be forced by the state, even as personal forgetting can be a survival strategy for diasporic peoples. Considering that the memory of the Middle Passage as a legacy of Black Atlantic culture has been mediated and sometimes almost erased by colonial history, Brand also notes the ways in which the trace of such memory is re-experienced in the bodies of diasporic peoples, or to use Bergson's terms, the ways in which a body is "an ever advancing boundary between the future and the past … a pointed end which our past is continually driving forward into our future" (*Matter and Memory* [1991] 78). Proposing fifteen poems as paper "ossuaries" that become the repository for lives scattered like bones, Brand explores the limits of reclamation and remediation, while maintaining an awareness of the ironies inherent in a globalized and culturally constructed memory that tends—like its storage box metaphor—to equate memorialization with locality. So it is important to remember that the "bone cabinets" of the poems do not serve as sites of memory so much as they function as rhetorical structures, which Brand uses to contain dialectics about the efficacy and uses of memory: the ways that memory can imprison as well as liberate, the ways that memory can enervate as well as enliven. In doing so, Brand debates the terms of modern memory through what Toni Morrison, in a 1993 interview with British critic Paul Gilroy, has called the way "slavery broke the world in half":

> It's not simply that human life originated in Africa in anthropological terms, but that modern life begins with slavery [...] From a woman's point of view, in terms of confronting the problems of where we are now, black women had to deal with "post-modern" problems in the nineteenth century and earlier [...] Certain kinds of dissolution, the loss of and the need to reconstruct certain kinds of stability. Certain kinds of madness, deliberately going mad [...] in order not to lose your mind. These strategies for survival made the truly modern person. They're a response to predatory Western phenomena. (Morrison 178)

Morrison's location of strategies of dissolution and deliberate madness as responses to the cultural legacy of slavery is absolutely at play in what Brand calls the "steady spill of enjambment" (*Perfect* 25) that comprises *Ossuaries*. Brand's unnamed lyric narrator, and the character of Yasmine, a woman who lives her life on the run after a single enraged criminal act in the 1970s, both struggle with ways to live on "the thin diagonal between then and now" as they try to realize "the fragile, fragile promise of humanity" within the "limitless vicinities / which made all land perilous" ("ossuary XI," 82–83).

Ossuaries challenges the mediation of images of violence, exemplified at a point early in the text when Yasmine, a woman who doubts and revives her own revolutionary spirit throughout the text, sees the televised images of the World Trade Center towers collapsing on 11 September 2001, "the spectacular buildings falling limpid, to nothing" and notes "it's done, someone had done it, someone, / had made up for all the failures" (26). Yasmine remains bitterly, even righteously, defiant in her belief that "it is not enough to change the bourgeois state ... / you have to bring it down" (29), and refuses to give credence to the call for public mourning: "she had mourned enough for a thousand / broken towers, her eyesight washed immaculate and / caustic, her whole existence was mourning, so what?"

("ossuary II," 30). From this point, weary dissolution becomes a force in *Ossuaries*, and the unnamed lyric speaker takes up the point to suggest that an ossuary must be more than a site of remembrance. An ossuary can include a living legacy of toxicity in the bones of the living worn thin with moral, political, or quotidian effort in the present day: "I drowned in vats of sulphurous defences // the crate of bones I've become, good / I was waiting to throw my limbs on the pile, / the mounds of disarticulated femurs and radii" (49). Although the invocation of the mass grave—an ossuary that attempts to eradicate memory rather than memorialize loss—is shocking in these lines, the narrator notes wryly that this wish to join the pile of bones is less shocking than it is a tenet of slavery: "But perhaps we were always lying there, / dead on our feet and recyclable, / toxic and imperishable, the ways to see us" (49). Marx's dictum from *The Eighteenth Brumaire* that the "tradition of all the dead generations weighs like a nightmare on the brain of the living" is particularly apropos to the kind of memory that Brand proposes to examine in *Ossuaries*: not memory as a grateful or reparative return, but memory as a living, physical, political pressure, made of equal parts nightmare and surging defiance. Brand's diction is important; calling bones "recyclable" suggests the capitalist commodification of slavery with people as infinitely renewable objects, but when the same bones are considered "toxic and imperishable," the scattered bones take on a resistant power as a poisonous reminder of the price, and the legacy, of modernity. This legacy meets with the kind of postmodern subjectivity that Morrison suggests: a way to assert that history is exactly as present as it is past, and that any strategy for survival must understand that the institutionalized archaeology of memory favours violence over completeness.

Ossuaries is undeniably a book about memory, but it is also a book about the difficulty of locating memory, and about the cultural and historical fallout of living with such difficulty. The metaphor of scattered and dishonoured bones as the material evidence of memory, and the recollection (both metaphorical and literal) of said bones as a device by which oppressed populations may reclaim and materialize their history, have become popular tropes in Canadian literature since the 1990s. Works by First Nations authors and Chinese Canadian authors have also begun to address the need to bring the bones of ancestors back to specific cultural communities. For example, Thomas King's *Truth and Bright Water* and Gregory Scofield's *Singing Home the Bones* both assert the importance of reclaiming bones of First Nations people who have been lost either to the anthropological displays in museums or through the scattering of peoples who have become separated from their cultural history. Sky Lee's *Disappearing Moon Café* is bracketed by a search for the bones of Chinese railway workers who died before being able to bring their families to Canada: an act that appeases the ancestors and makes a hero and patriarch out of the "bone searcher" Gwei Chang.

These literary projects of collection and re-collection link the scattered bones to scattered memories, much as *Ossuaries* does. But unlike these texts, *Ossuaries* refuses a reification of memory from the gathering of bones. In fact, Brand's lyric narrator reappropriates the scattering of bones as an earned refusal to re-collect herself, and instead proposes a kind of unity among the scattered bones as a diasporic symbol. In "ossuary V," she grows so tired of the "efferent blood // petitions" of life in the twentieth century that she is "down to the last organ and happy to be there ... // bone dry // ... scatter bones, losing all relation to myself" (48). Part of the power of *Ossuaries*—the poems as bone cabinets that display the violence of history—is that the subject matter challenges the containment proposed by the form. Brand's subject is the legacy of the Atlantic slave trade, and the bones of the title are the bones of dead Africans who were sold into slavery, and who died violent deaths either in transport or far from home, and whose memories are not situated in either graveyard or ossuary. When the scattered remains of peoples whose forced and commoditized diasporic movement means a shearing away of—or at least a drastic reduction in—available sites of memorialization, "memory" in this context becomes removed from official histories and so must be actively reasserted, often through a search for material evidence as a way of situating memory and reasserting lost histories.

The problem that Brand addresses again and again in this text is not the problem of remembering trauma, but rather the problem of living with a history of the body that is both unlocatable and omnipresent. If "the Door of No Return," as Brand calls it, is a place of both memory and no-memory built by gargantuan public and private losses as well as by capitalism's investment in and debt to the enforced labour of enslaved peoples, how then shall a Canadian-Caribbean writer like Brand write about memory as a site, or a metaphor, or even a trope? Brand's career-long engagement with the tenets of Marxism reminds us that no metaphor is unmediated, and considering what Brand is offering when she situates the human skeleton as a central metaphor for *Ossuaries*, it is hard to believe that she would devote herself to thinking about bones as an uncomplicated spur to recovering memory. In fact, the most arresting and most discomfiting aspect of *Ossuaries* is that as much as the text seems to insist on the materiality of bones, it also resists a romanticized reading of bones as either the site or the trope of memory. And although Brand works with bones as the metaphor both for memory and for the loss of memory, *Ossuaries* distinguishes itself from feminist discourse about how or what "the body remembers" by situating the problem of memory in the black body as an important legacy that has been overwritten by imperialism and a narrow view of modernity. With the "ossuaries" referring at once to resting places and the lack thereof, the poems become repositories for toxic ideologies and for the recollection of the past, and the bones function as metaphors for simultaneous presence and absence:

> as if we could exhume ourselves from these mass graves,
> of ships, newly dressed
>
> if we could return through this war, any war,
> as if we needed redemption, instead of
> this big world, our ossuary ("ossuary XI," 81–82)

Though the metaphors for memory in *Ossuaries* reach toward what poetry does best—the imaginative actualization of concepts and the animation of the insensate through metaphor—they also refuse the ease of those associations and stretch instead toward constructions like "rhetorical metatarsals": "speaking bones" that must be located in the past and the present.

In the epigraph to her 2001 book *A Map to the Door of No Return*, Brand defines the "Door of No Return" as "a spiritual location [and] a psychic destination," one that has been "illuminated in the consciousness of Blacks in the Diaspora." With its subtitle, *Notes to Belonging*, this book discusses the legacy of the Middle Passage as a loss of memory, anchored by Brand's retelling of a repeated event in her childhood when her grandfather struggles on several occasions to recall the name of his ancestors' tribal affiliation and every time cannot do so. Brand notes that the older man's inability to remember became for her a moment that "revealed a tear in the world" (4) and drew her attention to "a rupture in history, a rupture in the quality of being. It was also a physical rupture, a rupture of geography" (5). As a way of extending the conversation she began in *A Map to the Door of No Return*, what Brand proposes in *Ossuaries* is not so much a recovery of memory by a symbolic or actual recollection of bones, or even a healing of that rupture, but instead a bold gesture that points to the ways in which the metaphor of remembering through the body plays out in lived experience. What if, Brand asks, the rupture in history creates irreparable gaps in kinship and family narratives, even as rupture itself endures in the bones of the dead and the living? What if historical toxicity is a sign for remembrance? Writing can embed toxicity as well, and Brand's question at the end of *A Map to the Door of No Return*, "Does all terror become literary?" (223), echoes throughout *Ossuaries*. Remembering the terror of the Middle Passage has become, in part, a literary dynamic that forces a mediation of the historical rupture in memory, that rift in memory that has been passed down through generations.

Ossuaries is not a gentle book, historically or metaphorically, and the work that it does is perhaps described best by Raymond Williams's definition of "structures of feeling":

> practical consciousness is almost always different from official consciousness, and this is not only a matter of relative freedom or control. For practical consciousness is what is actually being lived, and not only what it is thought is being lived. Yet the actual alternative to the received and produced fixed forms is not silence: not the absence, the unconscious, which bourgeois culture has mythicized. (130–31)

Williams clarifies that structures of feeling do not impose a primacy of feeling over thought, but rather suggest an exchange between the two: "thought as felt and feeling as thought: practical consciousness of a present kind, in a living and interrelated continuity" (132), or more simply, a "structure of feeling is a cultural hypothesis" (133). Working with her own cultural hypothesis, Brand reasserts the historical trauma of the Middle Passage against what she has called the "stupefying innocence" of Canadian culture (*Bread* 191). In doing so, she considers the metaphor of bones in quite a different way than do current readings of the "feminist post-colonial gothic" that use ghosts and haunting as primary symbols of a buried history (Kulperger 97). Instead, Brand proposes the "ossuary" of writing as a post-colonial archive that refuses the haunting metaphor of the Gothic mode and favours instead the paradox presented by the rupture of history. The Gothic mode depends upon psychoanalytical criticism in its evocation of a "return of the repressed," but Brand's paradox of bones relies upon a more political reading: Morrison's modern black consciousness through Marx's "circumstances directly encountered, given and transmitted from the past."

The text of *Ossuaries* explores, in part, a third-person narrative of Yasmine hiding from her criminal past, someone who evades captivity but is paradoxically trapped by the need to efface her identity. Alternating with Yasmine's narrative are the first-person poems that take on an oracular tone and that will be familiar to readers from Brand's earlier book, *Inventory* (2006), and the Governor General's Award–winning *Land to Light On* (1997). This series of urgent tercets offers an anaphora of indictments against geopolitical and colonial travesties, or a "catalogue of harms" in Brand's terms. In *A Map to the Door of No Return*, Brand notes, "to live in the Black diaspora is I think to live as a fiction—a creation of empires, and also a self-creation. It is to be a being living inside and outside herself [...] To be a fiction in search of its most resonant metaphor" (18–19). One of the "resonant metaphors" that Brand takes up in *A Map to the Door of No Return* is the "caged body": body as captive not only to the narrative of the past, but also and equally to what has been forgotten, wilfully and sometimes even usefully, about that past. Brand notes: "our cognitive schema is captivity ... In the Diaspora, as in bad dreams, you are constantly overwhelmed by the persistence of the spectre of captivity" (29). Brand picks up on that metaphor of captivity in the very beginning of *Ossuaries* with the text's opening lines: "I lived and loved, some might say, / in momentous times, / looking back, my dreams were full of prisons" ("ossuary I," 9). The sensuality of the body is couched in this text as another kind of prison, and in "ossuary III," the lyric narrator makes it clear that she is not interested in exploring love or sexuality as the wellspring of hope:

> I tried love, I did,
> the scapulae I kissed, I did
> ...
> the curve of clavicles, I dug artesian wells of kisses there,
> utensils of kisses,
> spoons of kisses, basins of kisses, creeks of kisses
> ...
> so don't tell me how love will rescue me
> ...
> since living was all I could do and for that,
> I was caged in bone spur endlessly ("ossuary III," 37–38)

For the narrator of *Ossuaries* who is "caged in bone spur," the imprisoned body is the living mirror of the "disarticulated femurs and radii" (49), and the stated wish to free the body from history is strung between the motifs of caged and the scattered bones: "to undo, to undo and undo and undo this infinitive / of arrears, their fissile mornings, / their fragile, fragile symmetries of gain and loss" (21).

Invoking the image of a mass grave that claims the bones of the weary living, Brand challenges the public images of atrocity, the culture of memory, and the sometimes problematic term "post-memory" as generationally or culturally inherited, as Marianne Hirsch proposes the term. While the mass grave has been firmly established in the public imagination by the heavily mediated images of twentieth-century genocides in Germany and in Rwanda, to name only two, a mass grave is distinguished by its wilful and deliberate lack of care for human remains, while an ossuary is a historically and socially organized repository for bones, often bones that have been transported from their original burial sites for a variety of reasons. The nineteenth-century municipal ossuary beneath Paris, known as the Catacombs, attracts more than a million tourists per year; in part, they are attracted by its historical significance, and in part by the strangely ordered display of the bones. While the bones in the Parisian Catacombs are organized and displayed in symmetrical patterns, disorder is the rule at the Verdun ossuary. Since the Verdun ossuary houses bones of First World War military personnel from both sides of the conflict, mixed together along with those of civilians who were killed on the battlefield or in close proximity to it, the lack of order is maintained to emphasize the common properties of the bones, and to underscore the fact that each of these bones was dug up from the surrounding fields long after any identification was possible. These two examples of ossuaries, one a civic repository and the other a memorial site to violent conflict, suggest two of the elements that Brand's poetic ossuaries interrogate: civic acknowledgement and the place of memory in such acknowledgement.

Metaphors for the ossuary in works by black Canadian writers include M. Nourbese Philip's *Zong!* (2008), a poetic reconsideration of a legal document that names 150 enslaved Africans who were drowned in 1781 for the insurance money their deaths would yield to the slave merchants. Philip uses the legal text as the "bones" of her poetic text, and it is no surprise that *Zong!* features a line drawing of a human femur on its cover. In his novel *The Book of Negroes*, Lawrence Hill suggests that the ossuary of enslaved African people can be found in the Atlantic Ocean, and his narrator, Aminata, warns against sailing into the west:

> Pink is taken as the colour of innocence, the colour of childhood, but as it spills across the water in the light of the dying sun, do not fall into its pretty path. There, right underneath, lies a bottomless graveyard of children,

mothers and men. I shudder to imagine all the Africans rocking in the deep. Every time I have sailed the seas, I have had the sense of gliding over the unburied. (7)

For Brand, the conception of the bones themselves, subtracted from geography, is the ultimate ossuary; "each bone has its lost dialect now" in this "genealogy ... made by hand" (*Ossuaries* 50, 52). The lyric narrator of *Ossuaries* articulates the bones—in both senses, speech and anatomy—as structures of feeling that can transcend mediated images of memory. Or as Brand puts it, they will "glitter beyond these ages / ... burn beyond the photographs' / crude economy" (51).

The repository for bones in *Ossuaries* exhumes memory even as it urges a more consciously political engagement with history. For example, in "ossuary XI," in her discussion of Jacob Lawrence's painting "Shipping Out"—part of his "War Series" of paintings that commemorate the military contributions of black soldiers in the Second World War—Brand suggests that the slave trade and the twentieth century are not so far apart. Although the painting is not included in the book, Brand notes how the image of the soldiers—sleeping on the ship in stacked bunks—recalls the organization of slave ships, and the ideology of the state that offers black soldiers as expendable bodies is a return to historical racism. Lawrence's "War Series" functions for Brand as a visual parallel to cultural memories of the Middle Passage; here she notes that the act of recovering memory is inevitably and painfully self-reflexive: "who could not see this like the passage's continuum, / the upsided down-ness, the cramp, the eyes compressed // to diamonds" ("ossuary XI," 81). Brand's prosody is nearly punctuation-free throughout *Ossuaries*, and the lack of a question mark after "who could not see" suggests in part an accusation that official history has expunged the history of the Middle Passage from contemporary memory and in part incredulity that the cramped shipboard quarters for black soldiers in the Second World War would offer such a visually transparent yet politically opaque return to that history.

But to return to Brand's discussion of poetry as a space of possibility, it is a good idea to think about the ways that poetry can interrogate memory outside the bounds of a prose narrative. Despite a few narrative anchors such as the character of Yasmine and an attenuated description of her years living outside the law, *Ossuaries* is determinedly, even defiantly, an exploration of what the lyric mode can do to confront and in some ways comfort what Brand calls the "angered, unknowable remembrance" of history for black people in diasporic space (*Map* 26). In *A Map to the Door of No Return*, Brand suggests that poetry is one of a handful of methods that can bring relief and create beauty: "Art, perhaps music, perhaps poetry, perhaps aching constant movement—dance and speed—are the only comforts. *Being* in the Diaspora braces itself in virtuosity or despair" (26). This continuum of virtuosity and despair appears again and again throughout *Ossuaries*, but perhaps is best represented in its relationship to memory and its mediations in this passage from "ossuary XIII," in which the speaker of the poem articulates the skeleton of "all the broken bodies" in a resurrection that recalls the raising of the dead in Ezekiel 37:

> look for nothing it will say, the cataclasite sacral crest,
> the gutted thorax, except the schistic rib cages,
> the feldspar wrists, the hyoid bone, what's left
>
> the prosthetic self and all the broken bodies,
> collapsed chest caves, will appear dressed, clattering
> down streets, in all fashions of all years,
>
> no one suspected the inventions,
> I felt my own acid hand on the knee joints,
> some gritty fluid on the mandible, the letter-writing finger (113)

The walking skeleton in these stanzas is not a Gothic image but a political one. Although it recalls the biblical passage in Ezekiel in which the prophet enters the valley of dry bones of those who died in slavery, this resurrection is not God's will, but is instead powered by the force of memory. Ezekiel is commanded by God to "prophesy upon these bones" and he does: "Come from the four winds, o breath, and breathe upon these slain, that they might live" (Ezekiel 37:9). When Brand "raises the dead" she does not put flesh upon the bones, but instead shows us the bare bones of those sacrificed to the slave trade "clattering / down streets" (113). The stanza immediately following returns to Brand's question in *A Map to the Door of No Return*—"Does all terror become literary?"—while offering a parallel question: Is all resurrection reparative? Using Toni Morrison's indictment in *Playing in the Dark* of "the hand that pours the acid" as being just as marked by the violent act as the hand that is splashed by the corrosive liquid, Brand notes the complicity of literature in offering metaphors that cannot locate the bones, let alone provide historical reparation. The raised skeletons in *Ossuaries* have petrified bones, which mark geological time and a material hardening of a "cataclasite sacral crest" and "feldspar wrists" (113). But it is in Brand's proposition of a "prosthetic self"—that which is supplemental to the aching reality of the "real" self—that *Ossuaries* proposes a more subversive resurrection, one that proposes a supplement to memory that offers, if not reparation, then a way to speak about Marx's "weight of dead generations."

In "ossuary XIII," with her invocation of "what's left / the prosthetic self," Brand reminds readers that what remains after atrocity may be viewed as "the remainder" or "the supplement," but it is also a trope of endurance (113). As David Wills suggests in *Prosthesis*, writing itself is prosthetic in that it is supplemental to the body and is "inevitably caught in a series of complex displacements; prosthesis being nothing if not placement, displacement, replacement, standing, dislodging, substituting, setting, amputating, supplementing" (9). The "prosthetic self" that Brand writes as a lyric entity is also a product of the paradox of memory, that which both can and cannot be retrieved, or a body that proves to be "toxic and imperishable." Alison Landsberg's conception of "prosthetic memory," though not always completely aligned with Brand's Marxist views of art, nonetheless provides a few useful ways to read *Ossuaries*, among them Landsberg's contention that prosthetic memory offers "a relationship to memory that facilitates, rather than prevents, the formation of progressive political alliances and solidarities" ("Prosthetic Memory" 145): "As memories that no individual can own, that individuals can only share with others, and whose meanings can never be completely stabilised, prosthetic memories themselves become a challenge to the 'total possession' of private property" (151).

Landsberg's focus on texts of mass culture and Brand's view of poetry as "the least commoditized art" seem to suggest opposing views of art, but both views of the value of the prosthetic lead back to Marxist "structures of feeling" in conjunction with a desire fostered by a text like *Ossuaries*—or Hill's *The Book of Negroes*, or Philip's *Zong!*—for diasporic and non-diasporic peoples to remember outside of a sometimes narrowly conceived Canadian national imaginary. In *Ossuaries*, memory is prosthetic in Landsberg's use of the term as simultaneously mediated by representation even as—or especially when—it is worn on the body. The structure of feelings incited in or located through reading poetry is different from the "public experience of the private" negotiated through the "mediated representations" that Landsberg discusses (149). There is a public memory at the marrow of Brand's "private" poetic structure of feeling, but the paradox persists, as paradoxes must. Brand's exhumation of a non-existent ossuary is as imperative as it is impossible.

Instead of eradicating hope for the future, Brand's paradox allows for possible political readings of memory. Brand shows memory as it is worn on the body, both in literary terror and in the contemporary diasporic context, as she notes in *A Map to the Door of No Return*: "The body is the place of captivity. The Black body is situated as a sign of particular cultural and political meaning in the Diaspora [...] [these ideas] remain fixed in the ether of history. They leap onto the backs of the contemporary—they cleave not only to the collective and acquired memories of their descendants but to the collective and acquired memories of the other" (35).

Brand's invocation of collective memory engages with another paradox: Maurice Halbwachs's classic description of collective memory as that which requires support by "a group delimited in space and time" (84), applied to a group that was deliberately scattered to serve the tenets of modernity's expansion of space and time according to the ideology of Manifest Destiny. Working with this conception of the captive body as caught in the ether of history, the bodies that appear in *Ossuaries* have the double life that Brand describes in *A Map to the Door of No Return*: they are simultaneously remembered and alive. Brand's use of the hyoid bone offers a slim hope for remediating memory in *Ossuaries*. The hyoid bone is the bone that makes human speech possible; variously called the "anchoring structure for the tongue" and the "lingual bone," the hyoid bone, which is positioned at the base of the mandible, is the "only bone [in the human body that is] not connected to any other" (Whipps). Violating the principles of anatomical relationship parsed in the spiritual "Dem Bones" (itself an allusion to Ezekiel 37), the hyoid bone is significantly *not* connected to the neck bone or to any other bone in the human body. Brand's choice of this bone in "ossuary XIII" is not incidental; *Ossuaries* explores a contemporary history of resistance that Brand links to a history of oppression, a history in which the hyoid bone was forcibly suppressed by neck irons that restricted speech between enslaved people and that was sometimes intentionally crushed by slave traders in order to silence people permanently.

The book's final poem, "ossuary XV," speaks from the ossuary itself as physical location and literary designation. Brand's speaker moves from the isolated and sometimes desperate "I, that slippery pronoun" (22) to an inclusive and elegiac "we" at last at rest in the ossuary:

> so here we lie in our bare arms,
> here the ribs for a good basket, a cage,
> the imperishable mandible, the rhetorical metatarsals
>
> ...
>
> here we lie in folds, collected stones
> in the museum of spectacles ("ossuary xv," 124)

In these final stanzas, Brand does not capitulate to any pressures for a complete closure of the narrative. The bodies are still offered through captivity metaphors with the pun on "ribcage," and the speaking "we" notes the considerable irony to be found in lying at rest in "the museum of spectacles" when these bodies were so long unlocatable in the national imaginary. However, the mandible remains "imperishable," and the metatarsals, as bones of the foot, have rhetoric of their own. The metatarsal bones are the bones of the foot that are most anatomically disposed to be broken in what is known in medical discourse as a stress fracture. The stress fracture that is specific to the metatarsal itself has a deeply metaphoric name, showing a historical poetics of bodily memory that endures even in scientific discourse. Some sources say that this metaphoric phrase originated in the First World War, when new and untrained soldiers were required to march long distances in ill-fitting boots. Other sources as old as Aristotle have identified "march fractures" to the metatarsals as the result of forced marches over rough ground without inadequate foot protection, the kind of fracture a captured African person would sustain when forced into a coffle, walking from the inland to the slave castles on the western coast of Africa. The rhetoric of these metatarsals is physical and epistemological; the memory of the lost body speaks through the metaphors for pain that return us to Brand's Door of No Return as a spiritual location that is also a psychic designation.

By contending that "The bone / is an organ like any other" (107), Brand reminds us of the body's fragility, but the pun on "organ"—an instrument with a voice—should not be ignored. *Ossuaries* explores the rupture of memory with the aid of literature's prosthetic devices to locate the irretrievable bodies of lost ancestors, the very people Brand's grandfather could not name when she asked. *Ossuaries*, as a text about memory and rupture, is a demonstration of John Frow's proposal that "the time of textuality is not the linear, before-and-after, cause-and-effect time embedded in the logic of the archive but the time of a continuous analeptic and proleptic shaping" (229). Brand's closing remarks in *A Perfect Kind of Speech* note that her political and poetic work remains inspired not by the idea that change will occur within her lifetime, but instead by her knowledge that "change is now only a negotiation with memory" (27): a shaping of bone.

6

Mediation and Remediation in Carlos Fuentes's *The Old Gringo*

John Dean

National communities are constructed by memories of being a people—a social group sharing a common language, ethnicity, and ideology. Both official history and historical fiction depend on the narrative arrangement of select details to support the legitimacy of a national community's social order. Once history is confined to the written word, its selected memories are archived so that they, and only they, will be remembered.[1] Historical fiction, however, speaks from history's gaps in memory and revisits the consciously deselected memories that have been constructed in a national community's dreams of reality; it then remediates them into alternative possibilities—not to deny history, but to open for question the guiding assumption that the past can be told objectively, that recorded data can be disinterestedly arranged to tell a narrative truth based on empirical evidence and causality. Carlos Fuentes remediates history in *The Old Gringo* by weaving historical events into consciously fictive reconstructions to expose the fictive nature of history. In doing so, he demonstrates that there *is* no history; there are *histories*, and no narrative of history is definitive.[2]

The official history of the Mexican Revolution situates *The Old Gringo* in historical time that, as Henri Bergson notes of most records, has a date and is therefore "incapable of being repeated" ("Matter and Memory" 113). Historical discourse can only revisit or revise events contained in historical time. Events that do not validate official historical narratives often go unrecorded, and unrecorded events are officially forgotten. Matthew Graves and Elizabeth Rechniewski note that "forgetting is the silent, unacknowledged partner of remembering," as "official narratives overwrite private memories without acknowledging them" (12). Fuentes visits the archive of historical memory and writes over events, disclosing private histories (the extratextual documents of Ambrose Bierce and of Mexican self-representation) to evaluate history's closures. Historical figures Pancho Villa, Emiliano Zapata, William Randolph Hearst, and Woodrow Wilson, whose historical time has passed, people the novel, yet the fictional character Harriet Winslow remediates their histories in her memory and—here I borrow a phrase from John Frow as he describes cultural memory—"evokes [historical memory] into presence" (*Time and Commodity Culture* 150).[3] Rather than repeating history as an archival dissemination of cause and effect, Winslow *performs* history by first absorbing official accounts of the Mexican Revolution, then by experiencing that revolution first-hand, and ultimately by remediating it in personal memory and, in doing so, overwriting the pages of history's archive. Fuentes uses Winslow's memory to narrativize the past, in which the old gringo, a retracing of Ambrose Bierce, plays a large part.

When the old gringo crosses the Rio Grande from Texas into Mexico, history melds with historical fiction and the bridge he crosses explodes into flames. In crossing the geographical border, he has simultaneously crossed a matrix of psychological borders: the discursive border between official history and historical fiction; the dominant Euro-American ideological border separating American from Mexican culture; and the liminal border between life and death. These three psychological borders coincide with the three successive explosions of the material bridge connecting El Paso with Juarez. The first explosion is heard only by the old gringo, suggesting that it has significance in relation to him alone: "he heard the explosion and turned to see the bridge in flames" (Fuentes *Old Gringo* 10). This explosion signals a disruption between the official history of Ambrose Bierce—which reports his crossing into Mexico in the winter of 1913 and his disappearing in January 1914 (many historians believe he was killed during the siege of Ojinaga)—and, through Winslow's memory, Fuentes's dream of what Bierce experienced in Mexico.

Chalene Helmuth, an expert in the writings of Fuentes, explains that Fuentes "does not let the reader forget that his character is not Bierce himself but rather the Old Gringo. This represents a disruption of traditional readings that accept the historicity of a novel that situates itself within a historically accurate context" (117). Fuentes's fictive construction of history demonstrates that truth in fiction is no less accurate than truth in official history; both create stories out of collected data, and both make speculative connections to bridge gaps among data. Helmuth discusses the implications of historical reconstruction in *The Old Gringo*, which represents "the subjectification of history through the exposure of its constructs": In its "incorporation of 'facts' that are now redefined as constructs, [*The Old Gringo*] suggest[s] that there exists no single, valid, or natural mode of narration" (126). Helmuth concedes Linda Hutcheon's argument in *A Poetics of Postmodernism* in which Hutcheon notes that "this does not in any way deny the value of history-writing; it merely redefines the condition of value" (qtd. in Helmuth 126). Therefore, Helmuth concludes, "the underlying dynamic of reading historical accounts is not resolving which version is true, as there are many truths, but seeing the theoretical frameworks guiding each supposition into a position of truth and authority" (126). The old gringo continues to cross between the seemingly objective history of Bierce's life and the subjective fiction of his own experiences, both of which speculate and expand upon collected data—accounts from witnesses, conjecture, and dreams. The hyperbolic explosion of the bridge between history and fiction illuminates the imagined separation of the two.

The second explosion on the U.S.–Mexico bridge signals communal experience, as "everyone's attention was diverted by the explosion on the bridge" (Fuentes *Old Gringo* 11). Unlike the first explosion, which, as the wording suggests, only the old gringo hears, this second explosion involves the American and Mexican border communities. The fire on the bridge linking the two countries brings the ideological differences between them into clear focus. *The Old Gringo* takes place in 1913 as the Mexican Revolution is entering its second year. America's Western frontier had reached its geographical limits at the Pacific Ocean more than thirty years earlier, yet the American collective memory of mobility and cultural expansion as divine rights continued to inform the American character.[4] Americans depended on frontiers to mark their peripheries, which articulated American culture as central. Those frontiers also served as borders to be crossed in the name of progress. In "The Significance of the Frontier in American History" (1893), Frederick Jackson Turner had declared that the American frontier was officially closed. Without the hope of further geographical expansion, the American mythos of cultural advancement through be colonial dissemination might be relegated to the past. Turner noted that the American character had been nurtured on the promise of free land and unlimited resources, both of which offered unlimited opportunity. In *The*

Old Gringo, Mexican revolutionary Colonel Frutos García explains to his men the continuing American drive to cross frontiers: the gringos "spent their lives crossing frontiers, theirs and those that belonged to others" (5). Nineteenth-century Americans' identity and development hinged on crossing the geographical and psychological frontiers that defined their limits.[5]

The old gringo has absorbed the archive of U.S.–Mexican history and reconstituted it in a collective memory that has relegated Mexico to the past. He has come to visit the archive, not the country or its people. Colonel García discerns in the old gringo a misrecognition of Mexico and its progress. He says that Mexico is "a family memory" for the old gringo, whose "father had been here, too, as a soldier, when [the U.S. military] invaded us more than a half century ago" (Fuentes *Old Gringo* 6). The old gringo is crossing into Mexico to travel back in time, as if Mexico's history has not progressed since the U.S.–Mexican War. Of course, it is he, not Mexico, who is trapped in archival memory. In his first battle fighting for the *villistas*, he re-enacts the American Civil War by imagining he is a Union Army soldier fighting his father, whom he imagines is a Confederate in that civil war. The old gringo remembers that during this war, fathers had "serv[ed] in the opposing army ... bidding their sons: 'Carry out your duty. Fire upon your fathers'" (79). Jane Creighton notes that this scene is linked to Ambrose Bierce's "A Horseman in the Sky," in which a Union sentry sees a Confederate soldier—a horseman on a cliff overlooking a Union troop detachment. This Confederate soldier is the Union sentry's father. The Union sentry shoots him so that he will not warn the Confederates of the Union troops' position. Creighton clarifies that Fuentes, by using Bierce "to tell a story about the Mexican Revolution," creates "a fusion of seemingly disparate pasts that are to be considered as complex events reaching into the present, rather than as settled and reduced verities. Bierce provides him with a history linked to U.S. interventionist policies that have been an integral part of Mexican politics" (71–72). The old gringo carries his nation's identity crisis into Mexico, and at times, this internal conflict overshadows his understanding of the present-day Mexican conflict between federalists and revolutionaries. In Mexico, he experiences "[t]he frontier of our differences with others, our battles with ourselves" (Fuentes *Old Gringo* 5). Just as official history often imposes its own understanding on other places, reflecting upon the Self to articulate the history of the Other, the old gringo imposes his superego on Mexico to manage his experience there. He misreads Mexico's present in the archive of American historical memory.

Winslow, like the old gringo, imagines that Mexican history has failed to progress. But unlike the old gringo, who sees a Mexico whose history is in permanent stasis, Winslow believes she can help bring Mexico into the modern world. She imagines, and therefore sees, a Mexico whose meaning is authorized by an accumulated Western fantasy of the disordered Other and whose existence depends on Euro-American articulation. This is the official history of U.S.–Mexican relations. She constructs a Mexico in need of colonial rule and then articulates it as she looks at *villista* General Tomás Arroyo's men, their women, and their children. She tells the old gringo, "Look at them, what these people need is education, not rifles. A good scrubbing, followed by a few lessons on how we do things in the United States, and you'd see an end to this chaos" (Fuentes *Old Gringo* 41). When the old gringo asks her, "You're going to civilize them?", she responds, "Precisely. And starting tomorrow" (41). Winslow is attempting to transmit dominant U.S. ideology onto Mexico and thereby perpetuate the colonial legacy handed down to her through the American collective memory of the American Revolution, the Texas Revolution, and the U.S.–Mexican War. This collective memory is what entitles boundary-busting Americans to expand what they believe is their central knowledge beyond cultural and geographical borders.

In Mexico, Winslow is responsible for hacienda owner Señor Miranda's property, which, except for the Miranda ballroom lined with mirrors from floor to ceiling, is being burned down in front of her by Tomás Arroyo's revolutionaries. In response to Arroyo's men destroying the hacienda, where she had been hired to teach the children, Winslow tells the old gringo, "Señor Miranda paid me a month in advance. I shall be responsible for seeing that his property is respected during his absence. I tell you, I am responsible" (Fuentes *Old Gringo* 40). She does not consider the oppressive history of the hacienda system, in which the majority of Mexicans—who are peasants—have few rights and no agency.[6] Where the revolutionaries see the fire as a victory over class oppression, Winslow sees the destruction of civilization by child-like barbarians who know no better. She has carried with her into Mexico the Euro-American history of paternalism, and she feels that it is up to her—the responsible Euro-American who knows how the world works—to make sure that Mexico does not degenerate into further chaos. Just as U.S. president Woodrow Wilson attempted to save Mexico from itself at Vera Cruz—attempting to oust General Victoriano Huerta, who had become a replacement dictator for Porfirio Díaz—Winslow "felt it was her duty to come to Mexico"

(41).⁷ There, "she would be able to teach everything she knew to Mexican children" (47). Winslow not only intends to teach the Mexican children to live in Euro-American time, which is marked by stages of progress, but also believes that English, whose structures speak dominant European and Euro-American values, is the language Mexican children should learn in order to become civilized. If her civilizing mission succeeds, these children will then expand American knowledge claims and further spread the Euro-American Empire of Western history and civilization.⁸

The old gringo anchors Winslow to Euro-American constructions of Mexico, the distorting lens through which she initially sees the country. In the Miranda ballroom, Winslow and the old gringo do not look at their own reflections in the mirrors. Both are "doubtlessly conditioned to ballrooms" (Fuentes *Old Gringo* 39), as each comes from middle-class Victorian society, but neither is accustomed to examining the guiding assumptions inherent in their shared dominant Western subjectivity. Thus they do not reflect upon their shared complicity with a U.S. colonial legacy of ethnocentrism that imposes its civilizing mission onto cultures it imagines to be backward and chaotic. The official history of U.S.–Mexican relations is often a colonial performance in which the twentieth-century historical discourse community creates a national community that knows itself by its difference from other national communities. Post-colonial scholar Abdul R. Jan Mohamed argues in "The Economy of Manichean Allegory" that speaking of the Other is speaking of the Self, since one can only know the Self and project mysterious parts of it onto the Other. In such a projection, the Self becomes a subject only as it recognizes itself in the Other. The Mexican Revolution heightened U.S.–Mexican encounters both as American troops intervened to keep Huerta's forces from receiving arms and as thousands of Mexicans migrated to the United States to escape the violence between federalists and revolutionaries. Many Americans could come to terms with Mexicans only by projecting the "dark" qualities they perceived in themselves onto the seemingly incomprehensible Other. Such Americans did not see Mexicans; rather, they saw undesirable parts of themselves and imposed them onto the Mexicans in an attempt to recognize them. Without this projection of the Self onto the Other, these Americans would not have recognized anything in the Mexicans, and the Mexicans would not have existed in the Euro-American colonial imagination. The old gringo and Winslow exemplify this tendency, projecting undesirable parts of themselves onto the Mexican revolutionaries and thereby denying each revolutionary's subjectivity. This colonizing (and dehumanizing) impulse to speak for the Other is the discourse of the American national archive, which itself stands on the shoulders of the European national archive. In "Literatura de Fundación," the introduction to *Puertas al Campo,* Octavio Paz expresses the need for Latin Americans to create their own reality: "Before we had any existence of our own, we began by being a European idea" (qtd. in Taylor 17).

In the Miranda ballroom the Mexican revolutionaries first "see" and attribute value to themselves while ignoring the old gringo and Winslow's gaze, thereby taking away the old gringo and Winslow's power to assign misrecognized Euro-American values to them. When the Mexican revolutionaries enter the ballroom, Winslow sees them only in relation to herself; she believes they are searching for the old gringo and her, the only valuable presence in the room. She moves close to the old gringo for protection and says, "They have seen us" (Fuentes *Old Gringo* 39). The Mexicans, however, "indifferent to the presence of the two gringos," focus on their own reflections in the mirrors and say, "Look, it's you" ... "it is me" ... "it is us" (40). In seeing their reflections they endow themselves with a subjectivity that subverts the imagined objectivity projected onto them by Euro-Americans. Maarten van Delden, in *Carlos Fuentes, Mexico, and Modernity,* argues that the Mexican Revolution made Mexican self-identity construction not just possible but inevitable, since the revolution caused Mexicans to look at themselves as subjects with historical agency rather than as subjects responding to an image that the United States had constructed of *and* for them. For the first time, they recognized themselves, their whole bodies, not as they had been articulated in Western fantasy or by privileged classes, but as they understood themselves: as mobile and capable of creating their own histories. Because of the Mexican Revolution, the labouring peasants could see and articulate themselves.

In "Re/Visions: Mural Painting," Paz explains how the Mexican Revolution signified Mexican self-realization: "The Mexican Revolution was the discovery of Mexico by Mexicans. [...] The Revolution revealed Mexico to us. Or better put: it made us look back so as to see it. And it made painters, poets, and novelists all look back" (114). Rosemary A. King notes that *The Old Gringo* "provides a 'look back' at the Revolution [...] as revolutionaries see the ideal, whole nation they want to claim, a vision captured figuratively by their reflections in the mirrors" (47).[9] The revolutionaries have been oppressed for decades by the hacienda system and the elitist Mexican government; their taking over the Miranda ballroom signifies their right to see themselves, and to be seen by others, as Mexican citizens with a hand in their country's destiny. They are not footnotes in a dusty archive. Like common Americans, common Mexicans are now mobile, as is Mexican history. Fuentes writes that before the Mexican Revolution, "Mexicans had never moved, except as criminals or slaves. Now they were moving, to fight and make love" (*Old Gringo* 102). The revolution's effect on the Mexican people is made clear when Winslow imagines what they would say in remediation: "We never knew anyone outside this region, we didn't know there was a world beyond our maize fields, now we know people from all parts, we sing our songs together, we dream our dreams together and argue whether we were happier isolated in our villages or now, whirling around everywhere, dizzied by so many dreams and so many different songs" (163–64). The Mexican Revolution opened new opportunities for Mexican peasants—who might otherwise have been relegated to a static past—to participate in a more dynamic future, yet they were not in search of a Euro-American future; rather, they were in search of a national community based on self-realization without outside intervention.

Maarten van Delden points out that, in his review of John Mason Hart's *Revolutionary Mexico: The Coming and Process of the Mexican Revolution*, Fuentes disagrees with Hart's argument that the Mexican Revolution's significance was that of "'a war of national liberation against the U.S.'" (qtd. in van Delden 32). Rather, Fuentes believes that the revolution reflected "a nation searching for itself" and coming to know itself through "the cultural perception of self" that "would have happened with or without the United States" (Fuentes "History out of Chaos" 12). American intervention was misguided: it came in the form of oppressive imperialism exemplified by William Randolph Hearst's vast land and commercial holdings in Mexico and by Wilson's forced occupation of Veracruz. When the old gringo burns the papers that Arroyo had been keeping for his people—papers that the King of Spain had written to grant "a handful of hardworking men" communal lands and "protection against the encomienda system" (Fuentes *Old Gringo* 29)—he is continuing this legacy of intervention. In burning these papers, the old gringo is not only enforcing his nation's archival hegemony, which discursively silences the Other so that the Euro-American may tell, and own, the Other's history, but also creating a historical gap to fill in with his own eternal presence. He knows that Arroyo will kill him for this act, and he expects that his death in Mexico will be remembered more than Arroyo and his people's histories.

The American national archive has conditioned the old gringo to imagine that his presence is more valuable than the Mexican presence. Mexico is, for the old gringo, merely a place to die, as he imagines its history is in stasis.[10] His first impression of Mexico is of an immobile past that can be reduced to one sentence:

> [I]n the old man's clear eyes were fused all the cities of gold, the expeditions that never returned, the lost priests, the nomadic and moribund tribes of Tobosos and Laguneros that had survived the epidemics of the Europeans and then fled the Spanish towns to master the horse, the bow, and later the rifle, in an endless ebb and flow of beginnings and dissolutions, mining bonanzas and depressions, genocides as vast as the land itself and forgotten as the accumulated bitterness of its men. (Fuentes *Old Gringo* 11–12)

The old gringo believes that if he can name—and thereby control—Mexico's past, he can name and be "in control of [his] own destiny" there (17). His past is one of disillusionment, for he has lost his ability to connect with others. The third bridge explosion after the old gringo crosses into Mexico signals his complete separation from his life in the United States. In the moments leading up to this explosion, he recognizes that he is "a voluntary fugitive" from his past (12). His two sons have died, one by suicide and one by alcohol poisoning; his wife has died after a long illness, during which he and she separated; and he has permanently alienated his daughter. These four events correlate with the "four successive and irreparable blows" that have driven the old gringo to Mexico to die (13). Fuentes writes, "Now all that was left was the open south, the only door open to his encounter with the fifth, blind, murderous blow of fate" (13). The old gringo anticipates this fifth blow to be his death in front of a Mexican firing squad. The revolutionaries remember him saying that "to be stood up against a Mexican stone wall and shot to rags was a pretty good way to depart his life. He used to smile and say: 'It beats old age, disease, or falling down the cellar stairs'" (7). He wants the husk of his story, his corporeal self, to die heroically so that his essence—his story immortalized in its telling—may be set free. Mexico is the tablet on which he wants his story to be written because, as he imagines it, it represents a "time before" and offers him a place to relive his former heroism in both public and private battles. More than once he says, "To be a gringo in Mexico [...] ah, that is euthanasia" (145). He has come to Mexico, not to engage with the country, but to be heroically mythologized in collective memory.

The old gringo's death in Mexico does more to perpetuate U.S. intervention in Mexico than it does to turn Mexico into the old gringo's ideal palimpsest. Winslow's witnessing and reporting of Arroyo's shooting of the old gringo becomes an almost international incident: American reporters spread word that one of Villa's men has shot the old gringo in cold blood, and the *Washington Star* calls for the return of the old gringo's body. Although Pancho Villa expertly fields American journalists' questions about his diplomatic relations with another revolutionary leader, Venustiano Carranza, and about the American occupation of Vera Cruz, when he is asked about Arroyo's killing of the old gringo, he is caught off guard. A journalist asks him, "Is it true you had an American officer shot in the back? That a captain in the United States Army was killed in cold blood by one of your own men, General?" (Fuentes *Old Gringo* 172). Villa, who has not heard about this incident, can only respond, "What the shit ...?" (172). The reporter continues by authorizing and universalizing the American narrative account of Villa and, by extension, Mexico, as an abject place of death: "*Responsible* sources in the United States have branded you as nothing less than a common bandit, General Villa. *Public opinion* questions whether you can guarantee safety here in Mexico. Do you respect human life? Can you deal with civilized nations?" (172; italics mine). Such dogmatic claims of universality, and such presumptions that a Mexican revolutionary is the antithesis of civilization, coincide with the American national archive's treatment of all Mexicans. This is exemplified by Walter Prescott Webb, who claims historical authority when he states that Mexicans have "a cruel streak" in their nature: "This cruelty may be a heritage from the Spanish of the Inquisition; it may, and doubtless should, be attributed partly to the Indian blood" (14).

Villa, who is media savvy and therefore conscious of the need to construct his own narrative presence before one is imposed on him, orders Arroyo to exhume the old gringo and bring his body to Camargo. There, behind Villa's headquarters, Villa's men execute the old gringo "for the second time" (Fuentes *Old Gringo* 177); in doing so, they remediate American newspapers' record that the old gringo was shot in the back by one of Villa's cold-blooded men. Villa plans to tell the American media that the old gringo "died in a battle against the Federales" who "captured him and shot him" (177); Villa has successfully remediated his own history to imagine new possibilities. He tells Arroyo that he "didn't want to be dragging around the body of any gringo that could give Wilson an excuse to recognize Carranza or intervene against Villa in the north" (177). Villa, like the old gringo, wants to be in control of his own history, which, as stated earlier in this chapter, depends on the narrative arrangement of select details to support a chosen emphasis. Villa has omitted some details and added others so that he may be written into history as a man of the people rather than as a brutal bandit.

Although Arroyo and his people's history had previously been mediated through their land grant papers, once these papers were destroyed, Arroyo and his people had to remediate their history by performing it in collective memory. Winslow remembers that they "would have to speak now because the papers with their history would no longer speak for them" (Fuentes *Old Gringo* 163). The story does not depend on the material text for its recovery; rather, it depends on the Mexican people's telling, which is the essence of Mexico. In collective memory, a culture continues. History, on the other hand, sentences cultural memory to death, for it assumes that "the subject is already too distant in the past to allow for the testimony of those who preserve some remembrance of it" (Halbwachs 139). The old gringo destroys a historical text; in doing so, he tries to destroy Arroyo and his people's memory. However, Arroyo values these papers only as an artifact, for he is illiterate. He says, "I may not be able to read, but I can remember. [...] I know what my papers mean better than any who can read." He does not confine his people's history to the past; he performs it in the present: "[A]ll of the stories, all the histories, are here in my head, a whole library of words; the history of my people, my village, our pain: here in my head" (Fuentes *Old Gringo* 30). Perhaps Fuentes is suggesting that, like official history, Arroyo and his people's papers create borders that suppress the story by restricting its meaning and value to a dead past. Once the story crosses the border between mediated history and communal memory, however, its essence is made available to speak the complexities of a people's meaning and value. The written account, then, loses its authority to contain the story.

Unlike the old gringo's encounters with Arroyo, Winslow's encounters with the general free her memory of official historical confinement. She comes to understand that the Mexicans she had relegated to the past "have simply mobilized their old pasts, hoping that she would do the same and join them" (Fuentes *Old Gringo* 3). The implication here is that Mexicans are not, as Winslow had earlier imagined, restricted to U.S. official historical accounts; rather, just as American history progresses for Americans, Mexican history progresses for Mexicans. In engaging with Arroyo, Winslow is transformed into a self-reflexive being. Early on, Arroyo forces her to question her own presumptions about Mexico by asking her if the Mexico constructed by the United States is definitive: "Did you see anything different from what you saw in Washington; is the image always the same?" (59). At times, she does see in Arroyo the stereotypes she had been conditioned to see in a Mexican: "She saw him now once more in his unlearned, spontaneous poses, a bullfighter in a vacant ring at night, surrounded by the dead smell of carcasses, an unsuspecting tenor in one of the Italian operas she had seen with her mother at the National Theater" (138). In Arroyo, she often sees "a child almost," who is in need of her nurturing and guidance (138). As she continues to engage with Mexico, however, she puts aside her paternalist lens, and through her personal memory, she remediates what archival memory had conditioned her to see.

The Old Gringo is a performance of Harriet Winslow's personal memory. Remembering her experience in Mexico, she reflects on the competing knowledge claims of *the* Self, informed by the discursively constructed American national community that creates *the* Other in mediation, and of *a* Self who, among Others, witnesses and remediates the past to defer history's closures of meaning and value. Here I distinguish between what critic Mary Louise Pratt terms the "seeing-man" who "creates the otherness between the seer and the seen" without questioning his or her subjectivity as witness (180), and the witness who removes his or her historical lens to see both himself or herself and others as coequal participants in creating meaning out of the past.[11] Winslow's remediating memory attempts to negotiate the binary construct of Self and Other.

Rosemary King notes that when Winslow dances with Arroyo in the Miranda ballroom, "she sees herself for the first time in mirrors because his presence as a Mexican makes her own Anglo identity visible to her" (47–48). Through her paternalist lens, Winslow had seen backward Mexicans suspended in official historical time rather than Mexicans continuing in the present. Her denial of their subjectivity is reflected back to her by Arroyo, whom she attempts to dominate with oral sex: "[S]he took that uneasy, rising, half-grown thing between her lips," yet Arroyo "refused to come" (Fuentes *Old Gringo* 138). Her attempt to possess him in her mouth signifies the colonial act of silencing and owning the Other in order to speak for him. He refuses "to shrink and be beaten, refusing to acknowledge that in her mouth he was her captive" (139). Arroyo mimics Winslow's colonizing impulse to deny his subjectivity, to impose objectivity onto him as an Other. In doing so, he reflects back to her an image of her own official distortions of Mexico and its people.

Later, reflecting on her guiding assumptions, she admits, "Arroyo, I know, I have not looked at all of your people, I wish I had, I have certainly missed something. [...] I have learned. I am making an effort, I swear it. I am trying to understand all this, you, your country, your people" (Fuentes *Old Gringo* 190). Winslow is changing from the Anglo colonialist subject, "whose imperial eyes passively look out and possess" (Pratt 9), to a person who is open to active and direct experience, an experience that negates colonialist naming, knowing, and owning. In other words, Winslow's subject position had been that of the dominant Euro-American who sees only what Western travel books and authoritative historical accounts have conditioned her to see. She had expected to teach Mexicans their abject position in the dominant order constructed in previous Euro-American travel accounts, yet she realizes, "[A]lthough I came to teach, I am the one who is being taught" (Fuentes *Old Gringo* 148).

As she crosses back into the United States, she realizes that "the next frontier of American consciousness" is "the most difficult frontier of all, the strangest, because it was the closest and therefore the one most often forgotten, most often ignored, and most feared when it stirred from its lethargy" (Fuentes *Old Gringo* 186). J. Douglass Canfield explains the significance of Winslow's realization: "Through the materiality of her memory, Harriet must try to negotiate the Border, to turn it from the wound, the [scar] Innocencio still sees it as when he delivers Harriet and the coffin carrying the Old Gringo to the Border crossing" (195). If she can begin to live with her self—an identity now reconstituted by American and Mexican memories—she can find vital meaning and value outside of archival memory. When she arrives on the U.S. side of the border, she remembers responding to the American journalist's question, "Don't you want us to save Mexico for democracy and progress, Miss Winslow?" with, "No! No! I want to learn to live with Mexico, I don't want to save it" (Fuentes *Old Gringo* 187). She had wanted to add "that what mattered was to live with Mexico in spite of progress and democracy, that each of us carries his Mexico and his United States within him" (187). Winslow's crossing from Mexico into the United States signals her crossing from misrecognition to the recognition of meaning and value in the Other and, by extension, the Self. This internal crossing is punctuated by the bridge's "burst[ing] into flames" behind her. She thinks, "I have been here. This land will always be a part of me" (187). Canfield suggests that this scene signifies Winslow's refusal "to burn bridges" (195). The bridge connecting the old gringo and Winslow's First World home with the revolutionaries' Third World must be crossed not with mediated monologue, but with *re*mediated dialogue. Otherwise, the border will remain a wound, a painful reminder of nationalist discourse that creates and separates two nations.

Fuentes has constructed a fictive account of the old gringo to emphasize the antagonistic relationship between the United States and Mexico. Due to official accounts of backward citizens carrying out meaningless violent acts, the Euro-American imperialist imagines Mexico as a place of death.[12] The Mexican remembers the United States as an invading army that took a large portion of Mexican territory in the U.S.–Mexican War. General García speaks to the deceased old gringo and, by extension, to the United States: "Haven't you ever thought, you gringos, that all this land was once ours? Ah, our resentment and memory go hand in hand" (Fuentes *Old Gringo* 9). Mexican collective memory resists historical closure and cartographical articulation imposed by the Treaty of Guadalupe-Hidalgo.

Fuentes writes that the border is a "wound" that, when crossed, reopens in a flaming explosion of histories and memories (*Old Gringo* 8). The official U.S.–Mexican border, drawn by a treaty that closes a war's meaning and a national community's access to previously held lands, cannot be closed in historical narrative. Gloria Anzaldúa describes the U.S.–Mexico border as "*una herida abierta* [an open wound] where the Third World grates against the first and bleeds. And before a scab forms it hemorrhages again, the lifeblood of two worlds merging to form a third country—a border culture" (25). This culture is not in historical stasis; it lives its present as it mediates and remediates history and, thereby, negotiates competing memories of the past that continue into the present. In *The Old Gringo*, Fuentes has revised our positions in the Self–Other interplay and clearly vindicated the need to revisit the history of U.S.–Mexican relations so that a new story of mutual understanding can be written, if not for the past, then at least, one hopes, for the future.

NOTES

1 I am indebted to John Frow, who in his "Toute la Mémoire du Monde: Repetition and Forgetting" (1997), introduces the "archive" of history, which treats time as "linear, before-and-after, cause-and-effect." The archive determines an event's "meaning" and "truth" by "its status as an event" (Frow 218–46).

2 Linda Hutcheon makes this argument in her seminal work *A Poetics of Postmodernism: History, Theory, Fiction*. After offering Peter Gay's famous analogy of a tree falling in the woods (a real event even without one or more historians to debate the details of the fall in mediation), Hutcheon concludes that

> while [Frederic] Jameson and [Haydn] White would agree that the past, obviously, did exist, they would contest our ability to *know* that past by any other

than textualized, interpreted "reports." White would go even further and argue that what we accept as "real" and "true" in historiography, as in fiction, is that which "wears the mask of meaning, the completeness and fullness of which we can only *imagine*, never experience." In other words, only by narrativizing the past will we accept it as true. (143)

3   Harriet Winslow was an American missionary (1796–1833). I will develop this connection as I expand this work in progress.
4   The term "American" may, of course, refer to anyone from the American continent. In this paper, I refer to Euro-American U.S. citizens as "American," not only to underscore the hegemonic distortion of the term, which erases South Americans and Central Americans *as* Americans, but also because Fuentes refers to Euro-Americans as "Americans" in *The Old Gringo*.
5   The *Congressional Globe* clarifies this imperialist version of Manifest Destiny as it reports on 11 February 1847:

> Mr. Giles, of Maryland—I take for granted that we shall gain territory, and must gain territory, before we shut the gates of the temple of Janus ... We must march from ocean to ocean ... We must march from Texas straight to the Pacific ocean, and be bounded only by its roaring wave ... It is the destiny of the white race, it is the destiny of the Anglo-Saxon race. (qtd. in Zinn 155)

6   It is interesting to note that Winslow, because she comes from Washington, D.C., is a Yankee, and therefore should be well aware of such a system, as it is similar to the southern plantations of the United States.
7   Steven Boldy notes that "Winslow is an anagram of W. Wilson."
8   The American national community, which has absorbed the official history of the American Revolution (1775–83) and of the Texas Revolution (1835–36), performs its cultural memory of American exceptionalism by imperialist transmission. American collective memory, as historical knowledge, is expanded by nation builders to educate and redeem Third World communities that have failed to progress as the United States has progressed. Historical knowledge has constructed Third World communities as backward and inarticulate. The American national community has been conditioned to believe that Third World communities are incapable of fending for themselves, so they need the United States to teach them how to survive. Edward Said describes this understanding of the place of the Other as "a locale requiring Western attention, reconstruction, even redemption" (206). Thus, the United States transmits its historical knowledge to the Other in order to save the Other, and in doing so, believes that it is performing an act of goodwill toward the unfortunate communities, which, it imagines, look forward to becoming civilized like Euro-Americans.
9   As Jane Creighton makes clear in "Bierce, Fuentes, and the Critique of Reading: A Study of Carlos Fuentes's *The Old Gringo*," Mexican self-identity constructed both in news photography published in mass during the Mexican Revolution and in the Mexican engravings by artists such as José Guadalupe

Posada made it possible for millions of Mexicans to live "within and among representations of themselves"—representations that "created an identity that could be read by them, or a fiction that simultaneously constituted reality" (72).

10 In the American collective memory, the Mexican Revolution solidified the image of Mexico-in-stasis. Webb writes that the Mexican Revolution was a period of "normalcy" and that the previous thirty-five years in Mexico, under Porfirio Díaz, had been an "'abnormal period'" because "Mexico made great progress" (474).

11 Examples of the "seeing man" are found in colonialist travel writing such as Joseph Conrad's *Heart of Darkness* (1899), Graham Greene's *Journey without Maps* (1936), and Evelyn Waugh's *A Tourist in Africa* (1960). These works demonstrate how Europeans witnessed and recorded subjective impressions of what they expected to see in encountering *the* Other. Their expectations were informed by what they had read in other colonialist travel writing and from both first- and second-hand stories told by other travellers, all of which were stored in the national-historical archive. Another example of the "seeing man" is the colonialist who witnesses *to* Others so that Others may become more like the witness, and thus recognizable or intelligible. We see such a "seeing man" in Daniel Defoe's *The Life and Most Surprising Adventures of Robinson Crusoe, of York, Mariner* (1719), R.M. Ballantyne's *The Coral Island: A Tale of the Pacific Ocean* (1857), W. Holman Bentley's *Pioneering on the Congo* (1900), and Henry Richards's *The Pentecost on the Congo* (1891).

12 For a thorough discussion of Mexico as a place of death for the American or European, see Daniel Cooper Alarcón's *The Aztec Palimpsest: Mexico in the Modern Imagination* (1997).

Part III

RECUPERATING LIVES: MEMORY AND LIFE WRITING

7

Resisting Holocaust Memory: Recuperating a Compromised Life

Marlene Kadar

This chapter is a meditation in progress on a primarily interdisciplinary archival biographical research project that takes as its starting point the unsavoury life of a former concentration camp guard, whose story is constructed from a/b fragments, news media sources, and, more recently, historical and legal documents. It has three parts: the first is a short, theoretical defence of the subject; the second is a short version of the journey of following Hermine; the third is a theoretical introduction to some of the conundrums and ambiguities such a project invites or requires, demonstrating the ways that various actors, readers, institutions, and cultures may be said to resist remembering even as remembering is, by its very nature, carried from my limited point of view as someone who is caught between the two poles of resisting and following. However, this state has helped me tolerate the incommensurable aspects of traumatic subjects (Lyotard) and the unfinished work of remembering Hermine, the betrayed, undecidable subject of my study.

A Defence

The subtitle of this chapter is "Recuperating a Compromised Life," in part as an answer to the response we see to certain kinds of feminist recuperation in this era, and in part to trouble the contradictions that wisely hamper our so-called "working through" the historical memory of one of Hitler's guards whose guilt has been established by a court of law, yet whose life still is a human one. Allan Meek proposes that historical trauma is found not in memory traces but in what is forgotten in the texts of academic critique, psychoanalysis, critical theory, and other activities. Nor can historical traumas be verified by empirical research; the requirement is to read the text of Hermine's life against the grain in order to demonstrate contradictions and difficulties in certainty as an intellectual option. Yet, as with all aporias, the way must be tried. Meek references Derrida: "[T]he rapidity with which 9/11 was spoken of as a 'traumatic event' effectively negated a deeper reflection and more gradual working-through of its political significance" (4–5). But to every time there is a season, and it may be the time is *still* not right to consider the deeper questions Meek anticipates, including the question of the ordinary killer about whom we have been cautioned since Hannah Arendt's satiric essay "We Refugees" in *1943*! I have tried to represent the in-between, unfixed, constantly changing middle ground on which I have encountered Hermine because it seems the only way to adapt to new grey-zone knowledge when, as Omer Bartov has stressed, "the historiographies of the victims and perpetrators rarely overlap" (118). But, as Sayner responds, their histories certainly do ("Memories of Victimhood" 312).

I do not in any way want to suggest that the events of the Holocaust deserve forgiveness. What I want to explore is the possibility that the tender, poignant ambiguities of life writing (life writing writ large) "complicate and dissemble the victim/perpetrator dichotomy in ways that encourage us to think through alternatives" to what Jill Scott calls "blame and hatred," even while it is clear where culpability lies.

In his autobiography, when discussing the analyst's role in interpretation, Freud wrote that "the *fundamental rule of psychoanalysis* [is] bringing into consciousness of the repressed material which [sic] was held back by resistances. Uncovering the resistance [...] is the first step towards overcoming it. Thus the work of analysis involves an *art of interpretation*, the successful handling of which may require tact and practice but which is not hard to acquire" (*An Autobiographical Study* 45). Using this as a metaphor for our subject, I suggest there is repressed material in the stories we tell ourselves about evildoers and "the enemy among us," about their difference from us, about our national purity and/or safe borders, and about humanity. Hermine Braunsteiner's life is instructive because it may help uncover personal, historical, national, archival, and political resistances to her story in our reception of it and what it emblematizes. To uncover these things, we need to hone our skills at thick interpretation, and this will require tact and practice—which may lead to an outcome of "forgetting without amnesia and forgiving without erasing memory" (Whitehead 156).[1]

Following Hermine: The Journey

Hermine Braunsteiner was a concentration camp guard who, having worked double shifts at the Ravensbrück (near Fürstenberg, Germany) and Majdanek (Lublin, Poland) concentration camps during the Holocaust, fled Austria after the war. She was arrested in New York City in 1973 and extradited the same year to Germany, where she was convicted of war crimes for a second time.[2] After a trial that lasted nearly six years, she and seven other Majdanek guards were found guilty of "collaborative murder in 1,181 cases and being an accessory to murder in 705 cases" (Wiesenthal). Hermine in 1981 received two consecutive life sentences. In 1996, for reasons of poor health (she was diabetic), Hermine was released from a prison in Mühlheim by an act of reprieve signed by Prime Minister Johannes Rau. She went on to live a quiet life in an attractive seniors' townhouse residence in Bochum-Linden, Germany, supported by *Stille Hilfe* (Silent Help), a pro-Nazi front group in Munich. That group, which enjoyed official "non-profit club" (*Vereine*) status, had been founded by Heinrich Himmler's daughter, Gudrun Himmler Burwitz, to provide financial assistance for aged Nazis in their retirement years.[3] Between her birth in Vienna on 16 July 1919 as Hermine Braunsteiner and her death in Bochum-Linden in 1999 as Mrs. Hermine Ryan, many details of her life went unnoticed, though they pique our attention now.[4] Even when she was "found out" and extradited, the attention soon died down. There was no fuss made when she died, and her husband seemed to disappear from view as soon as she had passed away. We know his last address in Bochum-Linden, Germany, but that is all.

We do not know very much about Hermine Braunsteiner's early life in Vienna, but some facts were disclosed during various testimonies and trials. Hermine was raised Roman Catholic in the Nineteenth District of Vienna. Her father, Friedrich Braunsteiner, was a butcher; her mother, Maria Ann Knodn Braunsteiner, was a homemaker who took in laundry.[5] There is some confusion about Hermine's real name. Her birth name was Braunsteiner, not Braunstein[6] (the name under which she disembarked at Pier 21 in Halifax), and not Braunsdorfer, as it appeared in 1955–56 Austrian police reports.[6] Braunsdorfer circulated for a few years, but it seems to have been a "simple" typographical error. Such are the accidents and coincidences of archival research on a difficult and elusive subject: muffings (Goffman's term for mislabellings) and errors regularly interrupt the journey.

Like many female concentration camp guards, Hermine wanted to be a nurse (a "Blue Sister").[8] She would later recount that because it was impossible to secure such a position in the depressed Austrian economy of her youth, she had made a career choice that enabled a decent (if low) living wage for young women who wanted to work outside the home during the Reich's formative years.[9] According to Jack Morrison, in 1944 a twenty-five-year-old unmarried overseer could earn 185 reichsmarks per month whereas an unskilled textile worker earned approximately 76. Hermine was recruited to camp work from the floor of the Henkel factory in Berlin, where we can assume she earned a minimum wage. Hermine was one of at least 3,950 wardresses/matrons who "managed the hotel"[10]— that is, the Ravensbrück camp—between 1939 and 1945 (Schwarz 32; Brown 9). Ravensbrück's first prisoners arrived on 18 May 1939: 860 German women and 7 Austrian. On 29 May, 400 Roma women arrived from Austria; on 28 September, the first Polish women arrived. By late 1939, the camp population was 2,290; by the end of 1942, it was 10,800. By 1944, 70,000 had been added to the numbers and placed in one of Ravensbrück's thirty satellite camps; as of 1944 the main camp held 26,700 female prisoners, with a few thousand girls in the detention camp for youth/minors at the back corner of the site, Camp Uckermark. In total, 132,000 women and children were incarcerated at Ravensbrück: 26,000 were Jewish; the major nationality was Polish; roughly 92,000 died by starvation, execution, or overwork. Guards exterminated as many as possible in the final months of the war, including 130 babies and pregnant women.

New arrivals at Ravensbrück were instructed to address their supervisors as *Frau Oberaufseherin*, and never by a birth or married name, on pain of death. As a result, an accidental catalogue of nicknames and sobriquets developed; years later, these names were revealed in their fullness and "translated" when former prisoners recognized their jailers on the street or during the war crimes trials, the most important of which were the 1975–81 Düsseldorf Trial and the Third Majdanek Trial, where Hermine (Braunsteiner) Ryan was one of sixteen defendants. One of only eight found guilty, she was the only one to get a life sentence. She was identified in the courtroom as "Die Stütte von Ravensbrück" (the "Old"

Mare from Ravensbrück)—in Polish, "Kobyla" (the "Old" Mare). A Polish-speaking friend cautions, however, that "Kobyla" has another meaning that is less polite than "female horse" (Nycz).[11] Hermine's comrades Hildegard Lächert ("Bloody Brigitte"; "Krwawa Brygida" in Polish) got twelve years; Irma Grese ("The Beautiful Beast" or "the Beast of Belsen") was convicted of crimes against humanity and executed on Friday, 13 December 1945, when she was twenty-two years old (at Hameln).

The earliest English-language sources about Hermine are neither readily available nor necessarily scholarly. Among them are two journalistic articles: one in the *Washington Post* (6 August 1972), and a fuller piece by Dorothy Rabinowitz in *Commentary* (October 1976).[12] These are complemented by a series of short news items, including various updates in the *Toronto Star* (29 September 1971, 12 August 1972, 30 November 1974), largely because Braunsteiner had the singular distinction of being the first person to be denaturalized in the United States for lying on her visa application (made in Halifax) and then extradited to Germany on the premise that she had likely committed horrible crimes in a concentration camp. One Majdanek witness, Hanna Mierzewska, testified that Hermine and Hildegard Lächert were the worst, the "most brutal" of the guards, and would use anything to beat them, including a whip and a riding crop. In a Majdanek protocol, "Protokól przsłuchania świadka," taken in 1964 from survivor Danuta Brzosko-Medryk, a Warsaw dentist, special attention is once again given Hildegard Lachert and Hermine Braunsteiner. Brzosko-Medryk writes: "From the same time period [1943] and from field five I also remember Auseherin [sic] Braunsteiner. I personally saw her come to the women's field with a dog, a huge German Shepherd, and she would bait him against the working prisoners whom he would bite, causing pain" (2).

For the purposes of denaturalization, the U.S. State Department had only to prove that Braunsteiner had lied on her application for a visa and citizenship; for the purposes of extradition, it had only to establish "probable cause" to believe that she had committed the crimes of which she had been accused. They did not have to prove, many years after the fact, that she had stomped old women to death (wearing iron boots) or hanged a fourteen-year-old girl as a lesson to other prisoners not to lie or steal food. The short version of the story goes like this: Braunsteiner was prosecuted for lying on her visa application; she was then extradited to Germany, the U.S. court having found sufficient evidence to sustain the German charges and that the charges were extraditable offences.[13]

Braunsteiner had applied for an immigration visa to the United States when she was thirty-nine years old. She did so at the American Consulate in Halifax, where she disembarked from the *Maasdam*, a vessel operated by Holland-America, a signatory transportation line, on 23 October 1958. There had been occasional mention that she had travelled by ship from Europe to Halifax, but no details were offered. Some survivors wrongly surmised that Braunsteiner had married an American soldier in Austria soon after her first release from prison, between 1948 and 1950. But Hermine had not married in Europe at all. It took me five years to figure out what really happened, partly because Canada could not help: there was no record of Hermine Braunsteiner in the immigration files kept in the National Archives of Canada (now Library and Archives Canada) (although there are reliable immigration summaries of other immigrants in those archives), and I was unable to procure any of the long versions of personal documents—visa, passport, marriage documents, ship manifests—from the Department of Vital Statistics in Halifax. As unbelievable as it may seem today, most of Canada's immigration files from the postwar period had been destroyed.[14] Hermine Braunsteiner had not been dead for fifty years, so I needed permission from her husband to procure more revealing documents. This turned out not to be possible: although I searched graveyards in Bochum-Linden, and phone directories and obituaries in New York, Russell Ryan has disappeared from any public record. I had no interest in Hermine's life until it became impossible to ask questions about her life. I wondered then: Who is hiding what, and why?

The Division of Vital Statistics, in Nova Scotia, allowed me to purchase the short version of her marriage certificate for C$26.50 in 2004. Although it looks like a benign piece of paper, it is an informative auto/biographical fragment, a trace that put me on the right track with Braunsteiner, her various names, and her great fortune (in the short term) to have gained safe haven in North America. The important markers are these:

1   Bride's Name: Hermine Braunstein
2   Groom's Name: Russell Ryan
3   Date of Marriage: 29 October 1958, six days after landing
4   Place of Marriage: Halifax

I surmised that Ryan and his fiancée had arranged to meet in Halifax and marry there, it being easier at that time for Russell Ryan, an American citizen, to cross the border into Canada than for Braunsteiner, a newly landed Austrian "fugitive from justice," to cross the border into the United States. Hermine Braunsteiner had been living with Ryan in Queens since arriving in New York City on the *Stavangerfjord A* on 21 April 1959 as a privileged "non-quota immigrant." The address is printed clearly on her visa application: 54–44, 82nd St. Elmhurst 73, Queens, NY.

We can assume that Ryan returned to Elmhurst to prepare the bridal home for his wife and settle down to a "normal" life. Mrs. Hermine Ryan must have thought that Miss Hermine Braunsteiner was now a mirage, a forgotten trace of a former life and not life itself. How wrong she was. U.S. bureaucratic practices ensured that INS case files related to Braunsteiner's extradition hearing and eventual deportation to Germany to stand trial (26 November 1975 to 30 June 1981) were held in storage in Kansas. I saw the files in New York City's National Archives and Records Administration (NARA) office in 2005. Copies of identity papers that had been filed at Halifax upon her arrival in 1958 were in the file box—so in the end, this life story remains, and the two identities as well.

For me, Hermine Braunsteiner Ryan's life has significant autobiographical and historical value for a number of reasons:

1   The anti-heroic nature of her life helps us fill in some important blanks as to the full scope of the tragedy that was the Holocaust unleashed by Hitler's Nazi regime.
2   The relative ease with which a low-level camp guard such as Hermine Braunsteiner was able to disguise the facts of her involvement in the Nazi genocide, even in the aftermath of its defeat, helps fill in some additional blanks with respect to Canada's and the United States's indifference to the migration patterns of such persons. Their "unauthorized entry" into Canada in this crucial period (1946 to 1959) has been documented by Howard Margolian, Alti Rodal, Reg Whitaker, and others.[15]
3   The creative and intellectual power of even the smallest trace of knowledge cannot be overlooked; sometimes, however that knowledge is only available through tedious archival research, supported by a research plan that is able to establish the story while always remaining open to its shifting shape, its ambiguities, and both productive and unproductive discoveries as time passes (Kadar).
4   Because one thing really does lead to another, the value of time passing must be highly respected, and conclusions must be provisional for

much longer than a scholar-biographer might prefer or easily tolerate. It is better never to assume that a trace is too faint to be plumbed.

5   Earlier radical-feminist claims about the ethical and moral superiority of women remain questionable in this context. At one time, theorists such as Andrea Dworkin and Catherine MacKinnon claimed a special place for women as nurturers, as better than men when it comes to treating our brothers and sisters well. I still meet students and colleagues who find it hard to believe that women were employed as guards in Hitler's camps, or that they could be "just as brutal as" or "worse than" their male counterparts. Yet they were, according to survivors Hanna Narkiewicz-Joklo and Helen Farkas. *New York Times* writer and memoirist Joseph Lelyveld captured Russell Ryan's sentiments: "My wife, sir, wouldn't hurt a fly. There is no more decent person on this earth."[16]

Gender, brutality, archival confusion, sobriquets, multiple languages and halting translations, errors of transcription, intentional misinformation, the passing of time, the frailty of human memory—all of these lead to a life writing subject, but a provisional one that not everyone will want to read.

Introduction: Resisting Remembering

When Hermine Braunstein/er ordered a Ravensbrück K-Z guard to push away the stool from under a nameless fourteen-year-old girl, that girl was heard to say in Polish to the assembled inmate-witnesses, "Remember Me."[17] After that, so it was reported, there was a "great silence."[18] That great silence has continued off and on until today; yet it was at the moment just described that HB sealed her fate. As Jill Scott writes in *A Poetics of Forgiveness*, the deafening silence is "symptomatic of the monumental interruption of the Holocaust itself, symbolizing the end of civilization and history as it had been conceived prior to 1933" (99). The woman who was ordered to translate instructions to the girl as she approached the gallows lived to tell the tale in testimony against the woman she now called "Mrs. Ryan." Mrs. Ryan, writes journalist Howard Blum, "wanted the girl to step up into the noose" (16–17). The nameless girl's invocation to remember her can also mean, "Remember this event, who was here, who did what." Seventy years later we can also say that there has been resistance to remembering the horror on a number of levels—we resist weighing the circumstances, assessing the desires at play, imagining the scene—yet several versions of this particular story about Braunsteiner and the girl do circulate in protocols and testimonies. Becoming Mrs. Ryan did not erase Hermine Braunsteiner; it just covered her up, veiling her identity for a time (with Canada's help).

This chapter is a response to the nameless girl's request, but here, she and her fellow prisoners of Ravensbrück are not my focus—an approach that has taken some working through on my part. At the girl's request,[19] I have tried to remember her in the name of other girls and women who, named and nameless, suffered at the hands of an army of *Aufseherinnen/* overseers/guards/matrons who managed the only large concentration (extermination) camp devoted primarily to women and youth in Hitler's prison system. I followed the trail of Hermine Braunstein/er that led from that spot on the *Appell* (roll call) grounds in 1943[20] to a farm road in Middle Musquodoibit, Nova Scotia, in 1956; and then on to Maspeth, Queens, New York, from 1958 to 1963, where the trail went cold for a time. Following Hermine has been an international cross-border project filled with detours that I could not have anticipated ten years ago—identity switches, inauthentic a/b identity markers, Nazi misinformation, and the politics of immigration and data collection and of remembering guilt and death.

Following Hermine gave me the opportunity to face personal resistance and fear, but also institutional and state-protected resistance, both accidental and intentional. The ironies of place and time haunt us: it is a belaboured but still fraught story of the wretched contradiction we witness between youngish women like Hermine, or "Kobyla," knowingly killing other young girls and women in Germany, Austria, and Poland, and women in Canada enjoying freedoms resulting from the employment "opportunities" of the war effort. Women like Kobyla appear to be protected by their employer, the *Politische Abteilung* (Command Headquarters, Political Department; casually, "Camp Gestapo") of the Third Reich/SS[21]—the same contingent that oversaw male commandants in Ravensbrück and other nearby camps, such as Sachsenhausen, a few kilometres to the south at Oranienberg. *Aufseherinnen* are often referred to by scholars as members of the SS, but this is an error. Female guards could belong to SS women's auxiliary units; the SS itself was exclusively male. We encounter a number of contradictions as soon as we speak these words: women were women and men were men, unless of course women had to stand in for men in the system. As we know from Sybil Milton, Claudia Koonz,[22] and others, the anti-feminist principle of "the 3 Ks"—*Kinder, Kuche*, and *Kirche*—applied to Aryan women unless, of course, a woman worked the *Lager* beat.[23] Although nobody would say that Rosie the Riveter found gender/racial equality in a Canadian munitions factory, let us not forget that Hermine was also never the equal of her male counterparts in the camp hierarchy and what the impact of that difference might signal.

Apart from my own impatience with this work of remembering, I bristle with confusion when I remember the resistance of national institutions that may find the facts too bold, too incriminating, or simply too painful to pull into a current memory. Here I speak of two major controversies relating to Hermine's story, one having to do with access to immigration screening documents in Canada, the other having to do with security in the U.S. Immigration Service:

1   As I mentioned earlier, none of Hermine's Canadian immigration documents exist (in Canada) because none from the period of German and Austrian immigration most pertinent to our work (1945 to 1960s) have been saved in the national archives. Alti Rodal has written about the tragedy of the 1982–83 destruction of records in Annex 4 of the government-commissioned *Nazi War Criminals in Canada: The Historical and Policy Settings from the 1940s to the Present* (1986). This loss became public when the RCMP could not locate identity documents in the extradition case of Helmut Rauca (1982–83). The RCMP wrote: "The loss of these records, whose destruction should not have taken place, has seriously impaired the ability of Canadian authorities, notably the RCMP, to investigate and take effective action against war criminals in Canada" (4).[24] We learn through the commission that IMM. O.S. 8 forms—Application for Admission to Canada—were routinely destroyed, but that original case files were not destroyed until the 1980s.

2   When it became clear to Victor Schiano and Tony De Vito that someone was betraying their cause—stealing De Vito's summaries of interviews with survivor-witnesses of Majdanek (incriminating Hermine)—the prosecuting attorneys in the United States decided they had to carry all their files on their person. Seven of the twelve summaries had been removed from "the bottom drawer of one of the chief trial attorney's filing cabinet" the next morning (Blum 15).

The Austrian amnesty of 1957 resulted in the quashing of a large number of proceedings and, as a consequence, in the downplaying of Nazi crimes—a tendency that had been clear already for five to six years.[25] The same amnesty marked a turning point in Hermine's life. "Reborn" by her release from Austrian prison and her national pardon, Hermine planned her exodus from Europe quietly and cleanly, leaving no certain historical evidence about how that exodus transpired, or where or when. We might argue with Paul Ricoeur that both forgiveness and justice are, as a result, foreclosed upon, prevented—in other words, amnesty *does* mean amnesia or, as Ricoeur says, "commanded forgetting" (452–56). The idea here is that amnesty creates a new kind of double-bind memory—that is, Hermine could make assumptions about her past, and the mourning public could then either accept her amnesty or disregard it, since there was no one to touch, no person to address, no body to be held accountable. Hermine could easily evade the security radar, perhaps having been advised that Canada was a porous border. Irving Abella has suggested that Canada was "a Nazi Haven"—according to some, "Canada had the worst record among all western states in granting sanctuary to Jewish Refugees from Nazi persecution" (80). We also know that in the 1950s, 25,300 Austrian immigrants were allowed entry (Szabo 110–11) and that their numbers increased after 1955, after the Allies left Austria and the country was declared neutral. Among the newcomers were "likely 4000" men—war criminals (Abella D15). Was Canada a haven, as Irving Abella asks in his review of Howard Margolian's *Unauthorized Entry*? I cannot attest; but we do know that war criminals entered, that at least one of them was female, and that it was not difficult for her to cross the ocean on a signatory shipping line, disembark in Halifax, be married by Canadian authorities, change her name, and get farmwork on the east coast (as did Helmut Rauca).

As Ricoeur declares, "certain crimes should not be subject to statutes of limitation because they belong to the domain of justice ... [T]hese crimes themselves have long-lasting effects," and as a result, we remain "in a domain of complete confusion between the private world of forgiveness and the public world of justice" (Ricoeur and Anhohi 10). In other words, Hermine has put me in a difficult situation, in the middle of Deborah Britzman's difficult knowledge, which can no longer end. The social ego wants to console itself by "freezing" the events of history as if they did not have any present; we see this defence at its worst, in Holocaust denial, and at its best, in the separation of the present from the anguish about war criminals who entered Canada illegally (Ricoeur 473). The long reach of the Holocaust is current and deep, and mixed in with other issues—such as immigration, border security, refugee status, gender, Canada–U.S.

relations, anti-Semitism (both overt and subtle forms), and, much more recently, anti-Gypsyism (again raising the matter of a good refugee)—that complicate the key questions.

Standing in for auto/biography by or about Hermine is the idea of a life writing "limit-case"—to use Leigh Gilmore's juridical term—a limit-case "from the other side" of the courtroom but where representations of honourable actions and difficult forgiveness still operate (Ricoeur 457–58) even though no other just recourse is possible. A limit-case represents the victim's testimony when no court of law can "hear" a case because it is too old, or too frightening to repeat, or is in a form that does not comply with the rules of autobiographical writing. "In their exposure of the link between illegitimacy and fiction in self-representational projects, limit-cases expose the conditions in which alternative forms of knowledge about justice are compelled to appear, and how subjects who produce this knowledge are marked" (Gilmore 135). As all great life writing theorists have declared, "great auto/biographers have generally been heroes, personalities whose memoirs are justified by exemplary lives," even if the subjects's stories are "not without taint" (Rosen 553), but Hermine does not fit the mould, and this may be an incidence of a limit-case subject, although I am certain that Gilmore did not intend unsavoury characters to perform this role. If I am writing the limit-case about Hermine, we can hope that an alternative form of justice is the end result—a form in which Hermine's absent victims are acknowledged and questions of citizenship and belonging are hailed as complex representations that lend "substance to the national fantasy of belonging" (Gilmore 135), and its potential for forcing its cruel opposite—not belonging. In any case, Gilmore's theory allows the possibility that an auto/biographical subject leaks through "against-the-grain engagements" at the limit of autobiography—and limit is as pressing as a visa or a marriage certificate, generic types that reveal "what more conventional autobiographies [necessarily] obscure" (137).

Hermine's story is "characterized by a profound indecency" (Rosen 553) about a female subject who is guilty of crimes against women, children, babies, others. Why would Hermine write anything about herself, apart from filling in the applications for the visas and marriage certificates that became my limit-cases, the punch cards and shift forms that became evidence of work details, the addresses in Nova Scotia farm country and in the working-class districts of Queens that became my settings? The confessing murderer/war criminal must confront "greater resistance than any other category of writers" in order for "his assertions [to be] taken seriously" (Carl Lovitt qtd. in Rosen 553–54).[26] At the negative limit of biographical writing, following Hermine cancels out this resistance and replaces it with another: the resistance of the incredulous researcher who longs to know how it could happen. As Deborah Britzman gently suggests, the learning about and learning from that Freud distinguishes are all the more fragile in difficult knowledge insofar as the learner resists insight because what "tends to be projected is the learner's undisturbed present and not the way the learner's life has become her present" (118).[27]

Following Hermine is about following someone who tried very hard to prevent us from following. When prisoners blessed her with nicknames, they did so as a way of communicating with a future jurisdictional environment. Nicknames allowed prisoners to deliver warnings about their captors—that she was on the beat, or in a mood, or spying on the political prisoners, such as Gemma La Guardia Gluck, Genevieve De Gaulle, Nanda Herbermann, or Johanna Krause, without being "caught." They function as an epistle to us to remember. Sobriquets betray Kobyla; her trials really began when she ordered that stool to be pulled out from under the nameless fourteen-year-old girl who either stole food or denied she was Jewish.

Twenty years after the liberation of Ravensbrück camp, three Jewish survivors, upon recognizing Simon Wiesenthal in a Tel Aviv café, asked him: *Whatever happened to Kobyla?* At this moment, remembered sobriquets—*Kobyla*, or *Die Stutte von Ravensbrück*—ensured Hermine's place in the collective memory of Canada. Hermine kicked her victims to death; she used her whip and boots to harm other women. As Barbie Zelizer and Sara Horowitz tell us, this is not the way it is supposed to happen. Men abuse women; men are naturally violent; men are Nazis, not women. In a recent essay (2005), Horowitz tells us that women are still excluded from the realm of evildoing. She writes: "there is a particular anger reserved for the female collaborator, a special horror at something seen as particularly monstrous, above and beyond the act of collaboration itself" (172).[28]

Feminist scholars in Holocaust studies have made a huge contribution to helping us understand how gender constructs our subject when it is not always easy for history to assess the genocide in this way.[29] At the same time, we acknowledge that Hermine is subject to SS misogyny and postwar sexist practices. Can we talk about how she was a victim of the Third Reich's employment practices?

Liz Stanley writes that "if feminist auto/biography departs from [the conventional, coherent norm of a celebrated hero] … then it is no longer 'auto/biography' but something different in kind: an entirely different genre" (253). Most biographies mirror the "spotlight' approach" (216), but Stanley says that feminists have taken risks with the form and tried to do something else (162–65). Jana Evans Braziel suggests an "alter-biographical" form[30] that resists "the fixed relations of self, life, and writing in traditional conceptions of autobiography as a literary genre."[31] Victoria Glendinning's phrase alters the ground of the bios in genre—writers place under the spotlight one individual and cast everyone else into the shadows. I want to resist the biographical approach to Hermine's life, even as I follow her, because it is her context that interests us, the shadows and what memory or secret[32] they contain. However, Freud advised tact, and even a resisting construction of Hermine must be tactful because it is more importantly a response to the Holocaust, and thus a matter of ethics. Jennifer Geddes explains that there are two temptations that face ethical responses to the Holocaust:

1. The temptation to mythologize banal evil, à la Arendt, because it is relational and does not exist merely in the mind of an individual evil-doer (120). *Remember HB is a cog in the wheel so it is not helpful to demonize her.*
2. The temptation to domesticate suffering, to find good in it, or as Charlotte Delbo says, make good of the "useless knowledge" it provides. *Remember not to draw too much on sympathy for the suffering, as it is too close to pity (and more about the pitier) and makes us talk about useless knowledge.*

Following Hermine has made it possible for me to see these temptations more clearly. In addition, while pursuing the traces of history in this woman's life, I have tried to unlearn inherited "outsider" knowledge I may have harboured to protect myself from knowing what Agamben has called "the bare life" of *l'univers concentrationnaire*,[33] the other-world of the camps that Hermine maintained and repaired, training others to do the same. As Britzman writes, the "interminable work of social justice and ethical understanding," whether in literature studies or feminist activism, is only accomplished when the learner "comes to identify and dis-identify with difficult knowledge" (119)—by activating conundrums and contradictions, not always or only feeling the pressure to resolve them, especially when they cannot, in truth, be resolved. We want to avoid any focus on hope or courage as the "adequate lesson to be made from difficult knowledge," both of which are too often "seen as a bridge to continuity and expectation" (119) (my deepest wishes). Expectation would have us demonize Hermine; hope would have us punish her interminably, or delete her. Neither leads us back into the work of social justice, ethical understanding, or learning to look carefully at a dark side that is not just "over there," as many before me have demonstrated, including the late Sharon Rosenberg and Gina Feldberg, Yvonne Singer, Belarie Zatzman, and Brian Osborne[34] among others. This "dark side" is also Canada.

NOTES

I want to thank the Centre for Jewish Studies, especially Sara Horowitz and Marty Lockshin, and SSHRC for their kind support of this project. I also want to thank my dear colleagues in Miners Sabbatical Research Group, Humanities and Women's Studies, for listening and responding to my queries and concerns about Hermine over the years. Thanks also goes to my life writing colleagues in the MCRI Autobiography project and to wise readings by Jeanne Perreault, Susan Ehrlich, Gary Penner, Linda Warley, and Belarie Zatzman. Finally, I am grateful to Eleanor Ty and Russell Kilbourn for inviting me to be a featured speaker at "Memory, Mediation, Remediation: An International Conference on Memory in Literature and Film" 29 on April 2011 at Wilfrid Laurier University in Waterloo.

1. The complete quotation is: "both thinkers struggle with the uncomfortable but necessary distinction between forgetting without amnesia, and forgiving without erasing memory." By "both thinkers," Whitehead means Jacques Derrida and Paul Ricoeur. See Derrida, "On Forgiveness."
2. About her first trial, Ryan writes: "[Simon] Wiesenthal found that Hermine Braunsteiner had been convicted in 1949 by a low-level court in Austria for her role, not at Maidanek [Majdanek], but as an overseer at Ravensbrück. [...] She had been sentenced to three years' imprisonment. Because she had been in confinement awaiting trial, she was released shortly before her conviction" (46–47). More reliable are the Headnotes of Case No. 68-C-848, "United States of America, Plaintiff, v. Hermine RYAN, a/k/a Hermine Braunsteiner, a/k/a Mrs. Russell Ryan, Defendant, 360 F. Supp. 265; 1973 U.S. Dis. LEXIS 13916, 24 April 1973.
3. See Lebert and Lebert.
4. The address is Hattingerstrasse 44879. I thank my assistant, Violetta Damm, for this information.
5. Boxes 8-14, Case Files Released Under the Nazi War Crimes and Japanese Imperial Government Disclosure Acts, 1947–1994, RG 85, MLR Entry P-3, ARC 1766791.
6. Though unlikely, it is possible that another guard with the name "Braunstein" worked at the camps and was prosecuted. There is mention of a "Braunstein" in the Trial of the Major War Criminals before the Military Tribunal 452

1947, downloadable at HeinOnline http://heinonline.org. The reference to Braunstein and other supervisors is on page 452.
7   *Dokument 22.966 des Dokumentationsarchiv des österreichisches Widerstandes*, Vienna, Austria.
8   Under cross-examination, it was not uncommon for an indicted female guard to make this claim. The Blue Sisters Institute was devoted to the care of children and to a life of obedience to God and Christian values. More about the Religious Family of the Incarnate Word can be found at http://www.iveamerica.org.
9   Wages for female guards trumped average wages for women working in factories, such as at Henkel, where Hermine was working when she was "recruited" for duty at the "new camp for women," Ravensbrück K-Z. This camp was in Furstenburg, a quaint village around 87 kilometres north of Berlin, half an hour farther than Sachsenhausen K-Z at Oranienburg.
10 It is striking that on her U.S. visa application, under "occupation," Braunsteiner wrote "hotel manager."
11 My appreciation goes to Dorota Nycz, of Toronto, for conversations about the translations.
12 This article can be read online: Dorothy Rabinowitz, "Portrait of a Survivor" (October 1976), http://www.commentarymagazine.com/viewarticle.cfm/portrait-of-a-survivor-5719.
13 Canada has not had much success prosecuting war criminals. After its failure to obtain a conviction in the *Imre Finta* case, the federal government gave up on prosecuting Second World War criminals on the grounds that it was impossible to prove crimes to the criminal standard of "beyond reasonable doubt" fifty years after the fact.
14 See a cogent explanation of the "monumental blunder" in Cook.
15 Although Canadian historians did not seem to know about Hermine Braunsteiner Ryan's escape into Canada, they had analyzed the period and documented other war criminals' escapes. See Margolian; Rodal; and Whitaker.
16 See Lelyveld.
17 Mark Twain's oft-quoted quip points to the frailty of human memory: "When I was younger I could remember anything, whether it happened or not; but my faculties are decaying, now, & soon I shall be so I cannot remember any but the latter. It is sad to go to pieces like this, but we all have to do it" (210).
18 See Blum 16–17. This story, and the quoted lines, are taken from Blum's text in which he is telling the story of the prosecuting attorney, Tony DeVito, and what he heard in the Brooklyn courtroom that day in "Mrs. Ryan's" trial. Ryan had apparently "ordered an SS man, named Ender" to bring the stool (16–17).
19 Stories like this one are also to be found in a more recently published memoir by Lanckorońska.
20 Quoted in Protocol taken in 1964 in Warsaw by Hanna Mierzejewska (Majdanek Archives APMM, VII 135/173.

21 Commandant, Adjutant (the commandant was also the supervisor of the guards). Schutzhaftlagerführer ("head of protective detention camp"; in many camps, also the adjutant); Verwaltungsführer ("head of administration").
22 See Milton 297–307; Ringelheim "Women and the Holocaust" 243–64; Heinemann; and Koonz.
23 See Hutton.
24 There is more about this on pp. 230 to 241, missing from my manuscript copy.
25 See Garscha and Kuretsidis-Haider, presented at the 21st Annual Conference of the German Studies Association (GSA) in Washington, September 25–28, 1997, www.doew.at/thema/thema_alt/justiz/nachkriegforsch/warcrime.html#nazi.
26 See Abella.
27 See Britzman; Simon.
28 Horowitz, "The Gender" 172.
29 A few important references: Shaffer and Smith; Stanley "Moments of Writing"; Reid.
30 As Andrea C. Valente pointed out, Braziel defines the term "alter-biography" within a genre discussion by remarking that alter-biography is a "deconstructive or degenerative force within life-writing—one that erodes and contests the boundaries of genre as they are predicated on notions of genealogy, genius and race." *Caribbean Genesis* 13.
31 Braziel, "Proposal."
32 These are two variations of translations of titles of Philippe Grimbert's 2004 novel based on the French title, *Un Secret*.
33 "The Lager is a threshold in which human beings are reduced to bare life; and the torture this life suffers is nothing else but its exclusion from the polis as a distinctively human life. The bare life that is produced by this abandonment by the state is not biological life; not simple natural life, but life exposed to death (bare life or sacred life) is the originary political element" (2). This is the Muselmann as described by Primo Levi in *If This Is a Man*. One speaks of the Shoah as industrialized mass death, and of the camps as 'factories of death'. But the product of these factories is not death but, as Arendt puts it, a mode of life 'outside of life and death.' If for Arendt, however, the production of Muselmänner is anti-political, in that the camps are spaces in which plurality is foreclosed, for Agamben it is the emergence of the essence of the political." Andrew Norris, *The Exemplary Exception: Philosophical and Political Decisions in Giorgio Agamben's* Homo Sacer. See also Georgio Agamben, "We Refugees."
34 Osborne, with thanks to my late colleague, Barbara Godard.

8

"In Auschwitz There Is a Great House": The Location of Memory and Identity in the Roma *Porrajmos* (Devouring) or Holocaust

Sheelagh Russell-Brown

In Toni Morrison's novel *Beloved*, Sethe explains the idea of "rememory" to Amy, the white girl who helps her give birth to her daughter Denver while she is fleeing slavery:

> I was talking about time. It's so hard for me to believe in it. Some things go. Pass on. Some things just stay. I used to think it was my rememory. You know. Some things you forget. Other things you never do. But it's not. Places, places are still there. If a house burns down, it's gone, but the place—the picture of it—stays and not just in my rememory, but out there, in the world. What I remember is a picture floating around out there outside my head. I mean, even if I don't think it, even if I die, the picture of what I did, or knew, or saw is still out there. Right in the place where it happened. (43)

Morrison's novel portrays the mind's struggle between remembering or "rememorying" and forgetting the past. Memories are not only remembered, but rememoried and disremembered. The term "rememory" stands for the re-creation or representation of memory, not just the digging up of buried or repressed memories, but the re-living and re-experiencing of them in the present and the attempt to reach some resolution, some way of living with them. And each memory is in fact a plurality of memories.

It may seem strange to begin a discussion of the Roma and Sinti Holocaust with reference to a novel dedicated to the 60 million or more who died in the Middle Passage. However, it is this idea of "rememory" that I find myself constantly returning to when I consider the question of memory and forgetting in relation to what has been called the *Porrajmos* or Devouring.

Before continuing, however, it is necessary to say a word or two about terminology. In this paper, I refer to Sinti, Roma, and Gypsy, as well as to Gypsiness and Gypsy culture. The term "Sinti" refers to those Roma who arrived in Germany at the beginning of the fifteenth century, whereas "Roma" refers to those who arrived later, in the nineteenth and twentieth centuries, from Eastern Europe. For the most part, I will use the term "Roma" to refer to both Roma and Sinti, as well as to the Lovara, the Kalderash, and other Roma groups. Although many Sinti object to this ascription, this is the most commonly used term for the nation of those formerly called Gypsy, a nomenclature with negative connotations (for example, the derivative "gyp"), based on the now discredited tracing of their roots to Egypt. I use the term "Gypsy" when referring to those traditional and often stereotypical images that persist even today. In fact, some Roma prefer the term "Gypsy," as it connects them with the history of their people within the nation-states of Europe (Trumpener 846).

In conjunction with Morrison's (or rather Sethe's) words, I would also like to ground this discussion in two quotations from Holocaust survivors They have been chosen to capture the inherent complexities of pinning down the particular nature of Roma and Sinti memories (or lack of memories) and their location—inside or outside of the self. They also capture the fraught memory of Roma being in and out of history.

The statement "In Auschwitz There Is a Great House" is the first line of a song by the late Czech Roma musician Růžena Danielová, who was imprisoned in Auschwitz, where she lost her five children and her husband:

> In Auschwitz there is a great house
> And there my husband is imprisoned
> He sits and laments
> And thinks about me
>
> Oh, you black bird!
> Carry my letter!
> Carry it to my wife
> For I am jailed in Auschwitz
>
> In Auschwitz there is great hunger
> And we have nothing to eat

Not even a piece of bread
And the block guard is bad (Danielová)

The same song is heard in Algerian Roma filmmaker Tony Gatlif's *Latcho Drom*, sung by a Slovak Auschwitz survivor, Margita Makulová. Marlene Kadar reports that each of the many times that Danielová sang this song, she began with a prologue and ended with an epilogue. The prologue is as follows: "It is necessary that I say why I sing this song and I want the world to know about it. I was imprisoned for two years and I received the cruellest treatment." When she finished, she would say, "my five children were killed at Auschwitz: Jenda, Majduski, Thomas, Misanek and Suzanka, and my husband also. He was a very good man. I am the only survivor in my entire family" (qtd. in Kadar 241). The lyrics record an "unclaimed experience" (in the words of Cathy Caruth) to describe the belated experience of trauma ("Unclaimed Experience" 182). Even more significant, many versions of this song have circulated, at least three of them before the Second World War. Its roots appear to be ancient. Thus, Danielová's variant on the song represents a Romna's attempt to recover the lost history, not only of her family, but also of her people.

The timeless nature of this lament, along with the paradoxical caption that another Auschwitz survivor, the Austrian painter Karl Stojka, attached to a drawing of a Romani caravan, "We Sinti are in the gas chambers of Europe" (qtd. in Stojka *Gas*), are emblematic of the Roma attempt to assert identity and preserve memory even in the face of the ultimate extinguishing of identity.[1] The combination of picture and text here embodies a paradox. What we see are not the gas chambers, but a caravan. The caravan is empty. The Sinti are not in their traditional homes. Yet they *are*, and they have been defined by the Final Solution of the "Gypsy menace." They are in the gas chambers—in a place whose purpose is to bring about the Roma's *not being*. Nevertheless, Karl Stojka's words, "We Sinti are," can be read as those of resistance, as both a lament and an existential embracing of identity.

My previous research into Roma identity has focused on literary and artistic depictions of "Gypsiness" since the eighteenth century as they relate to the reality of Roma life. For the most part, such depictions were based on the Gypsy as representative of a way of life now lost to the *gadje* (non-Gypsy), a life rooted in nostalgia for the innocence and freedom of a romanticized past. However, as Alaina Lemon points out in her work on Gypsy performance and Roma memory, "there never actually lived an abstract Gypsy, 'nowhere and everywhere'" (4). Instead, the Gypsy reality is a multifaceted one. Gypsies have been nomadic; they have been settled and "assimilated"; they have been described as asocial and work-shy; they returned from the First World War as decorated heroes, and some even served in the German military in the Second World War; they have been musicians, horse trainers, fortune tellers, factory workers, shopkeepers, students. They have been German and Austrian citizens; they have been described as possessing *Artfremdes Blut* ("alien blood").

In my research, the abstract image of the exotic, mysterious Gypsy rover or femme fatale constantly collided with the fact that by 1945, around four-fifths of Europe's population of Sinti and Roma were dead as a result of Nazi policies. The exact number of victims will never be known; nor will we ever know the size of the pre-Nazi Roma population. This is for a number of reasons, among them, the fact that many lost their identity papers in the camps, and not all who died had been registered as Gypsies. Whatever the source, the numbers are significant. For example, Kecht tells us that 6,700 of the 11,000 Gypsies in Austria in 1938 died under Nazism (84). According to van Baar, 90 percent of the Czech Roma, some 6,000, were murdered by the Nazis (373). Toby Sonneman asserts that of the 30,000 German Roma and Sinti sent to the camps, only 5,000 survived (26). She writes that "[f]ive of every six Gypsies who lived in Germany before 1933 did not survive the Nazis" (83). Guenter Lewy contrasts the 8,000 Gypsies living in the Austrian region of the Burgenland at the time of the *Anschluss* with the 870 remaining in 1952, 636 of whom had survived the concentration camps (116). He estimates that of those Gypsies who arrived at Auschwitz, 85 percent did not survive (166). Of those who did, many had been sterilized in a procedure of "delayed genocide," suffering severe physical and psychic trauma in the process; others were maimed as a result of being used as slave labour, particularly after the "extermination by work" decree, or as subjects in medical experiments. Between 500,000 and 1,500,000 Roma and Sinti died in the concentration camps, including 250 children from the Czechoslovak city of Brno, who were the first human guinea pigs for Zyklon B gas. Yet such events have until recently received only passing notice. The Holocaust, as Dominick LaCapra reminds us, remains "a complex phenomenon at the intersection of history and memory with which we are still trying to grapple" (9). Now, close to seventy years after the liberation of Auschwitz and of Bergen-Belsen, few Roma victims remain to bear witness, thus making what accounts do remain even more crucial.

Roma themselves rarely use the term *Porrajmos*, coined by the American Rom academic Ian Hancock. In fact, until recent years—with the publication of some written memories, such as those of Ceija and Karl Stojka and of Otto Rosenberg, who have broken with the Roma tradition of silence to recount their experiences of Auschwitz—the Holocaust experience had not been commemorated by the Roma themselves, except through song. This can be attributed to a complex interweaving of factors that I discuss below.

Researchers such as Michael Stewart, Paloma Gay y Blasco, and Michaela Grobbel have posited various theories for this phenomenon. Stewart points to the lack of commemoration not as a lack of memory, but as recognition that there is no need for a communal memory, since the Roma are reminded every day by non-Roma of what it is to be "Gypsy" ("Remembering" 566). Similarly, Gay y Blasco, in her study of the Gitano of a Madrid neighbourhood, points to the Gitanos' compartmentalizing of "the life of before" and "the life of after" as a way to manage the painful memories of the past ("We Don't Know" 576).

One factor in the non-Gypsy attitude toward Gypsy memory of the Holocaust arises from our assumptions about commemoration as the only possible outward manifestation of memory. Stewart ironically uses the Platonic image of the shadows representing the ideal world:

> I came to feel that for many people the memory of the entire war was condensed into a few images that were normally kept deep in the shadows of the cave, illuminated occasionally and incandescently before being enveloped again in the penumbra of the past. ("Remembering" 564)

Stewart comments:

> Here then are the pieces of my puzzle: talk about the war was rare and moreover popped up in fleeting, fragmentary images. There were no forms of collective commemoration in which the historical memory of persecution was re-lived and recreated [sic] anew for each generation. I had come from a world where, as our common sense tells us, commemoration is the root of historical awareness. (565)

Such commemoration, however, requires both a sense of shared history and a social environment welcoming of such commemoration. Until recent years, these did not exist.

Grobbel sees the act of performance as a particular manifestation of Roma memory (149). In her examination of Roma autobiographies, she writes that the "texts reveal the unique configurations of memory, writing, and identity (both personal and national) and culture very clearly. What emerges is a notion of identity that it not essentialist but rather strategic and positional" (140). She comments that Roma autobiographies "raise questions about *where* memory traces are located and how memory is given a place in the present" (141). Along with the Sinti victims whose stories Toby Sonneman tells in her book *Shared Sorrows*, both Ceija Stojka and Otto Rosenberg grapple with identity, with what it means to both be and not be a German, a Berliner, an Austrian.

Lemon points out that the romanticized view of Gypsies as "living in an 'eternal present'" has crippled their ability to have their stories heard:

> [T]he fact that the world knows so little about Nazi liquidations of Roma is blamed on lack of Romany interest or even on alleged Gypsy taboos on remembering the dead. However, memory must be broadcast and magnified to become known, and not only have Roma lacked access to mass media, but most Roma who survived World War II have been living in states that prohibited memorials of atrocities that laid bare their racial logic. (3)

The battles faced by Roma and Sinti to have their suffering memorialized at the Berlin and U.S. Holocaust memorials and to build memorials on the sites of Czech concentration camps attest to the reluctance if not outright hostility of state forces. As Gay y Blasco perceives it, "the reluctance on the part of the European states to endorse the memorialisation of the Roma Holocaust can easily be seen as a refusal to allow them to belong to the nation" ("Picturing" 300). Absent a permitted site of memory, a social landscape that permits commemoration, the Roma have withdrawn their memories from the gaze of the Other.

For a long time after the war, the *Porrajmos* was not fully acknowledged, and thus few testimonies were available. One reason for this neglect was the assertion that, unlike Jewish victims, the Roma did not experience racial persecution, since they had been classified as "asocials" or criminals. Yet the Nazis bestowed the "asocial" classification even on law-abiding Roma. Initially, the Roma were imprisoned or sent to detention camps based on laws intended to combat crime that dated back to the 1920s, when the German Roma were first fingerprinted and photographed. So it was possible for the authorities to state that such laws, however bigoted, were not racially based, even though the terms "Gypsy plague" and "Gypsy nuisance" were used in the decrees. Thus, prior to 1933, any persecution was under the control of the police and other local authorities. Ironically, since the Indian ancestry of the Roma made them Aryan, another reason for their suppression and eventual elimination had to be found. It was Dr. Robert Ritter, who even prior to the war had been constructing genealogies of the Roma, who gave the Nazis their excuse. He posited that the Roma had become so interbred with European criminal elements that they had become "Mischlinge," and that the *Mischlinge* Sinti and Roma (some 90 percent of Gypsies), as opposed to those few of "pure blood," were biologically predisposed to crime and vagrancy. The terms "moral mental retardation" and "disguised mental retardation" were used to support a genetic basis for asocial criminality. From this, it was a small step to viewing the extinguishing of the Gypsy plague as a matter of eugenics. According to Roma historian and activist Ian Hancock:

> There are numerous Nazi policy statements available to us calling for the total elimination of the Romany population. [...] Thus in the Auschwitz *Memorial Book* we find "the final resolution, as formulated by Himmler, in his 'Decree for Basic Regulations to Resolve the Gypsy Question as Required by the Nature of Race,' of December 8, 1938, meant that preparations were to begin for the '*complete extermination* of the Sinti and Roma.'" In 1939 Johannes Behrendt of the Office of Racial Hygiene issued a brief stating that "all Gypsies should be treated as hereditarily sick; the only solution is elimination. The aim should therefore be the elimination without hesitation of this defective element in the population." (79)

When one considers the toll taken on the Roma and Sinti population as a result of such decrees, it is difficult to credit Guenter Lewy's statement that "[w]hether this treatment of the asocial is discrimination or racism is probably irrelevant" (40), particularly given the eventual refusal of reparations based on the denial that such treatment was racially motivated. The relevance of such attributions of innate social and criminal tendencies were painfully clear to the survivors.

On returning from the camps, Roma survivors were often told by their former neighbours, "You know, we suffered too" (qtd. in Stewart "Remembering" 570). Thus, they quickly learned to be silent. Often they were blamed for their own suffering due to their "criminal" or "asocial" lifestyle. Denied a chance for an education, they commonly returned to school years behind their peers. Sonneman describes a Sinti child who was teased and insulted by his classmates: "How could he respond? Could he explain that he was behind because he had spent the last two years in Auschwitz, Ravensbrück, Mauthausen and Bergen-Belsen?" (135). The Berlin Sinto Otto Rosenberg, who at nine was sent to the first racially defined fascist detention camp in Germany at Berlin-Marzahn and at fifteen found himself at Auschwitz, gives a straightforward account of how he sought compensation:

> In those days there was no talk yet of compensation or reparation. And when the time came, in the fifties, I had to go all the way to the superior court. They said I was not a true German and had no ties to the city of Berlin.
> "Gypsy. Wanderlust. Has no ties to the city of Berlin."
> I was entitled to twenty thousand or thirty thousand marks. Finally they offered me nine thousand marks out of a hardship fund. However, they wanted to deduct five thousand from this. Welfare that I had received because I had been ill. For my brothers and sisters who died in Birkenau, for my brother Max, for my brother Waldemar who was in the KZ in Bialystok and was killed, for my father who was in the KZ in Bialystok and about whose death I have conflicting reports, and for my mother who died as a result of her imprisonment in a KZ, I did not receive a single penny. [...]
> I then renounced all claims, just so that I would not have to be confronted with all this any longer.
> And that is what happened to many of us, often because they could not read and could not write and did not know what their rights were. (128)

Because Rosenberg had no proof in the form of birth certificates for the family members he had lost, he could not claim them in his application for reparations. The only recourse, he was told, was to have them exhumed, a desecration of memory too terrible for a Roma to contemplate.

The racializing of the Roma, then, continued after the war, with departments of the state often basing their decisions to refuse reparations on the very registration documents that had first sent the Roma to the camps. From a letter from March 1984 by solicitor Hartmut Wächter to the State Court of Munich, we learn that "[f]or their decisions on the applications for reparations by the victims, the courts drew upon former members of the 'gypsy office' in the Reichs Central Security Office and the 'racial hygienic research office' of the Reichs Health Ministry" (Rosenberg 157). Indeed, the victims experienced such difficulties until the 1980s, while some of those behind the racial stigmatizing of the Roma were rewarded.

Dr. Robert Ritter and his assistant Eva Justin continued their work, Ritter as Chief of the Welfare Office for the Emotionally and Nervously Disordered and the Juvenile Psychiatry Service in Frankfurt am Main, and Eva Justin as a "criminal psychologist" in Ritter's office. Not only did these perpetrators continue their work, but also the files they had created under the Nazis continued to be used until a public scandal threatened the relevant government departments in the 1980s, at which time they were destroyed.

After the war, Germany's Federal Supreme Court ruled that the racial persecution of the Roma and Sinti had begun only in 1943, and that any earlier incarceration and punishment had been solely on criminal grounds. The previous deadline to apply for compensation having expired in 1969, new rules for "compensation of hardships in individual cases for victims of non-Jewish descent" were announced (qtd. in Rosenberg 157). This compensation, however, was extended only to new applicants, not to those who had previously been denied. To summarize, after the end of the Second World War and the liberation of the camps, Roma survivors found that the new government administrations were imbued with the same attitudes as had led to their trauma. As Otto Rosenberg comments, after the war, "[t]he Nazis were still sitting behind the same desks they had always sat behind" (124).

Compounding the tendency toward forgetting is the fear among the Sinti and Roma that speaking up will lead the *gadje* to believe that perhaps the speaker is indeed genetically predisposed to asocial or criminal behaviour. The profound shame this threatens to instill inhibits discussion of life in the camps. Roma cultural taboos against immodesty and Roma hygiene laws were severely transgressed by conditions in the camps. Otto Rosenberg describes being forced to use a mixed-gender communal toilet: "Here one of the greatest taboos was broken. It was not a normal way of relieving yourself but a torture and insult to our people" (64). In Toby Sonneman's account of the Mettbach/Höllenreiner family, several survivors remember the shame of men, women, and children being forced to see each other's nakedness as they arrived at the camps and were ordered to remove their clothes. In addition, in a culture where a man's worth is dependent on his ability to father children and where motherhood is the highest role for women, forced sterilization shatters the psyche. Sonneman comments: "There are stories that cannot be told, stories that violate the sense of the self too profoundly. Stories that, if told honestly, would disintegrate boundaries of culture, of individual integrity [...] of humanity"

(192). Finally, there is the issue of survivor guilt: "Do you want to know what always makes me so pensive: Why did I survive? I do not know the answer to that myself" (Rosenberg 68). Ceija Stojka too wonders why she survived when her "little brother, seven years old, [had] to croak in the sick block [...] because we were not permitted to go to him" (Rosenberg and Stojka 19). At times, survivors were troubled by the thought that their survival had come about at the cost of their humanity. Rosenberg uses the image of the inoculation against feeling: "They gave us an injection up where the heart is. [...] Maybe it was a vaccination. It must have been a vaccination or I would not be sitting here" (86).

Since the late 1970s and early 1980s, with the publication of autobiographies written by the Roma that challenge traditional dualistic images of Gypsies as either asocial criminals or romantically idealized noble savages, we have witnessed a change in Roma culture. These writers are interested in how the past impinges on the present and in their role as, according to Grobbel, "cultural insiders and outsiders, doubly inscribed as Romany and as Austrian or German" (141). In addition, Romani activists are, according to van Baar, "contributing to the current reshaping of memorial landscapes in Europe" (153). He calls such commemorations "a present-day articulation of Romany memory and identity politics" (153). The *Porrajmos* has served in some ways to unite the Roma, the Sinti, the Lovara, the Kalderash, and other "Gypsy" groups as branches of a single culture. Sonneman refers to a Romani saying, "Our ashes were mingled in the ovens" (19). The written memories of Gypsy survivors have given their people a voice; among these contributions are the autobiographies of Ceija Stojka and Otto Rosenberg.

In her three volumes, *Wir leben im Verborgenen. Erinnerungen einer Rom-Zigeunerin* ("We Live in Seclusion: The Memories of a Romni," 1988), *Reisende auf dieser Welt* ("Travellers on This World," 1992), and *Träume ich, dass ich lebe? Befreit aus Bergen-Belsen* ("Am I Dreaming that I Live? Liberated from Bergen-Belsen," 2005), Ceija Stojka breaks the history of silence surrounding the persecution of the Roma in Austria, calling attention to her culture by making visible both its traumas and its victories. Her writings can be seen as a political act. The climate of the mid-1980s made Stojka's writing invaluable, given the increasing discrimination against those of an "alien" culture in Austria and Germany. Her autobiographical narratives were the first by a Romani author to be published in Austria, and she is the first Lovari musician to present her songs to a non-Gypsy audience. Her autobiography encouraged various

Romani groups to demand the political and social attention they had long been denied. She writes: "If I am a Roma woman from Vienna presented to the Austrian public, then it is a big risk for me. [...] But we have to be open. Otherwise it gets to the point that eventually they will be dumping all Romani into a hole" (*Leben* 154).[2] Like the Jewish Defense League slogan "Never Again," Stojka's words remind readers, and by extension her Roma community, that reluctance to bear witness, however dangerous such self-identification may be, could result in the greater danger of a return to genocide: "Someone must do it. Something from us must be noted in history. [...] Of the history of the Roma, or the gypsies, for the past centuries, you know very little. Their ancient culture is almost unknown. [...] It does not matter how you feel about awakening the memory, it is important that you give it" (*Reisende* 172). Only through revisiting the memories that continue to haunt her can Stojka ensure that her culture's contributions to Austrian culture are recognized and preserved.

Grobbel uses the prefix "re" (as in re-embody, revision, dare we say "rememory"), which she stresses as

> essential in performance discourse, because these "repetitions with a difference" allow for the possibility of transforming meanings of the past into the present or future. In this sense, the focus on the connection between memory and performance forces us to acknowledge the materiality of the memory process and, by extension, of the construction of history. It also encourages us to consider memory's potential for disruptive (re-)play and thus resistance to oppressive power structures. (141)

Against the authorities' denial of the harm inflicted upon her community, against the refusal of the Austrian public to consider the role of the Roma in Austrian society and culture, Stojka sets her words and her music, disrupting the complacency of the *gadze*.

Roma memory of the *Porrajmos* lives on in the hearts and minds of its survivors, some of whom are now giving it words. Some forty years after her release from Bergen-Belsen, Stojka stated that the experience "lives within me. When I speak about it, I taste the soup, the turnip" (Rosenberg and Stojka 19). To describe Stojka's art, Roxane Riegler invokes Andreas Huyssen's theory of "counter-memory," by which suppressed memories are brought to the surface: "Stojka [...] is counter-memory. As a survivor, she writes from under cover and struggles through. The effects are similar whether from the outside or the inside, whether from below or above:

repressed memory and history are retrieved and made visible" (276). Stojka herself uses the term *Rampenlicht* or spotlight: "[Y]ou think you will be the spotlight [...] It was buried deep in the darkness, but after the deep darkness for you will also be the light" (*Bilder*). Surprisingly, Stojka's trauma has not left her bitter. Rather, says Riegler, "her attitude is not naïve, but rather shows her capacity to forgive and still stay alert and aware of social realities" (264). Stojka does not deny the capacity of the *gadje* to once more attempt to "[dump] all Romani into a hole"; but she also trusts in the goodwill of those who will read her account and those of other survivors and determine to build a better future.

Stojka has stated in interviews that her family strongly disapproved of her writing about her experiences, viewing it as a transgression of her role as wife and mother. Even so, she began painting, writing, and singing as a coping mechanism. Referring to the political situation in Austria in the 1980s, she states:

> [Y]ou heard, "Auschwitz never existed." And I thought, "How can they say 'There was no Auschwitz'—I have it right on my arm." If someone says that now, what will happen in fifty years? A wind will eventually knock the barracks at Auschwitz over and blow everything from Bergen-Belsen and from Ravensbrück away so nothing stands, and then people will say, "There's nothing in it, it's implausible." So that idea doesn't grow, I wrote these pages. (Rosenberg and Stojka 19)

Writing these memories never ceased to be painful for her, so much so that at times she had to turn on the light behind her so that the sound of the approaching boots would diminish. As she says in the prologue to her most recent volume, "I turn around [...] and I am there again" (*Träume* 7).

Although she began writing as a means to hold on to her very sanity, Stojka's stated aim is to educate and to witness. Normally, such memories would have been passed on through Roma oral traditions. However, since the deaths in the *Porrajmos* of so many of those who would have passed on these traditions, survivors like Stojka and Rosenberg have preserved them in writing. As Stojka stated in an interview following the publication of her second volume, "[t]his book wasn't really for public consumption but for my children, so that when I'm no longer around they won't ever forget what was done to the Rom, the gypsies" (Rosenberg and Stojka 18). As a mother and as a Romna, she feels it is essential that her children remember, both for her and for their people.

I mentioned Stojka's family's disapproval of her writing of her story, an act they viewed as a transgression against her role as wife and mother. Yet it is precisely Roma women who have largely been responsible for rememory, for the location of identity, and for the preservation of traditions. Having grown up with the stories of her grandmother, Ceija Stojka is deeply rooted in the storytelling art of the Roma. In her autobiography, Stojka connects her story with her "mother tongue," the Romany language in which she presents her mother's words, before translating them into German. As Grobbel comments: "The return of her mother's voice represents the return of a silenced witness and lends expression to muted historical experience. [...] [T]he mother's voice and songs in Romani constitute a movement from the inside to the outside through the daughter's translation" (144). Thus Stojka constructs her memory in two forms. She remembers from inside the Roma community, while at the same time situating these memories within the larger community of Europe, in order to show "Europeans" that the Roma have long had a place in Europe.

The role of women is also prominently displayed in the accounts of music that Stojka presents in her writing. Singing is for the Rom, as for many oppressed peoples, both a way of maintaining tradition and a form of resistance against oppression. For example, Adelaida Reyes states that Roma music conveys a "socio-political message" that provides "insight into people as social beings who choose to mean through music" (qtd. in Hemetek 40). Stojka writes of the years before the war, when stories were often conveyed through music. She tells the interviewer Karen Berger that "the women would generally describe their lot in their songs: someone's death, a wedding, a child's illness" (Rosenberg and Stojka 19). She emphasizes the dynamic nature of Romany songs, stating that they are often revised during a performance, which may take hours to complete. According to Grobbel, "[t]he act of doing and undoing, of enacting her cultural tradition while reshaping it in the moment of performance and writing, demonstrates Stojka's memory work as an intervention in the history of silence surrounding Romany cultures in Austria" (147). Like Danielová's continuously revised Auschwitz lament mentioned above, Stojka's songs convey the continuity of Roma history, rather than a history interrupted by the singular event of the *Porrajmos*.

An autobiography that even more clearly blends writing with oral transmission is Otto Rosenberg's *Das Brennglas* or *A Gypsy in Auschwitz*, published in 1999, two years before his death. Rosenberg's account, told to Ulrich Ezenberger, is conversational, colloquial, almost stream of consciousness. It is a story of survival. Rosenberg too seeks to situate his narrative within the history of his country: "From the beginning, for as long as I can remember, and according to everything I had ever been told, we were German Sinti" (10). He concedes that "[y]es, that was long ago. We lived in peace" (18). However, his experience taught him that, contrary to what he had been told, he was not German: "The Reichs Germans were condemned prisoners too, but they were not treated as renegades like us. We were no longer allowed to be Germans" (75). Despite this admitted awareness, however, time and again he refuses to accept his non-German status: "How what the SS did and—as they say—Germans like you or me did was possible at all boggles the mind" (104). Rosenberg, as does Stojka, assumes a dual identity, here that of a Sinto and of a German, not that of the criminally inclined or the romantic noble savage. Only rarely is this an untroubled association. However, this very dual (or even triple) identification itself serves to underline the fact that, contrary to how they have sometimes been described (and frequently denigrated by their oppressors), the Roma do not normally perceive themselves as a people without a place of being. Instead, it is the *gadze* who have refused them such a place. As Lemon notes, "they *earnestly* see themselves as simultaneously Romani and a number of other things" (4). Hence the potential for a shattering of identity when their history and their role within their state are forcibly denied, when the story of Roma persecution is divided into unrelated periods—pre-1933, post-1938, post-1943—all in the name of avoiding the assumption of responsibility. However, Stojka and Rosenberg, as well as the many Romani activists, have focused the spotlight and the magnifying glass on what they claim must be remembered. Time and again, Rosenberg struggles to convey only the truth of his story: "But I do not want to say anything here that is wrong" (72).

Significantly, like Stojka with her "spotlight," Otto Rosenberg employs a governing symbol in the title of his work—the magnifying glass, *Das Brennglas*. While the magnifying glass is ostensibly the tool that the thirteen-year-old Rosenberg discovers, plays with, and is then brutally punished for "stealing" in the detention camp of Berlin-Marzahn (the guards considered his possession of it an act of "sabotage," he later discovered), it also represents the glass that he turns on his childhood trauma: "See, that is how things went" (62).

Rosenberg's account, like those of Stojka and Sonneman, stresses the importance of family continuity, particularly the role of the grandmother, for preserving the Roma in history: "She was the one who taught me, and from her I learned what had taken place before my time" (14). Similarly, Sonneman's interviews with victims who were also mothers reveal their anguish when their children were taken away from them or when, because of illness, they were unable to care for their families. They saw themselves and were seen by their children as the cement that held at bay the fracture of the family and of the psyche.

The Nazis too were interested in family matters as they applied to the Roma. Their agenda, however, was to trace the family relationships of the "pure" and the *Mischlinge* Roma and Sinti with a view to eventually eliminating the genetically mixed criminal nuisance. Rosenberg's account of the coming of Dr. Ritter and his assistant Eva Justin to the Gypsy camp at Marzahn is especially to the point, and it is chilling:

Eva Justin and Dr Ritter also came to our family:
"When? Where? Where? Where?"
Yes. What we knew we told them. (27)

Hampering recent research into Roma memory practices has been their desire to shelter memory from the communal gaze. This is a consequence of the Nazis' interviewing and registration practices. In fact, those interviews, combined with Justin's photographs of various Roma families and individuals, have been understood by the Roma as what Rosenhaft calls "[instruments] of genocide" ("Exchanging Glances" 311). As a child, Rosenberg was confused by how Justin could be simultaneously so kind and yet so cold. As an adult, he continually attempts to find the words to explain such a dichotomy, once referring to the gravestones on which the dead are always described as "good," and wondering how this can be.

Stojka's and Rosenberg's autobiographical narratives reveal the close connection between memory and performance. For both, rememory is also therapeutic. Rosenberg says:

Even now I could not just tell it like this if it were not so many years ago. In the beginning I had to take a break after every third word. That is how much it moved me. I was not able to tell anything about my parents or my brothers and sisters. That was not possible at all.

When holidays came I either sat in a corner, or I cried, or drank, and then it became even worse. That is only better now, only now is it any better. Now you

can talk about it better. Even though that will never pass anyway. I have some photographs, there I always light candles.
 That is the only consolation you still have: to remember your people. (103)

Given the use that has been made of Roma memories, it should not be surprising that until recently such remembering was an intensely private rite. Some of those who have studied Roma memory or supposed lack of memory of the *Porrajmos* attribute the lack of commemoration and therefore the ignoring of this event among the *gadje* to particular cultural taboos against reminders of the "beloved dead" (Fonseca; Clendinnen). While it is certainly the case that among some groups of Roma the passing on of the goods belonging to the dead and the keeping of photographs are both discouraged because they evoke too painful memories of the "beloved dead," such traditions should not be confused with a taboo against memory.

In their attempt to put into writing their experiences of the Devouring, the Roma are reclaiming their place in history, rewriting the history of their nation and of their countries. As Roudometof tells it, commemoration in whatever form "illustrates the appropriation of the historical record as a vehicle for the construction of national identity" (162). Sonneman describes interviewing one member of the Höllenreiner family who, when recounting his experiences in the camps, fears he will begin to stammer. Instead, he reads to her his written account, assembled as part of a 1993 exhibition on the Gypsies in Munich under the Nazis. His voice strained and angry, he reads:

"To this day, I still don't understand why they did that to us.
 "We were, and we are, German citizens. I have a family tree that shows we've lived for 500 years in Germany. We always had decent homes and jobs and we lived like any other citizens. I was a Munich boy, but it didn't count. I was a Gypsy." (136)

The "great house" at Auschwitz was, of course, not a place in which the Roma could truly "be" as a people, nor did many escape its gas chambers; however, the memories that have arisen from the *Porrajmos* and that have been recorded by its survivors are serving in some small way to return to them an identity and a history, not only in memory, but also "out there, in the world. [...] Right in the place where it happened."

NOTES

1 Stojka's drawing may be seen in the catalogue of an exhibition of his work, which was shown in the Künstlerhaus, Vienna, in February 1996. See K. Stojka, *Gas*.
2 Unless otherwise noted, the translations from Stojka's work were made for this author by Owen Rhys Brown.

9

Autobiography and the Validation of Memory: Neil M. Gunn's *The Atom of Delight*

K.J. Keir

Autobiography, more than any other literary genre, calls attention to problems regarding the function of memory in literature, the status we assign to memory in a text, and the modes of reading we employ. The most problematic texts are often those that illuminate the otherwise unconscious assumptions that govern our reading. Neil Gunn's autobiography, *The Atom of Delight*, is just such a text. The innovative way that Gunn approaches autobiography leads us to consider important questions, such as the status of memory in autobiographical fiction; the shifting reception of autobiography from modernism to postmodernism; the relation between spiritual autobiography and autobiography in general; and, lastly, the links between subjectivity and the depiction of memory.

The Status of Memory in Autobiography

Max Saunders (a critic of both modernist fiction and autobiography) has argued that in the autobiographical genre we see preserved "memory cultures[:] the ways in which memory was produced, constructed, written, and circulated" (323). Autobiography, Saunders argues, represents something of a "memory of memory," a record of differing conceptions of the status of memory in literary and critical history. "Memory cultures" are found not only in the way in which autobiographies are written, but also in the ways in which they are read. Assumptions about the nature of memory and its depiction inevitably shape our experience of reading, and

Saunders articulates contemporary assumptions when he writes that the "destabilizing of genres" in recent research "frustrates attempts to see life-writing as possessing a direct connection with subjective experience and individual memory" (322). Saunders skewers one critical paradigm (the romantic belief in the unmediated display of the self), but his own focus on "memory cultures" is not without its weaknesses. He neatly evokes the problems of an unselfconscious reading of autobiography, but his solution to these problems uses a methodology equally vulnerable to criticism. Essentially, he is proposing a meta-reading, a hermeneutics of hermeneutics. His "memory cultures" redirect attention from the indeterminacy of any and all readings of literary texts onto cultural history. Once we are made aware of the impossibility of grasping memory in unmediated form, we are left with a process of reading autobiography that is inherently uncertain: we do not (and cannot with absolute certainty) know how *reliable* what we read is. Saunders argues that a concern with "cultural memory" ameliorates this uncertainty. We need not worry about "actual events," because we are concerned with "cultural repercussions [...] memories as representations, and with representations of memories" (330).

Saunders seems to recapitulate a view that has come close to becoming critical orthodoxy in recent years. Various studies have looked at the formal properties of autobiography as representative of broader cultural assumptions regarding memory. Laura Marcus's book *Auto/Biographical Discourses*, for example, looks at how cultural mores regarding the purpose of autobiography have shaped autobiographical texts. At the end of her study, she links the writing of either biography or autobiography to the writing of another life. She writes that "[r]ecounting one's own life almost inevitably involves writing the life of an other or others; writing the life of another must surely entail the biographer's identifications with his other subject, whether these are made explicit or not" (273–74).

Looking at memory of the Other can be an immensely fruitful approach. Timothy C. Baker, for example, has recently explored the importance of the death of the Other in several modern autobiographies. Yet like Saunders's "memory cultures," Marcus's Other displaces the debate surrounding the mediation of individual memory onto a question of the collective. Both seek to avoid being drawn into a debate about the nature of memory, and instead look to a discursive analysis of representations. Both approaches are valuable, but both approaches also speak volumes about the tendency of some postmodern thinkers to reframe difficult questions about subjectivity as more neutral ones about discourse.

This kind of manoeuvre has been questioned by Duncan Bell, who has argued that the concept of collective or cultural memory is open to abuse. We should acknowledge, Bell argues, that "memory is [...] an individualistic psychological phenomenon *in so far* as it is a phenomenon that only individuals can possess properly" (72). This tension between reading memory as an individual phenomenon and as culturally conditioned is a fault line running through twentieth-century methods of reading of autobiography. At the core of these debates is the problem of mnemonic unpredictability, which some have read as indicating a type of modern consciousness. This "memory crisis," Richard Terdimann argues, "was never a complication to be solved" by any creative or hermeneutic approach (298). Using Proust as an unequalled example of a literary response to the problems of memory, Terdimann writes of "the unparalleled anxiety that [...] is indissolubly and unremittingly linked to the experience of recollection" in the modern world (159). This anxiety is perhaps a natural condition of human memory. James Olney has written of an apparently *inherent* mutability of memory that "distorts and [...] transforms; it causes some people pain and others happiness, or it brings both pain and happiness at the same time; it apologizes and it justifies, it accuses and it excuses [...] indeed, memory does virtually everything but what it is supposed to do: that is, to look back on a past event as it really was" (254).

Given this variety, any reading of autobiography will be attended by uncertainty regarding the validity of the memories presented within. This indeterminacy, where the reader is never certain what is distorted or transformed, is *radical*: literally, it is at the *root* of autobiography. It is this memorial indeterminacy that *The Atom of Delight* enthusiastically embraces.

The Atom of Delight, Modernism, and Postmodernism

Published in 1956, *The Atom of Delight* is situated in the middle of the transition from intense modernist subjectivity to a concern with discursive formations. This placement is not simply chronological; *The Atom of Delight* deploys tactics associated with both approaches. The book was a commercial failure and appears to have disappeared into a fissure between these two hermeneutics. Recovering *The Atom of Delight* from the bottom of this fissure is not only a task for the studious literary historian, however, because *The Atom of Delight* sheds vital light on the hermeneutics of autobiography.

Gunn was the foremost novelist of the Scottish Literary Renaissance, the flowering of modernist literature in Scotland from the 1920s onwards. Although it was a commercial failure, *The Atom of Delight* did influence a number of the next generation of Scottish writers: Kenneth White edited an anthology of Scottish haiku and gave it the title *Atoms of Delight* (2000); Alan Spence wrote an introduction to the only reprinted edition of *The Atom of Delight*, while one of the characters in his first collection of stories is enthusiastic about Gunn's symbolism (Gunn 1986; Spence *Its Colours* 219). Despite this influence, *The Atom of Delight* has never been given much attention by critics of Scottish literature. Gunn's biographers argue that readers were put off by *The Atom of Delight* because it frustrated their assumptions regarding autobiography; it was, according to Hart and Pick, "in no real sense" an autobiography (*Neil M. Gunn* 252). "Readers," they continue, "would have been willing to digest the philosophy [...] had the author in return opened himself to them. But he did not" (252–53). Hart and Pick's sense of Gunn failing to meet certain obligations to his readers seems to relate to the way in which Gunn seems to break what Phillipe Lejeune calls "the autobiographical contract" that guarantees "*identity in name* between the author [...] the narrator, and the one being spoken of" (200). In standard works such as the *Confessions* of either Augustine or Rousseau, this contract is honoured, but the twentieth century abounds in examples where writers have interpreted their obligations differently. Laura Marcus writes that critics have "charted autobiography's 'progress' into the novel form," a progress in which "any distinction between 'autobiography' and 'autobiographical' is effaced or elided" (239).

The Atom of Delight bears evidence of this elision. Gunn begins with standard first-person narration, conforming to Lejeune's tripartite identity: "Often when looking for a thing I find something else. I knew what I was looking for, but what I find is surprising. At once some part of life is resurrected; persons move about, I see their faces, the place, almost the air of that forgotten time" (7). He appears to be about to describe what happens when "some part of life is resurrected," recalled from "forgotten time" and formed into a first-person memorial narrative, but very quickly he begins to use the third-person to describe his past self: "The boy's world was entirely different from the adult's world. The grown man was a tall being moving amid the work and arrangements of life and death. For the boy, the funeral cortege passed, the school was left behind, the church door was shut—'I'm off!'—and he was into his own intense world" (31–32).

The third-person depiction of his own past reflects skepticism on Gunn's part about his ability to recollect and narrate the past. Seen in "his own intense world," Gunn's past self appears to be a foreign entity. In the act of self-memorialization, Gunn joins the reader as a spectator to his past and in doing so draws attention to the fact that these memories are being mediated. The reader is warned by the third-person narration to question the status of the memories Gunn depicts, alerted to the fact that both recollection *and* aesthetic transformation are present in *The Atom of Delight*.

Evaluating the validity or truthfulness of the memories Gunn depicts becomes difficult when Gunn uses the third-person. These parts of *The Atom of Delight* seem to belong to the genre of autobiographical fiction, a genre that also raises questions about the memories depicted within. Jerome Buckley suggests that the reader of autobiographical fiction should "assume [...] a likely relationship to an actual life-history known to us from other sources, which offer an extrinsic validation both of the speaker's voice and the 'reality' of the episodes he has chosen to re-create. Here, and perhaps to some extent in all autobiography, we knowingly accept some fictional distortion as a necessary adjunct to the teller's style" (116).

Buckley's vocabulary here ("assume," "likely," "perhaps," "some extent") points to either *probability* or a lack of precision. Even if we allow for some imprecision, there are still two problems with his "extrinsic validation" of autobiographical fiction. First there is a general problem, that other texts are not necessarily more reliable: memory depicted or recorded in non-fiction texts can also be faulty, biased, or even fabricated. Second (and more importantly), the modernist period as a whole seems to have been skeptical of "extrinsic validation," and this skepticism explains (at least in part) why the modernist period came to elide differences between autobiographical fiction and autobiography.

Gunn's attitude toward memory is in many respects based on this broadly held suspicion of received accounts of events. Paul Fussell argues that this skepticism was created by the First World War, which, he suggests, had the impact of eroding notions of historical order and destabilizing memorial art. Fussell argues that "the Great War was perhaps the last to be conceived as taking place within a seamless, purposeful 'history' involving a coherent stream of time running from past through present to future" (21).

Given this historical uprootedness, it is understandable that the modernist generation turned to fiction to substitute for the lost narrative wholeness of the actual world. With the possibility of remembering a past that has a bearing on the present (let alone the future) slipping away from them, modernist novelists turned toward art as a means of commemoration: fiction could bear more of the burden of shaping memory than fact could. The modernist marriage of fiction and autobiography suggests the primacy of aesthetic over experiential truth, a problematic and contentious suggestion. The modernist autobiographer stakes his text's memorial value on his realization of stylistic or aesthetic possibilities within his own text, not on fidelity to external realities.

It is thus fitting to invert Buckley's phrase and to speak of "intrinsic validation" in modernist autobiographical fiction or autobiography. The reader is aware of the text as self-mythologization, which is synonymous with self-memorialization. Memories are validated, or given worth, by their inclusion in an aesthetic project, not by being revealed as "real" by another text. The modernist use of the fictional form in autobiography, the seeking after memorial validity through art, is highly relevant to *The Atom of Delight* and to Gunn's career as a whole. The use of the third-person in *The Atom of Delight* is a confirmation of Fussell's theory of modern memory: Gunn inhabited a world of extreme epistemological doubt regarding history as a series of events amenable to recollection in linear narrative. The first-person "I" is tenable in this context only in the present; it does not have a historical existence.

Modernist memorial skepticism is not the only problem facing the Buckley-esque reader of *The Atom of Delight* who searches for "extrinsic validation." A reader might justifiably turn to an author's memoirs in search of some "extrinsic data" to validate the memories represented in his or her novels, but *The Atom of Delight* inverts this relationship. Gunn's reader is encouraged to look to his fiction as the "extrinsic data" that will verify the memorial status of *The Atom of Delight*. The reader is aided in making this curious manoeuvre by the fact that one of the central episodes in *The Atom of Delight* is largely a repeat of a key event from a novel, *Highland River*.

Gunn describes in *The Atom of Delight* how "the boy" catches a salmon by hand in a local stream:

> With his head tilted back to keep the water from lapping into his mouth, the boy feels for the bottom of the pool, and the big toe of his right foot comes gently against a surface that yields. As his eyes widen so does his mouth, and the water laps in. Choking and threshing the surface he rolls over, reaches blindly overhand kicks hard and grounds on the edge of the pool, where his

body goes into a slow compulsive squirm in its desperate effort to spew water and suck air at the same time. (37)

Readers familiar with Gunn's novels will immediately note the similarity between this chapter and the opening scene in Gunn's *Highland River* (1937). In this bildungsroman, the main character also manages to catch a salmon with his hands:

His hands went straight for the gills; one found a grip under a cheek, the other, slipping, tried for a hold on the body, and there and then began the oddest tussle that surely that river could ever have seen. (8)

The reader of *The Atom of Delight* therefore has the uncanny experience of hearing echoes of a fictional work in an autobiographic one. Ordinarily, the inclusion of an event in an author's autobiography would confirm the "reality" of an event in his or her fiction, but because of Gunn's use of the third-person this comparison cannot be performed. Even going so far as to detect the autobiographical within Gunn's fiction is a fraught process, as the dedication to *Highland River* indicates:

Dear John [Gunn's brother],
This can hardly be the description of our Highland river that you anticipated when, lying on our backs in a green strath, we idly talked the idea over. Certainly it is not the description I anticipated myself. Some ancestral instinct, at first glimpse of the river, must have taken control and set me off on a queerer hunt than we have yet tackled. Or am I now trying to cover up the spoor? You will early recognise that though there is no individual biography here, every incident may have had its double. Some of the characters seem to have strayed in from *Morning Tide*. I cannot explain this odd behaviour. (v)

To begin with, Gunn seems to admit the autobiographical nature of *Highland River*, even if his phrasing ("every event *may have had* its double") is evasive. Then, though, he diverts the question of memory in a number of ways. First, when he says that some of the characters "have strayed in from *Morning Tide*," he links *Highland River* with another of his novels, published five years earlier. If the reader has turned to *Highland River* for "extrinsic data" that is supposed to confirm the validity of memories presented in *The Atom of Delight*, Gunn's dedication sends them on to another text. The reader's need for supplementary verification is thus turned into a ceaseless chase after memory that is continually receding. Gunn's use of the third person forces the reader into the modernist mindset where the ultimate validation of represented memories lies in the quality of the art into which they are transformed.

Spiritual Autobiography

The third-person sections of *The Atom of Delight* are not the only ones that seem to deviate from conventional autobiography. Gunn also weaves together allusions and references to other texts. Sometimes this philosophizing seems to leave autobiography behind entirely as Gunn the man recedes into the web of discourse. Douglas Gifford has referred to *The Atom of Delight* as a "spiritual autobiography," a genre that in recent readings has been seen as inherently intertextual (101). Larry Sisson writes that spiritual autobiography "sets the self off centre and unsettles notions of individual, independent, or freely determined authorship. [...] [S]piritual autobiographers tend not to present themselves as points of artistic, religious, or narrative origin" (98–99).

We see this displacement of self in *The Atom of Delight* in Gunn's fictional treatment of episodes from his past life: Gunn presents himself not as a point of "narrative origin," but rather as a narrator grasping at a complex and fundamentally difficult memory. As Sisson argues, however, the spiritual autobiographer's chief tactic is *intertextuality*: "[The] individual's life is not simply the sum of his or her experience, nor is his or her history entirely 'personal.' Instead, the individual's identity takes shape within a network of references, and his or her story emerges from narratives other than the person's own" (99).

The spiritual autobiographer thus constructs his or her own narrative self-consciously as part of a larger collective narrative. In Sisson's examples, this collective narrative is Christian, the story of Paul's conversion in the Bible affecting Augustine's *Confessions*, for example. "Their lives," Sisson writes, "take shape in the light of others' lives; their lines abound with echo and allusion; their accounts share contours with previous books of faith" (100). This leads Sisson to describe spiritual autobiography as "highly intertextual, 'determined' in large part by previous self-portraits, and 'governed' by hermeneutics as much as by history" (102). He concludes that "[t]he form's open reliance on predecessors and patterns, its analytical reworking of past lives and perceptions, its imaginative echoes of others' works and worlds—all of these factors help clarify the centrality of hermeneutics to any act of life-writing" (104).

Such a postmodern concern with intertextuality quaintly echoes Jerome Buckley's emphasis on "extrinsic data" in the reading of autobiographical fiction: in both theories, the text is seen as insufficient for a full reading and the extrinsic need draws the reader out to other texts; yet as with Buckley, Sisson's intertextuality leads to a frustrating search for memorial validation.

To validate a given part of a text as mnemonically accurate, the reader is encouraged to read it as an echo of other texts. This echoing validates the text's memorial value by linking it to a grand theological narrative of past conversions and also to the biblical narrative. Yet Sisson seems to underestimate the importance of a specifically theological intertextuality. By being able to follow a series of intertextual echoes, the reader of Christian spiritual autobiography can trace echoes in one text back to another that claims absolute, divine, validity as a cosmological truth. Although Sisson claims that the same process of intertextual echoing is present in all autobiography, it is only when buttressed by theological authority that the memories represented in spiritual autobiography are validated.

The Atom of Delight is a spiritual narrative, discussing God and gods, religion, and the spirit or soul, but Gunn never invokes another text as a *validating authority* for his memories. For example, we have his discussion of being in church as a child giving way to a passage from Freud, the famous account of the emergence of religion in *Totem and Taboo*, which begins: "One day the expelled brothers joined forces, slew and ate the father, and thus put an end to the father horde" (Gunn 66; Freud 235). If *Totem and Taboo* were being employed in *The Atom of Delight* in the same intertextual relationship that we find in overtly religious narratives, then Gunn would end by pointing out that Freud's account of religion in *Totem and Taboo* matched his own experience. We would have before us a case of intertextual editing whereby Gunn's personal memory of being in church would be linked to and validated by a grander narrative relating to all religion. Yet Gunn chooses to disagree, and after following Freud's argument for some distance, lights upon Freud's admission that "I am at a loss to indicate the place of the great maternal dignities who perhaps everywhere preceded the paternal deities" (Gunn 68; Freud 247). Gunn then raises an account of maternal goddesses (Robert Graves's *The White Goddess*) before concluding that "[t]he drama of the father horde is a man-made drama for men, and all that follows from it may be expected to be bloody in a terrible and terribly dull way" (68–69).

Entering into this kind of discursive or responsive relationship with another text undermines Sisson's claims that spiritual autobiography is a paradigm for the "reworking" of previous narratives that we find in all autobiography. Here Gunn's usage is self-consciously constructed against some aspects of Freud's, but he also avoids endorsing Graves, writing that "it seems [...] we can choose our drama. There appears to be no certainty of how the god, male or female, or God, was first 'created' by those remote savages, our ancestors" (69).

While Gunn uses other texts in the representation of his memories of church attendance as a child, these other texts are not given the kind of authority that Augustine gives to biblical narratives. In *The Atom of Delight*, intertextual references raise possibilities that embellish Gunn's memory, but they provide no validating authority. The reader is left not with an instance of memory fully integrated into a wider cultural narrative, but one that seeks to engage with and question that wider narrative.

This is repeated even in those instances where Gunn evidently approves of the other text, and even where there is a discernible influence on *The Atom of Delight*. Gunn summarizes Eugen Herrigel's *Zen in the Art of Archery*, then begins the next chapter with, "While writing these words about *Zen in the Art of Archery* I remembered an experience which the boy had with a bow and arrow of his own manufacture that was anything but amusing at the time" (134–40, 141). The boy manages to mindlessly loose an arrow perfectly, in much the same way that Herrigel describes training to loose an arrow without engaging his conscious mind. "As a shot," Gunn says, describing his own effort, "it had been miraculous" (143). While earlier he disagreed with Freud's account of religion, calling it "man-made," he seems to acknowledge the validity of Zen (68–69). He writes: "The Great Doctrine, or any other doctrine, ideology, or system, remains susceptible in thought to any kind of criticism, for example to destructive criticism, to the charge that it is illusory or delusory, but the bull's eye containing the Master's two arrows [an incident from Herrigel] was not an illusion" (143).

Here *The Atom of Delight* seems to follow Sisson's model exactly. Gunn's vocabulary echoes Herrigel's, and he acknowledges that writing about *Zen in the Art of Archery* sparked a recollection of an event from his own life. Such a linguistic parallel mirrors Sisson's description of the spiritual autobiographer who constructs his narrative using others. Crucially, though, Gunn does not invoke Herrigel as an authority, nor does he use Herrigel to validate his childhood memory. As in the third-person sections, in the search for "extrinsic data," the reader who looks for intertextual references is frustrated by Gunn's tactic of denying authority to other texts.

The Second Self and the Otherness of Memory

The approach an author takes toward the task of representing memory in autobiography reflects his conceptions of both memory and the self. Gunn's treatment of memory as an indeterminable phenomenon is linked to a conception of the self as an entity that is hard to pin down or analyze. His term for this essentially *other* being is the "second self" (*passim*). Unlike references to "the boy," Gunn's descriptions of the second self sometimes use the first person, although his slightly strange syntax ("the self was me") marks the sense of dislocation. The second self is an internal other.

The concept of a second self or doppelgänger is to be found throughout Scottish literature. In the nineteenth century the concept was used to examine the nature of good and evil, for example in James Hogg's *The Private Memoirs and Confessions of a Justified Sinner*, or Robert Louis Stevenson's *The Strange Case of Dr. Jekyll and Mr. Hyde*. The same concept of division has been read by many as indicative of a Scottish mindset, perhaps most famously by G. Gregory Smith, who coined the phrase "Caledonian Antisyzygy": "a combination of opposites" (Smith 4). Gunn was aware of Smith's theory, referring to part of Edwin Muir's book *Scott and Scotland* as "one of the most signal instances of the Caledonian Antisyzygy run amok" ("Review" 125). Gunn's "second self," therefore, belongs in part to the tradition of doubling in Scottish literature. Gunn's use of the double is more modern, however, and he uses second self to distinguish between what Jung called the persona and a "truer" self. For Jung, the persona is "a kind of mask, designed on the one hand to make a definite impression upon others, and, on the other, to conceal the true nature of the individual" (Jung 94). For Gunn, the first self is equivalent to the persona, while the second self embodies "the true nature of the individual" (*The Atom of Delight* 158). When discussing memory, the second self is important because it is associated with experiences that have a "memorable quality" (*The Atom of Delight* 158). Gunn writes that "[t]he core of the difficulty" in describing the second self "lies in the remembering or the lack of remembering. I have had experiences so striking or unusual that I said to myself at the time I should never have forgotten them. Yet I have forgotten them. How can I know that I have forgotten? Because I remember saying to myself, Now, I shall remember that" (*The Atom of Delight* 157).

Perhaps this is the best explanation for the evasive tactics that Gunn uses throughout *The Atom of Delight*: the second self is the self that experiences "delight" in memorable experiences, but it seems to escape memory, leaving Gunn with only the memory *of having forgotten*. The second self is "like an uncharted island, where memory [has] forgot itself, or had abdicated" (*The Atom of Delight* 158).

Gunn's adoption of both third-person and intertextual tactics is an attempt to compensate for the inexpressible experiences of the second self. Neither aesthetic transformation nor overt philosophizing provides substitutes for memory, but Gunn argues for the value of the approach in a comment on the "difference between 'by the way' and 'on the way,'" which he says "may be the difference between not having any kind of philosophy and having one" (*The Atom of Delight* 10). Memory in *The Atom of Delight* is always somewhere between "by the way," spontaneously and unpredictably erupting into consciousness, and "on the way," leading the reader on to yet more reading. The experience is as wonderfully open-ended as any reading experience can be, in no small part due to the way in which Gunn refuses to claim or appropriate authority to finalize the meaning of his autobiography. In other words, and as he himself puts it in the final chapter of *The Atom of Delight*: "To say that the way has 'no end' is but to say that the adventure is open" (303).

Part IV

CINEMATIC REMEDIATIONS: MEMORY AND HISTORY

10

La Jetée and *12 Monkeys*: Memory and History at Odds

Amresh Sinha

"Memory is to one what History is to the other."
—Chris Marker in *Sans Soleil*

In this chapter I will provide a comparative reading of Chris Marker's *La Jetée* (1962) and Terry Gilliam's *12 Monkeys* (1995), which mentions *La Jetée* in the credits as an inspiration.[1] The structures of temporality in *La Jetée* and *12 Monkeys* are at odds with each other.[2] I will try to define a set of features that, in relation to the dialectics of time and space, define the different modes of representation of memory in these two films. According to Elena Del Rio, "*Twelve Monkeys* [sic] adopts a homogeneous visual style that levels out the difference between past, present, and future by saturating all of the times/worlds with the same 1990s-vintage gloss and dystopian dreariness" (392). She further suggests that the conception of temporality in *12 Monkeys* is essentially "spatial" in nature and that it thus "defeats the very purpose of time-travel itself" (392). Whereas in *La Jetée*, on the other hand, as David Rodowick suggests, "the image of time is *no longer* reduced to the thread of chronology where present, past, and future are aligned on a continuum" (4, emphasis added). It appears that *12 Monkeys* adheres throughout to a conception of time that can best be described as linear and continuous, in line with Hollywood's penchant for a seamless narrative flow without any apparent disjuncture. In a deconstructive reading of Gilliam's film, the ostensible trajectory of temporality hews to this conception of linearity, whose coextensive presence is perpetually subjected to the authority of narration. In a sense, the role of memory is eclipsed by the presence of narrative, which relies on the history of *La Jetée* as a film of exemplary status.

I begin with what remains undoubtedly an homage to the memory within *12 Monkeys* of *La Jetée*, with a tribute to the memory of a memory—for *La Jetée* evokes nothing but the very act of a memory frozen at the threshold of consciousness, whose meaning in *12 Monkeys* will be fully realized when this consciousness, which was held at bay in *La Jetée*, is eventually transformed into history (in the sense of the eternal return) in order to make amends with the apparent senselessness of memory's frozen silhouette. The image that haunts the protagonist, who remains unnamed in the *photo-roman* of *La Jetée*, is also the death of the narrative that begins *with* a memory, a memory that is anterior to consciousness. Even the temporality of the film is conceived in "the future anterior tense," which makes it an impossible film of an undecidable origin.[3]

In repetition we encounter the traces of memory that do not appear in consciousness but lie deep in the timelessness of the unconscious. To provide ourselves with a psychoanalytical foundation for memory-traces, we have to look into the behaviour of a time the determination of which lies in frequency rather than periodicity. Instead of in duration, which in itself is the sedimentation of time in past/present/future, the exact position of memory is located in the frequency, repetition, and breaching of the event. The first thing that the memory cancels is the consciousness of time. Therefore, instead of looking for memory in the chronological order, we ought to look into the topographical region, the environment where it actually occurs.

The significant difference between *La Jetée* and *12 Monkeys* is that the latter is a presentation of a recurring nightmare that has already taken hold of the unconscious in a quasi-narrative vein. The rest of the film is devoted to the explication and restitution of this dream, whose origin will no longer be determined by the cause *sui generis*; instead, the film's trajectory will be to progressively track down the motives and thus the principles of the originary trauma in the form of a dystopian tale of a time-honoured tradition of time travel.

In 1966, reviewer Ernest Callenbach called *La Jetée* "a film of heartbreaking nostalgia—nostalgia for ordinary life, the ordinary loves, of our present" (50). Marker's *La Jetée* is a *photo-roman*, or else a *ciné-roman*, a science fiction short film, which, since its inception, has captivated the film-viewing public in all parts of the world. *La Jetée* tells the story of a man (Davos Hanich) who is obsessed with the memory of a woman's face he once saw as a child on the jetty of Orly Airport, just before he witnessed the death of a man. What follows is a post-apocalyptic dystopian tale of the Third World War, with the complete destruction of the city of Paris. The survivors of the nuclear holocaust are driven underground, below the Palais de Chaillot, where they are ruled by a band of tyrannical German-speaking scientists, who are desperately seeking a way out from the "radioactive impasse." The historical significance of the location of the prisoners' camp under the ruins of Chaillot is a reminder that it was once used as a "storage space" for Henri Langlois's Cinémathèque Française (Lupton 94). The role of archives and museums and their relation to memory is perhaps best summed up in the film by the natural history museum the man visits with the woman: "the museum that is perhaps his memory." The subterranean cavern of the underworld dwellers also has its analogy in Plato's cave, the locus, figuratively speaking, of the first cinematic experimentation.[4]

In *La Jetée*, there is a prohibition against providing an image of the future. The future, after the destruction of the Third World War, appears only as the ruins of the present: shots of the destruction of the Arc de Triomphe and Notre Dame. There is no futuristic panorama that the camera captures. The destruction of the present suffices to picture the future, but the future as a sign that comes only after the present is fully negated, for it never makes the show. Gilles Jacobs has also remarked on the film's reluctance to portray the future through the means of images: "the voyage to the future is summed up with rare discretion in a few shots, a network of abstract lines reminiscent of Henri Michaux sketches; and in its evocation of the future itself, the film is carefully imprecise, both realistic and unrealistic" (166).

The scientists—or torturers—conduct terrifying experiments in time travel to find remedy in the future to appease the wrongdoing of the past. They search among the survivors for those who have some semblance of the past still intact in their minds that can serve as an anchor point for launching them into that time. The idea is "to project emissaries into time, to call the past and the future to the aid of the present."[5] The protagonist—the unnamed man—is selected because of his strong memory of the woman (Hélène Chatelain) he still loves. Although memory is selective, in this case the protagonist is selected *because* of his memory. The man is sent into the past numerous times as the experiments continue; initially briefly, then progressively longer as his sojourn in the past seems to garner success. He makes contact with the girl from his memory, and soon he spends longer periods with her in the present, which is also his past, for he comes from the future. His journeys into this past become more frequent and his relationship with the girl grows into a solid love affair. As soon as he realizes he is in love with her, the scientists discontinue the experiment and he is forced to return to the future, which is "defended better than the past" (Marker, *La Jetée*).

Before he surrenders himself to the men of the future who offer him a possibility of escape, he asks their permission to visit the girl for one last time.[6] When he arrives at the jetty of the Orly Airport, he realizes that the woman whom he had seen at the airport and whose image has been etched indelibly in his memory, is the same woman of his childhood memory (memory as recognition, as iteration), and as he runs towards her, probably to warn her of impending death, he is shot by a man who has accompanied him from the future. It was his own death that he had witnessed in the past, which had come to fulfill its prophecy in the future. Paul Coates explicates the protagonist's death as a "deferred moment" of memory that finally reaches its destination. He suggests that "here, as in Proust, the precondition of time travel is revealed to be the end of time [...]: the protagonist has pre-experienced his own death; or, rather, the entire film can be seen as the unfolding of the contents of the moment of death, in which memory ranges through time in search of a way out of the present moment of imminent demise, only to return to—having failed—that deferred moment" (309). The moral of the story is pronounced by the narrator in the last shot of the film, which depicts the protagonist's death: "There was no way to escape Time" (Marker, *La Jetée*).

12 Monkeys, like *La Jetée*, is a science fiction film of time travel, opening in the subterranean depths of Philadelphia in 2035, where the entire population has taken refuge after a deadly virus, released in 1996, has wiped out most of the earth's population. The film focuses on the existential crisis of a prisoner named James Cole (Bruce Willis), who, like his predecessor in *La Jetée*, is haunted by a recurring image from his primordial past of the shooting of a man at an airport terminal. His strong attachment to this single source of a traumatized past makes him a candidate for time travel, which he undertakes under the strict supervision of a group of scientists, the rulers of the dystopian underworld. His mission is to find the cause of the outbreak of the deadly virus and the possible remedy. His journey into the past brings him into contact with Jeffrey

Goines (Brad Pitt), the leader of a gang that calls itself the Army of the 12 Monkeys. In his visits to the surface, Cole kidnaps, befriends, and then falls in love with a psychiatrist, Kathryn Railly (Madeleine Stowe), who has written a book on the so-called Cassandra complex (a premonition of future disaster coupled with helplessness to prevent it from occurring). The rest of the film involves a complex narrative of time travel in which Cole's ultimate realization of his obsessive past comes to a full circle of Cassandra-like prophecy in the future (his own death and the subsequent death of mankind).

La Jetée plays with different meanings of the French word *jetée*. In French, the transitive verb *jeter* means "to throw, fling, cast," but *jetée* means jetty, pier, which extends into the sea and simultaneously holds it at bay: it functions as a "breakwater [...] a wall designed to break the continual pounding of sea waves" (Cridland 130). Not only is the protagonist thrown or cast into the flow of time, like a projectile, but also, not ironically, his destiny seems intricately linked to the "projection" of the film, which gives it movement and thus the film a semblance of life. "As the film moves through the projector, the images become 'present' or *kinetic* (the root of 'cinema'); they give the impression of 'happening now,' which is the time of projection ('*jeter*' is the root of '*projeter*,' to project a film)" (Kawin 16). "Then another wave of Time washes over him" and takes him back to the future from which *he* is continuously trying to escape through the obscure path of his memory which clings to a single image that stands like a "breakwater," *jetée*, against the "waves of Time" (Marker, *La Jetée*).

History and Memory

Critics of *La Jetée* have not yet provided a satisfactory explanation for the crucial distinction between the past and the present in the film. And the significance of that distinction cannot be exaggerated, *especially* since the relation of memory and history hinges precisely on the differentiation of past and present. As Jacques Le Goff contends, "recent, naive trends seem virtually to identify history with memory, and even give preference in some sense to memory, on the ground that it is more authentic, 'truer' than history, which is presumed to be artificial, and above all, manipulative of memory" (xi). For social historians like Le Goff, the relationship between memory and history is already perfectly expressed in the sentiment that "memory is the raw material of history [and] the discipline of history nourishes memory in turn" (xi). What such a sentiment establishes is a connection between history and memory that historians must take into account in their project of historiography, in other words, the history of history. They must remember to go back to the source of memory, whether mental, oral, or written, in order to distinguish it from the project of historical writings as contemporary, which is to say, that the past must be viewed from the perspective of the present. For the historical work to continue in an objective manner, the opposition between *past* and *present* ought to be regarded as both "fundamental" and "essential," because "the activity of memory and history is founded on [precisely] this distinction" (xii). If the opposition between memory and history is based upon the distinction between past and present, objective and subjective, private and public, then we should also extend this analogy to film studies and apply this distinction to the genres of fiction and documentary as well.

I tend to both agree and disagree with Le Goff in that the cinematic exploration of the relation between memory and history in *La Jetée* is not just a relation of identity between the past, or history, and the manner in which it is remembered, but also a matter of disruption, a disruption that occurs through memory's effort to escape internalization and confinement through narrativization in historical discourse. The conscious manipulation and exploitation of collective memory is precisely what the discipline of history seeks to destabilize in the contemporary project of historiography, which nonetheless believes in some kind of objective and historical "truth." Derrida characterizes such a view of history as essentially metaphysical: "The metaphysical [...] concept of history is not only linked to linearity, but to an entire *system* of implications (teleology, eschatology, elevating the interiorizing accumulation of meaning, a certain type of traditionality, a certain concept of continuity, of truth, etc.)" (*Positions* 57). History is often remembered and mediated through narratives—much too vividly, if I may say—in political and social contexts of nationalistic and other types of mass movements.

The current obsession with memory is an indication of the renewed interest in the question of history, the representation of which is being increasingly fictionalized in order to expose the mythological foundations of its institutional character. According to Pierre Nora, the constitutive role of memory in modern society is prepared by history, whose function is to "organize a past," in a constantly changing time ("Between Memory and History" 2). If history, on the one hand, as Nora claims, is responsible for the conquest and eradication of memory, then on the other hand, it has also produced a break in the "ancient bond of identity," a break in the equilibrium of memory and history (2). A break in consciousness, readily perceivable with the rise of industrialization, which also marked simultaneously the disappearance of the present culture, brought about some very disturbing factors, resulting in the loss of historical memory. Memory, indeed, as it had always lived in the experience of preindustrial culture as collective memory (see Maurice Halbwachs), found itself displaced by the expansion of "democratization and mass culture on a global scale" (2). Such a break has caused us to shift our lives from the endless repetition of ancient ritual, in which each act is the resemblance and remembrance of the same act, to live in a historically discontinuous spontaneity, or, in other words, in history, which appears in the form of trace, mediation, and distance.

Walter Benjamin pointed out in "Some Motifs in Baudelaire" that the structural change in people's experience, both empirically and biologically, was caused by the rise of "big-scale industrialism" (*Illuminations* 157). He considered the explanation given by Bergson in *Matiere et memoire* far superior to Dilthey's *Das Erlebnis und die Dichtung*, and to Klages, and to Jung, whose philosophies completely undermined "man's life in society" in favour of "true experience […] of a philosophy of life" (157). What attracted Benjamin to Bergson was the latter's outright rejection of "any historical determination of memory" in "facts" (157). Thus, "it is less the products of facts firmly anchored in memory than of a convergence in memory of accumulated and frequently unconscious data" (157). The "standardized, denatured life of the civilized masses" had entered a historical phase that clearly marked its discontinuity from the so-called calm of history in which Hegel's Spirit was triumphantly self-absorbed (156).

Benjamin's comment here reflects first of all the inadequacy of historical experience, which relegates everything to the past by shutting it out, by closing it, and by enclosing it within a certain duration of historical determinacy, thereby pronouncing upon it a certain judgment, as in the final judgment, a death sentence, from which the object gains currency only posthumously. History, the great arbiter from which each generation has drawn lessons for future happiness, and which leaves everything behind itself, is not a backward-looking driving force. The face of history, unlike Benjamin's Angelus Novus, is not turned backward. Although this face may be looking forward, however, his feet are dragging him backward. Thus, to "shut out" history means to stop the pretension of forward progression, to decelerate the acceleration of time in a linear past–present–future continuum, and to liberate sight from its inward trance to the present scene that demands the release of the *instant* from the historical moment. Benjamin's *Erfahrung* (experience) professes to that sentiment that properly conveys the sense (as invoked in Proust's *mémoire involontaire*) of the temporality of *La Jetée*, which also extracts the instant of the man's death as an experience outside the continuum of linear and inward progression of time.[7]

The concept of time in *La Jetée* is conceived on the basis of singularity because of its iterability in death, a singular and unique event whose repetition is nonetheless realizable in the time (that is, first) of death as the death (that is, last) of time. "[E]ach time its first and only chance. Consequently, each time is the last," Derrida tells us (*Politics* x). On a different tune, Jean-Louis Schefer postulates a theory that the death of the protagonist in *La Jetée* marks the occasion of a "reconciliation or a coincidence of time and images" (102).

Terry Gilliam's *12 Monkeys* begins with the construction and reproduction of a recurring trace of memory, one that haunts its protagonist for the rest of the film until its transmigration into a global catastrophe. In this we see the merging of the personal or private, singular and thus unique, memory of an individual being progressively integrated into the collective historical narrative of the future of mankind. Although history as narrative is continuously evoked through flashbacks, the dynamics of social memory and its infrastructure (archives, museums, libraries, monuments, and other sites of memory) have not been fully articulated in the film as its corollaries. In *La Jetée*, on the other hand, to escape from the narrative, from his predetermined history as such, the prisoner will have to use the "loopholes" of time, which are presented in an enigmatic fashion in the film as dissolves and fades.[8] Réda Bensmaïa describes the composition of *La Jetée* as "a series of heterogeneous photograms [...] a succession of images that are frozen, as if suspended in time" (149). In other words, "*La Jetée* is really constituted by the destruction of what we would call the drifting [*la dérive*] of the fiction effect" (143). Furthermore, these dissolves and slow fades to black operate as "holes" in our perception (143). The dissolves and fades "at the intersection of any two images" in *La Jetée* are the fusion and/or tearing away of the past (retroactive) and the future (after-effect) that momentarily appear at a standstill in the *Nachträglichkeit* of deferred present.

Cinematic codes, such as the dissolves and frequent fades to black in *La Jetée*, render the status of the "photograms," that is, freeze-frames, virtually indeterminate.[9] The indeterminacy of the freeze-frame is much like the unpronounceable name of Hitchcock spoken in silence in *La Jetée* as an indirect gesture and a direct homage to the sequoia tree sequence in *Vertigo* (1958). The photograms themselves are so heterogeneously disseminated throughout the narrative of *La Jetée* that any effort to establish some kind of a linear and syntactical continuity between them might seem a bit far-fetched due to the irreducible difference in the constitution of the images predicated upon "the absence of the reproduction of the movement" (Bensmaïa 140). On the other hand, the shots' shared basis in photographic representation creates a difficulty in breaking them down into "well-defined segments" (140). Bensmaïa cites Roger Odin, who states that "*La Jetée* operates in the mode of a generalized freeze-frame," where the movement, in its absence, cannot be "reproduced," but can only be "represented" or "symbolized" solely in the imagination of the viewer (139).[10] The indeterminacy of the freeze-frame, the "*photogramme*," has led Philip Dubois to muse upon the undecidable ontology of this unpronounceable film as something that is "simultaneously beyond photography and before the cinema, more than the one and less than the other, while being a little of both at the same time" ("Photography *Mise-en-Film*" 153).

Part of *La Jetée* "resides," in a non-phenomenological sense, in the absence of a narrative because of the *presence* of the commentary, which functions as a supplement compensating for the "lack," the "loopholes" and gaps, in the non-linear spatial structure of the narrative. The visuals are opposed to the authorial voice in a far more entwined sense than has been imagined by the critics. The visuals force the commentary to stumble into a false tone of reconciliation. Schefer has eloquently surmised that "the part that makes this story come alive for [me] remains invisible and necessarily deprived of images" (106).[11] On the other hand, it has also been argued by Odin, as Bensmaïa reminds us, that the narrator's off-screen commentary, from an elsewhere place, provides continuity to an otherwise visually fragmented and displaced text, a certain presence of narrative authority that is most amicably suited to the spectator's desire for coherence (140). Through the voice-over the film incorporates the need for subjectivity and identification, the apparatus of the cinematic desire that holds the spectator in its thrall. For Odin, "the commentary organizes the *totality* of the film elements into a signifying continuity" (141). It brings mobility into immobility, transparency into opaqueness, order into chaos.

The memory as an image has not yet found its voice: it cannot speak of itself in *La Jetée*. It can only be signified with its association with death. In *12 Monkeys*, the "consciousness" of the world appears to have existed prior to the destruction of the Third World War—or, at least, the end is already known—due to the constant emphasis on the boy's point of view, which becomes part of the narrative strategy for identification and subjectivization, unlike Marker's ubiquitous narrator, whose authority is sacrificed as an autochthonous/autobiographical voice by translating it into an image/text, that is, writing.[12] The writing as a trace or form or text appears in the narrator's voice, which according to Schefer "borrows its script from the narrative mode of a Kafka" (Schefer 102).

12 Monkeys instead stays within the realm of perception, that is, presence.[13] The role of the narrator, who remains non-diegetic in *La Jetée*, is compromised by the presence of the young boy in *12 Monkeys*; the latter's point of view comes to determine the subjective dimension of the film. The fact that the psyche continues to exist after the self has been liquidated (the film's last scene depicts the young boy leaving the airport after Cole has been shot dead) is more of an instance of the teleological summation of the spirit that prevails in the Hegelian self-consciousness. The death here figures as an act of a transcendental consciousness of the Spirit (the mode of becoming History) that recognizes itself in the act of apprehension rather than a disavowal or an impossibility of knowledge that the experience of death itself signifies.[14] What else is achieved, if not this very awareness that one has already witnessed (historicized), that one has already been present not only as a victim but also a witness, *istor*, to one's own death in an "outer body" experience (and here we can think of the spectres from *Hamlet* and *Macbeth*, but these spectres are enigmas of injustices, not simply presences of spirit's absolute control over its own historical determination)?[15]

It has been an intriguing problem for me to explain how one can be a witness to one's own death by actually realizing it in one's life. How can one be both present and absent, living and dead, at the same time? Constance Penley provides a rational answer for why, in the last scene of *La Jetée*, we never see the boy in the present witnessing his death as an adult in the future: "In the logic of this film," Penley argues, "he has to die, because such a logic acknowledges the *temporal impossibility* of being in the same place as both adult and child. In *La Jetée* one cannot be and have been" (138, emphasis added). Furthermore, the insertion of the spectral voice of the narrator in *La Jetée* into the figure of a young boy in *12 Monkeys*—that is, the substitution of an actor for the narrative voice—pushes the film into an anthropomorphic dimension at the expense of the formal and aesthetic experiments of *La Jetée*.

Memory and Photography

The spirit of *La Jetée*, however, proceeds from the perspective of memory in which time is continuously brought to a halt. There no longer exits the possibility for staging the primal scene of the Lacanian "mirror image" as its own alterity in the images of *La Jetée*—the processes of primary and secondary identification through which the homogeneous subject is constituted in the psychoanalytical discourse of the cinema.[16] Such possibility is either forgotten or renounced in the film, because the filmic itself never appears (barring one instance) in the film except in the absence of the narrative, which requires our complicity as long as we are "completely removed from it" (Bensmaïa 141). This lack of specularity only proves that in the photographic image there is no after-life, only silence. As Roland Barthes says, "each reading of a photo, and there are billions worldwide in a day, each perception and reading of a photo is implicitly, in a repressed manner, a contract with what has ceased to exist, a contract with death" (*The Grain* 356).

La Jetée is a *photo-roman* whose closest ally arguably is the comic book, which also works on the principles of arrested motion. The subject of photography in *La Jetée* is, however, neither static nor still.[17] It is not the study of features, the art of portraiture, which demands a perfect *stillness* from its object, be it a human being or a passing cloud—the subjects of photography are always already in dynamic motion—they are caught *in the act*, so to speak.[18] In the photographic image, this act of supreme negation becomes an affirmation of death, in the Nietzschean sense of the "eternal return." If the "eternal return" in Nietzsche signifies a continual affirmation—"the highest formula of affirmation"—then is it possible to affirm death in its absence, that is, in life (Nietzsche 70)? What sort of affirmation will this be, when death is negated for the sake of its meaning in the continuity of life? We shall witness that Marker in *La Jetée* is mainly engaged in this process of releasing photography from its death-like immobility. Therefore, for photography to be released from the figure of death to which it is bound by absence, it must, once again, witness its own death in the movement of memory. The image is nothing without memory.[19]

Memory and Trauma

As far as the subject of memory and its origins are concerned, the most disturbing factor is the cause of the memory attributed to a traumatic event—the witnessing of the killing of a man in broad daylight at an airport. How to underscore the trauma in both of these films? In *La Jetée* the trauma is not instigated by an extraneous causality. This is a story of a man encountering his *own* death in the absence of meaning. That is because, in any event, the meaning itself cannot be annihilated in its own presence without cancelling itself. The condition of the possibility of the photograph exists in the absence of the thing that no longer exists. Then how shall one pursue the absence that only appears in relation to the non-existent, that is, that which is not yet forgotten? Moreover, in *La Jetée*, the cause of trauma is not yet marked by a prior event; instead, the trauma and its cause are not determined in the past, but as a trace of memory whose existence is prior to its realization in consciousness.

The anchor memory or the archaic memory, the memory of memories, this image of a beloved's face, remains a fixity, a point that becomes the ontological source of the film. Catherine Lupton traces the origin of this image of a beloved's face as a fixation in Marker's cinematic career to his primal childhood memory. "In *Immemory*," she writes, "Chris Marker reveals the origin of this primordial association of a woman's face with cinema, in his childhood memory of the face of the actress Simone Genevoix in Marc de Gastyne's *La Merveilleuse Vie de Jeanne d'Arc* (1928)" (95). Raymond Bellour traces the origin of the photograph in Jacques Feyder's film *L'Image* (1923–25), which is "dedicated to the image-woman, the object of the strongest desire, the sign of the most poignant reality" (119). According to Benjamin, "what prevents our delight in the beautiful from ever being satisfied is the image of the past [...] which [is] veiled by the tears of nostalgia" (187). Benjamin suggests that "what prevents our delight in the beautiful from ever being satisfied is the image of the past ... veiled by the tears of nostalgia" (187). What photography cannot achieve is built into its structure, for it cannot "faithfully" reproduce the image of the past, which is only possible through the involuntary illumination of a memory that remains repressed at the unconscious level.

The obsession with the image with which the unnamed protagonist of *La Jetée* both lives and dies in the end is the reckoning of a premonition that triggers the desire for memory, which is the same as desiring one's own death. Unlike the river of Lethe, the river of oblivion, of forgetting, this fountain, this fulcrum of memory, has strong ties to a fixed anchor that serves as the provocative beginning of a desire to become a perpetual forgetting in the name of the most sacred memory, the memory of all memory, from which the desire to live itself becomes detached from the moment and becomes a privileged discourse of the Bergsonian *dureé*, in which time is stretched to its metaphysical limit (Bergson *Introduction to*

Metaphysics 56–58). Face to face with the memory—the other (in a Levinasian sense)—the man recognizes, which is the same as remembering, his own death as the signature of a forestalled image that he was unable to relinquish, for it had already ordained his destiny from the very beginning: "He understood there was no way to escape Time" (Marker).

La Jetée has a relation of absence with itself and an absence of relation with itself, because as a series of photographs its indexicality is presupposed by the absence of the referent; furthermore, an absence of relation here signifies that the film itself is mediated through memory, as a trace of the absence. *La Jetée* situates the "trauma" as the bedrock of its existence. There is no absolute beginning for a prior traumatic event whose existence becomes the source of memory's malady. One thing is clear: the time travel into the past is not determined by his memory, for he is not "sent into his memory, rather his memory is used as a force that helps him enter the past" (Kawin 16). Here it should also be acknowledged that Marker's film clearly marks a difference between the identity of the past and the memory of it. In this memory a part of him is constituted, or, is he a part of that memory? An unsure ground; an uncharted territory—is he a prisoner of his own memory? Or, is he the prisoner of his image?

12 Monkeys, by contrast, projects a relationship that could best be designated in chronological terms as the representation of (a) a past that is present; (b) a present that is already past; and (c) a past that is already contained in the future (the young protagonist relates to these three stages with his own perpetual presence). The appearance side by side of the young boy and Bruce Willis in the present, the latter hailing from the future, represents "a tragic syllogism" of past, present, and future (Schefer 102). It is a misfortune to align in a linear fashion the radical ruptures of time in terms of its tense, past, present, and future. In a sense, the past is regrettably watching the present as the death of the future. *12 Monkeys* is full of such traumatic references that seem to trigger the operation of memory in a mechanical manner without reflecting on the mechanics of memory evoked by thinkers as diverse as Hegel and Augustine.[20]

Mémoire volontaire and *Mémoire involontaire*

In *La Jetée* the emphasis, as far as the nature of memory is concerned, is Proustian, the personal side of the memory; whereas *12 Monkeys* seems to privilege the totalizing and universalizing form of memory that resembles history in a public sense. In the essay "On Some Motifs in Baudelaire,"

Benjamin takes up the issue of aura in relation to *mémoire involontaire* (*Illuminations* 155–220). He compares the Proustian *mémoire involontaire* (involuntary memory), the most exemplary and enigmatic experience of auratic writing, with the *mémoire volontaire* (voluntary memory), "perpetual readiness of volitional, discursive memory," the "one that is in the service of the intellect" (186; 158). Simply put: the difference between these two types of memory is that the former has an accidental but full relationship to the past, whereas the latter, *mémoire volontaire,* although clearly present in its "attentiveness" to the past, happens to retain no trace of it. In historical terms, both these memories imply the "atrophy of experience" (159). Prompted by the destruction of the traditional experience of a community, for instance, of storytelling—a specific mode of communication that passed on the experience of the storyteller to the listener— the new experiences that *mémoire volontaire* encompasses are certainly not geared toward retaining that element or trace of the past. In its experience, *mémoire volontaire* has ceded its ineffectual and intellectual domain from personal to impersonal information, which is "encouraged by the technique of mechanical reproduction" (186).

It is quite possible that, without upsetting Benjamin's definition of *mémoire volontaire* as the "perpetual readiness of volitional, discursive memory," the "one that is in the service of the intellect," we can safely assign Cole's persistent nightmare to that category or kind of memory. Although Cole's persistent nightmare is not necessarily, in a strict sense, the effect of voluntary reproductions of his conscious mind, the workings of his unconscious seem to be truly engineered by "the technique of mechanical reproduction" (186). Rather than an image, a photogram, whose identity exceeds the discursive specificity of the narrative at heart of the enigma of *La Jetée*, in *12 Monkeys* Cole's nightmares have the whole narrative of death already interiorized in a manner that sets a new standard for valuing information over experience. On the other hand, the protagonist of *La Jetée* betrays all those symptoms that take a Proustian turn toward *mémoire involontaire*.[21]

Involuntary memory finds its trace in a moment in history in which the personal and individual past can no longer be reconstituted by a recourse to the experience of the traditional past. Such memory already crystallizes outside the conscious experience of the individual who has no control over it. Involuntary memory, thus, can no longer be associated with the inventory of an individualized objective memory, because it reflects upon the contingency of the chance encounter with the objective world that lies "beyond the reach of the intellect" (Benjamin 158). The contingency of involuntary memory evades the "prompting" of voluntary memory and gives access to a past that is beyond the reach of the intellect. Benjamin says of *mémoire volontaire*: "it is its characteristic that the information which it gives about that past retains no trace of it" (158). And thus to restore the experience of the individual past with the material of collective past, at a time when it is increasingly difficult to reconcile these two antagonistic tendencies, voluntary memory comes to our aid, but not in order to reconstitute the order of the past that no longer has its home in the individual consciousness. Instead it is present, as Proust would say, in "some material object (or in the sensation which such an object arouses in us)" (158).

For instance, the difference between a photogram, a frozen image, and the slow-motion sequences, the privileged trope of rendering the nightmares in *12 Monkeys*, can best be thought of in the conceptual treatment of the deaths of the protagonists in both films in terms of voluntary and involuntary memory. It appears that in *12 Monkeys* the destruction of the human race is treated in terms of inevitability, as an abstract and quantitative death. By contrast, in *La Jetée* the destruction of the human race is already a *fait accompli*. The film avoids at all costs any concrete representations of human mutilation and portrays a concrete manifestation of death, which Marker himself has described elsewhere as "a moment stopped [that] would burn like a frame of film blocked before the furnace of the projector."[22] But one should not fail to register that the protagonist of *La Jetée* too has access to *mémoire volontaire*, and his memory has already been put to the service of the intellect, albeit not his own, but to that of the masters, his tormentors. And if we concede that the image of the woman that he carries from the past is a sign of that *mémoire volontaire*, for which Proust had so little patience, then this has its own peculiar logic in the film. As I stated earlier, the access to one's own past in *mémoire volontaire* is limited to the "promptings of a memory which obeys the call of attentiveness." Voluntary memory fails to conjure the image of the past, because instead of the past, what we get from it is only the image. That is why one encounters in the photograph a memory that retains no trace of the past. Nonetheless in Proust's *mémoire involontaire* (involuntary memory), Benjamin finds a redemption and reconciliation of the two elements of memory. In the protagonist of *La Jetée*, we discern that "the voluntary and involuntary memory lose their mutual exclusiveness" (160).

In *La Jetée* the memory procedure of the protagonist has much in common with the ancient art of mnemotechniques, with its sites (*loci*) and images (*imagines*).²³ First the place and then slowly the images appear; first they are almost illegible, but with time these indistinct mental images acquire definite imagistic form, a truly legible image character. And this process is, to a large extent, reciprocated in Gilliam's *12 Monkeys*. Cole's dream or nightmare scenes are also disclosed in fragmented sequences that only acquire clarity (legibility) in the last dream scene, which transforms into reality, thus clarifying and condensing the bits of information strewn across the film in a rather dislocated fashion.²⁴

While watching *La Jetée* we are seldom, if ever, conscious of the fatalistic encounter with one's own death, a death that is forever deferred because it signifies the nullification of consciousness that is affirmed in death. And thus the outcome of *La Jetée*, in this particular situation, is not pre-determined, as in *12 Monkeys*, which negates the critical possibility of creating resistance, or at least results in a different outcome. Of course, the entire film is geared toward resisting the meaning of the past through the intervention of a future that seeks to overcome it by revealing the impossibility of the possibility of memory's incarnation into history as a resistive force. Memory fails to disentangle itself from the inevitability of historical time, but its pockets of resistance lie in the interstices of history itself, which can neither determine nor predict its originary and fleeting encounter with the other. In *12 Monkeys*, Cole's hapless death could be interpreted (by the young boy that is Cole himself, by Railley, and by scores of other witnesses in the airport) as the transformation from the act of memory to the passivity of spectating upon history. Cole experiences his death not through an activation of memory in the affirmative sense, but as a victim of history, who witnesses his past die with passivity—an act transformed into stasis. This culminates in a passage from observing or experiencing to spectating upon one's own death as "fate," or as a fact of history.

La Jetée struggles against this inevitability of history pronounced as a judgment at the end of the world, which continues to exist only historically for all kinds of mediated representations. What the protagonist's death captures in the face of the woman on the jetty is the image of that time, and memory is the trajectory through which that time is regained, as in either Proust or Hitchcock's *Vertigo*. A twice-lived time is only possible within the sanctuary of the mnemonic walls, because time in memory is split from itself; as Derrida, following Hamlet, would say, it is "out of joint." Time is no longer part of that vast continuum that exists in (in)difference to the transcendental consciousness of the subject. Time here is ruptured or fractured in memory. Memory obliterates time, in a fundamental sense, by simply negating it in consciousness but without subjecting it to the logic of reason. In *La Jetée* the man sees his own death in the image of her face, to which he is glued because it is his death that the face expresses as an image. And in that image, in that face, his memory will find its final abode, its final destination. The story of his life that has become his memory is expressed in the face of that woman on the pier of the airport at Orly. It is this face that holds the secret of his death, the meaning of which finally dawns upon him as he sees her again on the same spot: *the space has become time*. In memory, time and space are intertwined in a radical heterogeneity; the relationship is arbitrary, and the logic confounding.

Conclusion

The rationale for organizing this article has been to explore the trajectories of these two forces—memory and history—always at odds with each other within culture. The simple difference between memory and history can be found in their representations. "Memory," according to Nora, "is a perpetually actual phenomenon, a bond tying us to the eternal present; history is a representation of the past. [...] Memory takes root in the concrete, in spaces, gestures, images, and objects; history binds itself strictly to temporal continuities, to progressions and to relations between things. Memory is absolute, while history can only conceive the relative" (8–9).

The crucial question, then, is how does the difference between memory and history translate into a filmic text? In *La Jetée*, the images form a presentation; in *12 Monkeys*, the images are represented as being secondary to a primary organization of perception. "'Presentation' differs from 'representation,'" explains Edward Casey, "by virtue of not having as its primary feature an indexical or iconic sign in relation to what it signifies. To represent something is to offer a second something that has the self-effacing function of directing the mind or the senses back to the first something, with which it is connected in various ways" (210). *12 Monkeys* is a retrospective look through the element of time travel in which history is a *representation* of temporal continuities inscribed within the narrative structure, whereas *La Jetée* "goes above and beyond representation" to become ultimately "unrepresentable" (Bensmaïa 144).

NOTES

1 According to Terry Gilliam, in an interview on Channel Four on BBC, "*12 Monkeys* [...] wasn't going to be a remake of *La Jetée*—it was going to be inspired by it. *La Jetée* is the Acorn, in a sense, and *12 Monkeys* is the Oak,

and they are both finite things and one did become the other." http://www.smart.co.uk/dreams/monkfact.htm, 13 March 2010. The inspiration goes back from the predecessor to Hitchcock's *Vertigo* (1958), which originally "inspired" *La Jetée* for Marker.
2. Contrary to my assertion, which will unfold later, that *La Jetée* avoids the trap of linear storytelling, both Catherine Lupton (91) and Alain J.-J. Cohen (150) advance the opposite view. Both claim that in *La Jetée* a linear narrative movement can be perceived through the means of classical norms of editing (fades, dissolves, cuts, etc.), despite the absence of movement in and between images in all but one shot.
3. *The Overlook Film Encyclopedia—Science Fiction*, 21 March 2007, http://www.csie.ntu.edu.tw/~b2506017/sf/3.htm.
4. See Lee, http://www.sensesofcinema.com/contents/00/4/jetee.html.
5. I have throughout this chapter used the script of *La Jetée* reproduced from Marker: http://www.scifiscripts.com/scripts/lajette.txt. The book is out of print.
6. For a very interesting reading of the implications of this escape offered to him by the men of future from a Platonic idealistic perspective, see Lee.
7. "Here the term *Erfahrung* designates experience, but experience understood [...] as the traversal of a danger, the passage through a peril (from Lat. *Experiri*, to undergo, whose root *periri* is found in *periculum*, peril, danger; *Erfahrung*, from old high German *fara*, danger > *Gefahr* = danger)" (Sandro 121).
8. Sandro suggests that "the search for a loophole in time is an effort to prevent the death of History conceived as a blockage in the movement of humanity toward its destiny" (117). Similarly, Harvey Roy Greenberg also suggests that *La Jetée* evokes "the paradoxes and the fractures of consciousness" (123).
9. For another interesting discourse of the photograms as freeze frames ("the interruption of movement") in *La Jetée*, see Raymond Bellour.
10. I am following Réda Bensmaïa's reproduction of Roger Odin's text. See Odin.
11. I am using the online version of the text translated by Paul Smith.
12. Marker has been classified as a "writer-*cinéaste*," an "essayist," a man who writes with his camera, from Siberia (*Letter from Siberia*), Africa (*Les Statues meurent aussi*), China (*Dimanche à Pekin*), Cuba (*Cuba Si*), Japan (*Le Mystère Koumiko*), France (*Le Joli Mai*), and Israel (*Description d'un combat*)—from "anywhere in the world where there is evidence." André Bazin in 1958 described *Letter from Siberia* as "an essay on the reality of Siberia past and present in the form of a filmed report" (Bazin 44).
13. See Del Rio's comments on "visibility" and "presence" (384).
14. According to Hegel, in *Phenomenology of Spirit*, Spirit's "fulfilment consists in perfectly *knowing* what *it is*. In knowing its substance, this knowing is its *withdrawal into itself* in which it abandons its outer existence and gives its existential shape over to recollection" (emphasis in original) (492).

15 For an illuminating discussion of the protagonist in *La Jetée* as a spectre/revenant that "like a phantom [...] comes from a nameless, distant land," see Coates (311). He is referred to at one point in the film as "*mon spectre*" ("my ghost") by the girl.
16 On the other hand, Constance Penley argues precisely from a Freudo-Lacanian perspective by evoking the primal scene fantasy in *La Jetée*, the desire to return to the childhood in an Oedipal struggle to possess his mother at the Orly airport. The death itself is conceived as "a symbolic castration" (138).
17 On the other hand, For Gilles Jocob, "the static quality of the images suggests the stratification of memory. To remember something is to halt time" (167).
18 Walter Benjamin has noted in his "Artwork" essay that the camera arrests the flow of perception and captures the subtlest physiognomical gestures (*Illuminations* 217–51).
19 The point I am making here is, perhaps, best enunciated by Roland Barthes in *Camera Lucida: Reflections on Photography*.
20 See Hegel *Encyclopedia* 221–22. See also Augustine *Confessions* X:210–84; Hegel, *Encyclopedia of Philosophical Sciences*, 221–22.
21 Lupton, too, notes the involuntary nature of *La Jetée*'s memory: "*La Jetée*'s also evokes tensions between the action of involuntary memory returning to the past in its entirety, and the experience of memory as a series of images removed from the continuous flow of time" (96).
22 Marker's alter ego, Sandor Krasna in *San Soleil*: "I am writing you all this from another world, a world of appearances. In a way, the two worlds communicate with each other. Memory is to one what History is to the other. An impossibility. Legends are born out of the need to decipher the indecipherable. Memories must make with their delirium, with their drift. A moment stopped would burn like a frame of film blocked before the furnace of the projector."
23 For an exhaustive study of the ancient art of mnemotechniques, see Yates.
24 For an illuminating and detailed analysis of the nightmare sequences in *12 Monkeys*, see Cohen (152–57).

11

The Traces of "A Half-Remembered Dream": Christopher Nolan's *Inception* (2010), Wong Kar-wai's *2046* (2004), and the Memory Film

Anders Bergstrom

> Nothing sorts out memories from ordinary moments. Only later do they claim remembrance when they show their scars.
> —*La Jetée* (1962)

> All film images are memories of their own inscription.
> —Maureen Turim, *Flashbacks in Film* (1989)

The New Memory Films: An Expanded Genealogy

By representing and projecting images of the past onto the screen, cinema raises questions about how memories form the narratives of our lives and how cinema can itself constitute a mode of memory. Christopher Nolan's *Inception* (2010) thematically and formally explores memory recollection and formation, as psychic spaces are made concrete in lucid dreams. In the film, Dom Cobb (Leonardo DiCaprio) seeks an escape from the past and some measure of forgiveness by navigating complex narrative and memory constructions. In the process of creating its world, *Inception* pushes the boundaries of the commercial action film and challenges traditional modalities of cinematic representation of the past. *Inception* is not the only recent film to address the role of memory in our lives. Wong Kar-wai's formally challenging, international art film, *2046* (2004), explores the weaving of memories and stories in the life of writer Chow Mo-wan (Tony Leung). Although both films explore themes of loss and how memory constitutes our identity in relation to others, *2046* offers an interesting contrast to *Inception* in terms of its mode of production and reception.

Cinema, as a fundamentally visual medium, shapes how human beings see themselves. Its simultaneously *indexical* and *iconic* qualities make it a privileged site for the reliving of memories: indexically, the photographic nature of cinema testifies to the existence of objects and past experiences; iconically, cinema is able to reproduce them with verisimilitude. Thus, it should come as no surprise when cinema, whether international art cinema or the Hollywood blockbuster action film, takes memory as its subject. The commonalities between *Inception* and *2046*, in how they enact memory cinematically, demonstrate the need to recontextualize their reception within the history of the memory film, rather than the action film or art film genres. These films share thematic concerns but also reveal the trace of memory on cinematic practices, challenging the possibility that there is any fundamental difference between memory and other cinematic spaces.

One way to contextualize *Inception* and *2046* is to propose that each is a meditation on the central theme of Chris Marker's landmark film, *La Jetée* (1962): there is no escape from time. This "cinematic meta-theme" connects "narratives of individual desire, death, and mourning and, above all, memory. [...] In other words: the problem of temporally conditioned *identity*, individual or collective" (Kilbourn 47). *La Jetée* is an exemplar of the relationship between cinema and memory. It tells the science fiction story of a man who, in the aftermath of a devastating war, is chosen by mysterious captors to travel back through time in an effort to save the world. The unnamed protagonist is chosen because of his vivid memories of the past, which cushion the jarring psychological impact of time travel. One particular memory is the visage of a woman he glimpsed as a child on the jetty at Orly Airport the same day he witnessed a man's murder. The significance of this is only made clear in the startling, elliptical ending of *La Jetée*. In a series of (mostly) still images, Marker's film explores the nature of time and memory, and how memories indelibly mark their presence upon our identities: key themes that continue to resonate, both thematically and philosophically, throughout world cinema today.

Marker's exploration of "the paradoxes and complexities of perception and the subconscious" has had a clear influence on memory-related international cinema (Sellars), in both art films and blockbusters. Two of *La Jetée*'s memory film predecessors, Alfred Hitchcock's *Vertigo* (1958) and Alain Resnais's *Last Year at Marienbad* (1961), also serve as key intertexts for *Inception* and *2046*. These films form a rough genealogy of a Borgesian cinema[1]—the corpus of the memory film—that "explores the process and problems of cinematic narration: how stories are told, and especially the relationship of characters to the narrative process" (Peña 230). While transcending genre labels, they also explore the labyrinths of human memory, through reduplication and repetition. Like *Last Year at Marienbad*, *Vertigo*, and *La Jetée*, *Inception* and *2046* are films about men who are marked by the image of a woman from the past. In *Inception*, Cobb is a specialist in a particular form of corporate espionage in which he infiltrates people's dreams and performs acts of "extraction" and "inception." This dream technology leads to the death of his wife, Mal (Marion Cotillard), whose *mnemic avatar* haunts the dreamscapes where Cobb and his team perform their work. *2046* follows Wong's *In the Mood for Love* (2000), continuing the story of Chow. Chow moves into a room in the Oriental Hotel and writes a series of stories constructed around the idea of "2046," a time and "place where one can recover lost memories because nothing ever changes" (*2046*). The memory of Chow's lost love So Lai-chen (Maggie Cheung) haunts his present romances and the stories that he writes. Both *Inception* and *2046* use the logic of cinema to represent various memories and embody Gilles Deleuze's "theory of cinema as conceptual practice" (*Cinema 2* xv).

The disparate modes of production and reception of the two films belie the numerous overlapping points of contact between them. On a thematic level, the relationship between these films seems obvious. *Inception* and *2046* reveal and revel in the constructed nature of memory, cinematically representing through memories and dreams the protagonist's personal traumas and histories. Resituating *Inception* and *2046* as participants in the history of the memory film demonstrates how, by visualizing philosophies of memory on the screen, cinema has shaped and continues to shape our conceptions of how memory operates. Such cinematic explorations are not limited to the classically defined art film or to Western cinema. What is represented in the films is a reconciliation with the past; Cobb and Chow use dreams and narratives to constitute and reconcile their identities in relation to the past. More radically, they recall a Bergsonian recollection of the past in the present as mnemic images intrude into dreams and as stories disrupt the distinction between time and space. In *Matter and Memory* (1988), Henri Bergson writes about a distinctly human relationship to memory, which he contrasts against the impulse to live only in the present. He comments on the danger: "he who lives in the past for the mere pleasure of living there, and in whom recollections emerge into the light of consciousness without any advantage for the present situation [...] here we have no man of impulse, but a *dreamer*" (153). *Inception*, *2046*, and other memory films challenge us by presenting us with such dreamers, whose respective recollections are manifested cinematically. Memory films are interested in exploring how such recollections, or memory-images, constitute cinema. Ontologically, all of cinema becomes a form of remembering. However, these films are particularly interested in the repetition of this pattern within their narratives. To paraphrase *La Jetée*, the scars of the past reveal themselves only in remembrances that form the affective cores of the films. Or, as Mal says in *Inception*, "Pain is in the mind."

Genre and Narrative Form

To recontextualize *Inception* and *2046* as representative of cinema's ability to deal with memory, it is helpful to begin by looking at each film's relation to its respective genre and mode of production. Despite the films' thematic similarities, genre marks the most distinct difference between *2046* and *Inception*: both have a complex relationship with their respective modes of production and reception, while at the same time displaying certain generic concerns.

In many ways *Inception* epitomizes the dominant mode of film production and consumption of the early twenty-first century. The movie was sold and designed as a summer "tent pole" film, combining popular genres. It is an action film, and thus follows the genre convention of having action set pieces that unfold at regular intervals, such as the Mombasa chase sequence and the snow fortress assault. *Inception* also draws on the "heist film" structure (Nolan "Dream Work" 32): a team is assembled to do a specific job, in this case infiltrate the dreams of Robert Fischer (Cillian Murphy) and plant an idea in his mind that will cause him to break up his father's powerful energy consortium. Most importantly, *Inception* fits into the category of "blockbuster" in terms of its mode of production and reception. Its status as a blockbuster action film is anchored in how it capitalizes on the success of Nolan's previous film (*The Dark Knight* [2008]) and on the reputation of international star Leonardo DiCaprio (*Titanic* [1997]).

2046 is representative of the contemporary transnational art film. It was shot and financed outside of Hollywood by a recognized international *auteur*. While 2046 sits outside of "the definite historical existence" of the art film, it still follows "a set of formal conventions, and implicit viewing procedures" (Bordwell "The Art Cinema" 774–75). Thus, "art film" can be seen as a mode of cinematic production and consumption that, borrowing from David Bordwell, sets itself up through "deviations from the classical canon" (779), rather than being limited to a particular historical moment in the history of film. These deviations include a focus on radical self-reflexivity (or "authorial expressivity"), psychological realism, and ambiguity. 2046 can also be viewed as a transnational postmodern film, one that uses the imagery both of the past and of an imagined future and that combines a century of art films about memory with the history of Hong Kong cinema. In 2046, Wong's eschewing of clear establishing shots means that "Asia is only evoked after having gone through *mneme*, that is, through the director's personal memories of Asia" (Botz-Bornstein 73). For Wong this means movies about Asia, intertexts drawn from both his own film *oeuvre* and the wider history of Hong Kong and Asian film. The film's shooting locations, which are scattered throughout Southeast Asia and China (Macau, Bangkok, and Beijing standing in for Hong Kong and Singapore), add to its déjà vu effect. The locations stand in for a 1960s Hong Kong that no longer exists; 2046 embodies temporality in its very mode of production, as the particularity of a specific era in Hong Kong's history is repeated and scattered across Asia.

For both the character of Chow and, by extension, director Wong Kar-wai, Hong Kong evokes a particularity of time and place, as does the room "2046" within the diegesis. Personal experiences of uncertain liminality are explored cinematically—both Chow's interactions with his own memories of love affairs in 1960s Hong Kong and Wong's position as a post-colonial Chinese filmmaker working in Hong Kong post-British handover but before the full assimilation of Hong Kong into Mainland China. Wong's uneasiness can be compared to the paralyzing power of Chow's melancholic inflected nostalgia. As Stephen Teo notes, "Wong looks at the history of Hong Kong and its cinema, and how this plays out through time and memory, which is his most effective theme. Like the narrator in Proust's *Remembrance of Things Past*, Wong strives to achieve a transmutation of memory into being, setting his memory in motion in the medium of the cinema" (5). Wong's films have always played with the genres that constitute classic Hong Kong cinema from the past century: romance-melodrama (*In the Mood for Love*), cops and robbers (*Chungking Express* [1994]), *wuxia* (*Ashes of Time* [1994]) and, in 2046, a pastiche of styles with a science fiction element. Wong's various intratexts establish Hong Kong as the postmodern city *par excellence*: as a cosmopolitan, international city perched precariously between East and West.

While certainly not an "art film" in any classical sense, *Inception* borrows some of the pseudo-genre's formal elements, especially in its use of film style and ambiguity. The presence of these "art film" elements legitimizes our interpreting *Inception* and *2046* as characteristic examples of the memory film. These films negotiate complex representations of time and space by adopting styles and narrative structures typical of the "art film."

The use of science fiction in *2046* and *Inception*—whether literal or metaphorical—to inscribe the personal histories of Chow and Cobb links standard genre elements within each film with their place in the history of the memory film. Memories in *2046* are experienced in ways similar to how we experience them in life: colours, movements, and names remind us of the past and weave a complex memory fabric. The science fiction element in *2046* is found in the stories that Chow writes, which have a complex relationship to his memories; the science fiction element in *Inception* is found in Cobb's ability to actually enter a representation of his memory. *Inception* uses the science fiction conceit of "shared dreaming" to investigate the concept of visualized memory spaces and takes a literal bent on the visualization of memories. Appropriating Bahktin's notion of *chronotope* (literally, "time space") is one helpful way to describe the complex, nested structure of the dreams-within-dreams. Bahktin described *chronotope* as "the intrinsic connectedness of temporal and spatial relationships that are artistically expressed in literature [or other narratives]. [...] Time, as it were thickens, takes on flesh, becomes artistically visible; likewise, space becomes charged and responsive to the movements of time, plot, and history" ("Forms of Time" 84).

Inception's use of complex *chronotope* can be seen in how, as one descends further and further into the film's dream constructions, the time–space relationship warps and leads to the mysterious "limbo" where mere minutes of "actual time" are transmuted into the experience of decades within the dream. The lucid dreams that Cobb's team enters are created via a combination of a dream architect, who creates the Escher-like dream-spaces, and the dreamer, who populates the dreams with manifestations of his or her unconscious. Those who enter the dreams bring with them whatever psychological baggage they have. Thus, Cobb, whose recollections of the traumatic loss of his wife constantly interfere with his ability to act as an architect, hands over the creation of the architectural spaces to Ariadne (Ellen Page), whose mythological namesake recalls her narrative function of helping Cobb navigate the labyrinths of his own mind.

In an inversion of the way that Chow cannot escape his painful memories in his science fiction stories about "2046," Cobb chooses to use the dream technology to revisit his own memories of the past where Mal is still alive. Very literally, through the ability to visualize both complex diegetic levels in 2046 and virtual spaces in *Inception*, the cinematic apparatus becomes the way that characters, and by extension viewers, interact with memory. The onscreen relation between characters is temporal rather than spatial. Film techniques such as crosscutting and music change the way the viewer understands character relations between separate diegetic levels: the normal relationship between diegetic levels, in which characters are unable to communicate with nested dreams or narratives, is transformed. In an interview in *Film Comment*, Nolan expressed that one of the things that initially intrigued him about the ideas in *Inception* was the idea of "a shared, genuine, human interaction in a virtual space" (32). *Inception* goes beyond even its director's idea of virtual human interaction, calling into question the way actual memories are formed through collaborative processes. Characters are able to relate temporally as well as spatially in the dreamspaces. Cobb and Mal experience decades of life alone together in "limbo," creating memories that are no different from any other memories. This very fact—that nothing marks the dream memories from ordinary moments—becomes the twist or conceit of *Inception*: characters can become literally lost in their own memories. As a character remarks to Cobb in Yusef's (Dileep Rao) dream den, "[t]he dream has become their reality. Who are you to say otherwise?" (*Inception*).

One complaint about Nolan's dreams in *Inception* is that they lack cognitive scientific or psychoanalytic verisimilitude, but such a complaint neglects *Inception*'s generic and thematic concerns. The science fiction idea of entering other people's dreams allows for the exploration of how human beings literally become one another's memories and identities. Mal has become a permanent part of Cobb's psyche. Such a literalized notion of collective memory becomes a complex metaphor for how memories are actually formed. The science fiction genre in *Inception* is the vehicle for exploring real philosophical notions of the relationship between the self and other, challenging a notion of what constitutes a legitimate memory or reality.

Similarly, through a complex diegetic structure, 2046 explores the nature of memories and how one constitutes reality temporally. Rather than literalize the science fiction element, however, 2046 negotiates a more complex relationship between its parts. On one level, we are given the story of Chow in Hong Kong in the 1960s and the relationships he has with various women. On another, we are given access to the visualizations of the stories that Chow tells. However, the relationship between the two is not as simple as a story-within-a-story conceit. The relationship between *Inception*'s diegetic levels is actually simpler, despite its seeming complexity. *Inception* being a blockbuster action film, its viewing procedures aim to clearly explicate the rules of its narrative, hence the excess of explanatory dialogue in the film. Ambiguity comes not through form, but rather through the nature of the questions the film asks. *2046*, by contrast, offers its viewers no simple structures to hold on to. The film opens with an initial narration in Japanese introducing Tak (Takuya Kimura), a time traveller on a train coming back from "2046," before we meet Chow in the 1960s. Thematically, "2046" operates as a place where "nothing ever changes" (*2046*), and the introduction of the time-space at the beginning of the film sets it up as a central metaphor for the rest of the film. Similarly, *Inception* opens with Cobb washing up on the shores of "limbo." While initially disorienting, *Inception*'s opening can be explained—the following two hours are the memories of "a half-remembered dream" (*Inception*): a two-hour flashback. The nested structure of the diegesis echoes the nested levels of the dreams. Thus, *Inception* and *2046* play with temporal manipulations, such as the flashback, literally "locating them within the psyche" of the characters (Turim 16).

The flashback is constitutive of memory in cinema: it frames and focalizes historical elements in subjectivized ways and structures memory into a narrative, as Maureen Turim argues in *Flashbacks in Film* (1989). Turim contends that the flashback narrativizes memories, putting them into temporal and spatial order within the framework of the overall film. She points out that, as a structuring device, the filmic flashback has had a great influence on other representations of memory, further blurring the distinction between how different memory images operate. The memory images in *Inception* and *2046*, as in *La Jetée*, are "problematic as flashbacks" (221), for they challenge Turim's statement that "[i]maginary and potential future spaces," the kinds of memory images explicitly explored in *Inception* and *2046*, "are obviously less available to 'visualization' than are the events of the past" (219). Turim notes that such "manipulations of narrative temporality can serve to self-consciously expose the mechanisms of filmic narration" (16), but these films take further advantage of cinema to expose the very mechanisms of memory itself.

2046 is not content to explore memory purely through narrative temporality. After the film moves to the 1960s plot, where we meet Chow and the mysterious gambler, Black Spider a.k.a. Su Lizhen (Gong Li), a viewer encountering the film for the first time cannot help but wonder about the diegetic relationship between the earlier science fiction elements and this scene, and, likewise, the mysterious nature of the relationship between the two characters. Subsequently, we flash-forward within the 1960s to Christmas Eve 1966, where Chow meets a character from his past, Lulu/Mimi (Carina Lau), whose character nostalgically recalls Wong's second film, *Days of Being Wild*, and who seems unable to remember who he is. In a scene recalling the complex mystery at the centre of Renais's *Last Year at Marienbad*, Lulu/Mimi cannot be sure whether she did meet Chow before.

Thus, *2046* raises similar questions about memory and certainty as *Inception*. What is the legitimacy of memory vis-à-vis change? Both Chow and Cobb are paralyzed by the fear of change and would prefer to dwell in a single memory. Like Scottie in *Vertigo*, Cobb and Chow prefer their recollection image to the actual person. All of these characters epitomize Bergson's *dreamer*, the person who is unable to dwell in the present and who prefers the "virtual" to the "actual." These films crystallize Deleuze's formulation of Bergson: "It is in the past as it is in itself, as it is preserved in itself, that we go to look for our dreams or our recollections, and not the opposite" (*Cinema 2* 80). Cobb spends his "off-the-clock" dreamtime reliving past experiences with Mal. Memory operates through a constant comparison between actual events and the virtual, present past. Thus, Cobb suffers from an inability to control the intrusion of Mal into his dreams, while Chow invents the world of "2046" where nothing ever changes. However, one thing that memories confirm is that we are never the same. On one level, Lulu/Mimi is right to question her memory of Chow. Chow is not the same as his character in Wong's *In the Mood for Love* or *Days of Being Wild*. In *2046*, Chow has transformed into a rakish womanizer markedly different from his earlier personas. So different that it is not until late in the film that viewers can be sure that he is indeed the same character. Later in the film, Bai Ling (Zhang Ziyi) asks Ping: "Was he always like this?" The answer is, of course, no. The emotional distancing that Chow has undergone has prevented him from emotionally engaging in new relationships; it has also changed who he is. We might consider whether his lost love, So Lai-chen, would even recognize or want him if he were to get her back.

2046 moves back and forth in time and between diegetic levels: those of Chow the writer, and the fictional world of "2046" and "2047" (the stories that Chow writes where he incorporates the various female characters who will later be brought into the story). Though we begin with the assumption that the Japanese time traveller, Tak, is modelled on Jing-wen's (Faye Wong) boyfriend, we learn that in reality Chow had "begun to feel it wasn't about her boyfriend at all. Rather, it was more about me" (*2046*). Chow's writing of the science fiction stories conflates the personal and historical; there is no straightforward flashback structure. Instead, we are given Chow's personal imaginings of his stories. In *2046*, the distinction between the thought-image and the memory-image is blurred, emphasizing the difficulty of distinguishing between the two.

Recursion, Repetition, and the Image of Memory

Through stylistic choices that embody memory functions and interrogate the ways we experience time, *Inception* and *2046* reinforce the idea that there is no escape from time. Examples of these choices include editing techniques such as complex crosscutting between temporal and diegetic moments. These films also manage to shrink and expand time, not merely though cinematographic effects like slow motion, but through the reorganization of spatial relationships through montage and *mise en scène*. *Inception* expands time through the complex intercutting of the various dream levels as Cobb attempts to perform "inception" on Robert Fisher. *2046* makes special use of similarities and repetitions within the *mise en scène* and events within the diegesis to highlight the persistence of memory and create a déjà vu effect.

Wong blends these motifs of recursion and repetition thematically, exploring Chow's obsession with the past and his perception of his own memories and history. The year from which the film takes its title is the forty-ninth year after the 1997 British handover of Hong Kong to the People's Republic of China, the expiry date of subsequent Chinese assurances that Hong Kong would remain unchanged for fifty years. So "2046" refers to the end of a period in which Hong Kong will remain "frozen" or unchanged. Chow's memories of Su Lizhen/So Lai-chen have shaped his life as a lover and a writer. One of the difficulties in approaching the film is the seeming repetition of scenes, which in terms of narrative evoke Hitchock's *Vertigo*, as, like Scottie (James Stewart), Chow is unable to escape the grip of the memories of past loves: So Lai-chen, and then later the gambler Su Lizhen. For Chow, one woman becomes all women. Thus, in *2046* both personal and collective memory recursively circle back in upon themselves, preventing a moving forward or any real engagement with the past.

Recursion and repetition manifest themselves through the presence of *mise en abîme*—literally "placing into the abyss"—the formal technique of repetition within a frame using mirrors or fractal imagery. Wong's command of film style, through the use of elements such as composition, lighting, and camera movement, is key to establishing the themes. Visually, recursivity is seen in the film's dozens of mirror shots that fracture the frame: there are many shots of characters looking in mirrors and of characters reflected in mirrors. The framing repeats the motif of infinity literalized in Chow's stories of "2046." In a striking passage of the film, the intertitles flash, "One hour later. 10 hours later. 100 hours later. 1000 hours later" (*2046*), while the android character played by Faye Wong stares into the mirror-like windows of the train for what could be eternity. In this respect, the delayed emotional responses of the android characters in the science fiction story also manifest aspects of Chow's identity, instead of the various women in his life on whom they are visually modelled. The repetition of lines of dialogue or states of being allows us to understand the science fiction sections as Chow's thought-images: the significance of those sections lies in what they reveal of him. Earlier, when we are introduced to the character of Jing-wen, the physical model for the android character, she is tracing elliptical shapes on the floor of room 2046. Is there a connection between *mise en abîme* and this physical movement? Her behaviour prefigures aspects of the stories that Chow will write later in the film. Thus, the mirroring is built into the very visual structure of the framing and acting, between different scenes and diegetic levels.

In the final stretch of the film, the recursive nature of the narrative presents itself one last time. As Bai Ling (Zhang Ziyi) says goodbye to Chow, he recounts—in one of the film's more straightforward flashbacks—his relationship with the mysterious Su Lizhen, a.k.a. Black Spider. Through this repetition, the film essentially asks which Su Lizhen he is pining after ("Su Lizhen" being the Mandarin pronunciation of the name So Lai-chen, whom we see only briefly in a black-and-white scene in a taxi). Chow leaves his reminiscences by saying to Su Lizhen, "Maybe one day you'll escape your past" (*2046*), but this statement could also be for Chow himself. Will he ever escape the past? And more importantly, given his dwelling in nostalgia, does he even want to?

Recursion and repetition are literalized in *Inception* and bind memory to cinema through the images in the film. The viewer experiences the repetition of setting as Cobb revisits key memories with Mal, and *Inception* alludes to the train's place in the history of cinema, recalling the Lumière brothers' *L'arrivée d'un train à La Ciotat* (1896). The train also plays a significant role in *2046*. Chow's chronotope, "2046," can only be reached by a mysterious train that the time traveller Tak rides to move between Area 1224 and Area 1225, once again transforming and conflating a time into a place (the numbers being the dates of Christmas Eve and Day as well as the respective "zones" within the story). However, the film suggests that no one can quite escape time in this way, as no one has ever come back from "2046." Trains become the metaphor for the transversal of the temporal rather than the spatial, or for the spatialization of time. In *Inception*, Cobb's first extraction job takes place while they are sleeping on a train. The train *later* becomes a mechanism for moving between time-spaces, as Mal and Cobb lay their heads on a train track in order to perform the "death" that will return them from "limbo" to their actual world. Later in the film a train becomes a destructive force in the dreamscape, shattering the illusion of images. Given this metaphorical nature, the train that smashes its way through the cityscape of the first dream level during the Fisher job shows that Cobb has internalized this lesson too well. The train becomes associated with his inability to move past his memories. Thus, paradoxically, trains, modes of transportation, actually reinscribe the idea in these films that one cannot escape from memory: the train in *2046* never reaches its destination. To be constantly moving yet never really getting anywhere seems to be the fate of those who cannot make the leap that is "an act of trust in possibilities beyond their present comprehension" (Bogue 121). Both films concretize the lessons that Deleuze takes from Kierkegaard and Nietzsche, regarding the "leap of faith" and "repetition," appropriately embodying them in cinematic terms (121).

As noted earlier, Cobb prefers to dwell in the past upon the images of his dead wife, Mal; the film intercuts between his reminiscences of his time spent with her in "limbo," where Cobb planted the idea that caused Mal to kill herself, and his present. Beyond the idea of nested dreams-within-dreams, the idea of the recursion and repetition of memory is expressed through the act of inception. Cobb plants the idea that "the world we inhabit isn't real" (*Inception*) in Mal's mind, which recalls the Platonic notion of "anamnesis," a re-remembering of "eternal truths that one once knew but had forgotten" (Bogue 117). In *Inception*, this idea, this prevention of "becoming" through the stasis of memory, is the very thing that leads to Mal's suicide and Cobb's guilt over planting the idea in her head. The conceit that the temporality of "limbo" can be escaped by "death" in the dream state reflects the idea that death is ultimately the only escape from time, or at least the static time of "limbo."

Inception embodies cinema's non-distinction between the "virtual image" and the "actual image," eschewing conventional flashbacks when Cobb uses the dream technology to actually re-experience time with Mal. The extent of Cobb's obsession is only made apparent when Ariadne follows Cobb into the "basement" of his unconscious where he "keeps" Mal. Ariadne exclaims, "These aren't just dreams, these are memories. You told me never to use memories" (*Inception*). Here, as Cobb continually relives his moments of regret, the film also plays on the idea of collective memory. As Ariadne tells Cobb, "You've asked me to share dreams with you" (*Inception*). Cobb is reminded that he cannot simply relive these memories over and over again without considering how they affect others in the shared dreams, which they do as Mal becomes a more and more malevolent force within the dreamscapes.

Inception also manifests recursivity visually through *mise en abîme*—in this instance, the technique of repetition within a frame using mirrors or fractal imagery. *Inception* visually plays with these concepts, utilizing mirrors in a sequence that exemplifies *mise en abîme*. In the course of her training in the creation of dreamscapes, Ariadne creates two giant mirrors suspended opposite each other. The result is an infinite regression of images, indistinguishable from one another. The mirror acts as a visual metaphor for the layering of levels in the dreams-within-dreams in much the same way that Resnais's *Last Year at Marienbad* incorporates recursion in both its mirrored, labyrinthine chateau and its repetitive voice-over narration. Deleuze describes such a proliferation of virtual images as an illustration of the "indiscernibility of the real and the imaginary" (*Cinema 2* 69). The indiscernibility of reality and memory is a key theme in both *Last Year at Marienbad* and *Inception*, causing some to speak of *Inception* as the action film remake of *Marienbad*.

This "indiscernibility" is the "objective characteristic of certain existing images," in this case both the memory-image and cinema-image (*Cinema 2* 69). Deleuze describes how the situation of two facing mirrors is "prefigured in *Citizen Kane*, when Kane passes between two facing mirrors," but notes that it "comes to the fore in its pure state in the famous palace of mirrors in *The Lady from Shanghai*, where the principle of indiscernibility reaches its peak" (70). Actuality in Welles's film is only re-established upon the smashing of the mirrors, which is also how Ariadne ends her illusion in *Inception* and thereby repeats the notion that destruction and death can re-establish certainty. The dream states of *Inception* become an entire palace of mirrors, again recalling the chateau from *Last Year at Marienbad*: virtual images proliferate, thrusting memories into the present in very literalized ways and blurring the distinction between past and present. To break the mirrored *mise en abîme* is to wake the dreamer from the dream, as the train does earlier when Cobb and Mal rest their heads on the train tracks in limbo. *Inception* is as much about cinema as it is about memory or dreams: it reaffirms the lesson that cinema "is not merely one of the most effective metaphors for memory but that cinema—alongside photography—is *constitutive* of memory in its deepest and most meaningful sense" (Kilbourn 1). In *Cinema 2: The Time-Image,* Deleuze reaffirms the role of self-reflexivity in cinema, not only because, quoting Wim Wenders, it is "able to tell only its own story," but also because cinema offers the crystal-image, Deleuze's term for the way that cinematic images contain both the *indexical* pastness of the photographic image and the *iconic* presentness of its viewing (*Cinema 2* 76). In visualizing the effects of the past upon the present, films like *Inception* and *2046* concretize such a philosophical concept.

Inception, in particular, embodies the point of indiscernibility between the virtual and the actual. Deleuze writes that

> [w]hat causes our mistake is that recollection-images, and even dream-images or dreaming, haunt a consciousness which necessarily accords them a capricious and momentary allure, since they are actualized according to the momentary needs of this consciousness. But, if we ask *where* consciousness is going to look for these recollection-images and these dream-images or this reverie that it evokes, according to its states, we are led back to pure virtual images of which the latter are only modes or degrees of actualization. (*Cinema 2* 80)

Here Deleuze re-establishes the relationship between perception and memory. Film embodies the notion that the perception of the actual inevitably requires the calling up of the past in virtual images. Every act of perception depends upon the past, thus the crystal-image of cinema visualizes time. *Inception* ends with a moment of ambiguity, a deliberate cut on the spinning top, Cobb's "totem" (appropriated from Mal), his guarantee that what he perceives is "actual" rather than "virtual." In the end,

Cobb chooses to believe, to turn his back on the still-spinning totem, and embrace his children. The final shot of the film, with its frustrating cutaway from the spinning top imposing the ambiguity of the art film on the frustrated audience of the action blockbuster, makes Cobb's choice clear. Rather than try to arrest the passage of time, he accepts the ambiguity of his reality.

Conclusion

2046 opens with a pre-credits shot of what appears to be a hole in a tree, which the viewer later learns is the place where one whispers secrets that one cannot tell anyone (the hole and this mystery refer intratextually to the ending of *In the Mood for Love*). Wong's Director's Statement for *2046* frames how this image concretizes some of the themes of the film:

> [T]here is a need in all of us to have a place to hide or store certain memories, thoughts, impulses, hopes and dreams. These are part of our lives that we can't resolve or best not act upon but at the same time we are afraid to jettison them. For some, this is a physical place; for others, it is a mental space, and for a few it is neither. (Wong, "Director's Statement," qtd. in Brunette 105)

This ties the image of the hole in the tree as a place to store secret memories to the idea of "2046" as a place where one can live in a frozen memory. Both are impossible spaces, and the film thematizes the effect of attempting to find such spaces. *Inception* too thematizes the impossibility of remaining in such a state of paralysis instead of jettisoning the past in order to embrace "becoming." While it is not a typical "Hollywood ending," as Cobb comes to terms with his reality and himself as a memory subject, *Inception* offers a kind of philosophical closure. *2046*, on the other hand, resists granting Chow the kind of closure that *Inception* grants Cobb, despite the enforced ambiguity of the final shot of the spinning top.

Deleuze wrote in the mid-1980s that "[i]n the cinema, there are perhaps three films which show how we inhabit time, how we move in it, in this form which carries us away, picks us up and enlarges us" (*Cinema 2* 82). The films he cites are Dovzhenko's *Zvenigora* (1928), Hitchcock's *Vertigo*, and Renais's *Je t'aime je t'aime* (1968)—once again reaffirming the place of Hitchcock's and Resnais's films as essential entries in the genealogy of the memory film. While it is perhaps too bold to find them places on that rarefied list, both *2046* and *Inception* deserve to be recontextualized and given their place within the history of the memory film, as these films dramatize the role of cinema in the constitution of memories and visualize philosophical concepts of temporality and identity.

NOTE

1 Richard Peña surveys the influence of Jorge Luis Borges on cinema in "Borges and the New Latin American Cinema," noting "the influence of Borges on a number of European, principally French filmmakers: Alain Resnais, Alain Robbe-Grillet [the creative force behind *Marienbad*], and especially Jacques Rivette" (229). Both Nolan and Wong have also expressed a specific admiration for Borges in interviews and cited him as an influence on their work. See "A Man and His Dream: Christopher Nolan and *Inception*" on *The New York Times Arts Beat* blog and Stephen Teo in *Wong Kar-wai* p. 46, respectively.

12

"You must remember this ...": Watching *Casablanca* with Marc Augé

Graeme Gilloch

Introduction

The complex and convoluted play of remembrance and forgetting has been a long-standing theme in the writings of the contemporary French ethnographer and cultural theorist Marc Augé, although his focus until recently has tended to be on the spatial conditions and configurations of such processes, practices, and possibilities. For instance, in his insightful and intriguing set of reflections on the Parisian metro system, *In the Metro* (1986; trans. 2002), he recounts how certain subway stations and lines (above all, the Auteuil–Gare d'Orléans–Austerlitz line) remain for him to this day so inextricably bound up with particular phases of his life, so imbued with personal memories, that these toponyms themselves serve as mnemonic prompts, setting in train whole series of intimate remembrances. Indeed, the book opens with what remains for him one of the most startling images from his Parisian childhood: the unforgettable sight of a grey-clad German soldier standing guard at the Maubert-Mutualité station in 1940, Augé's first direct encounter with the Nazi occupation.[1] Moreover, it should also be recognized that the work for which Augé is perhaps best known in Anglo-American circles—his conceptualization of the "non-places" (*non-lieux*)[2] proliferating in our age of "supermodernity"—identifies and characterizes precisely those banal everyday environments deemed bereft of meaning and memories—all those anonymous fast food eateries, motorway service stations, waiting areas of all kinds, hotel lobbies and airport lounges, scenes that we swiftly pass through, are made to endure on occasions, but seldom remember.

While the spatial aspects of recollection are certainly significant in his poetic and at times painful book *Casablanca* (2007; trans. 2009 as *Casablanca: Movies and Memory*), this study is something of a departure for Augé in its exploration of the relationship between the work of memory and the medium of film. As will become apparent, this involves two key aspects: on the one hand, as might be expected, Augé is intrigued by the role and representation of memory in the narrative structure of Michael Curtiz's classic 1942 Hollywood romantic drama *Casablanca*, a film now on general re-release in celebration of its seventieth anniversary; and on the other, Augé is concerned with unravelling his own memories occasioned by watching this film today, a film that he first saw as a child on its first release in Paris in the immediate aftermath of the Second World War. Framing his reflections and reminiscences with the deeply nostalgic pleasures of cinema-going in the Latin Quarter, Augé elegantly and intricately interlaces a series of family narratives prompted by the film: he recounts how the traumatic historical events—war, displacement, and exile—in which the main characters of *Casablanca* are caught up resonated with his own childhood experiences of the Nazi invasion and occupation: of leaving Paris in 1940 with his mother and suffering weeks of privation and uncertainty on the road in the south and west of France as they sought to remain close to his conscripted father; of a charismatic uncle who happened to live in Casablanca, who was to distinguish himself during the war as an intrepid submarine captain and Free French hero but whose life was then blighted by the death of his young wife; there are even a few tantalizing fragments of Augé's own experiences as a young national serviceman in North Africa in the 1950s and 1960s during the Algerian War; and finally, most importantly, most movingly, returning to the present there is his precious and poignant relationship with his dying mother, as he seeks desperately to augment and corroborate his own limited childhood memories with her now failing recollections of times past before it is too late. Watching *Casablanca* one more time invokes all these family stories, biographies and destinies.

My purpose in this chapter is not to unpick and follow each of these threads in turn. Instead, I want to explore Augé's fascination with *Casablanca* as a film that captures the vicissitudes and vagaries of memory. To do this, I suggest one might usefully turn to one of his earlier studies, indeed his most explicit and sustained analysis of remembrance and forgetting, *Oblivion* (1998; trans. 2004), for in many ways that book provides the theoretical and conceptual framework for Augé's cinematic memories and, moreover, for a distinctive way of reading this classic Hollywood film itself as melodrama—"melodrama" understood here not as exaggerated or extravagant play of excessive emotions and events, but rather in its now archaic sense of a drama imbued with music and song (from the Greek: *melos*, "song"). To be clear: this is not so much Augé's own reading of the film but more a reading *with* or *through* Augé (with a little help from motifs borrowed from Walter Benjamin).[3]

"For old times' sake"

And so let us begin with a song:

> Di die di die di die
> Di die di die di die
> Di die di die di dum ... (Curtiz)

With this, surely the most famous hum in movie history, Ilsa Lund (Ingrid Bergman) prompts Sam (Dooley Wilson) to play a song he claims to have forgotten, a song that ironically insists on the work of memory. Reluctantly, Sam picks up the theme and starts to sing:

> You must remember this
> A kiss is just a kiss
> A smile is just a smile
> The fundamental things apply
> As time goes by. (Curtiz)

What deliciously, doubly ambiguous lyrics this supposedly forgotten, in truth unforgettable, verse has! On the one hand, its opening line is an injunction, an instruction, an imperative: "you must remember this" can be taken to constitute a demand or duty to retain in memory what was, a requirement to preserve a past moment. Forgetting is forbidden; remembering is configured as obligation or necessity.

On the other hand, this "must" may also be understood as an emphatic: "you *must* remember this" expresses a sense of astonishment and incredulity that some particular thing, some past incident or instance, could ever be forgotten. *Surely* one remembers, even if one would prefer not to—how could it be otherwise? Forgetting appears here as impossibility.[4] And what exactly is it that has to be remembered, that certainly cannot have been forgotten? Once again, the song presents us with a conundrum. Are "smiles" and "kisses" those "fundamental things" that "apply" during and despite the passage of time? If so, then why are they preceded by the word "just," seemingly diminishing their significance? If "smiles" and "kisses" are really no more than "smiles" and "kisses," then how could they truly be the "fundamental things"? And in any case, is it really the "fundamental things" that we remember? Surely our memories are never so tidily sorted and sifted, so easy classified and categorized into important and trivial matters, the "fundamental" and the frivolous. Indeed, meaning and significance change in retrospect, that is to say, these are the very things that are constructed and reconstructed "as time goes by." And so it is that all those insubstantial and inconsequential "smiles" and "kisses" may very well compose the very stuff of memory, gestures and moments that we cannot but remember, that we must not forget.[5]

Sam's song, like Ilsa's humming, is cut short. Rick Blaine (Humphrey Bogart) storms in and silences him with an angry, "I thought I told you never to […]" (Curtiz) before being silenced himself, before his interruption is itself interrupted by the sight of Ilsa to complete the chain of unfinished phrases. And in bringing these former lovers together with his song one more time, Sam's work is now almost done. We will hear "As Time Goes By" played only twice more: once, after hours, for Rick in his Café Americain, ushering in the sweet and sour memories that compose the flashback sequences of Paris; and once during the flashback itself, in some French café where Sam, Ilsa, and Rick are finishing off the last of the champagne and arranging to flee the French capital together on the night train south. With Ilsa's arrival in Casablanca, Sam takes a long, last bow as reluctant musical matchmaker, and then curiously disappears from the film's finale just as he inexcusably vanishes from the film's main credits. We do hear the song in the background at the very end of the film. It is played as the lovers say a last farewell and the Lisbon plane departs, but Sam is no longer singing. The absence of the voice reminds the viewer of Sam's own premature disappearance.[6]

Figures of Oblivion

While stressing Sam's key role as witness, as onlooker in a love triangle, Augé curiously neglects Sam's song in his reflections on *Casablanca*. This is surprising given that it is surely "As Time Goes By" that he has in mind when in *Oblivion* he notes the unforgettable, entrancing entrance of

Bergman and then, on the same page, muses on the decisive role of music as a mnemonic:

> Music (which frequently plays a major role in our perception of the film image) is, more than any other art perhaps, in its various forms, apt to bring those it takes by surprise back towards shores they do not always recognise very well but of which they are suddenly, thanks to the music, sure to have known and loved once, before leaving them. The refrain, the old tune, the melody of the "three little notes" the song mentions, have that re-creative ability, that poetic power—independent of musical genres, except that "popular" music has the widest audience and therefore offers a much more diverse and extensive humanity than the specialised music-loving public the possibility of feeling the subtle adaptability of time, the feeling of "strange familiarity" (*unheimliche*) that Freud associates with repetition, but about which we have learned with Proust that, in its most felicitous forms, being more familiar than strange, it may also be aroused by the obviousness of the return. (73–74)[7]

Oblivion provides the lens through which one may read Augé's fascination with *Casablanca*, in its emphasis on the fundamental interdependence and interplay of remembering and forgetting in the constitution of memory. This is most memorably captured in a littoral or marine image:

> Memories are crafted by oblivion as the outlines of the shore are created by the sea [...] For millennia on end, the ocean has blindly pursued its work of eroding and remodelling: to those who know how to read, the result (a landscape) really has to have something to say about the resistance and weakness of the shore, of the nature of its rocks and soil, of its faults and its fractures, and whatever else [...] Something, too, of course, about the pressures of the ocean; but the strength and direction of these pressures also depends on the shapes of the submarine relief—that extension of the earthly landscape [...] On the whole, then, something of the complicity between earth and sea, which have both contributed to the lengthy work of elimination of which the present landscape is the result. (20–21)

In developing this topographical trope into an ethnographic theme, Augé identifies and explores three formations or "figures of oblivion," each linked to moments of narrative fiction and marked by practices of ritual, each involving a different configuration of past, present, and future:

1. The figure of "return": by this, Augé means the concern to "find a lost past again by forgetting the present" (56), in other words, a complete immersion in what has been, such that any sense of the present and

future is dissipated or subordinated. Or perhaps the past exerts some inescapable, irresistible compulsion upon the now (to avenge a previous injury or injustice in the feud, for instance). Augé's exemplary anthropological form is that of "possession" (of the shaman, of the afflicted) by the spirits of long-departed ancestors.
2. The figure of "suspense": this, by contrast, involves the forgetting of the past and the deferral of the future for the sake of an intense and absolute preoccupation with an enduring "now," a sense of timelessness and living in and for the present only. This is that extraordinary or ecstatic moment of *carpe diem* in which, perhaps, everyday rules and obligations are fleetingly set aside in some kind of "state of exception" (Augé's example is that of the festival or carnival in which customary norms are temporarily reversed or displaced).
3. The figure of "re-beginning" or the notion of a new start or fresh "departure": this, Augé notes, is typically enacted in initiation ceremonies or other rites of passage, and involves a forgetting and/or leaving behind of the past and the present so as to enter into a new phase of life, a new state or condition, one often marked by the promise of good fortune ahead, by optimism and the *promesse de bonheur*.

We will return to these three figures in due course. Suffice to say here that, although Augé himself never explicitly puts it in these terms, my contention is that *Casablanca* contains each of these three moments—or, more precisely, imagines (turns them into images) and thereby screens these differing configurations of oblivion.

As I have already indicated, however, Augé's *Casablanca* study is about far more than the film itself. Indeed, he interlaces at least three distinct lines of thought in the composition of a veritable latticework of memory, history, and film text. Or perhaps a cinematic metaphor is more apt here: these are sets of reflections that are spliced into one another in the form of a montage of movies and memories.

First, Augé is concerned with the relationship between cinema and memory.[8] And it is important to note the term *cinema*, not just film: Augé's book opens with an early evening visit to the local independent cinema, not a contemporary multiplex, but one of those small, seductive little cinemas that once flourished on the Left Bank and in the Latin Quarter and that continue to eke out a living somehow, specializing in art house movies, retrospectives, and reruns of all-time classics.[9] He is at pains to stress the ritualistic aspect of this excursion: the booth in the foyer where the cashier sits, selling tickets and chatting a little with regulars; the impassive usherette with her torch who conducts you promptly but wearily to your seat; entering the already darkened space of the auditorium; squeezing past the various knees and bodies of those already seated; the sense of expectation as the trailers give way to the main feature. All this reminds Augé of his childhood visits to the movies. Indeed, this is not all. For Augé, the form of the cinematic medium itself—the concatenation of film images, their sequencing and editing, their staging as montage—is in some way analogous to the work of memory. Film-images are, he suggests, not unlike memory-images in significant ways. He is interested in the way that, for instance, film images are unchanging, the stars themselves do not age, while the viewer and the context of watching are never the same. The film presents us with the always-the-same amid the ever-new. The film does not alter, yet we, the viewers, are apt to find something different each time, to have our attention caught by some small details that we do not remember from previous screenings, by that "tiny spark of contingency"—as Walter Benjamin famously puts it in his "Little History of Photography" (*Selected* II: 510)—that appears only in the "now" of its recognizability by the spectator. And this leads Augé to reflect upon one particularly memorable film that he saw as a boy way back in 1947 and that continues to haunt him to this day: *Casablanca*.

And then there is Augé's half-remembered childhood itself. Although it was not released in France until after the war, the film's main themes (of escape, exile, fear, waiting, and displacement resulting from the Occupation of 1940) mesh with Augé's memories of that traumatic historical moment. The agitated comings and goings of the refugees in the movie bring to mind his own convoluted journeys with his mother—perilous nocturnal expeditions undertaken so as to be close to his father, who had been called up and then stationed in various training camps and garrisons southwest of the Loire until the armistice and demobilization. And Casablanca itself, perhaps the only city in the world better known as a movie, indeed as a Hollywood set,[10] than as an actual place,[11] had a special significance for Augé: it was home to his aunt and uncle, the latter a charismatic figure whom, as a renegade submarine captain and Free French war hero, Augé to this day still thinks of as some kind of Bogart-like figure.[12] And so it is that the adventures and escapades of Augé's relations, coupled with his own early experiences—a Parisian childhood around 1940—compose a set of remembrances, of odysseys and encounters, to which he seeks to bring a degree of coherence, some sense of sequence, some possibility of narration. For this he turns to his aging, dying mother, and between her failing memory and his imperfect one, they try to piece together their story of enforced migration, one that Augé himself recalls only as a set of suggestive toponyms (Champagne, Tarbes, Canejan, Le Mans, Bourdeaux) interspersed with the names of other refugees encountered *en passant*.[13] All this and more[14] forms the second narrative thread to Augé's book.

And of course there is the third theme: the film *Casablanca* itself, and it is this that I wish to focus upon in this chapter. Not only is *Casablanca* a film about the plight of those in flight, but it is also, as I have hopefully already intimated in my reflections on Sam's song, most profoundly and perplexingly a melodrama of remembering and forgetting.

Casablanca: Melodrama and Memory

Casablanca opens with a mapping of the escape route taken by Europeans fleeing the German advance: from Paris to Marseille, then by ship across the Mediterranean to Oran, then overland to Casablanca. And there they wait for the opportunity to reach Lisbon and the transatlantic liners that will take them to safety in the New World. But those lacking the necessary documentation wait in Casablanca, "and wait and wait," as the voice-over intones. Casablanca has become a giant holding bay, a seedy Kracauerian hotel lobby of waiting.[15] We see (the Hollywood version of) the city's streets, alleyways, and bazaars filled with the desperate and those who prey upon them—tricksters, black marketeers, thieves and swindlers; we enter the lobby of a certain Café Americain and hear of its elusive owner, a man who begins to intrigue us as much as he intrigues his various clientele; and finally we gain access to the backroom where Rick himself is to be found, sitting playing chess against himself (against time, perhaps? against death?), a veritable Minotaur at the heart of this labyrinth, this amnesia palace, or a monarch sitting in the silent central chamber of this teeming anthill called Casablanca. Rick is not stuck in this city; he is stuck in his own recent past. He is not waiting to escape to his American homeland, he is brooding over what he has left behind in Paris. Who is Rick? What has happened to him? The unfolding of these mysteries is, of course, the key to the story of *Casablanca*.

Combining memory and melancholy, melancholy (according to Freud) being the enduring love for the impossible love object, Rick is a figure of "return" in his absorption by the past. The present and the future hold no charms for him. Until, that is, unexpectedly and against all the odds, the very source of his brooding, the impossible beloved herself, arrives in Casablanca, chances upon Rick's café, and, spotting Sam, asks him to play "As Time Goes By," the mnemonic, the signature of their love.

"You must remember this [...]" (Curtiz): as if Ilsa and Rick could possibly have forgotten.

That night, Rick stays up drinking, waiting for Ilsa to return once more. And as he waits, the images that preoccupy him, that preoccupy them both, the images of their brief but passionate love affair in Paris, are screened as a flashback sequence. In many ways, this is a conventional flashback sequence,[16] in which a character's memories are transformed into and screened as film images.[17] One should perhaps appreciate then that it is not simply a crude use of back projection or calamitous continuity problem when Rick and Ilsa's drive through the city suddenly becomes an excursion into the countryside and day gives way abruptly to night. The suddenly changing rather than subtly dissolving backdrops are not a clumsy failure but rather the clearest indication that these are configured as memory-images, that is to say, images that blend seamlessly into one another, images of love in which one is oblivious to time and place. When was it exactly? Where were we exactly? Who notices such things when one is so entranced by love? Love is here configured as a moment of dream-like suspension. Rick and Ilsa seek to live only in the present in Paris, no questions about the past, no thought for the future; indeed, the very moment Rick starts making plans, the spell has been broken.[18]

The flashback is also a moment of punctuation, of interruption and counterpoint. Ilsa tricks Rick into leaving Paris without her. This is the first of at least three acts of self-sacrifice, each occasioned by love, and each enhanced and ennobled by the backdrop of corruption and selfishness against which they take place. True, while the notion of self-sacrifice in love is central to Eco's reading,[19] for me, it is significant that this altruism first appears in the Paris flashback, that is to say, in a tale within a tale. For readers of Walter Benjamin, this cannot but call to mind his immanent critique and distinctive reading of Goethe's famous novella *Die Wahlverwandtschaften (Elective Affinities)*.[20]

Benjamin's essay contrasts illusory love, the superficial attractions and fleeting infatuations of the novella's four main characters, with genuine or "true love" ("*wahre Liebe*") (*Selections* I: 345) as displayed by the young couple in a story recounted one evening by a visitor: "The Curious Tale of the Childhood Sweethearts." In this remarkable narrative, we learn of a boy and a girl, constant childhood companions who grow to be bitter rivals and enemies in their youth, such that their concerned families, which both had once harboured happy expectations, decide to separate them for good. He joins the army and distinguishes himself as a daring and courageous officer in distant lands. She blossoms into a beautiful young woman and attracts many suitors, eventually accepting the attentions and marriage proposal of one among them. The day of the wedding arrives, and their celebrations are to be held on a riverboat chartered for the happy occasion. The young man returns from his regiment to join in the festivities and pay his respects. Then things take an unexpected turn. The bride-to-be realizes she has made a terrible mistake: she has loved the young man, the soldier, all along. In a mixture of love and anguish, she throws herself from the boat into the surging waters of the river. The young man, similarly struck by the realization of love, does not hesitate and throws himself into the torrent after her. The currents are kind: they are both brought to shore; they are reunited with the other guests and reconciled. And who could refuse the entreaties and tears of these two young lovers? Who could not forgive them their follies and bless their future together? And so the tale ends.

For Benjamin, "wahre Liebe" risks everything and, trusting in God and good fortune, the beneficence of fate, wins through. The readiness to die for love, for self-sacrifice, leads not to death but rather to happiness; by contrast, the timid emotions and shallow conformity of the characters in the novella itself inevitably result in misfortune and loss.

Another of Sam's songs invites good luck and combines a sense of interruption with an invocation of benign fortune: "Knock on Wood."[21] And indeed there is one figure who enjoys both love and luck in Casablanca, a figure who seems marginal to the storyline but whose readiness for self-sacrifice for the sake of love reminds Rick of what "wahre Liebe" might mean. Annina (Joy Page), a young Bulgarian newlywed, asks Rick for advice: lacking the necessary money, she is prepared to sacrifice herself and gratify the sexual advances of the corrupt and comic Prefect of Police, Louis Renault (Claude Rains), in order to procure the necessary travel documents that will ensure their escape. Instead, Rick tips off the croupier to fix the roulette table so that her husband wins not once but twice on 22, thereby securing the funds required and saving her from Louis. It is not exactly good fortune that saves the newlyweds—the table is rigged, even luck in Casablanca is not innocent. But the readiness for self-sacrifice is decisive and receives its unexpected reward. Annina is saved from doing "a bad thing" by Rick doing a "beautiful thing" (Curtiz).

The third and final instance of self-sacrifice for love occurs, of course, at the end of the film. Instead of using the special travel documents to escape Casablanca with Ilsa, Rick does the thinking for both of them and gives them to her so that she and Victor can leave together on the Lisbon plane. This is a sacrifice not only for love but also for memory—or rather, more specifically, for the sake of the remembrance of love. The memories that set Rick brooding in our first encounter with him are now transformed by the recognition of "wahre Liebe." This is Paris restored, love in the past redeemed through an act of love in the present. The future of their memories is ensured and confirmed in perpetuity: they will always have Paris.[22] And so the film concludes with two images of departure, that is to say, of new beginnings: as Ilsa and Victor fly off to Lisbon, Rick famously speculates on the start of a beautiful friendship with Louis.

In this way, *Casablanca* screens the three figures of oblivion for Augé, although this is never made explicit in his study. But I would want to go somewhat further than this in any case and suggest that the whole cinematic experience itself—the ritual of entering the same dark chamber time and again; of immersing and losing oneself in the fictions, times, places, and characters on the screen; and then of emerging afresh into the light of day once more—all of these also replay the structure of oblivion, of return, suspense, and re-beginning.

Epitaph

In synthesizing the different strands of his study—family, childhood and film, past and present, the remembered and the forgotten—Augé's concluding chapter is elegiac and beautiful. It begins with a memorial act: he lays flowers on the grave of his mother in Brittany, his mother who had helped him make sense of his disparate childhood memories, the mother for whom all of this has been written but who will never now read it. And then he takes the train home to Paris, where, arriving as darkness begins to fall, he hurries to his beloved local cinema and takes his seat just in time to watch a film, what else but *Casablanca*, one more time. This is a book then not just about forms of memory and melancholy but finally about the work of mourning too. It is, in retrospect, imbued with grief and bereavement for a beloved mother. *Casablanca*, this little book, is for Augé what *Camera Lucida* (1993) is for Roland Barthes, but with a cinematic film not a Wintergarden photograph at its heart. *Casablanca*, this enduring film, has become one long *punctum* that wounds him and will continue to wound him as time goes by. Augé cannot but remember this.

NOTES

1 See Augé *In the Metro* 3. For his reflections on these reflections some twenty years later, see Augé *Le Métro Revisité*.
2 See Augé *Non-Places* 96.
3 Lauded as "[t]he director's one enduring masterpiece [...] the happiest of happy accidents and the most decisive exception to the auteur theory" (Andrew Sarris qtd. in Maltby 47), and as "a modern film classic, perhaps the favourite picture of World War Two" (Koppes and Black 287), *Casablanca* has not surprisingly become one of the most discussed films in cinema history (see Maltby 489–90). Based on the theatrical script *Everybody Goes to Rick's* by Murray Burnett and Joan Alison, and adapted for the screen by Julius and Philip Epstein with Howard Koch (Koppes and Black 287), the film has conventionally been perceived in two ways: one the one hand, in its studio conception, cinematography, and star casting, it is a classic and utterly conventional Hollywood romantic drama. Accordingly, it is "regularly cited as exemplifying the ways in which the Hollywood movie constructs and explains its storylines" (Maltby 476), and, indeed, may be seen as "the Forties most characteristic single film" (Higham and Greenberg 19). On the other hand, and despite the skeptical stance taken by, for example, Colin Shindler ("it has little to do with the war"; 67), the movie is widely recognized as an exercise in wartime propaganda and a powerful endorsement of the American entry into the European theatre of war, even though the U.S. government's Office of War Information was troubled both by Rick's overlong equivocation and by the depiction of a corrupt and compliant French Vichy administration (see Koppes and Black 290). As Maltby observes, the film has "a propagandistic message which seems utterly unambiguous to present-day audiences" (479). Perhaps the most distinctive and provocative discussion of the film is to be found in a 1984 essay by Umberto Eco in his *Travels in Hyperreality*. In seeking to understand how this "very modest aesthetic achievement" (197) has managed to become revered as a "cult movie," Eco's highly ironic essay recognizes *Casablanca* as the most perfect of imperfections, as "ramshackle, rickety, unhinged in itself" (198), as a "reunion" (209) of every cinematic cliché, as an assemblage of every archetype. And this is what makes it inimitable in all its own imitations, every line endlessly quotable, every scene open to parody, the whole thing utterly enchanting, unforgettable, "Sublime" (209). Eco writes: "Casablanca became a cult movie because it is not one movie. It is 'movies.' And this is the reason it works in defiance of any aesthetic theory" (208). The film's charm requires a certain naïveté on the part of the spectator. It would not, could not, withstand serious theoretical scrutiny—and Eco

concludes with the hope that it will never have to: "It will be a sad day when a too smart audience will read *Casablanca* as conceived by Michael Curtiz after having read Calvino and Barthes. Perhaps we have been able to discover here, for the last time, the Truth" (211).

4 This tension between love as that which must not be forgotten (as duty—marital) and that which cannot be forgotten (as intoxication—romance), is of course, the fundamental dilemma of the film.

5 And so it is that when, recalling the Wehrmacht's entry into Paris, Rick juxtaposes the important and the incidental and tells Ilsa: "Not an easy day to forget. I remember every detail. The Germans wore grey, you wore blue." But which is which here?

6 For brief discussions of Sam's role in the context of the portrayal of African Americans by Hollywood films at the time, see Shindler (41) and Koppes and Black (180).

7 Augé's concern with music in film is both unusual and welcome. As Philip Drake observes: "With a few exceptions film theorists examining the relationship between history, memory and film have focused upon visual images" (qtd. in Grainge 185). Drake's own reading of music in *Sleepless in Seattle* includes discussion of an intertextual moment in the film in which Meg Ryan is shown watching *Casablanca* on television and listening to "As Time Goes By."

8 Augé is, of course, not the only writer to explore cinema-going and spectatorship as lived and remembered experiences. See, for example, Kuhn, as well as Stubbings qtd. in Grainge 65–80.

9 See his *Casablanca: Movies and Memory* [hereafter *CMM*] 1–3.

10 However phony these sets may seem to us now, Augé writes: "*Casablanca* was really something else. If the stereotypical exoticism of the streets of the Casbah in the film has always left a strong impression on me, it's because it corresponds to the images that from early childhood the name of this African city had awoken in me, along with a few others with strange sounds, such as Diégo Suarez or Djibouti" (*CMM* 5).

11 For a study of the visual culture of the actual city of Casablanca, see Ossman (1994).

12 See *CMM* 5; *CMM* 57; and *CMM* 65.

13 As part of this process, Augé comes to recognize the failings and confusions of his own memory: he discovers that his sense of the trajectory of his travels with his mother is hopelessly wrong; indeed, he realizes that he has mixed up these painful journeys with earlier holiday excursions to the Atlantic coast of France.

14 Augé also notes his own military experiences of North Africa during the Algerian War. See *CMM* 66–69.

15 Part of his wider study of the detective story, Kracauer's reflections on the hotel lobby identify it as the "inverted image of the house of God," a transient home only to the flotsam and jetsam of modernity, an intermediate space that "accommodates all those who go there to meet no one" (175). In Augé's

terms, it is a non-place. And this is what Casablanca has become: a way station, a transit camp, a stopover in which the exiles have become trapped. It is a whole city as *non-lieux*.

16 For a discussion of the flashback as a formal temporal technique of Hollywood movies, see Bordwell et al. 42–43. Interestingly, the authors point out that "[f]lashbacks are rarer in the classical Hollywood film than we normally think" (42).

17 In her study of the use of flashback in films, Maureen Turim points out how individual and collective memories are spliced together: "flashbacks in film often merge the two levels of remembering the past, giving large scale social and political history the subjective mode of a single, fictional individual's remembered experience" (2). This is precisely the case in *Casablanca*, as she notes later: "the Paris segment depicts not only Rick's disappointed expectations but also the Fall of France to the invading Nazi army" (126). She adds: "For the American audience this flashback became both a reminder of scenes they had witnessed in newsreels and through newspapers, the collective memory of history now inscribed through visual and textual sources, and a supplement to that memory" (127).

18 Of their love story, and desperate at least to preserve its purity and beauty in memory, Ilsa says: "I don't know the finish yet. We knew very little about each other when we were in love in Paris. If we leave it that way then we will remember those things and not Casablanca, not last night."

19 Eco astutely recognizes the leitmotif of sacrifice in the film: "The idea of sacrifice pervades the whole story, Ilsa's sacrifice in Paris when she abandons the man she loves to return to the wounded hero, the Bulgarian bride's sacrifice when she is prepared to give herself to help her husband, Victor's sacrifice when he is prepared to see Ilsa with Rick to guarantee her safety" (207). And then there is the last, the "Supreme Sacrifice" (208) by Rick at the film's conclusion.

20 See Benjamin *Selected Writings* I:297–361. See in particular 330–33.

21 There is a third key moment of song in this melodrama: when Victor Laszlo conducts the café orchestra in a rousing impromptu version of "La Marseillaise," a moment of patriotic fervour and propaganda in a scene that is both "one of the most powerful and memorable in World War Two films (Koppes and Black 289) and "a scene no one but a team of Hollywood script writers could have conceived" (Higham and Greenberg 86).

22 Rick tells Ilsa, interestingly, almost reversing her earlier utterance (n19): "We'll always have Paris. We didn't have, we lost it until you came to Casablanca. We got it back last night" (Curtiz).

13

The Cinema of Simulation: Hyper-Histories and (Un)Popular Memory in *The Good German* (2006) and *Inglourious Basterds* (2009)

Stefan Sereda

Rather than offering objective reflections of history, Hollywood films that represent past eras and historical occurrences always do so through a process of mediation and subjective interpretation.[1] According to the philosophers Jean Baudrillard and Fredric Jameson, the (re)production of historical images in this context is a dilemma symptomatic of advanced capitalist postmodernity. For Baudrillard, nostalgic films, and films that take actual historical events as their subject matter, from the 1970s "Hollywood Renaissance" director's cinema—including *The Last Picture Show* (Bogdanovich, 1971), *Chinatown* (Polanski, 1974), *Barry Lyndon* (Kubrick, 1975), *All the President's Men* (Pakula, 1976), and *Apocalypse Now* (Coppola, 1979)—commodify history as a mythological "retro scenario" detached from any historical reference points or political relevance to the present (43–46). Despite these films' period-specific *mise en scène*, Baudrillard finds no more relation to a "historical real" in them than an "*invocation* of resemblance," which he labels "the flagrant proof of the disappearance of objects in their very representation: *hyperreal*" (45).[2] Jameson concurs with Baudrillard's reading of these films' retreat from contemporary politics, arguing that nostalgia films instead "restructure the whole issue of pastiche and project it onto a collective and social level" (*Postmodernism* 19). For Jameson, this is true of films about the past in which narrative determines audiovisual style, such as *American Graffiti* (Lucas, 1973), as well as in films such as *Star Wars* (Lucas, 1977) and *Body Heat* (Kasdan, 1981), which are *metonymically* nostalgic in their form.³ *Body Heat* in particular—a film noir with a contemporary setting as well as formal-stylistic markers that associate it with the genre's 1940s origins—prompts Jameson to observe that it is

> exceedingly symptomatic to find the very style of nostalgia films invading and colonizing even those movies today which have contemporary settings: as though, for some reason, we were unable today to focus our own present, as though we have become incapable of achieving aesthetic representations of our own current experience. But if that is so, then it is a terrible indictment of consumer capitalism itself—or, at the very least, an alarming and pathological symptom of a society that has become incapable of dealing with time and history. ("Postmodernism" 117)

If one agrees, with either Jameson or Baudrillard, that filmic nostalgia typically occurs at the expense of historical understanding, aesthetic innovation, and a more politically motivated cinema, then Hollywood films that deign to represent history are faced with challenges to their validity and use value.

An increasing number of Hollywood films that originate as commodities nevertheless take up these postmodern challenges. In reference to historical films from the 1970s, Baudrillard insisted that "a whole generation of films is emerging that will be to those one knew what the android is to man: marvellous artefacts, without weakness, pleasing simulacra that lack only the imaginary, and the hallucination inherent to cinema" (45). Film scholar Robert Burgoyne articulates the future of history on film in more positive terms, anticipating "a whole new genre of visual history, or history as vision [...] with its own rules, its own regimes of credibility, and its own sort of truth" (234). A genre of films that, over fidelity to any historical record, intentionally favours an understanding of history as always-already mediated and therefore malleable, has already emerged as a new American film form. The films in this *cinema of simulation* fashion novel aesthetic arrangements through which to engage with history for contemporary ethico-political purposes. The cinema of simulation, therefore, is a late capitalist development in film-historical representation that Baudrillard and Jameson failed to predict.

The cinema of simulation is the latest filmic permutation of *la mode retro*, or the style and language of nostalgia. A long tradition of films set in the past—including biopics, historical epics, traditional westerns, and period piece costume dramas—as well as films that are nostalgic in their form, contributed to the development of this vernacular throughout the twentieth century. These earlier films, genres, and styles stand as necessary forebears to the cinema of simulation. This most recent phase in the representation of history on film has emerged out of late capitalism as a response to postmodernism, as an "attempt to think the present historically in an age that has forgotten how to think historically in the first place" (Jameson *Postmodernism* ix). As such, the cinema of simulation requires the postmodern nostalgia found in those films that Baudrillard and Jameson describe as necessary points of departure from which to devise a new historical mode. The term "cinema of simulation" is best applied to films that self-consciously provoke intersections among fiction, history, and media, particularly the cinema. These films understand history as being reified by media representations, recognizing, as Baudrillard did, how the image replaces the real thing it once signified, and treating history as a "malleable fiction" (Kilbourn 46). Unlike most period pieces and early nostalgia films, most entries in the cinema of simulation do not claim to represent historical truth, but instead convolute official narratives by imparting overt fictionalizations of historical persons and events that have already been mythologized by the media. Therefore, these films vacillate between a fidelity to the mediated historical record and a paradoxical self-conscious departure from official historical narratives. Films that represent history according to how it has been mediated through popular memory via intertexuality often do so with a motivated, contemporary use value in mind. Still, these revisionary engagements with history do not always run counter to contemporary American political or historical discourses.

The cinema of simulation surfaced after the 1970s, becoming especially prevalent in the first decade of the twenty-first century. Films produced in this mode structure their aesthetics through an accelerated form of pastiche that borrows from a time period's cultural artifacts to represent the era. The Hollywood Renaissance nostalgia films *American Graffiti* and *Chinatown* exerted an especially strong influence on the cinema of simulation in this aesthetic regard. The cinema of simulation also adapts history as a series of objects that are already recorded, represented, and remembered to manipulate and mythologize the past in a way that has use value for the contemporary moment. Woody Allen's mockumentary, *Zelig* (1983), pioneered this tactic, although *JFK* (Stone, 1991) and *Forrest Gump* (Zemeckis, 1994) revolutionized its deployment in the 1990s. While constituting a popular media form, the cinema of simulation speaks to a history that is indebted to popular media artifacts. Moreover, films in the cinema of simulation present history as a re-presentation, which the media then commodify for consumption, thereby acknowledging the collapse of history as a metanarrative capable of offering an objective account of the past. Therefore, the cinema of simulation understands history not as epistemological truth, but as the discursive construction, "history." This "historical" (or, in some cases, anti-historical) sensibility is evident in a host of recent films that simulate the past through intentionally hyperreal representations, including Todd Haynes's *Far from Heaven* (2002) and *I'm Not There* (2007) and Steven Soderbergh's *Che* (2008).

The cinema of simulation's mechanics are displayed in two films from the last decade that revisit the Second World War, namely, Soderbergh's *The Good German* (2006) and Quentin Tarantino's *Inglourious Basterds* (2009). Both films exhibit cinematic simulation as a style through intertextual referencing that treats mediated historical records and fictions as artifacts in their own right, and, in their practicality, as valid fragments of the respective histories that the films revise. Furthermore, Soderbergh deliberately poaches documentary archival footage, which he inserts into *The Good German*'s diegesis as a tactic that reflects what Jameson and Baudrillard would describe as the disappearance of the real into the hyperreal in late-capitalist society.[4] The blending of documentary footage with "historical" re-creations in the cinema of simulation confuses the boundaries between representation and truth, simulation and document, hyperreal and real. In assuming history's hyperreal mediation and recontextualizing its commodified images for ideological purposes, these films recognize how cinema and memory have become related to each other in the postmodern. The cinema of simulation treats cinema as "memory, or 'meta-archive'" and memory as "(cinematic) intertextuality, in which cinema's own past (and ever-present present) constitutes an archive potentially accessible within or through any film, but which tends to operate in specific, motivated instances of intertextual appropriation and recontextualization" (Kilbourn 45). In other words, the cinema of simulation depends on popular media forms to supply prosthetic memories, or personal memories that "derive from engaged and experientially-oriented encounters with the mass media's various technologies of memory" (Landsberg "Prosthetic Memory" 148–49) for redeployment in the films. This approach to history marks the cinema of simulation as a post-prosthetic memory form that communicates an awareness of history as being a discursive construction and cinema as being capable of manipulating historical meaning. In other words, films in the cinema of simulation present *hyper-histories* that combine historical records with dramatizations, fabrications, and media artifacts from and about the periods being depicted, as well as other media artifacts that contribute to the films' overall aesthetics. The hyper-historical representations offered throughout the cinema of simulation surpass Baudrillard and Jameson's expectations for the nostalgia mode. Since films aligned with the cinema of simulation assume history's malleability as they redirect prosthetic memories to establish political commentary with relevance to the contemporary moment, they present a solution to the postmodern inability to confront the present found in earlier attempts to depict history on film. The cinema of simulation can therefore be interpreted as being postpostmodern in its hyper-historical manoeuvrings.

When examined in relation to each other, *Inglourious Basterds* and *The Good German* show how films in the cinema of simulation can generate hyper-histories to forward radically divergent political agendas. Whereas *Inglourious Basterds* depicts the American military as the primary force of international justice during the Second World War, *The Good German* attempts to expose the linkages between America's postwar empire and the spectre of Nazism. Both films communicate ideological sentiments that resonate with political currents in the present-day United States. Yet Soderbergh's film reconstructs a historical discourse to counter the popular narrative of the Second World War and recall how Americans turned its atrocities to their benefit. Tarantino's film, by contrast, offers a vengeful fantasy retelling of events so attuned to American popular memory of the war that it participates in the same sort of historical forgetting that Soderbergh's film so adamantly opposes. Taken together, these films display how the cinema of simulation reconstitutes history to produce narratives that can challenge or reinforce hegemonic political discourses in the contemporary moment.

From Allusion to Simulation: *La Mode Retro*'s Evolution in American Film

If prosthetic memories culled from various popular media forms shape the hyper-historical films that make up the cinema of simulation, then this simulation aesthetic necessarily depends on historical allusion through intertextuality. The cinema of simulation inherits this tactic for representing history from the Hollywood Renaissance nostalgia film cycle. Jameson distinguishes nostalgia films from earlier historical films according to their stylistic poaching, arguing that the nostalgia film "was never a matter of some old-fashioned 'representation' of historical content, but instead approached the 'past' through stylistic connotation, conveying 'pastness' by the glossy qualities of the image, and '1930s-ness' or '1950s-ness' by the attributes of fashion" (*Postmodernism* 19). Of course, costume dramas have always relied on objects in the *mise en scène* to evoke earlier historical periods. Hollywood Renaissance nostalgia films expanded on the historical film's representational strategies by developing new formal techniques for summoning an impression of the past. Sometimes, these techniques recalled earlier film styles; for example, the black-and-white cinematography employed in *The Last Picture Show* to depict a 1950s Texas dust bowl serves a nostalgic function in that it resurrects an outmoded visual style. *Butch Cassidy and the Sundance Kid* (Hill, 1969) opens with a similar aesthetic deployment in the form of a silent film short, which replicates a filmmaking style that is specific to the early twentieth century in which the film's action is set. This film also applies intermediality to generate a sense of nostalgia in a sepia-toned photomontage sequence.[5] Whereas *Butch Cassidy and the Sundance Kid* demonstrates how media technologies can cultivate an impression of "pastness," *American Graffiti* shows how intertextuality and cultural appropriation can metonymically characterize an era. A coming-of-age film whose tag line asks, "Where were you in '62?", *American Graffiti* evokes the early 1960s through era-specific objects in the *mise en scène*, especially an assortment of classic cars, as well as a soundtrack comprised of popular hits from the 1950s and early 1960s. This soundtrack, which plays persistently throughout the film, is instrumental in producing the film's sense of nostalgia through intermediality. The songs featured in *American Graffiti* provide the film with memories of 1962 through its pop culture artifacts. The formal strategies found in these films have influenced the cinema of simulation's deployment of *la mode retro* as it is informed by intertextuality and intermediality.

In general, the nostalgia mode provides a necessary framework for the cinema of simulation, but *Chinatown* stands apart from the other entries in the 1970s nostalgia film cycle as a foundational film for the aesthetic of cinematic simulation. This neo-noir set in 1930s Los Angeles approximates its historical setting through pastiches of classical film noir, thereby displaying a formal strategy Paul Grainge terms "genre memory" (9). As such, *Chinatown* is emblematic of how the Hollywood Renaissance constitutes what Noël Carroll calls a "cinema of allusion," with the era's films sharing "a mixed lot of practices including quotations, the memorialisation of past genres, homages, and the recreation of 'classic' scenes, shots, plot motifs, lines of dialogue, themes, gestures, and so forth from film history" (56). Yet *Chinatown* adds a nostalgic dimension to the cinematic allusions found in Hollywood Renaissance films through its narrative as well as its pointed references to classical film noir. *Chinatown*'s use of filmic genre memory to approach its representation of an earlier period anticipates the style of the most historically focused films in the cinema of simulation. Both *Inglourious Basterds* and *The Good German* exemplify how this simulation aesthetic is put to use in the twenty-first century. The conflation of history with filmic genre memory in the cinema of simulation generates an intentionally reflexive hyperreal approach to the past that corresponds to Baudrillard's anxieties regarding the late capitalist hyperreal. Still, in *Chinatown*, history is not merely a retro scenario. Roman Polanski and Robert Towne's script about corrupt business dealings in Depression-era Los Angeles bears allegorical relevance to the Watergate Scandal, which corresponded historically to the film's production and preceded the film's 1974 release date by one year. This allegory is made apparent through water's connotative function as the narrative's site of misconduct. The historically oriented films within the cinema of simulation attempt formal-thematic approaches to the contemporary similar to the model provided by *Chinatown*'s compression of history, media, and political critique.

Several films from beyond the Hollywood Renaissance have also contributed to the simulation aesthetic found in contemporary films. Hollywood Renaissance films applied *la mode retro* in earnest to provide a sense of historical accuracy (*Butch Cassidy and the Sundance Kid*), to express a yearning for bygone eras (*The Last Picture Show*), to instill in the viewer a feeling of generational belonging (*American Graffiti*), and to supply allegorical meaning (*Chinatown*). By contrast, Woody Allen's mockumentary, *Zelig*, in its intertextual incorporation of documentary footage, which the film manipulates for the purposes of farce and ethico-political critique, is integral to the simulation aesthetic's development. This strategy infuses Allen's fictional narrative with prosthetic memories from the cinematic meta-archive. *Zelig* documents the life of the fictional Leonard Zelig (Woody Allen), a 1920s and 1930s personage who compulsively assimilates with those around him, even taking on their physical characteristics as a psychosomatic symptom of his illness. As a complement to Zelig's identity—which earns him the nickname "the Chameleon"—the film camouflages its original material amid the found footage. Allen deliberately casts aside historical accuracy in *Zelig* and instead relates a fabricated story by placing voice-over narration on top of the stock footage he employs. Moreover, Allen and cinematographer Gordon Willis simulate the film style of the period being depicted by using era-specific lighting, lenses, and cameras and then scratching the negative so that *Zelig*'s original footage matches its found footage.[6] In some scenes, Allen and co-star Mia Farrow are superimposed on the documentary footage through blue screen technology.[7] For example, one scene that relies on blue screen technology finds Zelig attending a party at Hearst Castle and hobnobbing with celebrities from the 1920s, including Clara Bow and a young Jimmy Cagney. The resulting film is an aesthetically seamless portrait of the era; its deliberately fictional material offers an intentional approximation of history that is not meant to convince the viewer of its truth, only of cinema's ability to mediate, manipulate, and manufacture historical fact. In this respect, *Zelig* parodies other documentaries that contribute to the proliferation of what Landsberg calls prosthetic memory.

Yet *Zelig* also directs its stock footage in such a way that the film takes advantage of the prosthetic memories offered therein. According to Landsberg, prosthetic memories can "bridge the temporal chasms that separate individuals from the meaningful and potentially interpellative events of the past" (148). Thus, prosthetic memories have a contemporary use value in their ability to connect individuals to history, especially since they can mark trauma, recall political struggles, and generate empathy between disparate social groupings over time (148–49). Moreover, Landsberg's model, in its recognition of capitalism as a positive force in the dissemination of prosthetic memories (149), contradicts Jameson's and Baudrillard's arguments that regard late capitalism as a force that not only obscures memory but also confounds any clear division between memory and history in the contemporary moment. Although *Zelig* is not a valid historical document, its hyperreal qualities relate the schizophrenic zeitgeist of American capitalism during the Roaring Twenties. The film also calls attention to the historical traumas of racial and ethnic oppression. At one point, the narration jokes that Zelig, who is "a Jew that can turn himself into a Negro and an Indian," is a triple-threat to the Ku Klux Klan. On a more serious note, Zelig recalls through hypnosis the anti-Semitism that contributed to his need to feel safe through conformism, so it is both poignant and ironic that his final transformation results in his becoming a Nazi. Documentary images of Nazi party rallies accompany this climactic moment in the film. *Zelig*'s deployment of *la mode retro* does not offer mere escapist nostalgia, but a historically informed contemporary message regarding the traumatic social dangers of conformity. As such, the film reminds the viewer of historical traumas, while demonstrating the need for empathy among different social factions; for Landsberg, these are the purposes of media commodities that trade in prosthetic memory.

Zelig anticipates the twenty-first-century films in the cinema of simulation, as Allen self-consciously dilutes the mediated historical artifacts he adapts into a hyperreal myth with use value in the contemporary moment. The film's confounding of the boundary between fiction and documentary predates by several years the similar strategies employed in subsequent, more popular period pieces that attempt hyperreal aesthetics, such as *JFK* and *Forrest Gump*. While *JFK* is more blatantly political than *Zelig*, its covert blending of archival and original footage results in a more manipulative aesthetic than the mockumentary style found in Allen's film. *Forrest Gump*, with its digitally enhanced scenes that show Tom Hanks interacting with famous deceased personalities in earlier decades, exemplifies for Burgoyne how cinema becomes "the emblematic expression, not of the real, but rather of the hyperreal" (220). Although Tom Hanks's insertion into archival footage from the 1960s and 1970s violates the historical record as much as Allen's appearance at Hearst Castle, *Zelig*'s parodic, mockumentary elements can be viewed as less hyperreal than *Forrest Gump* and *JFK*. According to Burgoyne, the latter films demonstrate how the cinema, "with its increasing use of morphing techniques and computer generated visual environments [...] would seem to be a medium that now refuses history in the traditional sense of origins, authenticity, and documentation" (223). Burgoyne's assessment is in keeping with Baudrillard's criticism that Hollywood Renaissance nostalgia films resemble the past without necessarily corresponding to any historical real.

Despite cinema's rejection of an authentic, documented history, Burgoyne observes that

> film in the present day appears to have strengthened its cultural claims on the past. The cinematic rewriting of history has, in the present cultural moment, accrued an extraordinary degree of social power and influence. Film appears to have acquired, more than ever, the mantle of meaningfulness and authenticity with relation to the past—not necessarily of accuracy or fidelity to the record, but of meaningfulness, understood in terms of emotional and affective truth. (223)

This dynamic, wherein film can influence people's interpretations of history without being faithful to the historical record, troubled Baudrillard, yet Burgoyne characterizes this paradigm shift toward hyperreal history on film as liberating. For Burgoyne, this new cinematic form of visual history, presented in films such as *Zelig*, *JFK*, and *Forrest Gump*, "challenges the sacrosanct nature of the document" by using documentary images from the cultural "image bank" to assist in "storytelling that freely mixes fictional, factual, and speculative discourses" (234). Accordingly, Burgoyne anticipates that this new cinematic genre of visual history could mean that "documentary images may no longer signify the facticity of past events, per se, but rather convey the sense that they are a representation of the past, a representation that may be employed for the purpose of metaphor, irony, analogy or argument, and that may be used in such a way that a certain poetic truth may emerge in the telling" (234).

The cinema of simulation embraces the strategic intersection of archival and original footage found in *Zelig*, *JFK*, and *Forrest Gump* and the epistemological confusion of truth and fiction produced through this approach to filmmaking. Yet, ironically, films in the cinema of simulation that are unfaithful to the historical record often display an high level of fidelity to the manner in which history has been recorded.

Hyper-History, Popular Memory, and Propaganda

The approximation of film styles through formal pastiche—often in combination with archival poaching and the use of era-specific filmmaking technology as well as digital imaging—is a necessary strategy of the cinema of simulation.[8] Film releases in this mode have been increasingly common in the twenty-first century. The hyperreal biopics *I'm Not There*, *Che*, and *Milk* (Van Sant, 2008) employ all of the above-mentioned techniques save for digital imaging, which is found only in Haynes's film. In *Far from Heaven* (2002), Haynes also demonstrates how a director's oeuvre can be recalled through a focused form of genre memory, that film represents the 1950s through an extended pastiche of Douglas Sirk's melodramas from the period.[9] Other films aim to evoke the past through stylistic connotation by extending *la mode retro* to their branding and marketing. For example, both *The Good German* and *Zodiac* (Fincher, 2007) bear outdated Warner Brothers logos hailing from the eras their narratives represent. There has also been a recent upsurge in promotional posters that employ pastiche to call to mind film marketing from earlier decades. Again, *The Good German*'s poster, which is modelled on a poster for *Casablanca* (Curtiz, 1942), partakes of this retro marketing trend to give the film a mythic and nostalgic resonance.[10] Similarly, *Grindhouse* (2007), which includes a double bill of the feature films *Planet Terror* (Rodriguez) and *Death Proof* (Tarantino) as well as a series of theatrical trailers, advertisements, and announcements, extends its simulation aesthetic beyond filmic pastiche to a simulation of the cinematic experience of 1970s grindhouse theatres.[11] All of these films exemplify Baudrillard's argument that "the cinema is fascinated by itself as a lost object as much as it (and we) are fascinated by the real as a lost referent" (47). Yet filmmakers also engage in simulations of styles that are very much alive, as evidenced in the talking-heads documentary sequence that opens *The Incredibles* (Bird, 2004), as well as in *Diary of the Dead* (Romero, 2007) and *Cloverfield* (Reeves, 2008), which fashion themselves as faux-cinéma-vérité digital home videos. In this way, the cinema of simulation enters into exchanges with film history at the levels of production and marketing, with the films made in this style intentionally presenting themselves as, rather than merely alluding to, a pre-existing type of film.

A paradigmatic example of how the cinema of simulation can flagrantly rewrite history to appeal to popular taste occurs in *Inglourious Basterds*. The film's tag line and first chapter title, "Once upon a time in Nazi occupied France [...]" heralds the film as a mythical fairy tale rather than a historical document. The narrative follows the titular characters—a "bushwhackin' guerrilla army" of eight Jewish American soldiers led by Lieutenant Aldo Raine, a Kentuckian with "a little Injun" in his blood—as they stage an "Apache resistance" against the Nazis in advance of D-Day. In a parallel narrative, Shosanna Dreyfus (Mélanie Laurent), witnesses her family's execution at the hands of a team of Nazis led by "Jew hunter" Colonel Hans Landa (Christoph Waltz). Posing as a French citizen, Shosanna plots to assassinate high-ranking party officials, including Hitler, by sabotaging a screening of Goebbels's latest propaganda film in the cinema she operates. Shosanna also produces a vengeful film of her own to play for her audience as she carries out her revenge through arson. The Basterds also plan to assassinate the officials by sneaking into the theatre and setting off a bomb; but Landa blows their cover and sneaks Raine and one of his men off to a meeting place. There, Landa and Raine make a deal that will ensure the bomb detonates when Hitler, Goebbels, Göring, and Bormann are all present, effectively ending the war, in exchange for Landa's freedom in America after the war ends. The two Basterds remaining at the scene shoot Hitler into a pulp, Shosanna's arson attempt succeeds, and the bomb explodes, killing everyone left in the cinema. In the film's coda, Raine carves a swastika into Landa's forehead before they cross the American lines together, proclaiming into the camera, which has taken on Landa's point of view, "this just might be my masterpiece."

Within the film's hyper-historical fabrication of the Second World War is a meditation on the role the media play in war, especially in relation to the dissemination of propaganda. From the opening scene, Tarantino establishes that propaganda fuels conflicts, with Landa self-consciously explaining to a French citizen who is suspected of harbouring Jews how Nazi propaganda relates Jews to rodents. The film's climactic event turns the cinema into a theatre of war, with Shosanna replacing the final reel of Goebbels's propagandist war film, "Nation's Pride," with her own film as a form of counterpropaganda meant to convince the Nazis, before they die, that they have committed atrocities. In a fashion typical of Tarantino's films, the plot to assassinate the Nazis in Shosanna's cinema is a self-reflexive fantasy meant to appeal to cine-literate audiences. In one narrative thread, the cine-literate viewer is represented onscreen through Lieutenant Archie Hicox (Michael Fassbender), a British soldier and film scholar. Hicox's careful film criticism, in which he relates Goebbels to David O. Selznick, sways the British High Command to send him on a mission to infiltrate the screening with Bridget von Hammersmark (Diane Kruger), a sexy German film actress who secretly operates as an underground resistance fighter. Although neither character lives to witness the screening, Hicox's narrative presents a fantasy for film buffs. Yet this fantasy wherein the film scholar can interact with movie stars and significantly affect the outcome of an important film's reception parallels Tarantino's fanciful engagement with history, wherein he can have American Jews kill Hitler in the cinema environment. Similar to Shosanna's burning her cinema with highly flammable nitrate film, *Inglourious Basterds*, then, is a hyper-historical work of political propaganda that enacts its vengeance upon Nazism through popular memory.

At face value, Tarantino's film is a radical rewriting of the Second World War as a historical narrative, with the Americans killing Hitler and thus ending the war, rather than the Russians, who reached Berlin first, shortly after Hitler's suicide. Yet *Inglourious Basterds* coheres with American anti-German Second World War–era propaganda, American popular memory of the war, and the nation's contemporary foreign policy. Tarantino's film reiterates popular American wartime fantasies, such as the cover of the first issue of Marvel's *Captain America* comic book, which shows the hero punching Hitler in the face. As an exercise in the production of post-prosthetic memory, the film approaches history via references to preceding films that recall the Second World War, including *The Great Escape* (Sturges, 1963) and *The Dirty Dozen* (Aldrich, 1967), and this aligns the film with Hollywood's predominant narrative of American heroism in the Second World War.[12] The film's climax, which erases the Eastern Front from its interpretation of the war, is also consistent with American popular memory of events. Russian Studies scholar Stephen F. Cohen argues that the American popular narrative of the war forwarded by films such as *Saving Private Ryan* (Spielberg, 1998), as well as other commercial projects, has "essentially deleted the Soviet War on the Eastern front," even though it was in that theatre that Soviet forces destroyed 80 percent of the German army.[13] Cohen maintains that America's popular memory of the war presents a version of history that shows the German army's defeat beginning with the landing of American forces in Normandy in June 1944.[14] The paramount concern of the film's highly reflexive final scene is to preserve the memory of Nazi atrocities, and in the process, Tarantino's film forgets the cooperation between the Allies and the Soviets, conveying instead a revenge narrative with American and Jewish heroes. Given the film's compression of history through its merging of the Second World War's historical record with the popular memory of the war as communicated in American media, the ethical and militaristic alliance between Americans and Jews, whether American or European-born, resonates in the contemporary international political climate as well. By offering a narrative wherein Americans commit overseas violence out of sympathy for their Jewish allies, Tarantino's film does not run counter to America's current alliance with Israel, only to the actual history of the Second World War, which America entered out of military and economic interests beyond any ethical motivations.

If *Inglourious Basterds* fashions a popular version of history, Soderbergh's *The Good German* is concerned with rewriting American popular memory of the war to expose historical truths. Tarantino's film offers a hyper-history by forgetting and disregarding the historical record of the Second World War as much as it commits the past to memory. By contrast, the thrust of *The Good German* is remembering the aftermath of the Second World War in minute detail to uncover the forgotten truth of how America privileged military, economic, and political gain over any ethical imperatives for making war with Germany. Set in Berlin against the historical backdrop of the May 1945 Potsdam Conference, this neo-noir follows American war correspondent Jake Geismar (George Clooney) as he investigates the death of his driver, Tully (Tobey Maguire). Meanwhile, Jake tries to reconnect with his ex-lover, Lena Brandt (Cate Blanchett), a German Jew who, at the beginning of the film, is Tully's mistress. While examining Tully's death, Jake discovers that both the Russian and American authorities are searching for Lena's former husband, Emil Brandt (Christian Oliver), whom she claims is dead. Jake decides he was assigned Tully as a driver so that he could find Lena and lead the Americans to Emil. Jake also discovers that Emil worked as secretary to Franz Bettman during the war, developing V-2 rockets in Camp Dora, where 30,000 slave labourers died, and that Emil's documents are the only proof of the atrocities committed there. Lena explains to Jake that she was able to survive the war as Emil's wife since this project required that Emil be designated SS like the other Germans involved in Camp Dora's operation. Driven by a desire to leave Berlin with Lena, on whom the American prosecutors have a file, Jake uncovers a conspiracy to bring the top Nazi scientists, including Bettman, off to America, where they will lend their skills to the U.S. government. Both Jake and the American intelligence authorities find out that Lena has been hiding Emil, who wants to expose the horrors of Camp Dora. After a German agent working for the Americans murders Emil and shoots Lena, she is taken to a hospital in the American zone and asked to turn over Emil's documents, thus eliminating any evidence of Bettman's involvement in the atrocities at Camp Dora. Jake promises Congressman Breimer (Jack Thompson) the papers, in exchange for Breimer's assurance that Lena will be allowed to leave Germany with Jake. Before boarding the plane, Jake confronts Lena about the American intelligence file on her and asks her how she managed to avoid the Holocaust in the years before her husband was given an SS ranking. Lena tells Jake that she tracked down twelve Jews for the Gestapo in order to secure her own immunity. Jake, stunned by this information, lets Lena board the plane without him.

It is stylistically fitting that *The Good German* returns to this era through a complex and focused simulation aesthetic that combines newsreel footage with an immaculate replication of Hollywood filmmaking during the war, save for its use of green screen technology and post-classical violations of the long-gone Hollywood Production Code. The film relies on black-and-white cinematography, wipes and other outmoded editing transitions, rear projection in the *mise en scène*, and musical cues featuring instruments commonly used in classical Hollywood but out of fashion in contemporary cinema, such as harps. Soderbergh even extended the practice of simulation beyond the frame by emulating classical Hollywood conditions of production: the film was shot on studio backlots and around Los Angeles, only incandescent lights and boom mikes were used on set, and the actors were directed to perform as though trained for the theatre (Kehr n.p.). The cinematography's pre-widescreen 1.66:1 aspect ratio and 32 millimetre wide-angle lenses were also period specific (Kehr n.p.). These techniques displayed a fidelity to Hollywood's historical methods of representation and thereby generated a self-reflexively hyperreal aesthetic.

The governing intertext that ties Soderbergh's film to Second World War history as it has been reified by the American media is *Casablanca*.[15] Beyond the poster, the film's narrative revolves around Jake's goal of securing exit papers for Lena's safe passage out of Berlin, just as in Curtiz's film Rick (Humphrey Bogart) chooses to help Ilsa (Ingrid Bergman) and her husband, Laszlo (Paul Henreid) escape Casablanca by hiding exit papers for them. In each film, a love triangle is formed by the male protagonist, his love interest, and the woman's husband, whom the protagonist believes is dead when the film opens. Each film ends with the protagonist sending the woman he loves off on a plane without him, with *The Good German*'s *mise en scène* replicating in detail the iconography of *Casablanca*'s final scene. Unlike *Casablanca* and *Inglourious Basterds*, *The Good German* is not a film about American heroism, military or otherwise, during the Second World War. Jake is appalled that Lena saved herself by rounding up Jews for the Gestapo, even while for selfish reasons he aids the U.S. government in burying the atrocities committed at Camp Dora. Tully, on the other hand, *enjoys* profiting from the war, as he makes clear in the following voice-over:

> You can say whatever you want about the war, certainly I would never have wished for all those millions of people to die, *but* the war was the best thing that ever happened to me, because when you have money there for the first time in your life you *understand* it, what money does for you. Where before all you understood was not having it, money allows you to be who you truly are.

Tully's speech offers a metaphor for all the Americans in the film, who behave arrogantly throughout as they take advantage of the trauma that devastated Europe and then promptly forget about it. After Lena boards her plane, the only "beautiful friendship" left to be forged is between the U.S. government and the Nazis it has adopted. Thus, *The Good German* is a disillusioned reworking of *Casablanca*'s altruistically patriotic narrative of American involvement in the Second World War.

In addition to *The Good German*'s intersections with Second World War cinema, the film also approximates history and, in doing so, addresses how historical narratives are constructed through representation. Bettman is the film's stand-in for Werner von Braun, the real-life SS scientist who designed the V-2 rocket before developing them through slave labour, and who later worked for both NASA and the American military. Conversely, the film's mention of Operation Overcast is a direct reference to the American project to bring German scientists into the United States, which later became known as Operation Paperclip. As with the other films in the cinema of simulation with which Soderbergh is associated, including his Che Guevera biopic, *Che*, and the Todd Haynes–directed, Soderbergh–executive produced *I'm Not There*, *The Good German* confuses fact with fiction. The film mingles the aforementioned historical truths with imaginary scenarios, particularly by blending documentary footage with staged scenes. In place of establishing shots, Soderbergh inserts newsreel footage from postwar Berlin, including shots taken at the Potsdam Conference. In some scenes, Soderbergh also uses the archival material as rear projection or green screen backdrops against which the actors are placed. Yet this combination of documentary and staged footage is not entirely seamless, as viewers should be able to tell that it is impossible for contemporary Hollywood stars to exist in the same space as people alive in 1945 Berlin. The effect alienates the viewer from the diegesis, reminding the audience that both the narrative and the newsreel footage are cinematically constructed in their own relative ways. Thus, the film's historical approximations expose how memory is produced through its mediation.

One of the film's most significant motives is to contrast the official interpretation of history with the realities filtered out of this hegemonic narrative. It is also telling that the film applies its historical scrutiny to the events surrounding August 1945, which included the Potsdam Conference, Operation Overcast, and the destruction of Hiroshima. By revisiting this period, the film returns to the origins of a New World economic and political order, and the roots of postmodernity, asking audiences in the tag line, "If war is hell, what comes after?" As the American Colonel Muller (Beau Bridges) tells Jake, the Potsdam Conference is not about "who gets Poland," but "the future [...] what do the next hundred years look like?" *The Good German* avoids treating history as a retro scenario (i.e., by exploring how Nazism and the Holocaust haunt the decades that have passed since the war), offering instead a reflection on the political and economic origins of late capitalism. Implicitly articulating the film's connection between the Nazi regime and the emergence of an American postwar consumer culture that has given rise to postmodernity, Muller asks Jake, "In a perfect world, doesn't a guy like Bettman end up building rockets for our side [while living in a] split level with a Ford in the garage, kids in the backyard playing in the sprinklers?" Jake's retort—"It isn't a perfect world, is it?"—calls into question the postwar American dream that links consumerism to domestic bliss and that believes capitalism to be globally benevolent. Soderbergh generates an ironic commentary on America's aims during the war by juxtaposing Jake's discovery of Lena's file and Operation Overcast with President Truman's radio-broadcast Potsdam speech, during which he told the American people,

> let's not forget that we are fighting for peace and for the welfare of mankind. There is not one piece of territory or one thing of a monetary nature that we want out of this war. We want peace and prosperity for the world as a whole. If we can put this tremendous machine of ours, which has made this victory possible, to work for peace, we can look forward to the greatest days in the history of mankind.

Of course, the collusion of America's military-industrial complex with its government, media, and citizens—this "tremendous machine"—was not put to work for peace in the latter half of the century, and the Americans *did* want to profit from the war, as metonymized in the film by Operation Overcast. Truman's official historical discourse is at odds with the film's positioning of America as indebted to Nazi war crimes. Here, at the Potsdam Conference, with global reconstruction commencing, late capitalism takes shape as a global system of order through America's wilful complicity in forgetting some of the trauma caused by European fascism. Suffering from survivor's guilt, Lena describes to Jake how the spectres of Nazism and the Holocaust will weigh on the world that comes after, when she tells him enigmatically, "you can never get out of Berlin." Lena wants to forget the things she did to survive the war, but an American official reminds her that "forgetting is a two-way street." *The Good German* endeavours to call attention to how this process of forgetting shapes historical narratives and popular discourses.

Ironically, *Inglourious Basterds* is more black-and-white than *The Good German*. While *The Good German* focuses on remembering how America overlooks its covenants with forces labelled as "evil" in its official history, *Inglourious Basterds* deigns to reinforce the popular Manichean discourse that separates American democracy from Nazism. Although it is true that Lt. Raine's Basterds carry out horrors of war on the Nazis, their actions are positioned in the film as the execution of Hammurabian justice. Raine articulates this justification in his introductory scene, during a speech to the Basterds:

> We will be cruel to the Germans, and through our cruelty they will know who we are. And they will find the evidence of our cruelty in the disembowelled, dismembered, and disfigured bodies of their brothers we leave behind us. And the German won't be able to help themselves but to imagine the cruelty their brothers endured at our hands, and our boot heels, and the edge of our knives. And the German will be sickened by us, and the German will talk about us, and the German will fear us. And when the German closes their eyes at night and they're tortured by their subconscious for the evil they have done, it will be with thoughts of us they are tortured with.

Raine's speech frames the Basterds' subsequent actions with the intention of absolving Americans for distributing justice in the face of historical evil, not to emphasize or expose American participation in war crimes. Meanwhile, Tarantino's film forgets the tenuous alliance forged between the United States and the Soviet Union, erasing this grey area from an otherwise black-and-white history of the Cold War, to represent Americans as more heroic. Soderbergh's film foregrounds this exchange by using the Potsdam Conference as a backdrop. By way of a comparable metaphor—a Nazi smuggled into America as a result of a plea bargain that is extremely profitable for the United States—the films deliver their contrasting historical perspectives. Both films assume that historical truth is always malleable in its mediation and demonstrate an acute awareness of cinema's power to render history into myth. Tarantino's rewriting of history functions in the same fashion as the "masterpiece" Raine inscribes on Landa's forehead, preserving a collective memory that vows never to forget how Americans combated evil in the Second World War. The narrative's hypothetical deal between Landa and the U.S. government is easy enough to forgive—and forget—because it did not take place in reality and is presented as a reasonable agreement to end the war in the film. For all of *Inglourious Basterds'* good Germans, vengeful French Jews, and Apache-inspired scalp-hunting American Jews paradigmatic of Tarantino's examinations of the connections between ethnicity, nationality, and violence, the film simplifies the Second World War as a historical conflict between good and evil. Soderbergh's film, which proved unpopular with American audiences, positions its fictional account of America's exchanges with Nazism in a manner that calls attention to real historical violations of justice and memory. *The Good German*'s mythical treatise on American arrogance in foreign affairs resonates in America's contemporary political environment, which officially denies involvement in historical atrocities. The contrasting interpretations of the Second World War offered by these films display how the cinema of simulation can manipulate history to either support or challenge America's official historical narrative.

Whereas *The Good German* is more concerned with fidelity to history than *Inglourious Basterds*, Tarantino's film is more faithful to America's popular memory of the war. *The Good German* is also more devoted to replicating 1940s film style than *Inglourious Basterds*, which compresses history by juxtaposing a range of cultural artifacts from different points in time. Yet both films display what Burgoyne calls history as vision, grounding their credibility in how meaningfully their hyper-historical narratives engage with the texts they deploy as prosthetic memories. In forgetting America's military and economic interests in the Second World War, *Inglourious Basterds* presents a narrative in keeping with America's current foreign policy, which situates the nation as an arbiter of international justice—particularly in the Middle East—despite the conflicts of interest that make America ill suited to fill this role. *The Good German*, by contrast, is a film about the failure of historical justice. Soderbergh's film, which proved unpopular with critics and audiences, dredges up Operation Overcast to counter America's popular memory of the Second World War. Therefore, *The Good German* is more invested in the production of prosthetic memory, to demonstrate to American audiences how America overlooks atrocities when such actions benefit the nation. Both films demonstrate the cinema of simulation's potential to move cinematic representations of history beyond retro scenarios and into the contemporary through the use of prosthetic memory and the intentional manipulation of premediated historical truth. The cinema of simulation assumes that history is already represented and interpreted as myth, that its cultural artifacts bear historical truth in a certain respect, and that the cultural-historical archive is most useful when it can inform discourses that affect contemporary politics.

As the latest filmic development of *la mode retro*, the cinema of simulation tempts critics to consider its status as a post-postmodern form. In one respect, the utter negligence towards historicity displayed in films such as *Inglourious Basterds* makes manifest Baudrillard's anxiety regarding the disappearance of authentic historical documentation under late capitalism. Furthermore, the cinema of simulation's reliance on earlier historical documents and representations speaks to Jameson's concern that postmodern art is incapable of dealing either with its own present or with its history in an original fashion. Yet the cinema of simulation does not treat history as a retro scenario, and the best films made in this style are acutely aware of how the media in the late capitalist era determine and thereby mitigate history through representation. Ironically, films made in this style are capable of novel approaches to history and poignant allegories that address contemporary politics because they embrace the cinema's tendency to reduce history to myth. The cinema of simulation does not merely attempt an escape to an idealized past; it also recovers useful elements from that past to produce new, commodifiable meanings that audiences can discover and apply to their own ethical belief systems. By deploying pastiches of earlier representations of history, the cinema of simulation fashions itself as a form of post-prosthetic memory that makes historical experience available as a filmic commodity while acknowledging how the recording of history depends on a process of representation that distances the historical text from its referents, thus producing a hyperreal myth.

NOTES

1 See Turim 17; see also 230.
2 In *Simulacra and Simulation*, Baudrillard defines the hyperreal as "the generation by models of a real without origin or reality," which describes a state of simulation (1).
3 According to Jameson, the latter type of nostalgia film "does not reinvent a picture of the past in its lived totality: rather, by reinventing the feel and shape of characteristic art objects of an older period [...] it seeks to reawaken a sense of the past associated with those objects" ("Postmodernism" 116).
4 See Baudrillard, *Simulacra and Simulation*; and Jameson, *Postmodernism, or the Cultural Logic of Late Capitalism*.
5 For another significant example of this technique, see Michael Cimino's *Heaven's Gate* (1980).
6 For additional information on *Zelig*'s production, see Allen's interview with Stig Björkman in Allen 137.
7 Allen 37.
8 Contemporary films may simulate other visual media styles as well. For example, *Elephant* (Van Sant, 2003), which does not dramatize the Columbine massacre directly, but offers a representation of similar events that transpire

as a simulacral version of the killings, uses first-person perspectives down the barrel of a rifle to simulate the perspective of first-person shooter video games. These shots connect the narrative to the media spectacle surrounding the Columbine massacre, including the video games some claimed inspired the massacre, but also to the media dialogue on this subject in the event's aftermath. Televisual aesthetics are also given to simulation, most significantly in *Pleasantville* (Ross, 1998), a film wherein television serves as a portal to the diegetic world of a syndicated program about small-town suburban America from the 1950s. Importantly, the film's characters are transported not to the 1950s, but only a representation of the 1950s, complete with all its formal codes, narrative myths and subtextual ideologies.

9 For an extensive analysis of how *Far from Heaven* comments on media saturation, see Joyrich.
10 Extratextual pastiche at the level of film marketing is also evidenced in the retro-1970s poster design for three 2008 films: *The Bank Job* (Donaldson), *The Strangers* (Bertino), and *Vicky Cristina Barcelona* (Allen). The posters for all three films feature a single image framed by a white border, a design feature common to 1970s film posters. This marketing strategy reflects *The Bank Job*'s 1971 setting, links *The Strangers* to the 1970s slashers from which it draws inspiration, and connects *Vicky Cristina Barcelona* to the films from Woody Allen's late-1970s heyday.
11 For a more thorough examination of how *Grindhouse* generates a hyperreal memorialization of grindhouse cinema, see Benson-Allott.
12 It is worth noting that the presence of anachronistic cultural artifacts hailing from long after the Second World War offers a reversal of the aesthetic found in films such as *Body Heat*—an aesthetic that crystallizes for Jameson the past's colonization of the present. *Moulin Rouge!* (Luhrmann, 2001), *A Knight's Tale* (Helgeland, 2001), and *Marie Antoinette* (Sofia Coppola, 2006), which deploy cultural artifacts in a similar fashion, all preceded *Inglourious Basterds*.
13 This material is derived from Cohen's interview with Peter Lavelle on *Cross-Talk LIVE*. See Cohen.
14 See Cohen.
15 *The Good German* also bears similarity to *A Foreign Affair* (Wilder, 1948), wherein a congresswoman visits occupied Berlin to investigate GI behaviour. Upon hearing rumours that a café singer is hiding her husband, a Nazi war criminal, from the authorities, the congresswoman recruits a military captain to help her investigate, not knowing that this captain is the café singer's lover. Although *Casablanca* figures more prominently in the film's marketing and resolution, it is possible to consider *The Good German* a mash-up of Curtiz's film and *A Foreign Affair*.

Part V

**MULTIMEDIA INTERVENTIONS:
TELEVISION, VIDEO, AND COLLECTIVE MEMORY**

14

The *Heritage Minutes*: Nostalgia, Nationalism, and Canadian Collective Memory

Erin Peters

The *Heritage Minutes*, a national memory project or *lieux de mémoire*,[1] are a series of seventy-four sixty-second-long television advertisements that ran on Canadian television stations. They were first aired in 1991, running from that date well throughout the 1990s, and are still seen, albeit infrequently, on Canadian television today. Made in both English and French, they amounted to forty-six hours of programming per month, with 30 percent of those hours running during network prime time (Lawlor 47). The *Minutes* were produced by the privately owned Historica Foundation, created by Charles R. Bronfman and the CRB Foundation to "enhance Canadianism" (Rukszto "Other" 74). In 1986, Canadian billionaire and philanthropist Charles R. Bronfman gave a $100 million endowment to the CRB Foundation, which he had set up with the explanation, "the history I learned in school was boring ... terrible. I didn't get enough about where we came from, enough about our heroes [...] We didn't get a sense of the excitement or romance of history" (Cameron "Heritage" 15). In other words, Bronfman believed that the usual means of passing on collective memories—namely, the education system and national celebrations and rituals—had failed, and so he took it upon himself to "fill in the gaps" (West 71).

In what follows, I address two closely linked questions: How can a nation's past be used as a resource to represent and redefine collective national memories in the present? And how can it do so while also acting as a nationally unifying tool? Through an examination of the *Heritage Minutes* advertisements, I explore the ways in which social memory gets constituted and reproduced; I also expose some ways in which the *Minutes* have been appropriated and adapted since their airing on national television, which has actually allowed the *Minutes* to inadvertently become pieces of Canadian cultural memory themselves.

The *Heritage Minutes* feature dramatized scenes of selected episodes in Canadian history and endeavour to encourage the Canadians watching them to assume these episodes as part of their own personal heritage. Thus, the *Minutes* can be seen as an attempt to "fill in the gaps of Canadian collective memory using the tools of popular culture" (West 67). Indeed, the *Minutes* exemplify how nationalist narratives can enter the realm of popular culture and the public sphere. Still, the notion of any form of Canadian collective memory is a fragile one at best. Canadian national identity has long been fraught with plurality, leading to a noticeable lack of any unifying national culture or distinctiveness. Perceptions of who Canadians are and what Canadian culture is abound within the nation, and Canada is often viewed as characterized more by regionalism than nationalism. Due to Canadians' perceived lack of identification with any particular form of collective history, Canada can be said to have a rather insufficient shared collective memory.

Marita Sturken has described collective memory, or cultural memory, as the way a group of people with shared experiences, history, and cultural identity construct ways of perceiving themselves (*Tangled Memories* 1–6). This definition is useful when considering Canadian collective memory. Canada has been an independent nation since 1867, but its vast territory, multicultural status, and high immigration prevent its citizens from having much of a shared experience, history, or cultural identity. Many Canadians, including the producers of the *Heritage Minutes*, mourn the deficiency of Canadian collective memory, not solely due to the fundamental value of a nation's past, but also because they see collective memory as "instrumental in bolstering a sense of national identity, and ultimately as a functional component of national survival" (West 68). In other words, collective memory projects such as the *Minutes* use the past to suit the purposes of the present. The decision of how to remember the past is made from a standpoint in the present, and in this way it permeates the past with present meaning. Collective memory is valuable for the maintenance and structuring of a national group, and it would be naive indeed not to notice the political agenda or, to phrase it differently, the politics of cultural representation at work in memory projects such as the *Minutes*.

Barbie Zelizer reflects that "at the heart of memory's study, then, is its usability, its invocation as a tool to defend different aims and agendas" (226). Regarding the uses of memory toward a nation, the purpose is typically focused on the survival of the group. Jacques LeGoff discusses the difficulties facing a nation that has an evident lack of collective memory: "[T]he known or recognized absence or brevity of the past can [...] create serious problems for the development of a collective mentality and identity—for instance in young nations" (2). It is important for the strength of the nation that its individuals feel some sort of collective attitude toward it and one another. In times of national turmoil or heightened national disunity, the need for sites of collective memory, or *lieux de memoire*, increases. Nora points out that "[t]hese bastions buttress our identities, but if what they defended were not threatened, there would be no need for them" ("Between" 12). The perception that the *Heritage Minutes* were a response to an apparent threat of national disunity is evident in their slogan, "Giving our Past a Future" (Historica website), which implicitly suggests that without the *Minutes*, or a parallel attempt to revitalize collective memory, Canada's future as a nation may be in danger of extinction (West 72). The 1980s and early 1990s were a time of great divisiveness within Canada for several reasons, most prominently the rising strength of the Quebec separatist movement, the continuing growth of American influence, and the realization of Trudeau's policy of multiculturalism. The *Minutes*, then, were meant to offset the apparent dissolution of the Canadian population and the fragile sense of nationality among Canadians. Thomas Axworthy, executive director of the CRB Foundation, explains that "what we remember, what we stress as significant, what we omit from our past, and what we don't know or understand about the stories of our fellow inhabitants, is critical to our ability to endure as a collective." Similarly, Canadian historian Desmond Morton writes that "[a] Canada once again threatens to disintegrate, a host of history and heritage organizations have emerged or revived with nation-saving concerns" ("Shared"). Therefore, this memory project was considered to be not only perhaps entertaining, but also in fact crucial for the survival and prosperity of the nation.

Heritage, Nostalgia, and Nationalism

In *Theatres of Memory*, Raphael Samuel explains the assumed difference between history and heritage—namely, that history is solely concerned with explanation and education, "the realm of critical enquiry," whereas heritage, the "antiquarian preoccupation," merely sentimentalizes and entertains (270). Samuel points out that critics of heritage charge it with being "the mark of a sick society, one which, despairing of the future, had become 'besotted' or 'obsessed' with an idealized version of its past" (261). However, Samuel has noted by then, "[w]e live [...] in an expanding historical culture" (25), and heritage, far from being imposed from above, is instead a popular collection of representations. Heritage is generally accused of lacking authenticity and of unashamedly sentimentalizing the past, yet "[t]here is no reason to think that people are more passive when looking at old photographs or film footage, handling a museum exhibit [...] as in any reading, they assimilate them as best they can to preexisting images and narratives. The pleasures of the gaze [...] are different in kind from those of the written word but not necessarily less taxing on historical reflection and thought" (271).

Taking into account Samuel's explanation of heritage, it is significant that the *Minutes* are called "Heritage Minutes" and not "History Minutes." The popularity of heritage rises, according to Samuel, with the onset of social or political upheavals. The *Minutes* and their contribution to a form of Canadian heritage arose at a time of great national tension and uncertainty, when Canada as a nation was certainly "despairing of the future."

National heritage strongly implies national unity, and for the *Heritage Minutes* to refer to their interpretation of Canada's past as "A Part of our Heritage" (Historica website) suggests that all Canadians share the same past and heritage, and also that they all consider this heritage to be worth preserving. For the *Heritage Minutes* to be truly all-encompassing of a Canadian heritage—if such a thing can be conceived of—the *Minutes* would have to take into account that the heritage exhibited in the vignettes is unquestionably one that is strongly focused on the present and highly selective. The fact is, "all recollections are told from a standpoint in the present [...] that demands a selecting, ordering and simplifying" (Samuel and Thompson 8). Using the past for the purposes of the present, as the *Heritage Minutes* have done, in this way alters the concept of heritage to mean not something that is necessarily of personal value to the individual, but rather something artificial that can be utilized to unify the collective in times of division.

Historian David Cannadine contends that "depression is the begetter of nostalgia" (qtd. in Samuel 261), but perhaps here we could substitute "disintegration" for depression. The threat of national disintegration in

Canada in the early 1980s and 1990s, arising largely from weak national unity, inspired a wave of nostalgia that can be seen in the *Heritage Minutes*. This confirms, as Samuel explains, that heritage and nostalgia "shore up national identity at a time when it is beset by uncertainties on all sides" (243). It is important to note, however, that nostalgia for the past is usually nostalgia for an *idealized* past and not a real one, especially when the notion of a collective national past and identity is fragile to say the least.

Nostalgia is an ambiguous concept; as Svetlana Boym observes, it "remains unsystematic and unsynthesizable; it seduces rather than convinces" (13). The term generally invokes reflections of the past when times were "good." Nostalgia, originally considered to be a medical condition, is today viewed an emotion, as a wistful or bittersweet yearning for the past. The word nostalgia comes from the Greek words *nostos*, "return home," and *algia*, "pain or longing" (Wilson *Nostalgia* 21). Thus, nostalgia literally translates as "homesickness," and although an individual remembers "the good times" with nostalgia, it is precisely those memories that cause the feelings of nostalgia. In this way, nostalgia is incurable, for it is not the past as a place that is longed for, but rather the past as a time. As Linda Hutcheon explains, "time, unlike place, cannot be returned to—ever; it is irreversible. And nostalgia becomes the reaction to that sad fact." Perhaps nostalgia relies on the irrecoverable nature of past time for its emotional impact, or what Hutcheon calls the "very pastness of the past" ("Irony" 3). In this case, if nostalgia centres on an idealized version of the past, then it is less about the past than about the present. Mikhail Bakhtin calls this idea "historical inversion" and explains that it is an ideal that is not being lived out in the present, and so is instead projected onto the past (*Dialogic* 147). Praising an idealized past is essentially a response to a feeling that the present is inadequate. Here it becomes very important to note, as Hutcheon reminds us, that to describe something as "nostalgic" is less a depiction of the thing itself than an attribution of a quality of response. Nostalgia is not something you recognize in an object or event, but rather something you feel ("Irony" 6). Nostalgia has had a history of being used as a protective withdrawal into the past to escape a threatening present or ominous future. Boym explains that "nostalgia inevitably appears as a defence mechanism in a time of accelerated rhythms of life and historical upheavals" (xiv). In Canada during the 1980s and 1990s, the threat of national disintegration and the discord within the country, largely due to the rising strength of the Quebec separatist movement, was possibly reason enough for the employment of a defence mechanism such as nationalistic nostalgia.

Nationalism, an ideology that focuses on the nation, can generally be thought of as the ties that bind citizens together by emphasizing the collectivity of their shared past for the purposes of the present. Indeed, it has been argued that "no ideology needs history so much as nationalism" (Hodgkin and Radstone 169). A nation refers to individuals and society as a collective unit incorporating such factors as shared language, history, and territory; these, however, are not the only factors that make up a nation. National identity, the sense of a countrywide community felt by individuals and societies, is crucially important, and nationalism "is not so much a discourse of origin as a discourse of identity" (169). Put another way, nationalism is "the simple manifestation of the natural and spontaneous solidarity that exists among members of a human group sharing a historical and cultural tradition from which the group derives its distinctive identity" (Collins 111). And as Katharine Hodgkin and Susannah Radstone have pointed out in *Contested Pasts*, nationalism is very much connected with the notion of contestation. This contestation is the result of a set of nationalist identifiers that demand that certain elements or characteristics of the nation be deleted. Over time, the criteria for what the nation entails change, and different priorities lead to different conceptions of what that nation is. However, in Canada, as in other multicultural states, there are highly diverse ideas about what constitutes the nation, and as a result, any notion of collective memory in a national context comes to be problematic as a consequence of the lack of a singular, culturally informed conception of the nation (170). This led Canadian historian Ramsay Cook to reflect that Canada is a "state without a nation," meaning that it has political organizations but no unifying homogeneous culture ("Interview" 1972). Hence, Canadian nationalism, or Canadian national culture, is elusive and in reality more regionalist than nationalist.

Canada's Identity Crisis

National culture is a difficult concept, especially in an era of cultural globalization. What makes the concept of a national culture so remarkable in Canada (but not exclusively in Canada) is that Canada has always lacked a singular, unifying national and cultural identity. Furthermore, as Canada does not have a language or symbolic culture shared by all its citizens, it does not "display the congruence between its political, cultural, and economic realms required of a nation state. [...] Canada does not have a national culture" (Collins 19–20). In fact, Canada is often referred to as a "nation of nations," and indeed, it includes several social groups that employ the language of nationalism, such as "Quebec Nationals" and "First Nations" (Sherbert et al. 3). Compounding this fragmentation is the high level of immigration to Canada, which brings people from all nations. In a country of so much cultural plurality, the concept of a universal Canadian cultural identity is controversial to say the least, and most certainly contested by Canada's many social groups. The enormous variance of ethnicities and subcultures has made it a challenge to create a singular, unifying cultural identity—a challenge that has not always been desired.

In 1971, Prime Minister Pierre Trudeau announced Canada's new policy of multiculturalism (a term coined in Canada), which was enacted largely as a consequence of pressure from cultural minorities. Before 1971, Canadian culture and identity had been recognized as "B&B," or bilingual and bicultural. This was based on the Royal Commission on Bilingualism and Biculturalism (1963–70), established by the Liberal government of Lester B. Pearson for the purpose of promoting an equal partnership within the nation between English and French Canadians (Haque 5). The B&B national identity changed with the advent of official multiculturalism, whose aim was to acknowledge a wider citizenship. Instead of promoting the mass assimilation of new immigrants (with mere pockets of minorities), multiculturalism celebrates Canada's diversity and allows citizens to "keep their identities" (Citizenship and Immigration Canada website). Trudeau claimed that "although there are two official languages, there is no official culture" (Meisel et al. 189). Multiculturalism and cultural tolerance are valued in Canada; however, the Citizen's Forum on Canada's Future noted in 1991 that "[w]hile Canadians accept and value Canada's cultural diversity, they do not value many of the activities of the multicultural program of the federal government. These are seen as expensive and divisive in that they remind Canadians of their different origins rather than their shared symbols, society, and future. [...] [M]ulticulturalism is often blamed for the lack of a clear national identity" (191).

The preceding quote raises an interesting question: If Canada is historically a nation of minorities and has never had a clear, unifying national identity, what led to the rise of an identity crisis in Canada in the 1980s and 1990s? Why did the lack of a Canadian identity become an obsession with policy makers and the political and cultural elite? There were several reasons for groups like the Citizen's Forum to become concerned about the lack of Canadian identity at this time. The rising strength of the Quebec sovereignty movement was a key reason, along with the heightening American influence in Canada as a consequence of the 1988 Free Trade Agreement and the American ownership of many Canadian corporations. The broadcasting of a large volume of American television in Canada was of enormous concern and led the Canadian Broadcasting Corporation (CBC) to point out in 1985 that "for every hour of Canadian drama on our English TV screens there are 45 hours of American drama. No wonder we are being culturally swamped" (qtd. in Collins 13). The increasing numbers of foreign immigrants who were neither French- nor English-speaking added to concerns about the weak Canadian identity, for these new cultures highlighted the lack of a single Canadian culture. But perhaps the most important reason why a Canadian identity crisis arose in the late 1980s and early 1990s was the realization of Trudeau's pluralistic, multinational policy in the late 1970s and early 1980s. That policy changed the way Canadians were asked to see themselves, from bilingual and bicultural to multilingual and multicultural. The policy and reality of multiculturalism allowed many subcultures to exist in Canada but resulted in a lack of cultural unity and overarching national identity. Indeed, a key objective of Trudeau's multiculturalism policy was to help cultural groups retain their own identity while participating in Canadian society and culture. However, as Canadians were no longer meant to see themselves as bilingual and bicultural, the notion of what exactly constituted Canadian culture was vague. Many Canadians were "unsure of what multiculturalism is, what it is trying to do and why, and what it can realistically accomplish" (Parliament of Canada website). Within the B&B identity structure, Canadians could see their national identity as a dualistic English/French combination and could declare their personal identity in that context as either English or French. The introduction of a more ambiguous multicultural identity structure blurred that division. For Trudeau's policy to function, much would have to be forgotten first. Of course there *is* a Canadian history, but it is one of colonial ties and regionalism; it was not a nationwide history based on a policy of multiculturalism. So that Canadians across the nation would relate to this new policy, which asserted a then unfamiliar multicultural national identity, Trudeau's policy called for the deliberate eradication of many repositories of an older collective memory based on regional rather than national collectivity. As Collins confirms, "Trudeau's goal for Canada involved a painful forgetting and that cauterization of memory is painful indeed" (131). The pain of forgetting arose from submitting to an enforced policy of pluralism, which necessitated the loss of certain aspects of regional culture. This in itself caused an identity crisis, for Canadians were thereby reduced to defining themselves by what they were not, rather than what they were. Tactics of denunciation do not actually shed light on what Canadians *are*; and as the Citizen's Forum pointed out, the lack of a singular unifying national culture and identity was divisive.[2]

This divisiveness within Canada was especially apparent in the matter of Quebec sovereignty-association. The Quebec referendums and their threat to fragment the nation helped spur a wave of pseudo-nationalism in what has been described as Canada's "unending quest for identity" (Begin 177). Out of these concerns came the recognition that Canada is essentially a nation of regional differences bound together through state-enforced national unity and that "the question of Canadian identity [...] is not a 'Canadian' question at all, but a regional one" (Frye i). Here, the regional is proposed as the true place for the formation of cultural identity in opposition to a national unifying collective Canadian culture. Linda Hutcheon adds that "Canada can in some ways be defined as a country whose articulation of its *national* identity has sprung from *regionalist* impulses" (*Canadian* 4). However, with the identity crisis of the 1980s and 1990s in Canada, the desire for a unifying national cultural identity began to grow; this soon became evident in many ways, most apparently through the medium of television.

The *Heritage Minutes*

The Historica Foundation's *Heritage Minutes* can be seen as an effort to create a Canadian collective consciousness. The unifying potential of a shared national consciousness is undeniable, so the *Heritage Minutes* can perhaps be described as a nation-saving quest fought with the tools of collective memory to forge unity in the face of disunity. Much has been said about their format and content; Cameron refers to them as a "vitamin pill" notion of history, writing that they are "sugar-coated, concentrated, easy-to-swallow, and good for the health of the nation. They were designed as an alternative to the history Bronfman (and many others) found so 'boring' and 'terrible'" ("Heritage" 17). There are historical inaccuracies in the *Minutes*, and while these are an important issue, they are outside the remit of this study and will not be discussed here. The *Minutes* are perhaps not exclusively concerned with the telling of truths, but rather with the creation a sense of Canadian cultural unity, or at the very least the creation of something "exciting" about Canadian history. As mentioned, when accelerated rhythms of life and upheavals occur on a national scale, an inevitable defence mechanism is to deploy nationalistic nostalgia. That the *Heritage Minutes* respond nostalgically to feelings that the present is inadequate by idealizing a unified past is apparent in their slogan: "Giving Our Past a Future" (Historica website). Evidently the fact that Canada never truly had a unified past to either idealize or give a future to is beside the point.

To use the nation's past as a unifying tool and create a set of collective memories of the past for the purposes of the present, the *Minutes* first had to identify a set of common connotations of Canadianism that "allowed individuals to see themselves in stories about 'their' social/historical contexts" (Lawlor 86). These connotations of Canadianism drew on nationalist characteristics, oscillating between occasional blatant stereotypes and vague representations, and combined them with highly dramatized and condensed examples of their occurrences in Canada's history. Deploying representations of past Canadians to portray what a Canadian is utilizes nostalgia, yet as Boym explains, nostalgia is not solely concerned with the past and can be "retrospective as well as prospective" (xvi). Thus, although the *Minutes* were eager to romanticize the past, they did so with an eye to idealizing the future's potential; they used the past as a resource for constructing a collective memory that would serve the present day's apparent needs. This is not to say that the *Minutes* succeeded in their quest—indeed, that judgment is not the purpose of this study. The concern here is simply to show how the *Minutes* applied the concepts of nostalgia and nationalism.

The topic of most concern to the producers of the *Minutes*—evident in the number of *Minutes* dedicated to it—was the relationship between Quebec and the rest of Canada; this was also the country's most pressing concern at the time the *Minutes* were produced. Several *Minutes* stressed how collaboration between English and French benefited Canada at the time of its founding; the *Minute* titled "Baldwin and LaFontaine" was an excellent illustration of the use of nationalistic nostalgia. This *Minute* opens with a scene of an election day in Quebec in 1841. A crowd of chanting French Canadians approach the voting area and demand the right to vote from the crowd of English Canadians already at the voting polls. Some fighting breaks out but is subdued by Louis-Hippolyte LaFontaine, who calls for "pas de violence." The scene cuts to LaFontaine receiving a letter from Robert Baldwin asking him to run for a seat in Ontario, then cuts again to LaFontaine and Baldwin meeting in Toronto.

Baldwin addresses his visitor: "Mr. Lafontaine, think of the history we'll make when a French Canadian runs and wins in York." The *Minute* closes by saying, "and they did make history" (Historica website). This *Minute* plainly emphasizes the past cooperation of English and French Canadians for the continuing good and prosperity of the unified nation. It depicts nationalistic nostalgia by dramatizing a past period of unrest between English and French Canadians and then stresses that the difficulties were easily and amicably overcome through collaboration that maintained national, not regional or linguistic-cultural, unity. Consequently, this *Minute* and others like it that portray French and English relations in Canadian history do succeed in highlighting Canada's dualistic past, albeit an idealized version of it, and they draw attention to the importance of that unified past for the present nation. These *Minutes* emphasize that the history of Quebec is in fact the history of Canada, and they are inclusive in their portrayals. No other province or territory is singled out in the *Minutes* as Quebec is; in the individual attention paid to it, Quebec is enveloped within the nation of Canada as a whole. This is a clear demonstration of how the *Minutes* intentionally used the nation's past as a resource for the needs of the present, by firmly securing Quebec's place at the centre of the nation and illustrating that it had always occupied that place, to the continuing benefit of all Canadians.

Another area of concern for the producers of the *Heritage Minutes* was regionalism and national geography. Canada's vast territory undoubtedly has been key to its national cultural identity. "If some countries have too much history, Canada has too much geography" (Bronfman qtd. in Kelly 8). That Canada is really more regionalist than nationalist was discussed earlier in this chapter. With regard to Canadian geography, the country can be divided into five regions: Atlantic, Central, Prairie, Pacific, and Arctic. The differences in lifestyle and culture between a Canadian from the Maritimes and one from the Rockies are considerable; as Lawlor explains, "regional self-definition is inevitable for a country which covers almost ten million square kilometres" (72). There are also cultural differences within each of Canada's regions. The *Minutes* sought to minimize regional differences by stressing commonalities and by implying that Canadians should adopt the experiences of their fellow countrymen from faraway parts of the nation as part of their own Canadian experience.

The *Minute* "Emily Carr," for example, portrays British Colombian artist Carr as she paints Canada's coastal rainforest. This *Minute* is geographically vague enough to suggest that an appreciation of Canada's natural beauty, and not just that of B.C., unites all Canadians. The *Minute* ends with a nationalistic dialogue spoken by Carr: "This is my country. What I want to express is here and I love it" (Historica website). Although Canadians from the Prairies may have difficulty identifying with the landscape of mountainous B.C., they are encouraged to contemplate that "other" region as part of their country, indeed as "part of [their] heritage."

Another *Minute* that illustrates the potentially divisive issues of regionalism and geographical distance is "Sir Sandford Fleming." Fleming was a nineteenth-century engineer and entrepreneur who initiated the building of three railways and invented the concept of standard time. This *Minute* emphasizes Canadians' ability to maintain a unified nation across enormous distances. In this *Minute*, Fleming exclaims: "We're not just building a railroad, gentlemen. We are building a country" (Historica website). The use of nationalism and nostalgia to serve the needs of Canada's uncertain present are evident in this *Minute*, in which, in an idealized version of the nation's past, national unity is achieved through hard work and cooperation.

These *Minutes* illustrate how the Historica Foundation reworked or idealized the past, tailoring cultural memory to accommodate present-day issues and requirements. Samuel tells us that "[m]emory is historically conditioned, changing colour and shape according to the emergencies of the moment" (x). This is especially true of collective or national memories, which can thereby transform a nation's collective past into a resource for present purposes.

The *Heritage Minutes* as Pieces of Canadian Cultural Memory

The popularity of the *Heritage Minutes* among Canadians was remarkable, and the *Minutes* have since been appropriated in many ways. In a particularly interesting turn of events, the *Minutes* have themselves become pieces of Canadian cultural memory. The Historica Foundation, by producing and distributing the *Heritage Minutes*, in effect *made* Canadian history by *making* Canadian history. The *Minutes*, which were "highly visible and widely consumed" (Rukszto 74), are familiar to Canadians who watched television during the 1990s, and the mere fact of their existence forged links among Canadians that led to a shared relationship and became part of a collective culture. Quite unintentionally, then, the *Heritage Minutes* became pieces of Canadian cultural memory, coincidentally serving as tools for national unity, quite apart from the Historica Foundation's original objectives.

After the original airing of the *Heritage Minutes*, "Mock Minutes" became a staple of Canadian comedy shows. This was predictable, considering the high visibility of the original *Minutes*. The Historica Foundation's website itself acknowledges that "[t]he *Minutes* have been a familiar part of Canada's cultural landscape for more than ten years. So familiar, in fact, they have been imitated and parodied by comedians" (Historica website). "Mock Minutes" are satirical versions of the *Heritage Minutes* and have been seen on Canadian television programs such as *This Hour Has 22 Minutes*, *The Royal Canadian Air Farce*, and *The Rick Mercer Report*. These parodic skits follow the same visual framework as the *Minutes*, lasting sixty seconds and closing with the "A Part of our Heritage" image. They range in purpose from simple jokes to political or social criticisms, and they communicate "the truths that cannot be accommodated within the heritage discourse but that speak to the complexities of national identity in contemporary Canada" (Rukszto 81). In this way, the "Mock Minutes" force viewers to question what gets incorporated into the real *Heritage Minutes* and what gets left out, perhaps to be included in the "Mock Minutes" instead. Thus, the "Mock Minutes" raise the issue of silence and omission in memory; in this regard, Luisa Passerini remarks that "any operation aiming to cancel memory cannot help being also an effort to produce another set of memories, to replace the previous ones" (241). If this is so, then inversely, any production of a new set of memories must also be an effort to cancel old memories. Here, then, the past is being reworked, or idealized, into a form that is acceptable to and supportive of the aim of the new set of memories. Clearly, in the *Heritage Minutes*, the new memories being presented are seeking to define the Canadian past through present-day issues. This act silences the actuality of the past in order to portray an idealized version for the purpose of constructing a desired collective memory for the sake of present and future.

Similarly, the "Mock Minutes" force viewers to consider the effects of nationalism and national heritage. A "Mock Minute" produced by *This Hour Has 22 Minutes* about Lucien Bouchard and the Bloc Québécois demonstrates how the "Mock Minutes" utilize nationalist discourse. This "Minute" portrays a weeping mother bringing her troubled young son to a therapist. The son plays with a maple leaf and quickly becomes more and more agitated until he tears it into little pieces. The boy then plays with two dolls, hitting the bigger one with the smaller one and shouting "vive le Canada!" The therapist diagnoses the situation, saying that the boy "seems to have some sort of block, a mental block, a bloc Québécois, if you will." This "Mock Minute" describes the Quebec separatist movement and English–French relations in the language of heritage (Rukszto 83). Instead of emphasizing a shared background and mutual respect as well as the potential for national unity and provincial cooperation as displayed in the *Heritage Minutes*, the "Mock Minutes" show Canadian political heritage as rife with disunity and regionalism and the nation as on the verge of dissolution. Yet even this spin on the past reflects the situation of the present while at the same time silencing former, more serious and optimistic accounts of the past in order to portray a satirical version of it. In place of "enhancing Canadianism"—which was Bronfman's original goal for the *Minutes*—the "Mock Minutes" subvert Canadian national pride. Nevertheless, in doing so, the "Mock Minutes" have created a point of commonality among all Canadians. Canadians recognize the satire in the "Mock Minutes," and these parodies have become, in a small way, a culturally unifying phenomenon. This phenomenon occurs as a result of Canadians' ability to highlight the "realities of Canadian life against the representations of imagined Canadian greatness" (Rukszto 85), and also through the humour they employ while doing so. Canada is more regional than national, and therefore the concept of a national Canadian identity is fragile; in this regard, "Mock Minutes" that stress the absurdity of Canadian national heritage are perhaps more unifying than the reality of any national heritage itself. This irony occurs because "what people laugh at, when and how [...] is absolutely central to their culture" (Palmer 2). Fascinatingly, the "Mock Minutes" have perhaps done more to create a sense of unity, national identity, and collective memory in Canada than the *Heritage Minutes* themselves ever could. This is because the former are able to unify Canadians with humour about their disunity and lack of national identity.

That said, the "Mock Minutes" are base allusions to the *Heritage Minutes*; as Hutcheon explains, "even in mocking, parody reinforces [the text parodied]" (*Theory* 75). Obviously, then, the *Heritage Minutes* have had an effect on Canadian culture. Hutcheon explains that parodies take the object of their study very seriously; this can be seen in the mirror-imaging style and structure of the "Mock Minutes" relative to the *Heritage Minutes*. Thus, "the anti-nationalist message of the 'Mock Minutes' is enabled by the original's message of national unity" (Rukszto 87). Inadvertently, the *Heritage Minutes* have become pieces of Canadian cultural memory through their very efforts to portray Canadian cultural memory.

A further way that the *Heritage Minutes* have unconsciously become pieces of Canadian cultural memory while attempting to portray that same memory is through mass communication tools, such as the Facebook website, which allows its members to meet online to exchange news and thoughts in public discussion groups. There is a Facebook group called *Heritage Minutes*, which discusses these texts. The fact that the *Heritage Minutes* project from the 1990s has a group dedicated to it on Facebook a decade after its era ended speaks to how deeply embedded the *Minutes* have become in Canadian collective cultural memory. The group's page describes itself to its 2,898 members thusly: "Do you feel like *Heritage Minutes* were a necessary part of your education (and development as a person)? Do you believe that it doesn't matter what the situation is, its [*sic*] never a wrong time to throw in some dialogue from a *Heritage Minute?* Did you learn all you need to know about Canadian history from these extremely well acted, realistic 60 second shorts?" (Facebook website).

This sarcastic introduction to the Facebook page is followed by a list of all the *Minutes*' titles and by a link to the Historica Foundation website. Also on this website is a link to a discussion board with topics such as: "What is your favourite *Heritage Minute?*", "*Heritage Minutes*—patriotic or propaganda?", and "*Heritage Minutes* that still need to be done." Perhaps most interesting, however, are the *Heritage Minute* quotations that appear all over the website. Members of the group are invited to quote their favourite lines from the *Minutes*, and under the section "What's your favourite *Minute* quote?", there are 211 quotes from the *Minutes* posted by Facebook members.

The number of posts by members directly quoting the *Minutes*' dialogue, or else discussing the quotes, is significant. Group members have left messages such as "so easy to drop into a conversation or joke [...] How do people from America have fun with their historical moments?!" (Facebook website). This posting exhibits how the *Minutes* have gone beyond their intended purpose of "enhancing Canadianism" to become a facet of Canadian cultural memory that Canadians nationwide can use to recognize and relate to one another while differentiating themselves from others (in this case, Americans). In accordance with this argument, another member writes, "I can't think of a single Canadian I know who doesn't crack up at the recitation of 'Now the people will know we were here'" (Facebook website). These posts on the group page are just two of many that express similar feelings toward the *Heritage Minutes*. Since cultural memory is defined as the way in which a group of people with a shared background construct ways of perceiving themselves (Sturken *Tangled Memories* 1–6), the manner in which the *Heritage Minutes* are being remembered, referred to, and utilized on Facebook as implements of cultural perception unmistakably permits them to be recognized as pieces of Canadian cultural memory.

Finally, the re-creation of the *Heritage Minutes* in Canadian high school history projects is worth mentioning in relation to how the *Minutes* have inadvertently created a Canadian collective memory. The Historica Foundation's website has a page dedicated to lesson plans, which invites visitors to "Make Your Own Minute." On this page are instructions to teachers across Canada detailing the methods and tools for producing *Minutes*. The same page supplies teachers with a list of topic ideas for the *Minutes* their students could select to create. What is significant here is that education in Canada is controlled provincially, not federally. This means that what a student studies in Saskatchewan, for example, can be very different from what a student studies in Prince Edward Island. The *Heritage Minutes* are not affiliated with any provincial education program; nevertheless, given that each province varies in its curriculum for students, the *Heritage Minutes* lesson plan is one of the few in Canada that can be implemented nationwide and tailored to suit each province in a way that discusses the nation as a whole. All of the topics selected by the Historica Foundation focus on nationally inclusive topics, not provincial ones.

A quick search on the YouTube website reveals the high number of student *Minutes* that have been created and shared. These unofficial *Minutes* come from students all over the country and vary from serious topics of Canadian history, such as the Terry Fox legacy, to light-hearted pop culture subjects, such as the stereotype that Canadians have a penchant for apologizing. The fact that classrooms across the nation have used the *Heritage Minutes* as a foundation for lesson plans in Canadian history highlights the extent to which the *Minutes* have come to be included in Canadian cultural memory. When used in this pedagogical fashion, the *Minutes* are arguably not exactly "enhancing Canadianism" through their own content, but in fact uniting students across the country by having them share in a common school project. Thus the content of the original *Heritage Minutes* vignettes may not be acting as a unifying cultural memory, but the resulting school projects that have been created because of them fulfill this purpose.

Conclusion

This study has investigated the concepts of heritage, nostalgia, and nationalism and has discussed how these can connect with and aid in the formation of national collective memories. Analysis of the Historica Foundation's *Heritage Minutes* suggests that they have used Canada's past as a resource in an effort to build a collective national memory in the present.

Selected episodes of Canada's history have been intentionally reactivated—and to some extent distorted—through the manufacturing of collective memories that seek to act as tools of national unification in a time of national disunity.

According to Elspeth Cameron, the *Heritage Minutes* read "contemporary values both backwards onto history and forwards to articulate nationhood" ("Heritage" 13). It is unsurprising, then, that the *Minutes* came into the Canadian cultural landscape during a period of political and social instability when aspects of the nation were threatened and questions about the definition of Canadian identity and nationalism proliferated. The *Minutes* present selected occurrences of Canada's past from a position highly influenced by contemporary circumstances. So it is noteworthy that several *Minutes* detail past cooperation between English and French Canadians, for example, whereas markedly few address Native issues. Thus, the *Minutes* can be considered a reaction to current events and are deliberate not only in what they depict but also in how they depict it. The *Minutes* utilize nostalgia; their very existence can be described as a defence mechanism. The Canadian nation depicted by the *Heritage Minutes* is a promising one, or, in Cameron's words, "a Canada characterized by responsible government and by compromise among conflicting rights and privileges and inventive problem-solving: a Canada inhabited by hardworking, self-sacrificing citizens from an array of ethnic groups interested in maintaining peace, order and good government" (18).

By projecting a romanticized view backwards onto the past and portraying how past national crises were overcome to the continued benefit of the nation, the *Minutes* themselves have become a nostalgic response to feelings of an inadequate national present by praising an idealized national past. That the *Minutes* are not wholly historically accurate—the historical consultant for the *Minutes*, John Herd Thompson, maintains "what we are guilty of is not 'inaccuracy' but *oversimplification*" (qtd. in Cameron "Heritage" 19)—allows for speculation that they were intended primarily not to explain historical events and facts, but to promote Canadian national unity and identity.

Collective memory projects such as the *Heritage Minutes* try to avoid rigid definitions and grand narratives (as evidenced in the "*A Part* of our Heritage" slogan) since they cannot fully resolve the pressures among competing national identities. However, such projects do still exhibit present-mindedness, which is an unavoidable aspect of remembering the past. The unifying potential of a shared national consciousness is undeniable;

however, when we analyze memory projects like the *Heritage Minutes*, we should remember that for each "memory" that is included, another is discarded or distorted. Therefore, no collective national memory project will ever be completely inclusive. Nevertheless, the *Heritage Minutes* can be viewed as an attempt to overcome the lack of national identity. Indeed, the *Minutes* demonstrate how the past can be enlisted to serve present interests, allowing Canada's past to be adapted and appropriated as a resource to represent and redefine a collective national memory in the present.

NOTES

1. French historian Pierre Nora coined the term *lieux de memoire* (sites of memory). He argues that these are artificial and deliberately constructed sites where "memory crystallizes and secretes itself" ("Between" 7) and that they are exclusively an occurrence of our modern time, a replacement for "real" memory, which no longer exists. Nora observes that *lieux de memoire* "originate with the sense that there is no spontaneous memory, that we must deliberately create archives [...] because such activities no longer occur naturally" (12–19).
2. Tony Wilden in *The Imaginary Canadian* refers to Canada as "Notland," stating it is "not English, not American, not Asian, not European, and especially not French" (1).

15

Disaster and Trauma in *Rescue Me*, *Saving Grace*, and *Treme*: Commercial Television's Contributions to Ideas about Memorials

John McCullough

My purpose in this chapter is to share some observations about the way commercial television shows serve as memorials. To put it another way, I will be considering the nature and characteristics of the memorial spaces that commercial television produces. My approach is not wholly located in the area of memory studies or trauma studies, although I will be relying on a number of the major themes that have emerged in research from these fields. Instead, I am interested in the sites of memorials, and, more specifically, in the way that memorials and memorializing produce spaces. I am interested in considering the ways that media dedicated to the representations of disaster and survival are designed and experienced as spaces. While my specific examples are drawn from commercial television, many of my conclusions are also applicable to new media and installation art, which share significant aesthetic and technological aspects with commercial television (e.g., screens, televisual aesthetics, "liveness" as an ethos and as a practice, digital archives, electronic interfaces).[1] By providing analyses of contemporary television's attempts to memorialize disasters, I hope to explore some of the spatial practices associated with traumatic mediation and remediation. In the process, I will draw attention to important distinctions between monuments and memorials and consider these television shows as prosthetics that actualize the processes of mediation and remediation. In trauma studies, the functions of such mediation typically include witnessing and translation, and while I will account for witnessing in the programs, I will pay particular attention to the ways that disaster and the associated traumas are translated for viewing experiences. In the process I hope to indicate the crucial role that fantasy has in the construction and experience of these memorial spaces.

The television shows that I am considering include *Saving Grace*, which memorializes the victims and survivors of the bombing of the Alfred P. Murrah Federal Building in Oklahoma City on 19 April 1995. This was a TNT Network series that ran for three seasons from 2007 to 2010. This program was produced by Fox Television and is distributed by 20th Century Fox Home Entertainment. The show was created by Nancy Miller and features the award-winning actress Holly Hunter as Grace, an Oklahoma City police detective who is a survivor of sexual abuse and who is tormented by guilt associated with the bombing. The audience learns in the pilot episode that the day before the event, Grace's sister had arranged for Grace to babysit her newborn while she went to pick up a birth certificate at the Murrah building. Since Grace was ill (we assume because of a hangover) and could not babysit, that errand was delayed a day, with the consequence that her sister became a victim of the terrorist attack. The boy, now a young teenager, quite regularly visits with Grace, and this relationship with her nephew provides many opportunities for discussions of trauma, guilt, and memory. The more important relationship in the show, though, is the one Grace has with an angel, who is bent on saving her from her downward spiral of guilt that has fuelled a lifestyle of self-abuse including promiscuous sex, overwork, aggressive driving, smoking, and drinking. Although the show is dedicated to the Oklahoma City bombing tragedy of 1995, its theme of redemption is deeply embedded in the post-9/11 context.

The second show under consideration is *Rescue Me*, which memorializes the efforts of the Fire Department of New York and the victims and survivors of the attacks on the World Trade Center on 11 September 2001. *Rescue Me* is an FX Network series that ran for seven seasons, from 2004 to 2011, and was produced by DreamWorks and distributed by Sony Pictures Television. The program's creator—actor and stand-up comic Denis Leary—stars as Tommy Gavin, a firefighter who lost several coworkers in the attacks, including his cousin, Jimmy Keefe. In the course of the series, Tommy also loses his son to a drunk driver. Believing that both losses were a result of his negligence, he takes them on as his cross to bear. The ghosts of his cousin and his son, as well as various victims of fire and the 9/11 attacks, overwhelm Tommy, who eventually spirals down much like Grace does. Both shows privilege Christian iconography and values, and in this sense, they can be viewed as part of a broader reaction in the cultural sectors to America's post-9/11 context.

Finally, *Treme* memorializes the victims and survivors of Hurricane Katrina, which struck New Orleans on 29 August 2005. This Home Box Office series recently ended its third season. *Treme* was created by David Simon, and some of its creative team (on and off screen) were lauded earlier for their work on the award-winning series *The Wire*. Like its predecessor, *Treme* aspires to present its narratives as sociologically accurate and tends to focus on the institutions at the heart of the crisis. Thus, *Treme* approaches the disaster as man-made rather than natural and is sharply critical of organizations such as the U.S. government, FEMA, and the Army Corps of Engineers, as well as a wide range of politicians and bureaucrats who failed to protect the city. The show suggests that American elites viewed parts of New Orleans as expendable. The series is not saturated with Christian meanings of the sort that drive the other shows, but there is a clear sense that most of *Treme*'s characters are seeking some form of redemption; although the show is mainly realistic, the traumas associated with the disaster often generate visions of phantoms and ghosts.

These shows take diverse approaches, but they are all melodramas, they all feature an ensemble cast, and they all play to a committed adult audience; in general, they all foreground aesthetic features that would be understood as characteristic of "quality television."[2] This is most true of *Treme*, with its HBO pedigree, its character-driven plots, its extensive socio-historical and cultural references, its location shooting and documentary realism, and its film-like aesthetic values, as well as its auteurist craft. *Saving Grace* and *Rescue Me* exhibit some of these characteristics as well, and moreover, all of these shows significantly foreground liberal humanism, although it might be argued that *Treme*'s social and political critique might actually work against this tendency by offering a structural analysis of social institutions. (In much the same way, Simon's work on *The Wire* could be said to undermine a naive commitment to liberal humanism.) All in all, these shows have much in common, and while their similarities are to be expected, given their common goal of memorializing disasters and survivors, their differences will nonetheless be useful in developing some conclusions about aesthetic strategies in memorial television as well as in new media memorials.

At this point, there is something to be gained from distinguishing between monuments and memorials, especially with regard to their effects on time and space (although my own emphasis will be on their production of space). The word "monument" denotes statues, buildings, or other structures erected to commemorate a famous or notable person or event. This includes the familiar case of a bust serving as a monument to a famous individual, as well as the more expansive case of an amphitheatre, for instance, serving as a monument to a specific emperor. Furthermore, a monument is typically built to endure, to be permanent and thereby achieve a victory over time. In this literal sense, the space of the monument is produced to remind us of the power and prestige of those it originally honoured, even after it has turned into a ruin. For Malcolm Miles, monuments "state a past or its imitation, but are erected to impress contemporary publics with the relation to history of those who hold power and the durability of that relation expressed in stone or bronze" (59–60). Monuments can also be understood to refer to a body of work or something that is representative of an extraordinary achievement. In this figurative sense, an igloo could be said to be a monument to pragmatic design, and a beehive is a monument to the productive capacities of a bee colony.

Monuments produce spaces by externalizing ideals that reside at their core. For instance, the Statue of Liberty and the National Monument in Washington, D.C., exert enormous force outwards from their centres; they extol virtues such as power, enlightenment, truth, freedom, and reason—values also extolled by the nation-state upon which the monuments' plinths stand. Ideally, monuments produce a space of assertion that immobilizes or *freezes* time. Lefebvre has commented that the level of repression in a monument is matched only by the level of its exaltation. In this sense, monuments expand their values outwards and over long distances (by virtue of their renown) but also exert a magnetic attraction that pulls people toward them because of the important values they express. That is the role monuments play in citizenship. Again, to cite Lefebvre: "Monumental space offered each member of a society an image of that membership, an image of his or her social visage. It thus constituted a collective mirror more faithful than any personal one" (220). In summary, monuments produce objects and spaces that project values that aspire to be timeless anchors of social, cultural, and political meaning.

Memorials, by comparison, are not only objects and spaces. In common parlance, they are also understood to be events, which is to say that a memorial, as much as it produces a space, is also associated with an unfolding of time or history within a practice and space of remembering. The temporal dimension of memorials lays significant emphasis on mourning as modest quotidian spatial practice. When we characterize memorials in this way, it is evident that the process of working through a trauma, for instance, encourages consideration of the effects of the passage of time and hence the role of the interval. Memorials are spaces that are marked by distinct temporal processes (life/death, daily/seasonal schedules, moon phases/fashions, wartime/peacetime, health/illness, working days/holidays), which pass in sequence and in a repetitive manner that mimics memory. As an example, a memorial event can happen the same time each year (e.g., as a tribute to a person) and thereby contribute to the year's overall structure, including its rhythm. If the memorial honours a deceased loved one, for instance, one's experience of a year may be so structured by it that other coordinates of time and place that would normally dominate perception are dislodged. In the example of a memorial day visit recognizing the day a parent goes to jail, all days before it are filled with enthusiastic anticipation and each day following returns to a sort of mundane routine. In such an example, depending on the nature and length of sentence, each subsequent memorial visit would assume a unique quality so that it could be said that the rhythmic pattern of that process has a life of its own, one that evolves over time. So it can be seen that the design of memorials produces intervals and that these lend texture to a memorial.[3] Axiomatically, it can be seen that the texture of a memorial is an impression of the passage of time.

Thus, the durability evident in the monument is, in the memorial, replaced by mutability; permanence by change; rigidity by rhythms; stasis by flows. From this perspective, television is particularly useful in suggesting ways to imagine memorials, including new media and installations, that would produce spaces of remembrance that feature vast digital archives and complex arrangements of content. In its packaging of various and heterogeneous programming elements (such as advertisements, various television shows representing a range of different genres, various styles of videographic information including text, graphs, and windows-in-windows compositions), commercial television excels at organizing an evolving series of bundles of information and affect. In Television Studies, this process has been characterized as flow, or more precisely segmented flow, in which the unfolding and packaging of space-time occurs (Williams *Television*; Ellis *Visible*). There is, then, a process to commercial television that encourages us to appreciate the memorial spaces that television produces—in particular, the way it designs intervals, creating rhythms and textured spaces filled with data and affect, or more provocatively, history and memory.

It is also apparent that the role of seriality in commercial television's design is useful in understanding memorials. In considering memorials that are designed to be interactive, site specific, and/or educational, we would want to make note of the function of seriality in commercial television. For instance, commercial television's ability to weave together disparate components of history/memory suggests how memorials that are in constant interface with users and that draw from a vast archive depend upon in-built serial design, emphasizing modules and interlocking blocks of images and sounds, organized around various thematic nodes. As well, since the computer and the television have converged in contemporary media culture, we can imagine rich scenarios of interaction between these tools and users. For instance, the proposed memorial at the site of the former World Trade Center includes an immersive experience that surrounds visitors with audio from cellphone calls made by victims on the two planes that were crashed into the towers. This example presents both a monument and a memorial. To the extent that the structure is meant to embody the virtues of those who died and those who survived, the new structures will serve as a monument in the traditional sense of a marker against time. And to the extent that the site also offers mediated access to the voices of those who died, it will serve as a memory tool that changes the proximity of the horror of that specific time depending on users' familiarity with the event. For some users, such as those who knew 9/11 victims, the memorial will feel very close, and one can imagine the space becoming suffocating to them due to an overabundance of the real. For others, the sound of those voices will be a complex weave of earnest expressions of love, sadness, and fear, but since these sounds will not be perceived as documents from loved ones, the effect will be less oppressive and, by contrast, more suggestive of the range of feelings and sentiments of the victims. In other words, for such users, the memorial will work to create a general sense of both human frailty and dignity. It is clear that the range of possible user meanings will be extensive, and this ambiguity will be attributable to the way in which the hundreds of mediated elements included in the memorial all exist as potentialities awaiting an encounter.

In much the same way, commercial television content lies as a field of potentialities that make sense and have effect only in relationship to viewers. This dynamic became a particularly potent theoretical insight when Television Studies and Cultural Studies, hoping to argue against the dominant view that popular culture produces "cultural dupes," began to account for the ways in which audiences strategically use media to construct meaning.⁴ In some cases these meanings were consistent with the authors' intentions, but at other times readings were produced that subverted the intended meaning. In terms of design, then, commercial television theory provides us with ways to think about the importance of seriality and intervals in memorials (see Sielke's chapter). By considering these design aspects of commercial television content and delivery, we can imagine memorials that would be interactive, user-centred, process-oriented, remediating, synaesthetic, and regenerative. For the duration of this chapter, I will turn my attention to the television shows to understand to what extent, and in what capacity, weekly commercial television programming produces memorial spaces.

The three shows under consideration provide numerous examples that illustrate the ideas discussed above. Each program is designed as serial television with the attendant focus on story arcs and character development. In addition, each show prioritizes popular entertainment style and provides audience-engaging performances. Furthermore, these shows negotiate commercial factors such as ratings competition and the creation of appealing contexts for consumer goods (including instances of product placement). The shows are made in an industrial context with stratified and hierarchically aligned labour, high-end technology, and strict mechanisms of control over talent and resources. While produced in a generic commercial context, their distinction derives from the fact that they are designed to be consumed in "boutique programming" contexts and DVD viewing, in keeping with the features of "quality television." The producers make regular use of those serial television conventions that are usually associated with "soap operas," in which characters develop in time-space, history and memory become integral to the narrative (flashbacks are common), and complex antinomies and contradictions are worked through in an extended—and not necessarily air-tight—narrative. As with much television programming, the sequence is prioritized, even above overall narrative coherence. In *Rescue Me*, for example, Tommy Gavin routinely moves between contradictory space-times: in the matter of a few minutes, he will be seen fighting fires in a realistic context, then fighting fires in slow motion as if he is in a music video, then fighting with his brother or wife in a domestic context, then counselling his godchild in a paternalistic moment, and finally blubbering to the phantom of his dead cousin, Jimmy Keefe, the godson's father and a victim of the 9/11 attacks. So, while these shows are narrative-oriented, story is not always the dominant category of experience, and it is important to recognize that, as with much commercial television (and unlike the novel, the short story, the epic poem, or the feature film), an inordinate amount of attention is paid to building a series of strong, sometimes overpowering scenes or sequences that work in an almost stand-alone capacity in the context of the series.

    The serial television form privileges an episodic structure that allows for the packaging of discrete aspects of character and narrative information while developing a story form that has been described as "an expanding middle." *Rescue Me* exemplifies how an episodic structure can serve a memorializing function. Certainly, the heterogeneous space-time that Leary occupies and that mixes fantasy and reality and past and present events and characters, as contradictory as it sometimes appears, is an effect of a central cause—9/11—and there is a suggestion inherent in the show that working through the trauma of that day's events is like experiencing a "soap opera." Although *Rescue Me* features men in masculine roles, it is not shy about situating these men in the emotionally raw world of "soaps." The show uses this form as its exemplary aesthetic model, and this is so obvious that, while the show survived seven seasons, one could safely argue that, as in "soap operas," there has been no real sense of development in the world of these characters. Over the course of the series, the same core of men occupy centre stage, the two women featured in the early episodes are still present, and, despite various breakdowns, the families and almost all the members featured in the early episodes are still around. Therefore, two of the most standard tropes of commercial television, the house and the family, remain predominant, including the metaphorical relationship that often links these figures to the workplace. For instance, while the Gavins and their relations constitute the formal family unit, the show makes clear how the firefighters constitute a family in their own right. For instance, each firefighter has a role in the family, with the Chief being the father, and Kenny Shea ("Lou" for lieutenant) as the mother figure who feeds and humours them, while the rest of the men in the "house" serve as various surrogate siblings, with the "probies" (probationary recruits) as the young brothers and the veterans as the older brothers. It is inevitable that the characters' domestic and work worlds collide, and this involves domestic strife that seeps into the workplace and, of course, just as many workplace events that impact the characters' home lives. The torturous integration of work and family is made explicit in the characters of Jimmy Keefe, Tommy's firefighter cousin, who dies in 9/11, and his son Damian, who is severely injured on the job shortly after joining the FDNY.

Additionally, the show's creators stress the importance of fantasy in the process of working through trauma, as visions, apparitions, and delusions are routinely showcased. These concepts are all part of what commercial television can usefully suggest about memorial design, and to this extent *Rescue Me* can be considered a good example of a memorial—even while it is often a highly offensive television show. For example, in one episode Tommy rapes his estranged spouse Janet (who is now living with his brother), and unlike his memories of his son's death or his cousin's demise in the WTC, the fiction does not comment on his actions. And on other occasions, Tommy expresses xenophobic and sexist opinions and there is no criticism of his self-pitying narcissism or white male rage. In fact, it might be argued that the show's attempts to serve as a memorial push its characters and plots to the brink of believability and moral acceptability. It is almost as though the need to focus the viewer's attention on the memorializing process demands heightened emotional expressions and an intensification of the affective capacities of the central scenes and sequences. These strategies, including the representation of rape as both a literal event and a metaphor, are consistent with the tradition of melodrama, and they do serve the memorializing process, even though this also means that any instances of retrograde behaviour by the characters are excused by way of honouring the traumatic event and the survival process.

A more progressive example of commercial television that serves as a memorial is David Simon's *Treme*. Many fans of the show are also fans of Simon's other work, especially *The Wire*. This attribution of authorship to Simon introduces a perspective that bears significantly on this subject—specifically, what is the role of authorship in the design of memorials? Authorship is a topic of broad interest in the area of public art and architecture and in visual culture generally. The reigning consensus is that, when considering memorials, a populist design by committee approach is routinely dominant; while the sign of the author continues to be significant (especially where it can produce prestige for the memorial), in effect, memorials are a collective effort. City planners and engineers, politicians and interested community groups, professional peers, marketing and real estate personnel, and security and police all have a stake in the development of such projects. The process can become extensive and highly complicated, and routinely, compromise is the order of the day. The rebuild planned for the site of the former World Trade Center is a case in point (Kaplan 136–47). The remediation of events associated with Hurricane Katrina, in the form of *Treme*, is also a good example of a collective work (despite it simultaneously being a David Simon television show and an HBO show). I am not just referring to the collective that makes the show, including the various producers, writers, and directors that Simon works with as well as all the below-the-line workers. It is important to also consider the show as a collective project on the basis that it uses documentary images for its opening sequence and samples real (archived) news broadcasts. Without this already-authored material, *Treme* would be a significantly different memorial. In this sense, there is a profound relationship between collective work and remediation. Although the two are not synonymous or mutually inclusive, they are connected to each other in important ways. For instance, a remediated work is collective in the sense that the labour it appropriates from the past always forms a collective with the current users. Still, a collective work is not always best described as remediated, although in some cases the translation of a group of contributions into one expression could be described as remediation (such as oral histories). In the television shows under consideration here, the ability to produce an affective memorial space depends on each show's willingness and ability to represent collective work, including the use of remediation as an aesthetic technique to link documents to affect.

By way of illustrating more of the dimensions of the collective and remediated nature of television memorial programming, we could consider *Treme*'s extensive use of location shooting. This aspect of the series is noted by most commentators, who also draw a connection between location shooting and community building. This is emphasized by the show's paratextual elements, such as Web-isodes, which regularly feature short documentaries that provide guided tours of the show's locations, including interviews with residents of the Treme neighbourhood.[5] Since *Treme* is shot on location, and because it captures a variety of musicians performing *on* location, the collective authorship of this commemorative show extends beyond the show's production group. Indeed, authorship must also be attributed to the musical performers (such as Allain Toussaint, Kermit Ruffins, Steve Earle, Lucia Micarelli, and Dr. John), who are authors in their own sequences. It can also be argued that the architects and citizens who painted their houses and trimmed their lawns are essentially the designers of much of the outside space encountered in the world of the show. On this count, then, commercial television again illustrates the ways that memorials are enriched by collective authorship.

In the context of commercial television, these types of questions really only matter to the sponsors and distributors to the extent that they effect viewership and ratings or subscriptions. For instance, the short lifespan of *Saving Grace* points to its inability to attract an appropriately large and desired audience. These types of commercial pressures were evident well before the show was cancelled; as ratings for the show began to plummet in the first season, the producers strived to make the show more conventionally popular. Thus, storylines became more predictable, Grace's idiosyncratic behaviour was significantly harnessed, and the more provocative aspects of fundamentalist Christianity were excised. So, while these shows are remediation *par excellence* and are recognizably collective in nature, it must also be noted that such television shows are characterized by their populism. The populism of *Saving Grace* and *Rescue Me* is positively ribald. Grace, for instance, impresses the viewer as a regular worker and a bit like an American stereotype: she works hard at her job, smokes profusely, drinks to forget problems, and has sex (on her mind) regularly. Grace's mirror in *Rescue Me* is Leary's Tommy Gavin, who also plays a tragic Dionysian figure. The libidinal force these characters develop is appealing on one level, offensive on many others, but perfectly an expression of American populist sentiment. Indeed, that sentiment devolves routinely into full-blown sentimentality and hence into some of the more familiar and denigrated tendencies of melodrama (e.g., the histrionics associated with Hollywood dramas, prime-time and daytime soaps, and movies of the week), in which heightened emotional crises and absurd processes of human redemption are a clichéd staple. By contrast, while *Treme* would also be considered a melodrama, its distinction lies in its interest in social formations—specifically, in the social and power relations that communities encounter during crises. Emotional crises and redemption take on a different role in this context—a less humanist one, more sociological, almost pedantic.

There is a consistency with regard to what the distributors assess as the value of these shows. For instance, David Simon's work is distributed by HBO, a premium cable service that features programming that is, in the words of one of its most quoted promotional slogans, "not TV. It's HBO." The premise is that the perception of greater value in the shows will attract a subscription audience that represents a desired demographic; for HBO, it is middle-aged, professional, upper middle class, bourgeois, and in possession of disposable income. This audience is interested in commercials for expensive and innovative automobiles, high-end clothing and fashion, financial services, and other premium products and services. Memorials, by contrast, produce aesthetic experiences that regularly aim to be independent of commercial demands. Memorial spaces, therefore, tend to represent a wider range of meanings relative to commercial spaces, and, consequently, there are significant contradictions between the values extolled by memorials and those of commercial television.

The thorny topic of value takes this discussion into territory that is regularly interrogated by critics of public art: the debate between elitism and populism. The idea of collective authorship necessarily introduces the idea of compromise, and this is always understood as compromising an individual artist's vision. As much as the three shows under discussion are nominally considered collective and populist works, they can also be understood as occupying various positions within the spectrum between cultural elitism and populist conformity. In each case, realism dominates as an aesthetic style, thus confirming a typical convention of North American popular television in which presence ("just the facts") is a celebrated norm. In attempting to argue for distinctions between types of programming, television scholars have claimed that realism is characteristic of, if not exclusive to, "quality television." As it has evolved, this is a broad (to the point of being almost useless) category of programming that is historically meant to designate television shows that reflect a "turn to relevance"—a phrase meant to designate programming that consistently and intentionally reflects current and significant social and political issues. This turn is illustrated by the appearance of such themes as racism, sexism, poverty, and sexuality as they were featured in particular shows beginning in the late 1960s with the Norman Lear sitcoms (*All in the Family, Good Times, One Day at a Time, Maude, Mary Hartman, Mary Hartman,* and *Diff'rent Strokes*) and MTM productions (*The Mary Tyler Moore Show, Rhoda, Lou Grant, Hill Street Blues,* and *St. Elsewhere*) (Nelson 179–85). Of the three shows under consideration here, *Treme* would likely be read as the most authentic representation and hence the most clear-cut example of "quality television." By contrast, *Rescue Me* and *Saving Grace* make regular use of obvious entertainment conventions such as chase scenes, pratfalls, and fantasy elements including dreams, phantom characters, visions, non-reality, and sometimes hyperreality. Because these types of elements appear unrealistic, the shows' respective meanings tend to be allegorical, rather than objective representations of the worlds they represent. The limited amount of location shooting in these shows underscores this impression. The alignment that develops, then, is between an authenticity represented in the elitist context of HBO programming and a populism that turns away from realism, particularly at the most socially and politically interesting points in the stories.

So, the category of "quality television," which generally characterizes all three shows, sheds little light on these shows' values as memorials. Nonetheless, in a way, the term "quality" is appropriate, albeit not in the way it was originally intended. It is clear that there is a perceived quality in *Treme*, for instance, to the extent that HBO recognizes its value in attracting a particular audience. At the same time, there are equally valid perceived qualities in the other shows that clearly represent exchange value in contemporary media markets. Considered in a more precise fashion, these shows' differing approaches to realism and fantasy are not so much indicative of their quality per se as they are symptomatic of two functions that are considered requisite—particularly within the field of trauma studies—in commemorative art and culture: witnessing and translating. This distinction can help illustrate the point that *Treme* is not a better memorial, or one of greater quality, so much as it is one that privileges realism and *witnessing*. While the power of such witnessing is undeniable, the other shows gain enormous force through their attention to *translating* their crises through fantasies.

On the one hand, documents of all types provide a fairly straightforward example of witnessing; on the other, fantasy and the construction of affect (sometimes through special effects) as means by which a trauma can be communicated or translated to others is a particular achievement of the "magic" of movies and television. The spectrum these shows move along can also then be understood as characterized by analogy on one end and allegory on the other. All these shows display an ease with which the narratives and the *mise en scène* intermingle fantasy with reality, allegory with analogy, and translation with accounting and witnessing. The shows are remediations of national traumas, and their similar designs suggest that memorials and the processes of cultural memory and working through can be resolved in the context of a series of form-problems. This is not to suggest that such traumatic memories are solved by a structuralist approach to human behaviour. But it can be seen that the ambivalence of commercial television, which is generated from a variety of substantial contradictions in its political economy and in its technological capacities, is useful to consider when estimating the value of remediations that are simultaneously history and its model. Necessarily, simulations dominate contemporary media culture and claims of authenticity are always qualified by this larger context. So, while the prosthesis that is commercial television is not likely to point in a prescriptive direction to authentic encounters with national traumatic memories, the effect of this prosthetic (and here it is good to remember that the word is derived from the Latin *pros* "in addition" + *tithenai* "to place," thus a phrase that describes a relation to place) is to create a space of memory and affect. In each of the shows, innovative *mise en scène* is often an element in a traumatic encounter (whether realistic or fantastical), and therefore the spaces of each show are quite distinct. For instance, in all three shows, but especially *Treme*, location shooting imparts a strong sense of place and community, so there is a sense of documentary realism that is referenced—images from the archive, as it were. In terms of fantasy, the shows often use narrative crises allegorically, and they certainly regard their source traumas as having allegorical relevance to daily problems, including domestic crises.

For instance, the angel that appears in each episode to save Grace is a fantasy figure that guides her through each daily crisis on the principle that she will learn to trust God so that she can eventually be redeemed for her guilt, which is associated with both private and public trauma. In many episodes of *Rescue Me*, especially season premieres and finales, sequences are composed as accompaniment to a song, with no noise or dialogue. In effect, these memorial moments become a music video. In such instances, the characters' actions often seem surreal and without motivation. At the same time, it is absolutely clear that these sequences are meant to represent heroic endurance, and this includes many shots of Tommy gazing painfully into the landscape and images of firefighters in an inferno (both literal and moral).

To cite a specific instance, consider the closing scenes of *Rescue Me*'s pilot episode, "Guts," which first aired on 21 July 2004. After Tommy has stormed out of a therapy session visibly upset about being asked to recall traumatic memories from his job, he drives around aimlessly while smoking. The smoking is important because it adds a sense of realism to the scene and also represents the character's adult but clearly "politically incorrect" behaviour. Notably, Grace is also seen smoking, and this signals something about the populist libertarian core at the heart of each series. Coldplay's song "Don't Panic" has gradually replaced all diegetic sound for these scenes, and as the song increases in volume, the view cuts away from Tommy to a montage of some of the other firefighters.[6] These characters are engaged in a variety of activities, some of which are clearly therapeutic. Franco Rivera, for instance, is punching a bag, while Lou is punching poetry into his computer (we get a glimpse of the title "Ode to the Heroes" and can read the opening lines: "Through the night into day / Risking life and limb were they / through smoke and flame and girders twisted / something gone that once existed"). In the meantime, Tommy has arrived at a beach and is drinking alone. The scene closes with two austere and foreboding shots. As a tracking shot moves slowly back from the beach and then pans to follow Tommy as he leaves, it reveals that he is not on the beach alone, but is shadowed by ghosts from his work life: Jimmy Keefe and three other firefighters, and a little boy and girl, all of whom show signs of distress and injury. The last shot of the sequence is a static high-angle shot framed so as to view down on the beach with the horizon at the top of the frame. This flattens the space so that as Tommy leads the other characters into the frame, they move up the screen to the horizon. As the song fades out, the feeling is one of bitterness and ambivalence. The image can be read to suggest that Tommy is leading these angels to heaven, foreshadowing his own demise; but this shot can also serve as a sign of rebirth. Similar to a music video or a modernist film, the meanings of this sequence do not depend on staples of commercial television such as dialogue or realist *mise en scène*. It is also worth noting that in *Rescue Me*'s non-realist sequences, the images that predominate are familiar to the point of cliché: they include flames engulfing spaces, hero characters carrying equipment and survivors, and structures crumbling.[7] In these sequences, the remediation of the crisis as a quasi-music video produces a space that is located allegorically in and around the event called 9/11, and this space contains crises and cataclysm and communities of victims and survivors; in short, this space is an image of the event's "unconscious" and provides a horizon of meaning that is structured through a complex interplay of reality and fantasy.

It is worth recalling Pierre Nora's observation that "modern memory is first of all archival. It relies entirely on the specificity of the trace, the materiality of the vestige, the concreteness of the recording, the visibility of the image" (Nora "Between" 13). The shows under consideration here illustrate Nora's point even though they include fantasy elements. *Treme*, with its heightened verisimilitude, may be said to be paradigmatic. In scene after scene, the show uses aspects of the real to verify for its viewers the authenticity of its stories. The images and the characters tend to provide a sense of what Janet Walker has called "situated testimony," or witnessing that is grounded in a real place of trauma (Walker 2010). According to Walker, in such processes, the acts of recalling, re-enacting, and rebuilding that are associated with working through trauma are connected specifically to an act of reclaiming a specific place, which is usually the site of a catastrophe. Walker argues that the ability of the survivor to speak from the place of trauma represents both a powerful moment of witnessing and an important act of reclaiming space. By celebrating the return to the Crescent City, *Treme* reflects this level of citizen empowerment, but it would be a mistake to suggest that the show's only value lies in its objective realism. An analysis of an important short sequence from the last episode of the first season will illustrate this point.

The sequence begins at a funeral service (one of several in the show) for LaDonna's brother, David Brooks. After following the search for David (Daryl Williams) since Episode One, and after a variety of clues have provided evidence of his location (all of this due to lawyer Toni Bernette [Melissa Leo] and her dogged pursuit of the truth), it is saddening, but unsurprising, to ultimately learn that the young man has died. For a variety of reasons, David was not properly identified, and was lost in the system, both while living and while dead. In Episode Nine, the viewer learns that David has been kept in cold storage for five months. At his funeral, LaDonna (Khandi Alexander) is framed in close-up, which shows that she is initially intent on the service, grief-stricken, and inward looking when a cellphone begins to ring. The ringing continues, creating a sense of awkwardness for the viewer, who anticipates that someone will have to apologize for interrupting the family's mourning. As it turns out, the sound is non-diegetic, which is established when the shot of LaDonna slowly pulls out of focus and transitions to a shot of a cellphone being answered by David in a house that the viewer may recall as his grandmother's. The viewer recognizes David, because he has already been identified in the refrigerated trailer and shown throughout the season in LaDonna's dreams. These dreams have been threatening: they feature David in a jail cell, sometimes alone and at other times with another inmate, whom the viewer knows (and distrusts) from an encounter with him in the course of the family's investigation.

It becomes apparent that what is being shown is a flashback to the day that Katrina hit New Orleans. That flashback follows David as he prepares to make a delivery that will lead to a traffic violation that will lead to an unjustified incarceration. These "facts" have been revealed in earlier episodes and are part of the official story that the family has been able to assemble. As to how the events of the day played out, these are left to everyone's imagination, as David has not survived to verify the truth. In this way, the show is able to suggest the absolute importance of the witness, who can verify the truth of history; but it is also quite clear that the show suggests that fantasy has an important place in memory. As LaDonna says in response to Toni's assistant, who is asking her to order an independent autopsy to determine cause of death, "What is there to find out that we can't already guess?" Almost as an illustration of that assertion, this sequence presents a fantasy that is being used to remediate the facts; this in turn allows LaDonna to stage a scene that helps her imagine, based on the evidence she has been presented with, how David spent the day that Katrina hit the city. Nonetheless, the show is ambivalent as to whether this process offers a positive outcome for LaDonna. On the one hand, by conjuring up this fantasy, LaDonna gets to share a moment with her brother, giving her a last chance to regain a sense of the order that structured their lives prior to the catastrophe. On the other hand, David's death suggests that whatever fantasy LaDonna conjures, she will likely also have to negotiate the more threatening and less reassuring images and stories of his humiliation, abuse, and murder as a series of fantasy scenarios that the show has already represented as nightmarish.

As the sequence continues, its design pertains to specific aspects of memorial spaces. When the images of David give way to those of other characters, the viewer realizes that what he/she imagined to be a continuation of the sequence from LaDonna's perspective is now increasingly not comprehensible as her fantasy. That is, the viewer is shown scenes that explain how all the central characters of the show dealt with the oncoming disaster. These scenes are provided not for LaDonna, but for the viewer, and as much as it is a pragmatic way of wrapping up the first season of a television show, it also achieves a powerful emotional affect. This affect is produced because the viewer is being encouraged to fantasize, like LaDonna, the order that existed before the crisis. The effect, then, is not precisely nostalgia, but a profound appreciation of the way that catastrophes change things forever. In this sense, the show as a fantasy itself directs viewers to a position of empathy and intersubjectivity with fictional characters (or at least the "situations" that those characters represent) who are going to experience trauma. The sequence is not intended to simply explain how the characters got to where they are, thus tying up some loose ends in the fashion of classical narrative style. Since its elements are based on reality and consistently refer to the extra-diegetic world, *Treme* has the ability to develop structures for empathy and compassion that connect to real communities of victims in New Orleans. So when the sequence returns to the present, the viewer is not reassured that this is the way things actually happened, but instead realizes that what he/she has experienced is LaDonna's model of empathizing, which has led the viewer to behave in a similar manner to these other characters. LaDonna's visions of what happened constitute her process of memory making; and the show makes it clear that she is not recalling something that is verifiable as fact; but by connecting her grief to other characters, the show encourages compassion in the viewer.

This sequence, then, provides a model of how memorial spaces use fantasy to encourage translation and intersubjectivity in an effort to work through trauma. This model is in keeping with those theorists who argue that successful memorials develop effective intersubjectivity through translating trauma that is, in the words of Frances Guerin, "at the heart of a process of bearing witness to the past" (119). This framework is also in line with ideas expressed by Walker, who describes the function of disremembering, which is not forgetting or repressing, but the contouring of memory through fantasies that often only tangentially reflect the objective reality of an event (*Trauma* 16–19). If the fantasies of these shows reflect a reality, it is not necessarily a direct transcription of witness accounts, so much as a translation or remediation or something disremembered. Disremembering is a strategy used by survivors, and its variegated texture (some reality here, some fiction there) would be evidence of the patchwork nature of working through trauma. As illustrated above, these shows use various strategies to encourage disremembering, creating contemporary memorial spaces composed of intervals of witnessing and imagining, analogy and allegory, and reality and fantasy.

NOTES

1   For an insightful discussion of the relationship between television and new media, refer to Murphy.
2   An early articulation of the concept is found in Feuer. Caldwell and Nelson revisit similar territory with their respective terms "boutique programming" and "high-end tv."
3   For a pioneering work in regard to the aesthetic experience of monuments, refer to Young.
4   For this intellectual history, refer to Nelson 164–70.
5   In particular, *Times-Picayune* writer David Walker champions the show's realism in his "Today on *Treme*" column by including visits to the locations used in the series, historical background pieces on these spaces, and interviews with New Orleans artists and residents featured in the series. That paper also runs a weekly column, "*Treme* Explained," that elaborates on local references in the show. A contrary view is expressed by Adolf Reed, Jr., who claims that *Treme* trades heavily in the touristic discourse that fetishizes authenticity,

with the consequence that real New Orleans city politics and culture are distorted for public consumption (*Three Tremés*).

6 The song lyrics are: "Bones, sinking like stones / All that we fought for / Homes, places we've grown / All of us are done for. / We live in a beautiful world / Yeah we do, yeah we do / We live in a beautiful world. / Oh, all that I know / There's nothing here to run from / And here, everybody here's got somebody to lean on."

7 These images are not unique to the show: they appear in films such as *World Trade Center* (Stone, 2006) as well as in numerous documentary images of the attacks. One significant early celebration of the heroic masculinity associated with such images is William Langewiesche's *American Ground: Unbuilding the World Trade Center*, originally published in three parts in *The Atlantic Monthly* from July to October 2002 and published as a book in October 2002. For a critical account of this and other such popular culture products, refer to Mead (57–68).

16

Creative Re-enactment in the Films and Videos of Omer Fast

Kate Warren

The desire to "experience" the past, whether through practices of fiction or documentary—a distinction that is increasingly difficult to maintain—is one key defining element of contemporary memory culture. Very often, the mode that facilitates such affective engagements with history and memory is re-enactment. Art historian Sven Lütticken has called re-enactments "historicist happenings" (27), a description that emphasizes the performative and experiential nature of such practices as well as their focus on the "now," on approaching "the past as present" (27). Re-enactments truly are "present"—indeed, they are pervasive in contemporary culture, observable in a multitude of media, representational strategies, social activities, and cultural objects. Popular films such as Steven Spielberg's *Saving Private Ryan* (1998) and Clint Eastwood's *Flags of Our Fathers* (2006) re-enact iconic images and events; documentaries and miniseries employ re-enactment incessantly to bring their subject matter to life for their viewers; "historical" reality television shows, a growing phenomenon, thrust participants into a re-created past; and re-enactment societies remain popular sources of entertainment and immersive history. Re-enactment practices characterize many living history museums, tourist sites, monuments, memorials, and museum exhibitions.

All these examples point to how, as Andreas Huyssen notes, "the desire for narratives of the past, for re-creations, re-readings, re-productions, seems boundless at every level of our culture" ("Present Pasts" 5). This chapter considers this cultural and historical phenomenon of re-enactment, some of its defining characteristics, and its role in the remediation of cultural memory. The gallery-based video installations of artist Omer Fast (born 1972, Israel) will serve as a focal point for most of the discussion.[1] Over the past decade, Fast has emerged as one of a number of contemporary visual artists who interrogate memory, history, representation, and remediation through an interest in re-enactment, revealing ways that the contemporary visual arts can offer alternative and critical approaches to mainstream and populist forms of this widespread phenomenon.

Historical Re-enactment: A Brief Trajectory

The urge to re-enact may be illustrative of present conditions, but it is by no means exclusive to contemporary culture. A thorough history would extend centuries; however, today's popular forms of re-enactment can largely be traced to a resurgence of interest during the nineteenth century and a reimagining of historical subjects in light of the historicism and Romantic sentiments that prevailed at that time (Lütticken 29). That era, which Friedrich Nietzsche described as possessing an "excess of history" (8), produced countless historical novels, artworks, revisionist architectural styles, and cultural modes of entertainment, which Sven Lütticken argues "helped to stimulate identification with the past and overcome the difference between it and the present" (29). These practices of re-enactment and repetition were not limited to refashioning events within living memory. One of the best-known examples took place in 1839, when the thirteenth Earl of Eglinton hosted a pageant that re-enacted a medieval jousting tournament; this hugely successful event "represented a distinctly nineteenth-century vision of the Middle Ages" (Rushton 5). Pageants, passion plays, and *tableaux vivants*, which grew in popularity around this time, were decidedly theatrical and performative approaches to mediating the past; thus they anticipated contemporary trends toward "experiential" and "affective" history (McCalman and Pickering 6–7). While re-enactment practices have been observed most often in the anglophone world,[2] they have been and remain a global phenomenon (Agnew 328). Continental Romanticism of the nineteenth century displayed such tendencies across art forms. Paintings such as Eugène Delacroix's epic masterwork *July 28: Liberty Leading the People* (1830) mixed "contemporary historical fact and poetic allegory" (Rosenblum and Janson 142), and the works of Baroque and medieval musicians were revisited by Romantic composers, such as Felix Mendelssohn's 1829 revival of Johann Sebastian Bach's *St. Matthew Passion* (Applegate).

Re-enactment practices and the wider culture of historicism later coincided with technological and aesthetic advances in realist representation. Unlike the broader aesthetic trajectory of Romanticism, which largely clashed with the increasing realist impulse, historical re-enactment has thrived upon realism, becoming intimately entwined with this dominant approach. From early naturalist developments in theatre scenography, such as panoramas and dioramas, to the invention of photography and the cinema, to contemporary CGI techniques (McCalman and Pickering 1–2), technological advances have made the re-creation and mimetic imitation of people, places, and events not simply possible but often desirable and expected. McCalman and Pickering characterize re-enactment as caught between two "reals," where there exists "a desire to learn from the literal recreation of the past and, at the same time, a yearning to experience history somatically and emotionally" (6). The cultural enthusiasm for re-enactments and re-creations of the past has intensified since the nineteenth century, bringing with it many questions and tensions concerning its relation to memory and history, its focus on affective modes of representation and experience for both participants and viewers, and its complex relationship to notions of authenticity, fidelity, and "the real" in its historical subject matters.

Re-enactment as Remediation: *Schindler's List* and *Spielberg's List*

Through his artistic practice in film, installation, and video, Omer Fast picks up on and evokes many of the tensions and defining features that dominate contemporary re-enactment practices. His artworks are often developed from interviews conducted with a range of people—from undertakers to soldiers, from asylum seekers to actors—yet when choosing subjects, he is often drawn to those whose memories, experiences, and personal narratives have been contested and compromised by processes of representation and remediation. He actively seeks people whose subjectivity is split in some way—what he calls "the duped/duping witness" (Fast and Lütticken 28). One of Fast's best-known works, *Spielberg's List* (2003)—a piece that largely established him internationally—keenly reflects these preoccupations with re-enactment, storytelling, memory, and bearing witness. For this work, Fast travelled to Kraków to interview Polish residents who had worked as extras on the film *Schindler's List* (Spielberg,

1993). Many of Fast's interviewees were old enough to have lived through the Second World War, and what is disconcerting about *Spielberg's List* is the way it reveals, constructs, and subverts the slippages that occur between past and present, between the real and the representation, and how the re-enactors articulate their experiences as extras in comparison to the original historical event.

The Holocaust has long been remembered, represented, and remediated across all art forms and media. The number of films, books, exhibitions, and memorials devoted to it seems endless, yet the incomprehensibility of the event persists, as does scrutiny about its limits of representation.[3] Upon release, *Schindler's List* generated new debates about these limits, particularly in relation to an equally epic piece of filmmaking, Claude Lanzmann's *Shoah* (1985),[4] with much of the contestation focusing on Spielberg's acts of re-enactment and re-creation. Scenes such as the sequence of female Jewish prisoners being ushered into what appears to be a gas chamber at Auschwitz, which is soon revealed to be a shower, and the film's tendency toward melodrama and pathos—for example, the girl in the red dress—reveal the power of a director like Spielberg to influence the cultural memory of this event on a global scale.[5] *Schindler's List* demonstrates the aspect of "immediacy" in Bolter and Grusin's "double logic" of remediation, whereby the representation aims "to erase or render automatic the act of representation" (33). Spielberg's precise re-creations of the Kraków ghetto, the Płaszów concentration camp, and Auschwitz-Birkenau strive for an experiential mode of audience reception,[6] and the film's black-and-white cinematography remediates the style of historical and documentary footage and photography.

Omer Fast's *Spielberg's List* continues and intensifies this complex process of remediation in the context of Spielberg's film and the broader legacy of Holocaust representation, yet his treatment is more akin to the flip side of Bolter and Grusin's double logic—"hypermediacy," which "acknowledges multiple acts of representation and makes them visible" (33–34). It reveals elements of remediation inherent in the act of re-enactment itself, and in doing so, it further obscures a situation that has already been temporally compromised through the re-enactment process. This is particularly evident in the language used by the extras to describe their experiences during filming. There are surreal and somewhat uncomfortable moments in Fast's film when the actors describe how they were chosen for their roles, with many of them using highly loaded terms like "selection" and "conscription" to describe the process. Many talk about being selected to play Jews because of their perceived Semitic-like features, and in doing so they mimic—consciously or unconsciously—the language that has developed over many years and that has been mediated through countless representations to describe the original horrifying event.

Of course, when talking to re-enactors about the events they re-perform, such temporal confusion is somewhat inevitable. Re-enactments can be highly emotionally charged environments that actualize the confusion between the "real" and the representation, sometimes producing a "period rush" where re-enactors have difficulty transitioning back into the present (Agnew 330; Horwitz 7). There are many such moments in *Spielberg's List,* and while the piece does not dismiss, condescend, or try to explain such moments, it actively exacerbates this tension through its editing and visual construction. Fast describes his interviewees as "authentic witness[es] to a representation" (Lewis-Kraus); thus he acknowledges that his interviewees, as extras, have had *real* experiences, albeit of a very *unreal* situation. The work itself is a dual-channel gallery installation, and its two screens reflect the multiple levels of doubling that occur throughout. The filmed interviews are intercut with present-day location footage from around Kraków and with snippets from Spielberg's film. For the Polish interviews, Fast hired two translators to produce the English subtitles, and he often incorporates both translations into the final work, alongside each other (Trainor 127). The subtle variations and mistranslations produced from the same utterance contrast with other passages of subtitles and dialogue that reveal themselves as being more overtly altered—"corruption" interchanges with "capitalism," "protesting" interchanges with "prospering"—and this subverts any assumption of subjectivity involved in offering, translating, and representing testimony. Fast's reworkings and alterations create fissures and gaps, allowing doubt and uncertainty to merge with the artwork's "real" and the "authentic"; the result is a piece that is deliberately ambiguous and ambivalent to forms of historical representation, documentary, and dramatization. *Spielberg's List* reveals complex feedback loops that emerge through and are produced by contemporary, multi-level forms of remediation. It also exposes the ways in which the practice of re-enactment can challenge the authority and the idea of the "witness" and compromise the nature of giving testimony.

As will be discussed, Fast uses re-enactment not simply as a subject matter but also as an expressive and critical device. The example of *Spielberg's List* has been introduced at this early stage because it articulates and problematizes the influence and power of large-scale, popular, and mainstream re-enactment projects as evidenced in a film like *Schindler's List*. Fast's subsequent remediation reveals and further complicates the aftereffects of Spielberg's historical spectacle, long after the cameras stopped rolling and the media event of the film's release subsided. The piece also incorporates footage shot during a *Schindler's List* "tour" of Kraków as well as interviews with the locals who started running such tours, revealing how, almost immediately after the film's release in America, tourists began visiting the sites depicted in the film and conflating cinematic representations with the real locations. Fast is not alone in his interest in re-enactment practices; many contemporary artists are increasingly drawn to them—notably, T.R. Uthco and Ant Farm, Rod Dickinson, Jeremy Deller, Pierre Huyghe, Irina Botea, Peter Watkins, and Christoph Draeger—and are producing artworks that often respond to events that are already highly mediated. In recent years, a number of international exhibitions have approached re-enactment as a popular curatorial theme.[7] These artistic and curatorial interests tap into the broader sense that re-enactment is a central technique and strategy in the continual remediation of memory and history.

Re-enactment: A Challenge to Memory and History

Re-enactments often address traumatic and dramatic events—moments of importance in national narratives—and in doing so, they play a significant role in the broader cultural memory of those moments. In contemporary society, most people's experiences of key historical events are mediated, often through television and radio and increasingly through the Internet and social networking sites such as YouTube, Twitter, and Facebook. Re-enactment is a crucial part of the diverse remediations and reiterations that follow, in the process of transforming media spectacles into events of memory and history.

Strategies of re-enactment straddle and pose challenges to our society's obsession with memory—or as Huyssen describes it, the "hypertrophy of memory" (3); at the same time, they confront historiographical concerns about how history is written. They reflect ongoing dialogues between memory and history that continue to be negotiated across different fields and modes of representation. Writer and filmmaker Steve Rushton describes artistic re-enactment as "the mediation of memory [...] Rather than being a form of representation [...] re-enactment is closer to a frame for varied critical approaches to the manipulation or restructuring of memory" (10–11). This position assumes a level of self-reflexivity and criticism, and while re-enactments can be used to present alternative histories that may have been forgotten by traditional history and mainstream remembrance practices, they are frequently used to reinforce already dominant and prevalent historical narratives, to maintain the status quo and offer a sense of endless and even compulsive repetition (Lütticken 45). In *Tourists of History* (2007), Marita Sturken analyzes the varied forms of re-enactment employed in the mediation, memorialization, and remembrance practices that have surrounded the terrorist attacks of 11 September 2001, arguing that "[r]epetition is a means through which cultures process and make sense of traumatic events. It is caught up in kitsch and the relentless recoding of trauma into popular culture narratives, yet it is also evidence of the ways that cultures reenact, sometimes compulsively, moments of traumatic change" (29).

Re-enactments are often employed as means of seeking closure and catharsis by prioritizing emotional and affective responses, and here lies one of its biggest challenges to traditional modes of history. Re-enactment is largely viewed with a level of suspicion within historiographical historiographical circles, illustrated by Greg Dening's characterization of it as the "present in funny dress" (qtd. in McCalman and Pickering 2). Re-enactment elicits such responses because it does not adhere to traditional academic and intellectual categories surrounding history. It prioritizes embodied and visceral experiences of history over analytical or distanced approaches. Re-enactment's promise—certainly not itself unproblematic—is to democratize historical knowledge (Agnew 335), to break down traditional categories and divisions between academic and non-academic pursuits of historical understanding, and to offer participants immersive access to history in ways that history books cannot.

Not all historians have been disinclined to ideas of re-enactment, and in the increasing study of this cultural phenomenon, the work of early-twentieth-century English historian R.G. Collingwood has received renewed interest. Collingwood argues that mental re-enactment is an essential element of good historical practice, insisting that the role of re-enactment is to enable the historian to imagine the world of the past from the perspective of historical agents and to understand their motivations. In *The Idea of History*, posthumously published in 1946, he asks, "how does the historian discern the thoughts which he is trying to discover? There is only one way in which it can be done: by re-thinking them in his own mind" (215). Such re-enactment of past experience and thoughts, Collingwood adds, is "not a passive surrender to the spell of another mind; it is a labour of active and therefore critical thinking" (215). Certainly Collingwood's approach to re-enactment is based on the desire to understand past actions specifically in relation to the *writing of history*, and his consideration of it is primarily as an intellectual pursuit, not a physical or artistic one. However, it is Collingwood's insistence that historians make a "strenuous imaginative leap into the past" (McCalman and Pickering 3) that becomes relevant for creative and critical re-enactment practices, such as the examples to be discussed of Omer Fast and of the previously mentioned artists. Collingwood argues that when a form of intellectual re-enactment is employed in the writing of history, "[a]ll thinking is critical thinking; the thought which re-enacts past thoughts, therefore, criticizes them in re-enacting them" (216). Contemporary artists who employ strategies of re-enactment are often motivated by a critical impulse, being less concerned with achieving dimensions of catharsis or historical understanding, and more interested in exploring the compulsive and obsessive dimensions of repetition, thus problematizing or undermining modes of representation and histories that may seek a *singular* truth.

Analogy, Equivalence, Experience

In his essay "Subject Positions, Speaking Positions,"[8] Thomas Elsaesser argues how, as various filmmakers have approached representations of the Holocaust and German postwar society, they have created distinct speaking positions for themselves and their films, in an effort to justify their "right" to speak about such topics (145–84). Through the vicarious encounters they offer, re-enactments allow their participants to form particular subject positions from which they can testify to their experiences. Re-enactors have had lived experiences of events or environments that, although simulated, nevertheless aspire to levels of historical fidelity, couched within a "hierarchy of the genuine" (Agnew 331). Thus, the speaking positions afforded to and assumed by re-enactors are complex and temporally compromised. As Vanessa Agnew argues, re-enactment often privileges *extremity* of experience, creating "a hierarchy of legitimacy; the most intense manifestation of suffering is most authorized to occupy the voice of history" (331). Thus, re-enactors often feel the need to testify and speak to the wounds and traumas they experience. We see this in *Spielberg's List*, in which one woman proudly shows the artist her scarred knee from when she was injured during filming. She adds that, in her belief, she experienced the reality of a concentration camp on a "mini-scale" (Fast). Another woman speaks of her genuine tears as her hair was cut on-camera, and while these extras were undoubtedly fully aware that their reactions were being formed within an environment of representation, such moments in the artwork reveal one of the problematic areas of re-enactment practice: *analogy*. The appeal of re-enactment is that it gives participants a sense of what the past was like. However, one of the dangers is that the re-enactors will assume that the emotions they feel are equivalent to those felt by the historical agents. Our knowledge of the contemporary world inevitably informs how we react to such situations, yet re-enactments are often highly affective experiences, where boundaries and distinctions between past, present, and future become blurred and porous.

The moving image is particularly well suited to capturing and emphasizing this sense of the past and the present colliding and conflating with each other. Such concerns around analogy in re-enactment observed in *Spielberg's List* are further explored in Fast's subsequent piece, *Godville* (2005). The artist visited the Colonial Williamsburg living history museum in Virginia and interviewed a number of "character interpreters" both in and out of character (Fast "Preface" 6), discussing both their fictional personas and their modern lives. Fast then subjected his filmed interviews to a vigorous and meticulous process of editing, a technique that can also be seen in one of his earliest pieces, *CNN Concatenated* (2002) and that has led Gideon Lewis-Kraus to call him the "Reanimator" (Lewis-Kraus). The stories recounted by the three interviewees are refashioned by Fast into new, alternative narratives and scripts through a compulsively detailed process—one of the most complex sections of the artwork took Fast two months to edit (Lewis-Kraus). At one point, one of the character impersonators describes a sense of "schizophrenia" (Fast) felt when two temporalities collide, and Fast magnifies this confusion by bringing implied associations into direct conversation, giving the impression that his subjects' historical characters are interchangeable with their contemporary selves. As the characters reminisce about memories from the past or talk about future aspirations, it becomes, at times, impossible for viewers to distinguish between past and present, memory and fantasy, real and fiction. References to the American War of Independence conflate with references to the War on Terror, and concerns about contemporary race relations resonate with references to the history of slavery. In the process,

Godville distinguishes not only an individual schizophrenia, but also a trajectory of political and cultural narratives that echo and reverberate across history and that have been used repeatedly to define American national identity. Thus, what begins on the personal level in *Godville* transforms into a feeling of equivalence and analogy that transcends and connects distinct historical periods, hinting at how the individual experiences of re-enactment practices extend to the broader historicization of events.

One crucial aspect of *Godville* is the way it has been purposefully installed in the gallery. Like most of Fast's pieces, *Godville* is typically installed in a "black box"—a darkened space usually fitted with carpet, sound insulation, and light locks—as opposed to the more common "white cubes" of contemporary art galleries. On entering the space, visitors see a large screen suspended in the middle of the gallery; projected onto it is footage of both "period" Colonial Williamsburg and the modern housing developments of the surrounding area. The voices of the character interpreters are heard as if in voice-over, but their images are not visible. Viewers must walk around the back of the suspended screen in order to discover the images of the interviewees projected on the other side; it is then that the highly edited and constructed nature of their testimony becomes immediately apparent through the jerky jump-cuts visible on-screen. Yet in a gallery setting many visitors do not explore the space, and thus they may miss this aspect of the artwork. Fast does not suppress or conceal his creative manipulations and interventions, but he does require his viewers to work in order to appreciate the multiple layers of meaning and construction. In this sense, the artwork seems to take a slight pleasure in ever so subtly contributing to the sense of cultural and historical schizophrenia—not only of the interviewees but also of the audience—a sense that lingers and persists after they have departed the gallery.

Challenges to Identification: *The Casting*

The seductive power of contemporary mass media, with their tendencies toward the spectacle and the experiential, is such that it is not just the participants of re-enactments whose memories and perceptions can be altered and influenced. Alison Landsberg argues for the cinema's capacity to produce in its viewers "prosthetic memories," which are not derived from lived experiences but rather are "sensuous memories produced by an experience of mass-mediated representations" ("Memory" 222). She argues that viewers are "brought into intimate contact with a set of experiences that fall well outside of their own lived experience and, as a result, are forced to look as if through someone else's eyes, and asked to remember those situations and events" (222). Following this logic, it is not simply the *Schindler's List* extras who have had an affective encounter with a re-enactment; so have the film's viewers, who can have an emotive engagement through the characteristics of the cinematic medium, which is particularly effective at influencing and positioning the viewing experiences of the audience. Landsberg's thesis is unashamedly utopian, focusing on the possibility that these affective encounters with the screen can stimulate a sense of increased empathic and political engagement within viewers. Certainly, she does not argue that such "radical democratic engagements" (228) are facilitated every time—or even most of the time—that an individual watches a film; rather, she advocates the more inherent possibilities of the medium. Undoubtedly, the cinema's power to influence the cultural memory of its viewers and even politically engage them is immense. However, running parallel to the positivist characteristic identified by Landsberg is the potential for the affective qualities of the cinema to offer simplified, uncritical forms of therapeutic closure.[9]

A tension lies at the core of the representational strategies employed by the cinema, namely the balancing act that films perform between potentially offering meaningful, emotive points of entry that engage viewers in modes of active spectatorship and critical understanding, and on the other hand promoting a sense of "easy catharsis," reducing infinitely complex topics to simplified narratives, or overshadowing them in politics or ideology. Rarely does a film fall solely into one situation or the other; the variety of human responses and interpretations alone ensures as much. That which for one person is cliché, is for another believable. This topic is too complex to consider in great detail in the scope of this chapter; however, this field of viewer identification is important to bear in mind when considering some of Fast's most recent artworks.[10] Fast displays a skepticism toward this cultural desire for empathic viewer responses—he has stated that he tries to resist catharsis in his work (Allen 216)—but at the same time, he is deeply aware of and indebted to the mechanisms of the cinema that promote engagement in his audience. His films rely on intelligently structured narratives, yet they do not disavow the constructed nature of these narratives. They reveal the mechanics and the elements of their fictionalization, only to often cycle and fold back upon themselves. His works are visually seductive, with recent pieces shot on film and produced using large film crews, yet in their aesthetic sophistication, they are constructed in ways that prevent the viewer from falling into the trap of easy identification.

Fast's 2007 piece, *The Casting,* was the artist's first attempt at constructing and filming a re-enactment. This work subverts ideas around the relationship between re-enactment and realism—already explored in this chapter—while continuing the artist's interest in challenging audience expectations and identification when viewing a filmic image. It is a four-channel video installation, projected onto the front and rear sides of two suspended screens, and arranged so that only two of the four projected images are visible at one time. *The Casting* is based on an interview that Fast conducted with an American soldier, and re-enacts two of the soldier's stories—the first about an uncomfortable date with a German girl, and the second about the accidental killing of an Iraqi civilian—as filmed *tableaux vivants*, projected on the front side. These memories are narrated by the soldier in voice-over, seamlessly blending and overlapping at points, alternating backwards and forwards between the two narratives and disrupting a straightforward linear flow.

There is an immediate disjuncture between the visual and the aural elements of *The Casting*. The two projections on the rear side display footage of the original interview, revealing that this dialogue has been substantially edited by the artist, so as to exaggerate elements of the soldier's stories, making up new narratives in the process. Fast's creative improvisations on his subject's testimony bring to mind a sense of artistic licence that is often levelled as criticism toward films (and other cultural representations) that stray too much from a text deemed to be "original" or "authoritative." By appropriating this creative technique, *The Casting* presents an immediate challenge to the preoccupation—and even anxiety—that re-enactments possess with regard to authenticity. The credibility of historical re-enactments is linked strongly to notions of the authentic and their fidelity to minute aspects of their period settings (Agnew 330), but as Maria Muhle observes, Fast "not only blurs the documentarian claim to truth and the fictional limitation to untruth, but he shows the absurd nature of this partition" (Muhle). The tendency toward realism in many re-enactment practices remains strong, yet contemporary media and cultural representations often negotiate desires for historical fidelity with the seductive power of a "good story."[11] *The Casting* actualizes this tension, offering viewers a narrative that is compellingly told and illustrated, while concurrently undermining any claims of being "based on a true story"—a phrase and signifier adopted so frequently as an invocation of truthful representation.

A sense of creative assemblage manifests itself in *The Casting* through Fast's seamless editing and sampling of the recorded testimony, acknowledging the artist's concern with the malleable nature of memory.[12] Like stories, which morph and change in each retelling through improvisation, exaggeration, and omission, so too do memories alter and shift as they are remembered, being "re-encoded in the context and mood of the present" (Markowitsch 279). Just as memories do not exist in the brain as preformed replicas of experience, Fast's practice argues that neither can the truth of any story or situation be pinpointed to a singular understanding or origin. Hence, by appropriating the mode of re-enactment with its associated connotations of authenticity and fidelity, and using it to re-stage events that may (or may not) have occurred, *The Casting* questions how events of memory or history can ever be faithfully re-created or represented. Fast's creative approaches parallel processes of remembrance themselves; just as memories are unstable and changeable, so too are the stories and testimonies in Fast's works fluid and unfixed.

The Casting challenges the construction of re-enactments as well as assumptions often made about realist representation, historical fidelity, and preconceptions of the authenticity of source materials. It also calls into question audience engagement with such popular forms of entertainment. The piece, which was shot with high production values on 35mm film (transferred to video), presents two scenarios that are staples of Hollywood genre filmmaking: a romantic encounter and a violent war scene. This, combined with the artwork's subtle humour and knowingly self-conscious structure, makes *The Casting* striking, recognizable, and pleasurable to watch. However, Fast does not offer his viewers an easy or uncomplicated pleasure, and his use of *tableaux vivants* profoundly illustrates this disjuncture. *Tableaux vivants* were a popular nineteenth-century medium that used people, props, and sets to restage historical paintings (Chapman 22), taking a still medium and "reanimating" it in a more performative capacity. Fast's use of this technique performs an inverse move, utilizing a medium already associated with movement and constricting the actors and images to static poses. In the process, *The Casting* impedes the flow of identification between the viewer and the images presented; rather than seeing a woman crying in grief, *The Casting* presents a figure paused midway in the action. The focus moves away from the associated emotional and affective possibilities that a moving image can engender in viewers—as per Landsberg's thesis—and shifts their attention toward the involuntary movements, twitches, and jerks of the actors' bodies as they struggle to maintain their poses.

Additionally, the compositions of the filmed *tableaux vivants* are based on images selected and accumulated by Fast through a Google image search (Michalka 13), and this lends them a recognizable yet somewhat clichéd quality, reflecting the way that certain types of images repeat through our visual culture. This further complicates the artwork's concern with audience engagement, in that it presents images that viewers may be familiar with, but only on a superficial level through endless repetitions on the news media and the Internet. *The Casting* engages viewers through levels of familiar cinematic genre conventions and image composition, while concurrently working to strain audience identification with its subject matter. As Fast says, "it is impossible [...] to create a direct translation of [the soldier's experience]; it is not possible to represent it, and so the work proposes a game of substitution" (Fast and Verhagen 4). The result is a re-enactment that acknowledges the inherently contested nature of personal and historical events, the intricacies and limits in representing such traumas and memories, and the complex levels of identification at play in such representations.

Talk Show and the Urge to Internalize and Personalize

Re-enactments are inherently collaborative affairs that involve multiple actors and participants and that have a broad impact on cultural and collective remembrance practices. Cultural memories do not exist in isolation from history and individual memories; rather, they constantly interact and become entangled within a "field of contested meanings" where "memories [...] move from one realm to another, shifting meaning and context" (Sturken *Tangled Memories* 2, 5). This fluidity of remembrance is keenly evident in Fast's performance-cum-video installation *Talk Show* (2009), harking to what Marita Sturken identifies as a defining element of cultural memory: the sense that "fantasies about what happened are as important in national meaning as any residue of the 'truth'" (29). *Talk Show* explores how individuals interpret and internalize stories and memories—including those of other individuals or collective remembrances—within the frameworks of the personal, often imbuing them with elements of fantasy and improvisation, which nonetheless contribute to, persist,and evolve in the diverse flow of retellings and remediations.

Talk Show originated as a three-night performance piece at New York's Performa Festival in 2009, with one of the shows being adapted into a subsequent three-channel video installation. The piece used the children's game of "broken telephone" as a structuring device. It took place on a small stage dressed to resemble a television talk show. Each night featured a different "guest," who recounted a detailed, personal story to an actor sitting alongside. The guest then departed, and the actor recounted, from memory, the story he or she had just heard to a second actor, with this pattern repeating and cycling through six different actors, until in the final retelling, the story had morphed into an almost unrecognizable distortion of the original narrative.

While not made explicitly clear in the performance or video, the three guests were chosen because they were linked to broader social and historical contexts, with their stories having received previous media coverage. One guest, David Kaczynski, is the brother of the infamous Unabomber Ted Kaczynski, while Lisa Ramaci (whose story featured in the video installation) was the wife of journalist Steven Vincent, killed in Iraq in 2005 (Trainor 125). Thus, the stories that the guests narrated—although told through a "framework of private tales of family trauma and loss, downplaying details of the broader context" (Trainor 125)—were already a part of the general collective consciousness and cultural memory of the audience and the general public.

What *Talk Show* presents compellingly is not a critique of mass media repetitions, remediations, and distortions, but rather an insight into how individuals internalize and personalize the stories they hear, absorb, and remember. The themes, motifs, and structures that persevere over the piece's retellings do not necessarily represent those narrative elements most crucial or pertinent to the original story; they reflect the elements that resonate most personally and are most memorable to the interpreting individual. The desire to "put oneself in another's shoes" is a strong cultural phenomenon, as Marita Sturken argues, and this is especially so regarding dramatic and traumatic events, when "[t]he question *How did they react to imminent death?* becomes *How would I react in the face of death?* This desire and the fantasies it produces are components of cultural memory" (*Tangled Memories* 36). Such imaginations may not enter official historical records, yet they remain crucial in the ongoing developments, understandings, and remediations of cultural memory.

This collision between the personal and the collective is revealed over *Talk Show*'s duration, as the actors are increasingly forced to work in a context that remains recognizable in its cultural significance, yet becomes ever-obscured and removed from the original story. As the performance progresses, their narrative inflections often verge on cliché and kitsch, resorting to culturally predetermined tropes of storytelling, stereotypes, and fantasies, as well as reinforcing a sense of play inherent in the artwork's "game" of origin. Implicated in this process is the audience, for their voyeuristic involvement in this spectacle of narrative evolution and mutation. While *The Casting* challenges the intricacies of engagement with memories as they are mediated, transmitted, and repeated through cultural devices such as the cinema, *Talk Show* confronts viewers directly with personal impulses and desires to live vicariously through the experiences of others. As James Trainor notes, the original performances of *Talk Show* elicited unease and even slight hostility among the audience (126). Some of this raw and immediate confrontation is lost as a result of the transfer of the work to video installation, but in that process it also gains an ironic appropriation and mimicking of the culture of televised trauma and victimhood, epitomized by television personalities such as Oprah Winfrey. This links *Talk Show* compellingly with the first artwork discussed, *Spielberg's List*, in the way that it refuses to privilege either the witness or the act of offering testimony. A previous quote from the artist about the earlier work resonates strongly in relation to *Talk Show*, where Fast describes how the piece "intentionally veers from the fetishized notion of the victim or survivor as a source of moral authority" (David and Fast). *Talk Show* reacts to a cultural context in which individual stories are not only transmitted and remediated but also, in the process, commodified and consumed by other individuals—a consumption that may drive personal imaginations and fantasies but equally has the potential to fuel distinct political, ideological, or cultural agendas. Fast's work calls to account the multiple acts of offering, transmitting, remediating, and receiving stories, memories, and testimony. Like all of Fast's artworks discussed here, *Talk Show* is neither aggressive nor overtly political in its approach; nonetheless, it taps into potent cultural and political undercurrents associated within the broad and multifaceted desires surrounding re-enactment and remediation of memory and history.

Conclusion

By acknowledging its long history and ongoing popularity, this chapter has placed re-enactment as a central approach to the mediation and remediation of memory and history. This popularity raises many questions about how re-enactment engages with, facilitates, and negotiates issues of identification, analogy, authenticity, improvisation, and fantasy. Creative and critical approaches to the topic of re-enactment are common, and certainly are not limited to the visual arts—consider Michael Winterbottom's *Tristram Shandy: A Cock and Bull Story* (2005) as an interesting cinematic example. However, as the discussion of the recent works of Omer Fast reveals, contemporary artists are often able to appropriate and exploit the defining characteristics of multiple media forms—historic and contemporary—in order to subvert contemporary concerns over representation.[13]

In his creative and critical approach to re-enactment, remembrance practices, and cultures of storytelling, Fast does not embrace overly didactic or analytical approaches. While his artworks employ distancing techniques and devices that undermine and draw attention to processes of audience identification, they do not aim to alienate or preclude engagement. Fast adeptly utilizes and appropriates the language and medium-specific techniques of the moving image to implicate how it transmits and transforms memory, history, and narratives, and to subtly implicate those who provide the stories and those who consume them. As the artist says, there are "rules we use when we consume filmed stories or dramatic narratives or the news. So for each piece I try to look at these rules when I edit and there is a pleasure in breaking them, or at least in articulating them and tweaking them and playing around with them" (Fast and Verhagen 3).

Fast understands the parameters and rules of the medium in which he works; he plays the game and subverts the process from within. His acknowledgement of the pleasure involved in the creation and reception of his work links to one of the simplest yet perhaps underacknowledged elements of re-enactment that Agnew notes—namely, that "reenactment is *fun*" (327, emphasis added). The pleasure of Fast's work is paired compellingly with his deconstructions and "bending" of the rules, imbuing the pleasure for the viewer with an edge of uncertainty and a requirement to "work out" what they are in fact watching. Fast does not exclude himself as an artist from the implications of his creative manipulations; he often inserts and critiques himself (or fictionalized versions of himself) within his artworks, thus completing a cycle of implication involving those who offer memories and stories, those who re-enact, re-interpret, and remediate them, and those who consume them. While re-enactment is but one line of inquiry applicable to the practice of Omer Fast, his multi-faceted interest in and approach to this widespread cultural phenomenon reveals the multiple cultural, social, and historical levels upon which re-enactments impact and resonate.

NOTES

1. Omer Fast is an increasingly prolific artist, having exhibited widely internationally, including at the 2011 Venice Biennale, the Whitney Museum of American Art, the Centre Pompidou, the Barbican, the Hamburger Bahnhof, and the Metropolitan Museum of Art. He was awarded the Bucksbaum Award at the 2008 Whitney Biennial and the 2009 Preis der Nationalgalerie für Junge Kunst. For an extended biography, bibliography, and artwork list and a selection of online videos, refer to the "gb agency" gallery website: http://www.gbagency.fr.
2. Defined as the United States, the United Kingdom, and other Commonwealth countries.
3. Articulated prominently by Saul Friedlander, who argues that "there are limits to representation *which should not be but can easily be transgressed*" (3, original emphasis).
4. For comparative analyses of *Schindler's List* and *Shoah*, refer to Hansen and Loshitzky.
5. These memorable filmic devices in *Schindler's List* are not without cinematic precedents. The motif of the girl in the red dress is found in *The Great Train Robbery* (Edwin S. Porter, 1903) and a similar device to the "shower scene" was used in the ABC miniseries *War and Remembrance* (Dan Curtis, 1988). For discussions on the reception of *Schindler's List* in different countries, including Israel, Germany, France, and the United States, refer to Loshitzky (*Spielberg's Holocaust*).
6. Spielberg considered shooting the film in Polish and German but decided against this, so as to increase audience engagement, stating "[t]here's too much safety in reading. It would have been an excuse to take their eyes off the screen and watch something else" (Royal).
7. Including *History Will Repeat Itself: Strategies of Re-enactment in Contemporary (Media) Art and Performance*, Hartware MedienKunstVerein, Dortmund, Germany, 2007; *Once More ... With Feeling: Reenactment in Contemporary Art and Culture*, Reg Vardy Gallery, The University of Sunderland, UK, 2005; *Life, Once More: Forms of Reenactment in Contemporary Art*, Witte de With, Rotterdam, The Netherlands, 2005; *Experience, Memory, Re-enactment*, Piet Zwart Institute, Rotterdam, The Netherlands, 2004.
8. The full title of this essay is "Subject Positions, Speaking Positions: From *Holocaust, Our Hitler*, and *Heimat* to *Shoah* and *Schindler's List*."
9. A film like *Schindler's List* has been strongly critiqued for its melodramatic approach and for ascribing to an (admittedly muted) form of the Hollywood "happy ending." For detailed analyses of the film, refer to Loshitzky (*Spielberg's Holocaust*).
10. Fast's most recent works, in particular *Nostalgia* (2009) and *5,000 Feet is the Best* (2011), display an even stronger tendency towards fictionalization and imaginative interpretation of testimony.

11 To use the example of *Schindler's List* again, the film, like the novel on which it is based (Thomas Keneally's *Schindler's Ark*), took "artistic license in presenting events" (Horowitz "But Is It Good" 119). Yet it also went to extreme lengths to ensure the minute accuracy of its re-enactments. As Fast's piece reveals, while filming the selection of Jewish arrivals at the concentration camp, extras playing German soldiers read from Xeroxed copies of the original historical documents that listed the names of real Jewish prisoners and victims. The replica Płaszów concentration camp included recreated Jewish burial stones, none of which were obvious in the final film, but which add to the film's sense of "verisimilitude."

12 McCalman and Pickering have identified improvisation as a problematic and complicated element of re-enactments, certainly worthy of further investigation, stating that "[the] uneasy relationship between realism, authenticity and affect is further evident in cases where the boundaries of reenactment are pushed towards improvisation" (9).

13 While not discussed here, Fast's 2008 piece *Take a Deep Breath* is another relevant example that deconstructs and critiques the practice of staging and filming re-enactments.

Works Cited

2046. Dir. Wong Kar-wai. Perf. Tony Leung, Gong Li, Zhang Ziyi, Faye Wong, Carina Lau, Takuya Kimura. Jet Tone Films, 2004. DVD. 20th Century Fox, 2004.

Abella, Irving. "Was Canada a Nazi Haven?" *Globe and Mail*, 20 May 2000, D15. Print.

Acton, Carol. "Writing and Waiting: The First World War Correspondence Between Brittain and Leighton." *Gender and History* 11.1 (1999): 54–83. Print.

Agamben, Giorgio. "We Refugees." Michael Rocke, trans. *Symposium* 49.2 (Summer 1995). European Graduate School. 15 Aug. 2011. Web.

Agnew, Vanessa. "Introduction: What Is Reenactment?" *Criticism* 46.3 (Summer 2004): 327–39. Print.

Ahmed, Sara. *The Cultural Politics of Emotion*. New York: Routledge, 2004. Print.

Alarcón, Daniel Cooper. *The Aztec Palimpsest: Mexico in the Modern Imagination*. Tucson: U of Arizona P, 1997. Print.

Allen, Jennifer. "Omer Fast." *Artforum* (2003), 216–17. Print.

Allen, Woody. Interview. *Woody Allen on Woody Allen: In Conversation with Stig Björkman*. New York: Grove, 1993. Print.

Alonso, Harriet Hyman. *Peace as a Women's Issue: A History of the U.S. Movement for World Peace and Women's Rights*. Syracuse: Syracuse UP, 1993. Print.

Anderson, Mark M. "Documents, Photography, Postmemory: Alexander Kluge, W.G. Sebald, and the German Family." *Poetics Today* 29.1 (2008): 129–53. Print.

Anzaldúa, Gloria. *Borderlands/La Frontera: The New Mestiza*. 3rd ed. San Francisco: Spinsters/Aunt Lute, 2007. Print.

Applegate, Celia. *Bach in Berlin: Nation and Culture in Mendelssohn's Revival of the St. Matthew Passion*. Ithaca: Cornell University Press, 2005. Print.

Arendt, Hannah. "We Refugees." *Menorah Journal* 31.3 (1943): 69–77. Print.

Assmann, Jan. *Religion and Cultural Memory*. Rodney Livingston, trans. Stanford: Stanford UP, 2006. Print.
Augé, Marc. *In the Metro*. Tom Conley, trans. Minneapolis: U of Minnesota P, 2002. Print.
———. *Non-Places: Introduction to an Anthropology of Supermodernity*. John Howe, trans. London: Verso, 1995. Print.
———. *Oblivion*. Marjolijn De Jager, trans. Minneapolis: U of Minnesota P, 2004. Print.
———. *Le Métro Revisité*. Paris: Seuil, 2008. Print.
———. *Casablanca: Movies and Memory*. Tom Conley, trans. Minneapolis: U of Minnesota P, 2009. Print.
Augustine, Saint. *Confessions*. R.S. Pine-Coffin, trans. London: Penguin, 1988. Print.
———. *Confessions of St. Augustine*. Rex Warner, trans. New York: New American Library, 1963. Print.
Axworthy, Thomas. "Memories Shape the Way We See Ourselves." *Toronto Star*, 26 September 1997, A28.
Bahktin, Mikhail. *The Dialogic Imagination*. Michael Holquist, Caryl Emerson, and Michael Holquist, eds. and trans. Austin: U of Texas P, 1981. Print.
———. "Forms of Time and the Chronotope in the Novel." *The Dialogic Imagination*. Austin: U of Texas P, 1983. Print.
Baker, Timothy C. "The Art of Losing: The Place of Death in Writers' Memoirs." *Life Writing*. Richard Bradford, ed. Basingstoke: Palgrave Macmillan, 2009. 219–33. Print.
Bal, Mieke, Jonathan Crewe, and Leo Spitzer, eds. *Acts of Memory: Cultural Recall in the Present*. Lebanon: University Press of New England, 1999. Print.
Bannerji, Himani. *The Dark Side of the Nation: Essays on Multiculturalism, Nationalism and Gender*. Toronto: Canadian Scholars' Press, 2000. Print.
Barthes, Roland. *Camera Lucida: Reflections on Photography*. Richard Howard, trans. New York: Noonday Press, 1991. Print.
———. *The Grain of the Voice*. Linda Coverdale, trans. New York: Hill and Wang, 1985. Print.
Bartov, Omer. *Mirrors of Destruction: War, Genocide and Modern Identity*. New York: Oxford UP, 2000. Print.
Bashevkin, Sylvia B. *True Patriot Love: The Politics of Canadian Nationalism*. Toronto: Oxford UP, 1991.
Baudrillard, Jean. *Simulacra and Simulation*. Sheila Faria Glaser, trans. Ann Arbor: U of Michigan P, 1985. Print.
Bazin, André. "Bazin on Marker." Dave Kehr, trans. *Film Comment* 39.4 (2003): 44–45. Print.
Begin, Monique. "From Beer Commercials to Medicare: In Search of Identity." *The Canadian Distinctiveness into the Twenty-first Century*. Chad Gaffield

and Karen L. Gould, eds. Ottawa: University of Ottawa Press, 2000. 173–81. Print.

Behrendt, Kathy. "Scraping Down the Past: Memory and Amnesia in W.G. Sebald's Anti-Narrative." *Philosophy and Literature* 34.2 (2010) 394–408. Print.

Bell, Duncan S. "Mythscapes: Memory, Mythology, and National Identity." *British Journal of Sociology* 54.1 (2003): 63–81. Print.

Bellour, Raymond. "The Film Stilled." *Camera Obscura* 8.24 (1990) 98–124. Print.

Benjamin, Walter. "Das Kunstwerk im Zeitalter seiner technischen Reproduzierbarkeit." *Gesammelte Schriften*. Rolf Tiedemann and Hermann Schweppenhäuser, eds. Frankfurt: Suhrkamp, 1989. Print.

———. *Illuminations*. Harry Zohn, trans. New York: Schocken, 1969. Print.

———. *Selected Writings*. Vol. 1. Cambridge: Harvard UP, 1996. Print.

———. *Selected Writings*. Vol. 2. Cambridge: Harvard UP, 1999. Print.

Bennett, Tony, Lawrence Grossberg, and Meaghan Morris, eds. *New Keywords: A Revised Vocabulary of Culture and Society*. Oxford: Blackwell, 2005. Print.

Bensmaïa, Réda. "From the Photogram to the Pictogram: On Chris Marker's *La Jetée*." *Camera Obscura* 8.24 (1990): 139–61. Print.

Benson-Allott, Caetlin. "*Grindhouse*: An Experiment in the Death of Cinema." *Film Quarterly* 62.1 (2008): 20–24. Print.

Bergson, Henri. From "Matter and Memory." *Theories of Memory: A Reader*. Michael Rossington and Anne Whitehead, eds. Baltimore: Johns Hopkins UP, 2007. 109–13. Print.

———. *Introduction to Metaphysics*. Mabelle L. Andison, trans. New York: Philosophical Library, 1961. Print.

———. *Matter and Memory*. Nancy Margaret Paul and W. Scott Palmer, trans. New York: Zone, 1988. Print.

———. *Matter and Memory*. 1896. N.M. Paul and W. Scott Palmer trans. New York: Zone, 1991. Print.

Berkman, Jane. "Feminism, War, and Peace Politics: The Case of World War I." *Women, Militarism, and War: Essays in History*. Jean Bethke Elshtain and Sheila Tobias, eds. Lanham: Rowman and Littlefield, 1990. 141–60. Print.

Berlant, Lauren. "The Subject of True Feeling: Pain, Privacy, and Politics." *Transformations: Thinking Through Feminism*. Sara Ahmed, Jane Kilby, Celia Lury, Maureen McNeil and Beverley Skeggs, eds. New York: Routledge, 2000. 33–47. Print.

Blättler, Christine, ed. *Kunst der Serie: Die Serie in den Künsten*. München: Fink, 2010. Print.

Blum, Howard. *Wanted! The Search for Nazis in America*. New York Quadrangle/ New York Times Book Co., 1977. Print.

Blustein, Jeffrey. *The Moral Demands of Memory*. Cambridge: Cambridge UP, 2008. Print.

Bogue, Ronald. "To Choose to Choose—to Believe in This World." *Afterimages of Gilles Deleuze's Film Philosophy*. D.N. Rodowick, ed. Minneapolis: U of Minnesota P, 2010. 115–34. Print.

Boldy, Steven. "Intertextuality in Carlos Fuentes's *Gringo Viejo*." *Romance Quarterly*. 39.4 (1992): n.p. *Academic Search Complete*. 30 May 2010. Web.

Bolter, Jay David, and Richard Grusin. *Remediation: Understanding New Media*. Cambridge: MIT Press, 2000. Print.

Bordwell, David. "The Art Cinema as a Mode of Film Practice." *Film Theory and Criticism*. Leo Braudy and Marshall Cohen, eds. 6th ed. New York: Oxford UP, 2004. 774–82. Print.

———, Janet Staiger, and Kristin Thompson. *The Classical Hollywood Film: Film Style and Mode of Production to 1960*. London: Routledge, 1985. Print.

———. *The Way Hollywood Tells It: Story and Style in Modern Movies*. Berkeley: U of California P, 2006. Print.

Botz-Bornstein, Thorsten. "Wong Kar-wai and the Culture of the Kawaii." *Films and Dreams: Tarkovsky, Bergman, Sokurov, Kubrick, and Wong Kar-wai*. Toronto: Lexington, 2007. 71–84. Print.

The Bourne Ultimatum. Dir. Paul Greengrass. Perf. Matt Damon, Julia Stiles. Universal Pictures, 2007. DVD. Universal Pictures, 2008.

Boym, Svetlana. *The Future of Nostalgia*. New York: Basic, 2001. Print.

Brand, Dionne. *Bread Out of Stone: Recollections on Sex, Recognitions, Race, Dreaming, and Politics*. Toronto: Vintage Canada, 1994. Print.

———. *Inventory*. Toronto: McClelland and Stewart, 2006. Print.

———. *A Map to the Door of No Return: Notes to Belonging*. Toronto: Vintage Canada, 2001. Print.

———. *Land to Light On*. Toronto: McClelland and Stewart, 1997. Print.

———. *Ossuaries*. Toronto: McClelland and Stewart, 2010. Print.

———. *A Perfect Kind of Speech*. Nanaimo: Institute for Coastal Research, 2008. Print.

Braziel, Jana Evans. *Caribbean Genesis: Jamaica Kincaid and the Writing of New Worlds*. Albany: SUNY Press, 2009. Print.

———. "Proposal." Faculty Research Grant Proposal. U of Wisconsin. 2001. Print.

Brittain, Vera. *Chronicle of Youth: Great War Diary 1913–1917*. Alan Bishop, ed. London: Phoenix, 2000. Print.

Britzman, Deborah. *Lost Subjects, Contested Objects: Toward a Psychoanalytic Inquiry of Learning*. Albany: SUNY Press, 1998. Print.

Brody, Florian. "The Medium Is the Memory." *The Digital Dialectic: New Essays on New Media*. Peter Lunenfeld, ed. Cambridge: MIT Press, 2000. 130–49. Print.

Brown, Daniel Patrick. *The Camp Women: The Female Auxiliaries Who Assisted the SS in Running the Nazi Concentration Camp System* (Schiffer Military History). Michigan: U of Michigan P, 2002. Print.

Brown, Wendy. *States of Injury: Power and Freedom in Late Modernity*. Princeton: Princeton UP, 1995. Print.

Brunette, Peter. *Wong Kar-wai*. Urbana: U of Illinois P, 2005. Print.

Buckley, Jerome Hamilton. *The Turning Key: Autobiography and the Subjective Impulse Since 1800*. Cambridge, MA: Harvard UP, 1984. Print

Burgoyne, Robert. "Memory, History, and Digital Imagery in Contemporary Film." *Memory and Popular Film*. Paul Grainge, ed. Manchester: Manchester UP, 2003. 220–36. Print.

Butler, Joseph. *The Analogy of Religion, Natural and Revealed*. London: Dent, 1927. Print.

Caldwell, John Thornton. *Televisuality: Style, Crisis, and Authority in American Television*. New Brunswick: Rutgers UP, 1995. Print.

Callenbach, Ernest. "La Jetée." *Film Quarterly* 19.2 (1965–66): 50–52. Print.

Cameron, Elspeth. *Canadian Culture: An Introductory Reader*. Toronto: Canadian Scholars' Press, 1997. Print.

Cameron, Elspeth. "Heritage Minutes: Culture and Myth." *Canadian Studies at Home and Abroad*. James De Finney, Gregory Kealey, John Lennox, and Tamara Palmer Seiler, eds. Montreal: Association for Canadian Studies, 1995. 13–24. Print.

Cameron, Elspeth, and Janice Dicken McGinnis. "Ambushed by Patriotism: The Wit, Wisdom, and Wimps of *Heritage Minutes*." *Canadian Forum* (March 1995), 12–15.

———. "Heritage Minutes: History, Culture, or Myth?" *Canadian Studies at Home and Abroad*. James De Finney, Gregory Kealey, John Lennox, and Tamara Palmer Seiler, eds. Montreal: Association for Canadian Studies, 1995. 9–11. Print.

Campbell, Sue. "Our Faithfulness to the Past: Reconstructing Memory Value." *Philosophical Psychology* 19.3 (2006): 361–80. Print.

"Canadian Multiculturalism." Citizenship and Immigration Canada. Web. 20 July 2011.

Canfield, J. Douglass. *Mavericks on the Border: The Early Southwest in Historical Fiction and Film*. Lexington: UP of Kentucky, 2001. Print.

Cannadine, David. "The Past in the Present." *Echoes of Greatness*. Lesley M. Smith, ed. London: Palgrave Macmillan, 1988. Print.

Carroll, Noel. "The Future of Allusion: Hollywood in the Seventies (and Beyond)." *October* 20 (Spring 1982): 51–81. Print.

Carruthers, Mary J. *The Book of Memory: A Study of Memory in Medieval Culture*. Cambridge: Cambridge UP, 1990. Print.

Caruth, Cathy. "From Trauma and Experience." *Theories of Memory: A Reader*. Michael Rossington and Anne Whitehead, eds. Baltimore: Johns Hopkins UP, 2007. 199–205. Print.

———. "Trauma and Experience: Introduction." *Trauma: Explorations in*

Memory. Cathy Caruth, ed. Baltimore: Johns Hopkins UP, 1995. 3–12. Print.

———. *Unclaimed Experience: Trauma, Narrative, and History*. Baltimore: John Hopkins UP, 1996. Print.

———. "Unclaimed Experience: Trauma and the Possibility of History." *Yale French Studies* 79 (1991): 181–92. Print.

Casablanca. Dir. Michael Curtiz. Perf. Humphrey Bogart, Ingrid Bergman, Claude Raines, Conrad Veidt, Peter Lorre, Sydney Greenstreet. Warner Brothers Pictures, 1943. DVD. Warner Home Video, 1999.

Casey, Edward S. "The Memorability of the Filmic Image." *Spirit and Soul: Essays in Philosophical Psychology*. Dallas: Spring, 1991. Print.

Chapman, Mary. "'Living Pictures': Women and Tableaux Vivants in Nineteenth-Century American Fiction and Culture." *Wide Angle* 18.3 (1996): 22–52. Print.

Chartrand, Tanya L., und Rick van Baaren. "Human Mimicry." *Advances in Experimental Social Psychology* 41 (2009): 219–74. Print.

Christ, Carol T., and John O. Jordan. "Introduction." *Victorian Literature and the Victorian Visual Imagination*. Berkeley: U of California P, 1995. xix–xxviii. Print.

Cicero, Marcus Tullius. *Rhetorica ad Herennium*. Harry Caplan, trans. Oxford: Oxford UP, 1954. Print.

Citizenship and Immigration Canada. *About the Multiculturalism Program*. 20 July 2011. Web.

Clendinnen, Inga. *Reading the Holocaust*. Cambridge: Cambridge UP, 1999. Print.

Coates, Paul. "Chris Marker and the Cinema as Time Machine." *Science Fiction Studies* 14.3 (1987): 307–15. Print.

Cohen, Stephen F. "Hollywood's War." CrossTalk LIVE. *Russia Today TV*. Interview. YouTube, 10 May 2010. 19 August 2010. Web.

Cohen, Alain J.J. "*12 Monkeys, Vertigo*, and *La Jetée*, Postmodern Mythologies, and Cult Film." *New Revue of Film and Television Studies* 1.1 (2003): 146–63. Print.

Collingwood, R.G. *The Idea of History*. Rev. ed. Oxford; New York: Clarendon; Oxford UP, 1993. Print.

Collins, Richard. Culture, *Communication, and National Identity: The Case of Canadian Television*. Toronto: U of Toronto P, 1990. Print.

Connerton, Paul. *How Societies Remember*. Cambridge: Cambridge UP, 1989. Print.

Cook, Pam. *Screening the Past: Memory and Nostalgia in Cinema*. New York: Routledge, 2005. Print.

Cook, Ramsay. *Canada, Quebec, and the Uses of Nationalism*. Toronto: McClelland and Stewart, 1995. Print.

———. "An Interview with Ramsay Cook." *CBC Digital Archives*. 28 May 1972. Web. 20 July 2011.

———. *French-Canadian Nationalism*. Toronto: Macmillan, 1969. Print.

Cook, Terry. "A Monumental Blunder: The Destruction of Records on Nazi War Criminals in Canada." *Archives and the Public Good: Accountability and Records in Modern Society*. Richard J. Cox and David A. Wallace, eds. Westport: Quorum, 2002. 37–65. Print.

Court case *re Ryan*, 360 F. Supp. 270, 273 (E.D.N.Y.), aff'd, 478 F.2d 1397 (2d Cir. 1973). Print.

Crean, Susan. *Who's Afraid of Canadian Culture?* Toronto: General, 1976. Print.

Creighton, Jane. "Bierce, Fuentes, and the Critique of Reading: A Study of Carlos Fuentes's *The Old Gringo*." *South Central Review* 9.2 (1992): 5–79. Print.

Cridland, Sean. "In the Twinkling of an Eye: Nietzschean Undercurrents in Terry Gilliam's *12 Monkeys*." *Film and Philosophy* 3 (1996): 130–37. Print.

Crownshaw, Richard. "On Reading Sebald Criticism: Witnessing the Text." *Journal of Romance Studies* 9.3 (2009): 10–22. Print.

———. "Reconsidering Postmemory: Photography, the Archive, and Post-Holocaust Memory in W.G. Sebald's *Austerlitz*." *Mosaic* 37.4 (2004): 215–36. Print.

Cunningham, Valentine. "The Sound of Startled Grass." *The Guardian*, 19 October 2002. 17. Web. 8 December 2012.

Cupchik, Gerald C., et al. "Viewing Artworks: Contributions of Cognitive Control and Perceptual Facilitation to Aesthetic Experience." *Brain and Cognition* 70.1 (2009): 84–91. Print.

Damousi, Joy. *The Labour of Loss: Mourning, Memory, and Wartime Bereavement in Australia*. Cambridge: Cambridge UP, 1999. Print.

Danielová, Růžena. "'In Auschwitz there is a Great House.' The Holocaust O Porrajmos." *Patrin Web Journal*. 23 September 2000. Web. 20 February 2011. n.p.

Das, Santanu. "'The Impotence of Sympathy': Touch and Trauma in the Memoirs of the First World War Nurses." *Textual Practice* 19.2 (2005): 239–62. Print.

David, Mia, and Omer Fast. "Interview." *51st October Salon* (2010): n.p. Print.

Davis, Fred. *Yearning for Yesterday: A Sociology of Nostalgia*. New York: Free Press, 1979. Print.

Del Rio, Elena. "The Remaking of *La Jetée*'s Time-Travel Narrative: *Twelve Monkeys* and the Rhetoric of Absolute Visibility." *Science Fiction Studies* 28.3 (2001): 383–98. Print.

Delacroix, Eugène. *July 28: Liberty Leading the People*. 1830. Oil on canvas, 2.6m x 3.25m. Musée du Louvre, Paris, France.

Deleuze, Gilles. *Cinema 1: The Movement Image*. Hugh Tomlinson and Barbara Habberjam, trans. Minneapolis: U of Minnesota P, 1986. Print.

———. *Cinema 2: The Time-Image*. 1986. Hugh Tomlinson and Robert Galeta, trans. Minneapolis: U of Minnesota P, 1989. Print.

———. *Repetition and Difference*. 1968. London: Continuum, 2004. Print.

DeLillo, Don. *White Noise*. New York: Penguin, 1986. Print.

Derrida, Jacques. *Archive Fever: A Freudian Impression*. Chicago: U of Chicago P, 1996. Print.

———. *Of Grammatology*. Gayatri Spivak, trans. Baltimore: Johns Hopkins UP, 1976. Print.

Derrida, Jacques. "On Forgiveness." *Cosmopolitanism and Forgiveness*. Mark Dooley and Michael Hughes, trans. London and New York: Routledge, 2001.

———. *The Politics of Friendship*. Georges Collins, trans. London: Verso, 1997. Print.

———. *Positions*. Alan Bass, trans. Chicago: U of Chicago P, 1981. Print.

Dewing, Michael. "Canadian Multiculturalism." *Parliament of Canada*. Rev. 15 September 2009. Web. 24 October 2012.

Dickinson, Emily. *The Poems of Emily Dickinson*. Variorum ed. 3 vols. R.W. Franklin, ed. Cambridge: Harvard UP, 1998. Print.

———. *The Letters of Emily Dickinson*. 3 vols. Thomas H. Johnson and Theodora Ward, eds. Cambridge: Harvard UP, 1986. Print.

"Dionne Brand Wins Griffin Poetry Prize." CBC News Online. Canadian Broadcasting Corporation, 1 June 2011. Web. 27 July 2011.

Druick, Zoe. "Framing the Local." *Canadian Cultural Poesis: Essays on Canadian Culture*. Garry Sherbert, Annie Gerin, and Sheila Petty, eds. Waterloo: Wilfrid Laurier UP, 2006. 85–98. Print.

Dubois, Philippe. "Photography *Mise-en-Film*: Autobiographical (Hi)stories and Psychic Apparatuses." Lynne Kirby, trans. *Fugitive Images: From Photography to Video*. Petro Petrice, ed. Bloomington: Indiana UP, 1995. 152–72. Print.

Eco, Umberto. "Serialität im Universum der Kunst und der Massenmedien." *Im Labyrinth der Vernunft*. Michael Franz and Stefan Richter, eds. Leipzig: Reclam, 1995. 301–24. Print.

———. *Travels in Hyperreality*. London: Picador, 1986. Print.

Ellis, John. *Visible Fictions: Cinema, Television, Video*. London: Routledge and Kegan Paul, 1982. Print.

Elsaesser, Thomas. "Subject Positions, Speaking Positions: From *Holocaust*, *Our Hitler*, and *Heimat* to *Shoah* and *Schindler's List*." *The Persistence of History: Cinema, Television, and the Modern Event*. Vivian Sobchack, ed. New York: Routledge, 1996. 145–84. Print.

Engel, Andreas K., and Peter König. "Das neurophysiologische Wahrnehmungsparadigma: Eine kritische Bestandsaufnahme." *Der Mensch in der*

Perspektive der Kognitionswissenschaften. Peter Gold and Andreas K. Engel, eds. Frankfurt: Suhrkamp, 1998. 156–94. Print.

Erikson, Kai. *A New Species of Trouble: Explorations in Disaster, Trauma, and Community*. New York: Norton, 1994. Print.

Erll, Astrid. *Memory in Culture*. Sara B. Young, trans. New York: Palgrave Macmillan Memory Studies, 2011. Print.

Erll, Astrid, and Ann Rigney, eds. *Mediation, Remediation, and the Dynamics of Cultural Memory*. Berlin and New York: de Gruyter, 2009. Print.

Eskin, Blake. *A Life in Pieces*. London: Aurum, 2002. Print.

Esposito, Elena. *Soziales Vergessen: Formen und Medien des Gedächtnisses der Gesellschaft*. Frankfurt: Suhrkamp, 2002. Print.

Eternal Sunshine of the Spotless Mind. Dir. Michel Gondry. Perf. Jim Carrey, Kate Winslet. Focus Features, 2004. DVD. Universal Home Video, 2004.

Evans, Suzanne. *Mothers of Heroes, Mothers of Martyrs: World War I and the Politics of Female Grief*. Montreal and Kingston: McGill–Queen's UP, 2007. Print.

Facebook. *Heritage Minutes Group*. Web. 20 July 2011.

Fast, Omer. *5,000 Feet Is the Best*. 2011. Single-channel digital video, colour, sound, 30 minutes.

———. *The Casting*. 2007. Four-channel video projection, 35mm film transferred to video, colour, sound, 14 minutes.

———. *CNN Concatenated*. 2002. Single-channel video, colour, sound, 18 minutes.

———. *Godville*. 2005. Two-channel video projection, colour, sound, 40 minutes.

———. *Nostalgia*. 2009. Video installation in three parts.

———. "Preface." *Godville*. Frankfurt am Main: Revolver, 2005. 5–7. Print.

———. *Spielberg's List*. 2003. Two-channel video, colour, sound, 60 minutes.

———. *Take a Deep Breath*. 2008. HD video installation, two synchronized channels, colour, sound, 27 minutes.

———. *Talk Show*. 2009. Video installation with three synchronized screens, 65 minutes.

Fast, Omer, and Sven Lütticken. "Email Extracts." *The Casting: Omer Fast*. Köln: Verlag der Buchhandlung Walther König, 2007. 27–41. Ed. (MUMOK), Museum Moderner Kunst Stiftung Ludwig Wien. Print.

Fast, Omer, and Marcus Verhagen. "Pleasure and Pain." *Art Monthly* 330 (2009): 1–4. Print.

Felman, Shoshana. "Education and Crisis, or the Vicissitudes of Teaching." *Testimony: Crises of Witnessing in Literature, Psychoanalysis, and History*. Shoshana Felman and Dori Laub, eds. New York: Routledge, 1992. 1–56. Print.

Feuer, Jane. *MTM: "Quality Television."* London: BFI, 1984.

Flags of Our Fathers. Dir. Clint Eastwood. Perf. Ryan Philippe, Adam Beach, Jamie Bell. DreamWorks SKG, 2006. DVD. Warner Home Video, 2007.

Fonseca, Isabel. *Bury Me Standing: The Gypsies and Their Journey*. New York: Vintage, 1996. Print.

Four Lights. New York: Women's Peace Party of New York City, 1917.

Franklin, Ruth. "Rings of Smoke." *The Emergence of Memory: Conversations with W.G. Sebald*. Lynne Sharon Schwartz, ed. New York: Seven Stories, 2007. 119–43. Print.

———. *A Thousand Darknesses*. Oxford: Oxford UP, 2011. Print.

Freud, Sigmund. *An Autobiographical Study*. James Strachey, trans. New York and London: Norton, 1952. Print.

———. *The Standard Edition of the Complete Psychological Works*. James Strachey, gen. ed. and trans. 6th ed. London: Hogarth, 1973. Print.

———. *Totem and Taboo*. A.A. Brill, trans. London: Routledge, 1919. Print.

Friedlander, Saul. "Introduction." *Probing the Limits of Representation: Nazism and the "Final Solution."* Saul Friedlander, ed. Cambridge: Harvard UP, 1992. 1–21. Print.

Frow, John. *Time and Commodity Culture: Essays in Cultural Theory and Postmodernity*. Oxford: Oxford UP, 1997. Print.

———. From "Toute La Mémoire du Monde: Repetition and Forgetting" (1997). *Theories of Memory: A Reader*. Michael Rossington and Anne Whitehead, eds. Baltimore: Johns Hopkins UP, 2007. 109–13. Print.

Frye, Northrop. *The Bush Garden: Essays on the Canadian Imagination*. Toronto: Anansi, 1971. Print.

Fuentes, Carlos. "History Out of Chaos." Review of John Mason Hart, *Revolutionary Mexico: The Coming and Process of the Mexican Revolution*. New York Times Book Review, 13 March 1988, late ed., 12. Web. 2 January 2011.

———. *The Old Gringo*. Margaret Sayers Peden, trans. New York: Farrar, Straus and Giroux, 1985. Print.

Fussell, Paul. *The Great War and Modern Memory*. Oxford: Oxford UP, 1975. Print.

Gaffield, Chad, and Karen L. Gould, eds. *The Canadian Distinctiveness into the Twenty-first Century*. Ottawa: Ottawa UP, 2000. Print.

Gammon, Carolyn, and Christiane Hemker. *Johanna Krause Twice Persecuted: Surviving in Nazi Germany and Communist East Germany*. Carolyn Gammon, trans. Waterloo: Wilfrid Laurier UP, 2007. Print.

Garde-Hansen, Joanne, Andrew Hoskins, and Anna Reading, eds. *Save As ... Digital Memories*. New York: Palgrave Macmillan Memory Studies, 2009. Print.

Garscha, Winfried and Claudia Kuretsidis-Haider. "War Crime Trials in Austria." *Dokumentationsarchiv des Österreichischen Widerstandes*. 25–28 September 1997. n.p. Web.

Gay, Peter. *Style in History*. New York: Basic, 1974. Print.
Gay y Blasco, Paloma. "Picturing 'Gypsies': Interdisciplinary Approaches to Roma Representation." *Third Text* 22.3 (2008): 297–303. Print.
———. "'We Don't Know Our Descent': How the Gitanos of Jarana Manage the Past." *Journal of the Royal Anthropological Institute* 7 (2001): 631–47. Print.
Geddes, Jennifer. "Banal Evil and Useless Knowledge: Hannah Arendt and Charlotte Delbo on Evil After the Holocaust." *The Double Binds of Ethics after the Holocaust: Salvaging the Fragments*. Jennifer L. Geddes, John K. Roth, and Jules Simon, eds. New York: Palgrave Macmillan, 2009. 119–32. Print.
Gifford, Douglas. "The Source of Joy: *Highland River*." *Neil M. Gunn: The Man and the Writer*. Alexander Scott and Douglas Gifford, eds. Edinburgh: Blackwood, 1973. 101–22. Print.
Gilmore, Leigh. "Limit-Cases: Trauma, Self-Representation, and the Jurisdiction of Identity." *Biography* 24.1 (2001): 128–39. Print.
Goffman, Erving. *Frame Analysis: an Essay on the Organization of Experience*. New York: Harper and Row, 1974. Print.
Gold, Peter, and Andreas K. Engel, eds. *Der Mensch in der Perspektive der Kognitionswissenschaften*. Frankfurt: Suhrkamp, 1998. Print.
Goldie, Peter. "Dramatic Irony, Narrative, and the External Perspective." *Narrative and Understanding Persons*. Daniel Hutto, ed. Cambridge: Cambridge UP, 2007. 69–84. Print.
Grainge, Paul. "Introduction: Memory and Popular Film." *Memory and Popular Film*. Paul Grainge, ed. Manchester: Manchester UP, 2003. 1–20. Print.
Grant, George. *Lament for a Nation: The Defeat of Canadian Nationalism*. Montreal and Kingston: McGill–Queen's UP, 2005. Print.
Graves, Matthew, and Elizabeth Rechniewski. "From Collective Memory to Transcultural Remembrance." *Journal of Multidisciplinary International Studies* 7.1 (2010): 1–15. Web. 9 Oct. 2010.
Graves, Robert. *Good-Bye to All That*. New York: Blue Ribbon, 1930. Print.
———. *The White Goddess: A Historical Grammar of Poetic Myth*. 1948. New York: Farrar, Straus and Giroux, 2000. Print.
Grayzel, Susan R. *Women's Identities at War: Gender, Motherhood, and Politics in Britain and France during the First World War*. Chapel Hill: U of North Carolina P, 1999. Print.
The Great Train Robbery. Dir. Edwin S. Porter. Edison Manufacturing Company, 1903. DVD. VCI Home Video, 2003.
Greenberg, Harvey Roy. "*12 Monkeys*: The Rags of Time." *Film and Philosophy* 3 (1996): 123–29. Print.
Grimbert, Philippe. *Memory: A Novel*. Polly McLean, trans. New York: Simon and Schuster, 2007. Print.

———. *Secret*. Polly McLean, trans. London: Portobello, 2008. Print.

———. *Un Secret*. Paris: Grasset and Fasquelle, 2004. Print.

Grobbel, Michaela. "Contemporary Romany Biography as Performance." *German Quarterly* 76.2 (2003): 140–54. Print.

Grusin, Richard. *Premediation: Affect and Mediality in America After 9/11*. New York: Palgrave Macmillan, 2010. Print.

Guerin, Frances. "The Grey Space Between: Gerhard Richter's '18. October 1977.'" *The Image and the Witness: Trauma, Memory, and Visual Culture*. Frances Guerin and Roger Hallas, eds. London and New York: Wallflower, 2007. 113–28. Print.

Gunn, Neil. *The Atom of Delight*. London: Faber, 1956. Print.

———. *The Atom of Delight*. 1956. Intro. John Pick. Foreword by Dairmid Gunn. Afterword by Alan Spence. Edinburgh: Polygon, 1986.

———. "Review of Scott and Scotland." *Landscape and Light: Essays by Neil M. Gunn*. Alastair McCleery, ed. Aberdeen: Aberdeen UP, 1987. 122–26. Print.

———. *Highland River*. Edinburgh: Canongate, 1996. Print.

Hacking, Ian. *Rewriting the Soul: Multiple Personality and the Sciences of Memory*. Princeton: Princeton UP, 1995. Print.

Halbwachs, Maurice. *On Collective Memory*. Lewis A. Coser, trans. Chicago: U of Chicago P, 1992. Print.

Hancock, Ian. "Responses to the Porrajmos: The Romani Holocaust." *Is the Holocaust Unique? Perspectives on Comparative Genocide*. Alan S. Rosenbaum, ed. Boulder: Westview, 2009. 75–102. Print.

Hansen, Miriam Bratu. "*Schindler's List* Is Not *Shoah*: Second Commandment, Popular Modernism, and Public Memory." *Spielberg's Holocaust: Critical Perspectives on Schindler's List*. Yosefa Loshitzky, ed. Bloomington: Indiana UP, 1997. 77–103. Print.

Haque, Eve. *Multiculturalism within a Bilingual Framework: Language, Race, and Belonging in Canada*. Toronto: U of Toronto P, 2012. Print.

Hart, Francis Russell, and J.B. Pick. *Neil M. Gunn: A Highland Life*. Edinburgh: Polygon, 1981. Print.

Haselstein, Ulla. "Die literarische Erfindung der Serialität: Gertrude Steins *The Making of Americans*. *Kunst der Serie: Die Serie in den Künsten*. Christine Blättler, ed. München: Fink, 2010. 17–32. Print.

Hegel, G.W.F. *Encyclopedia of Philosophical Sciences*. W. Wallace, trans. Oxford: Clarendon, 1971. Print.

———. *Phenomenology of Spirit*. A.V. Miller, trans. Oxford: Oxford UP, 1979. Print.

Heidegger, Martin. *The Concept of Time*. Oxford: Blackwell, 1992. Print.

Heinemann, Marlene. *Gender and Destiny: Women Writers and the Holocaust*. Westport: Greenwood, 1986. Print.

Helmuth, Chalene. *The Postmodern Fuentes*. London: Associated UPs, 1997. Print.
Hemetek, Ursula. "Applied Ethnomusicology in the Process of the Political Recognition of a Minority: A Case Study of the Austrian Roma." *Yearbook for Traditional Music* 38 (2006): 35–57. Print.
Henstra, Sarah. *The Counter-Memorial Impulse in Twentieth-Century English Fiction*. London: Palgrave, 2009. Print.
Herrigel, Eugen. *Zen in the Art of Archery* 1953. Intro. Daisetz T. Suzuki. New York, Vintage, 1999.
Higham, Charles, and Joel Greenberg. *Hollywood in the Forties*. London: Zwemmer, 1968. Print.
Higonnet, Margaret R. "Authenticity and Art in Trauma Narratives of World War I." *Modernism/Modernity* 9.1 (2002): 91–107. Print.
———. "The Great War and Female Elegy: Female Lamentation and Silence in Global Contexts." *The Global South* 1.1–2 (2007): 120–36. Print.
Higonnet, Margaret R., and Patrice L.R. Higonnet. "The Double Helix." *Behind the Lines: Gender and the Two World Wars*. Margaret Randolph Higonnet, Jane Jenson, Sonya Michel, and Margaret Collins Weitz, eds. New Haven: Yale UP, 1987. 31–47. Print.
Hill, Lawrence. *The Book of Negroes*. Toronto: HarperCollins, 2007 Print.
Hirsch, Marianne. *Family Frames: Photography, Narrative, and Postmemory*. Cambridge: Harvard UP, 1997. Print.
———. "The Generation of Postmemory." *Poetics Today* 29.1 (2008): 103–28. Print.
———. "Projected Memory: Holocaust Photographs in Personal and Public Fantasy." *Acts of Memory: Cultural Recall in the Present*. Mieke Bal, Jonathan Crewe, and Leo Spitzer, eds. Hanover: University Press of New England, 1999. 3–23. Print.
———. "Surviving Images: Holocaust Photographs and the Work of Postmemory." *Yale Journal of Criticism* 14.1 (2001): 5–37. Print.
Historica Dominion Institute. *History by the Minute*. Web. 20 July 2011.
———. *Your Place in History*. Web. 20 July 2011.
Hodgkin, Katharine, and Susannah Radstone, eds. *Contested Pasts: The Politics of Memory*. London: Routledge, 2005. Print.
Hoffman, Martin. *Empathy and Moral Development: Implications for Caring and Justice*. Cambridge: Cambridge UP, 2000. Print.
Horowitz, Sara. "But Is It Good for the Jews? Spielberg's Schindler and the Aesthetics of Atrocity." *Spielberg's Holocaust: Critical Perspectives on Schindler's List*. Yosefa Loshitzky, ed. Bloomington: Indiana UP, 1997. 119–39. Print.
———. "The Gender of Good and Evil: Women and Holocaust Memory." *Gray Zones: Ambiguity and Compromise in the Holocaust and Its Aftermath*. Jonathan Petropoulos and John K. Roth, eds. New York: Berghahn, 2005. 165–78. Print.

Horwitz, Tony. *Confederates in the Attic: Dispatches from the Unfinished Civil War*. New York: Vintage, 1998. Print.
Hoskins, Andrew. "Digital Network Memory." *Mediation, Remediation, and the Dynamics of Cultural Memory*. Astrid Erll and Ann Rigney, eds. Berlin and New York: de Gruyter, 2009. 91–106. Print.
———. "Launch of the Centre for Memory Studies." University of Warwick, n.d. Podcast. 28 January 2012.
Hutcheon, Linda. *The Canadian Postmodern*. Toronto: Oxford UP, 1988. Print.
———. "Irony, Nostalgia, and the Postmodern." *Methods for the Study of Literature as Cultural Memory*. Raymond Vervliet and Annemarie Estor, eds. Amsterdam: Rodopi, 2000. Print.
———. *A Poetics of Postmodernism: History, Theory, Fiction*. New York: Routledge, 1990. Print.
———. *A Theory of Adaptation*. New York and London: Routledge, 2006. Print.
———. *A Theory of Parody: The Teachings of Twentieth Century Art Forms*. New York: Methuen, 1985. Print.
Hutton, Margaret Anne. *Testimony from the Nazi Camps: French Women's Voices*. London: Routledge, 2005. Print.
Huyssen, Andreas. *Present Pasts: Urban Palimpsests and the Politics of Memory*. Mieke Bal and Hent de Vries, eds. Stanford: Stanford UP, 2003. Print.
———. *Twilight Memories: Marking Time in a Culture of Amnesia*. New York: Routledge, 1995. Print.
Imre, Anikó. "Roma Music and Transnational Homelessness." *Third Text* 22.3 (2008): 325–36. Print.
Inception. Dir. Christopher Nolan. Perf. Leonardo DiCaprio, Marion Cotillard, Joseph Gordon-Levitt, Ellen Page, Ken Watanabe, Michael Caine. Warner Brothers, 2010. DVD. Warner Home Video, 2010.
Jacob, Gilles, "Chris Marker and the Mutants." *Sight and Sound*. 35.4 (1966): 164–69. Print.
Jaggi, Maya. "Recovered Memories: The Guardian Profile." *The Guardian*. 22 September 2001. Web. 12 September 2011.
Jameson, Frederic. "Postmodernism and Consumer Society." *The Anti-Aesthetic: Essays on Postmodern Culture*. Hal Foster, ed. Seattle: Bay, 1983. 111–25. Print.
———. *Postmodernism, or the Cultural Logic of Late Capitalism*. Durham: Duke UP, 1991. Print.
Jan Mohamed, Abdul R. "The Economy of Manichean Allegory." *The Postcolonial Studies Reader*. Bill Ashcroft, Gareth Griffiths, and Helen Tiffin, eds. New York: Routledge, 1995. 18–23. Print.
Jay, Martin. "The Scopic Regimes of Modernity." *Vision and Visuality*. Hal Foster, ed. San Francisco: Bay P, 1988. 3-23.
Joyrich, Lynne. "Written on the Screen: Mediation and Immersion in *Far from Heaven*." *Camera Obscura* 19.3 (2004): 186–219. Print.

Jung, Carl Gustav. *The Essential Jung: Selected Writings*. Anthony Storr, ed. London: Fontana, 1986. Print.
Kadar, Marlene. "The Devouring: Traces of Roma in the Holocaust: No Tattoo, Sterilized Body, Gypsy Girl." *Tracing the Autobiographical*. Marlene Kadar, Linda Warley, Jeanne Perreault, and Susanna Egan, eds. Waterloo: Wilfrid Laurier UP, 2005. 223–46. Print.
Kaplan, E. Ann. *Trauma Culture: The Politics of Terror and Loss in Media and Literature*. New Brunswick: Rutgers UP, 2005. Print.
Kawin, Bruce. "Time and Stasis in *La Jetée*." *Film Quarterly* 36.1 (1982): 15–20. Print.
Kecht, Maria-Regina. "Three Media—One Story? Marie-Thérèse Kerschbaumer's 'Gypsy' Narrative." *Women in German Yearbook* 16 (2000): 83–103. Print.
Kehr, Dave. "You Can Make 'Em Like They Used To." *New York Times*, 12 November 2006. Web. 31 July 2011.
Kelly, Susan. *The CRB Foundation: The First Decade*. Montreal: Bowne of Montreal P, 1996. Print.
Khan, Nosheen. *Women's Poetry of the First World War*. New York: Harvester Wheatsheaf, 1988. Print.
Kidd, Kenneth. "A is for Auschwitz: Psychoanalysis, Trauma Theory, and the 'Children's Literature of Atrocity.'" *Under Fire: Childhood in the Shadow of War*. Elizabeth Goodenough and Andrea Immel, eds. Detroit: Wayne State UP, 2008. 161–84. Print.
Kilbourn, Russell J.A. *Cinema, Memory, Modernity: The Representation of Memory from the Art Film to Transnational Cinema*. New York: Routledge, 2010. Print.
King, Rosemary A. *Border Confluences: Borderland Narratives from the Mexican War to the Present*. Tucson: U of Arizona P, 2004. Print.
King, Thomas. *Truth and Bright Water*. Toronto: HarperPerennial, 2000. Print.
Kogan, Eugene. *Theory and Practice of Hell: The German Concentration Camps and the System Behind Them*. Heinz Norden, trans. New York: Farrar, Straus and Giroux, 2006. Print.
Kogawa, Joy. *Obasan*. Toronto: Penguin, 1981. Print.
Koonz, Claudia. *Mothers in the Fatherland: Women, the Family, and Nazi Politics*. New York: St. Martin's Griffin, 1981. Print.
Koppes, Clayton, and Gregory Black. *Hollywood Goes to War: How Politics, Profits, and Propaganda Shaped World War II Movies*. New York: I.B. Tauris, 2000. Print.
Kovács, András Bálint. *Screening Modernism: European Art Cinema 1950–1980*. Chicago: U of Chicago P, 2007. Print.
Kracauer, Siegfried. *The Mass Ornament: Weimar Essays*. Cambridge: Harvard UP, 1995. Print.

Kuhn, Annette. *An Everyday Magic: Cinema and Cultural Memory.* New York: Tauris, 2002. Print.

Kulperger, Shelley. "Familiar Ghosts: Feminist Postcolonial Gothic in Canada." *Unsettled Remains: Canadian Literature and the Postcolonial Gothic.* Cynthia Sugars and Gerry Turcotte, eds. Waterloo: Wilfrid Laurier UP, 2009. 97–124. Print.

LaCapra, Dominick. *History and Memory after Auschwitz.* Ithaca: Cornell UP, 1998. Print.

La Jetée. Dir. Chris Marker. Perf. Hélène Chatelain, Davos Hanich, Jean Négroni. Argos Films, 1962. DVD. Criterion Collection, 2007.

La Motte, Ellen N. "The Backwash of War." *Nurses at the Front: Writing the Wounds of the Great War.* Margaret R. Higonnet, ed. Boston: Northeastern UP, 2001. 3–75. Print.

Lanckoronska, Karolina. *Michelangelo in Ravensbrück: One's Woman War Against the Nazis.* Noel Clark, trans. Cambridge: Da Capo, 2005. Print.

Landsberg, Alison. "Memory, Empathy, and the Politics of Identification." *International Journal of Politics, Culture, and Society* 22.2 (2009): 221–29. Print.

———. "Prosthetic Memory: The Ethics and Politics of Memory in an Age of Mass Culture." *Memory and Popular Film.* Paul Grainge, ed. Manchester: Manchester UP, 2003. 144–61. Print.

———. *Prosthetic Memory: The Transformation of American Remembrance in the Age of Mass Culture.* New York: Columbia UP, 2004. Print.

Langewiesche, William. *American Ground: Unbuilding the World Trade Center.* 2002. New York: North Point Press, 2003.

Laplanche, Jean, and Jean-Bertrand Pontalis. *The Language of Psycho-analysis.* Donald Nicholson-Smith, trans. London: Hogarth/Institute of Psycho-Analysis; New York: Norton, 1974. Print.

Lappin, Elena. "The Man with Two Heads." *Granta* 66 (1999): 7–65. Print.

Last Year at Marienbad. Dir. Alain Resnais. Perf. Delphine Seyrig, Giorgio Albertazzi, Sascha Pitoëff. Cocinor, 1961. DVD. Criterion Collection, 2009.

Lawlor, Nuala. *The Heritage Minutes: The Charles R. Bronfman Foundation's Construction of the Canadian Identity.* Montreal and Kingston: McGill–Queen's UP, 1999. Print.

Lebert, Stephan, and Norbert Lebert. *My Father's Keeper: Children of Nazi Leaders—An Intimate History of Damage and Denial.* Julian Evans, trans. London: Little, Brown, 2001. Print.

Lefebvre, Henri. *The Production of Space.* Donald Nicholson-Smith, trans. Oxford: Blackwell, 1991. Print.

Le Goff, Jacques. *History and Memory.* Steven Rendall and Elizabeth Claman, trans. New York: Columbia UP, 1992. Print.

Lee, Sander. "Platonic Themes in Chris Marker's *La Jetée*," *Senses of Cinema* 4 (5 March 2000). Web. 22 March 2011.

Lee, Sky. *Disappearing Moon Café*. Vancouver: Douglas and McIntyre, 1995. Print.
Lejeune, Phillippe. "The Autobiographical Contract." *French Literary Theory Today: A Reader*. Tzvetan Todorov, ed. Cambridge: Cambridge UP, 1991. 192–222. Print.
Lelyveld, Joseph. "Breaking Away." *New York Times Magazine*, 6 March 2005. Web. 22 February 2011.
Lemon, Alaina. *Between Two Fires: Gypsy Performance and Romani Memory from Pushkin to Postsocialism*. Durham: Duke UP, 2000. Print.
Lewis-Kraus, Gideon. "The Reanimator: Omer Fast's Virtual Realities." *Nextbook* (2008). Web. 30 April 2010.
Lewy, Guenter. *The Nazi Persecution of the Gypsies*. Oxford: Oxford UP, 2000. Print.
Leys, Ruth. *Trauma: A Genealogy*. Chicago: U of Chicago P, 2000. Print.
Livingstone, Margaret. *Vision and Art: The Biology of Seeing*. New York: Abrams, 2002.
Locke, John. *An Essay Concerning Human Understanding*. Peter Nidditch, ed. 2nd ed. Oxford: Clarendon, 1975. Print.
Long, J.J. "History, Narrative, and Photography in W.G. Sebald's *Die Ausgewanderten*." *Modern Language Review* 98.1 (2003): 117–37. Print.
———. *W.G. Sebald: Image Archive, Modernity*. New York: Columbia UP, 2008. Print.
Luhmann, Nicklas. *Die Realität der Massenmedien*. Opladen: Westdeutscher Verlag, 1996. Print.
Loshitzky, Yosefa, ed. *Spielberg's Holocaust: Critical Perspectives on Schindler's List*. Bloomington: Indiana UP, 1997. Print.
———. "Holocaust Others: Spielberg's *Schindler's List* Versus Lanzmann's *Shoah*." *Spielberg's Holocaust: Critical Perspectives on Schindler's List*. Bloomington: Indiana UP, 1997. 77–103. Print.
Lupton, Catherine. *Chris Marker: Memories of the Future*. London: Reaktion, 2005. Print.
Lütticken, Sven. "An Arena in Which to Reenact." *Life, Once More: Forms of Reenactment in Contemporary Art*. Sven Lütticken, ed. Rotterdam: Witte de With, Centre for Contemporary Art, Rotterdam, 2005. 17–60. Print.
Lyotard, Jean-François. *The Postmodern Condition: A Report on Knowledge*. Geoff Bennington and Brian Massumi, trans. Minneapolis: U of Minnesota P, 1984. Print.
Maltby, Richard. *Hollywood Cinema*. Oxford: Blackwell, 2003. Print.
Marcus, Laura. *Auto/biographical Discourses: Theory, Criticism, Practice*. Manchester: Manchester UP, 1994. Print.
Margalit, Avishai. *The Ethics of Memory*. Cambridge: Harvard UP, 2002. Print.
Margolian, Howard. *Unauthorized Entry: The Truth about Nazi War Criminals in Canada, 1946–1956*. Toronto: U of Toronto P, 2000. Print.

Marker, Chris. *La Jetée: Cine-Roman*. New York: Zone, 1992. Print.
Markowitsch, Hans. "Cultural Memory and the Neurosciences." *Cultural Memory Studies: An International and Interdisciplinary Handbook*. Astrid Erll and Ansgar Nünning, eds. Berlin and New York: Walter de Gruyter, 2008. 275–83. Print.
Marshall, Catherine. *Militarism Versus Feminism: Writings on Women and War*. Margaret Kamester and Jo Vellacott, eds. London: Virago, 1987. Print.
Martin, Stewart. "W.G. Sebald and the Modern Art of Memory." *Radical Philosophy* 132 (2005): 18–30. Print.
Martin-Jones, David. *Deleuze, Cinema, and National Identity*. Edinburgh: Edinburgh UP, 2006. Print.
Marx, Karl. *The Eighteenth Brumaire of Louis Bonaparte* (1852). New York: International, 1963. Print.
McCalman, Iain, and Paul A. Pickering. "From Realism to the Affective Turn: An Agenda." *Historical Reenactment: From Realism to the Affective Turn*. Iain McCalman and Paul A. Pickering, eds. Basingstoke: Palgrave Macmillan, 2010. 1–17. Print.
McGinnis, Janice Dicken. "Heritage Minutes: Myth and History." *Canadian Studies at Home and Abroad*. James De Finney, Gregory Kealey, John Lennox, and Tamara Palmer Seiler, eds. Montreal: Association for Canadian Studies, 1995. 25–36. Print.
McRoberts, Kenneth. *Misconceiving Canada: The Struggle for National Unity*. Toronto: Oxford UP, 1997. Print.
Mead, John. "9/11, Manhood, Mourning, and the American Romance." *Reframing 9/11: Film, Popular Culture, and the War on Terror*. Jeff Birkenstein, Anna Froula, and Karen Randell, eds. New York and London: Continuum, 2010. 57–68. Print.
Meek, Allen. *Trauma and Media: Theories, Histories, and Images*. New York: Routledge, 2010. Print.
Meisel, John, Guy Rocher, and Arthur Silver. *As I Recall: Historical Perspectives*. Montreal and Kingston: McGill–Queen's UP, 1999.
Memory Studies. Periodical. Oakland: Sage, 2008. Print.
Michalka, Matthias. "'The Casting' Reviewed." *The Casting: Omer Fast*. Köln: Verlag der Buchhandlung Walther König, 2007. 7–24. (MUMOK), Museum Moderner Kunst Stiftung Ludwig Wien. Print.
Miles, Malcolm. *Art, Space, and the City: Public Art and Urban Futures*. London: Routledge, 2007. Print.
Milton, Sybil. "Women and the Holocaust: The Case of German and German-Jewish Women." *When Biology Became Destiny: Women in Weimar and Nazi Germany*. Renate Bridenthal, Atina Grossman and Marion Kaplan, eds. New York: Monthly Review, 1984. 297–307. Print.
Minority Report. Dir. Steven Spielberg. Perf. Tom Cruise, Max von Sydow. 20th Century Fox, 2002. DVD. DreamWorks Home Entertainment, 2002.

Morrison, Jack. *Ravensbrück: Everyday Life in a Women's Concentration Camp 1939–45*. Princeton: Markus Wiener, 2000.
Morrison, Toni. *Beloved*. New York: Vintage, 2004. Print.
———. "Living Memory." *Small Acts: Thoughts on the Politics of Black Cultures*. Paul Gilroy, ed. London: Serpent's Tail, 1993. Print.
———. *Playing in the Dark: Whiteness and the Literary Imagination*. New York: Vintage, 1992. Print.
Morton, Adam. "Emotional Truth: Emotional Accuracy." *Supplement to Proceedings of the Aristotelian Society* 76 (2002): 265–75. Print.
Morton, Desmond. "A Shared Past Is a Nation's Compass." *Toronto Star*, 26 September 1997, A28. Print.
Mountcastle, Vernon B. "Brain Science at the Century's Ebb." Special issue of *Daedalus* 127.2 (1998): 1–36. Print.
Muhle, Maria. "Omer Fast: Where Images Lie ... About the Fictionality of Documents." *Afterall* 20 (2009): n.p. 7 July 2011.
Murphy, Sheila C. *How Television Invented New Media*. New Brunswick: Rutgers UP, 2011. Print.
Nabokov, Vladimir. *Speak, Memory: An Autobiography Revisited*. New York: Vintage, 1989. Print.
Neisser, Ulric, and Robyn Fivush, eds. *The Remembering Self: Construction and Accuracy in the Self-Narrative*. Cambridge: Cambridge UP, 1994. Print.
Nelson, Robin. *State of Play: Contemporary "High-End" TV Drama*. Manchester: Manchester UP, 2007. Print.
Nick, James. "Time and the Machine—Terry Gilliam on Nostalgia, Bruce Willis, and the Look of *12 Monkeys*." *Sight and Sound* 6.4 (1996): 14–16. Print.
Nicks, Joan, and Jeannette Sloniowski, eds. *Slippery Pastimes: Reading the Popular in Canadian Culture*. Waterloo: Wilfrid Laurier UP, 2002. Print.
Nietzsche, Friedrich Wilhelm. *The Use and Abuse of History*. Julius Kraft, ed. New York: Macmillan, 1957. Print.
Nolan, Christopher. "Dream Work." Interview by Amy Taubin. *Film Comment* (2010): 30–35. Print.
———. "A Man and His Dream: Christopher Nolan and *Inception*." Interview by David Itzkoff. *Arts Beat*, 30 June 2010. Web. 12 April 2011.
Nora, Pierre. "Between History and Memory." *Realms of Memory: The Construction of the French Past*. Arthur Goldhammer, trans. Laurence D. Kritzman, ed. New York: Columbia UP, 1996. 1–20. Print.
———. "Between Memory and History: *Les Lieux de Memoire*." Marc Roudebush, trans. *Representations* 26 (Spring 1989): 7–24. Print.
Norris, Andrew, ed. *The Exemplary Exception: Philosophical and Political Decisions in Giorgio Agamben's Homo Sacer*. Durham: Duke UP, 2005. Print.
Odin, Roger. "Le film de fiction menacé par la photographie et sauvé par la bande-son (à propos de *La Jetée* de Chris Marker)." *Cinémas de la*

modernité, Films, Théories: Colloque de Cerisy. Dominique Château, André Gardiès, and François Jost, eds. Paris: Editions Klincksieck, 1981. Print.

Ogden, C.K., with M.S. Florence. *Militarism versus Feminism: An Enquiry and a Policy*. London: George Allen and Unwin, 1915. Print.

Oliveira, Michael. "Griffin Poetry Prize shortlister Dionne Brand has no fear for poetry's future." *Kitchener Record*, 5 April 2011. Web. 23 April 2011.

Oliver, Kelly. *Witnessing: Beyond Recognition*. Minneapolis: U of Minnesota P, 2001. Print.

Olney, James. "The Ontology of Autobiography." *Autobiography: Essays Theoretical and Critical*. James Olney, ed. Princeton: Princeton UP, 1980. 236–67. Print.

Orwen, Patricia. "Soon on TV: The 60 Second History Lesson." *Toronto Star*, 1 April 1991, A2.

Osborne, Brian S. "The Place of Memory and Identity." *Diversities* 1.1 (Summer 2002): 9–13. Print.

Ossman, Susan. *Picturing Casablanca: Portraits of Power in a Modern City*. Los Angeles: U of California P, 1994. Print.

Ouditt, Sharon. "Myths, Memories, and Monuments: Reimagining the Great War." *The Cambridge Companion to the Literature of the First World War*. Vincent Sherry, ed. Cambridge UP, 2005. 245–60. Print.

———. *Fighting Forces, Writing Women: Identity and Ideology in the First World War*. London: Routledge, 1994. Print.

Palmer, Jerry. *Taking Humour Seriously*. London: Routledge, 1994. Print.

Pankhurst, Sylvia. *The Home Front: A Mirror to Life in England during the World War*. London: Hutchison, 1932. Print.

Parfit, Derek. *Reasons and Persons*. Oxford: Clarendon, 1984. Print.

Passerini, Luisa. "Memories Between Silence and Oblivion." *Contested Pasts: The Politics of Memory*. Katherine Hodgkin and Susannah Radstone, eds. London: Routledge, 2003. 238–54. Print.

Paz, Octavio. "Re/Visions: Mural Painting." *Octavio Paz: Essays on Mexican Art*. Helen Lane, trans. New York: Harcourt Brace, 1993. 113–68. Print.

Peña, Richard. "Borges and the New Latin American Cinema." *Borges and His Successors: The Borgesian Impact on Literature and the Arts*. Edna Aizenberg, ed. Columbia: U of Missouri P, 1990. 229–43. Print.

Pence, Jeffrey. "Postcinema/Postmemory." *Memory and Popular Film*. Paul Grainge, ed. Manchester: Manchester UP, 2003. 237–56. Print.

Penley, Constance. *The Future of an Illusion: Film, Feminism, and Psychoanalysis*. Minneapolis: U of Minnesota P, 1989. Print.

Philip, M. Nourbese. *Zong!* Toronto: Mercury, 2008. Print.

Plato. "From *Theaetetus* and *Phaedrus*." *Theories of Memory: A Reader*. Michael Rossington, Anne Whitehead, and Linda R. Anderson, eds. Baltimore: Johns Hopkins UP, 2007. 25–27. Print.

Pratt, Mary Louise. *Imperial Eyes: Travel Writing and Transculturation*. New York: Routledge, 2007. Print.

Proust, Marcel. *In Search of Lost Time: Swann's Way*. C.K. Scott Moncrieff, trans. Vol. 1. London: Vintage, 1996. Print.
Rabinowitz, Dorothy. "Portrait of a Survivor." *Commentary Magazine* (1976): n.p. Web.
———. *New Lives: Survivors of the Holocaust Living in America*. Indiana: Universe, 2000. Print.
Radstone, Susannah, and Bill Schwarz, eds. *Memory: Histories, Theories, Debates*. New York: Fordham UP, 2010. Print.
Reed, Jr., Adolf. "Three Tremés," nonsite.org. 4 July 2011. Web. 17 January 2012.
Reid, Donald. "America so far from Ravensbrück." *Histoire-Politique*, mai–août 2008. Web. 24 June 2011.
Rescue Me. Season 1–7. Prod. FX Network, Dreamworks, Denis Leary, and Peter Tolan. Dist. Sony, 2004–11. DVD.
Ricciardi, Alessia. *The Ends of Mourning: Psychoanalysis, Literature, Film*. Stanford: Stanford UP, 2003. Print.
Richards, Janet Radcliffe. "Why the Pursuit of Peace Is No Part of Feminism." *Women, Militarism, and War*. Jean Bethke Elshtain and Sheila Tobias, eds. Lanham: Rowman and Littlefield, 1990. 211–25. Print.
Ricoeur, Paul. *Memory, History, Forgetting*. Kathleen Blamey and David Pellauer, trans. Chicago: U of Chicago P, 2004. Print.
Ricoeur, Paul, and Sorin Anhohi. "Memory, History, Forgiveness: A Dialogue Between Paul Ricoeur and Sorin Anhohi." *Janus Head* 8.1 (2005): 14–25. Web.
Riegler, Roxane. "The Necessity of Remembering Injustice and Suffering: History, Memory, and the Representation of the Romani Holocaust in Austrian Contemporary Literature." *Studies in 20th and 21st Century Literature* 31.1 (2007) 260–84. Print.
Ringelheim, Joan. "Women and the Holocaust: A Reconsideration of the Matriarch." *Signs* 10.4 (1985): 741–61. Print.
———. "Women and the Holocaust: A Reconsideration of the Matriarch," in Jewish Women in Historical Perspective. Judith R. Baskin, ed. Detroit: Wayne State UP, 1991. 243–64
Rodal, Alti. *Nazi War Criminals in Canada: The Historical and Policy Setting from the 1940s to the Present*. Prepared for the Commission of Inquiry on War Criminals. Canada: Commission of Inquiry on War Criminals, 1986. Print.
Rodowick, D.N. *Gilles Deleuze's Time Machine*. Durham: Duke UP, 1997. Print.
Rose, Steven. *The Making of Memory*. New York: Vintage, 2003. Print.
Rosen, Alan. "Autobiography from the Other Side: The Reading of Nazi Memoirs and Confessional Ambiguity." *Biography* 24.3 (2001): 553–69. Print.
Rosenberg, Karen, and Ceija Stojka. "They Couldn't Take Our Thoughts: A Conversation with Ceija Stojka." *Women's Review of Books* 12.6 (1995): 18–20. Print.

Rosenberg, Otto. *A Gypsy in Auschwitz*. Helmut Bögler, trans. London: London House, 1999. Print.

Rosenblum, Robert, and H.W. Janson. *Nineteenth-Century Art*. Upper Saddle River: Pearson Education, 2005. Print.

Rosenhaft, Eve. "Exchanging Glances: Ambivalence in Twentieth-Century Photographs of German Sinti." *Third Text* 22.3 (2008): 311–24. Print.

———. "A Photographer and His 'Victims' 1934–1964: Reconstructing a Shared Experience of the Romani Holocaust." *The Role of the Romanies: Images and Counter-Images of "Gypsies"/Romanies in European Cultures*. Nicholas Saul and Susan Tebbutt, eds. Liverpool: Liverpool UP, 2004. 178–207. Print.

Rossington, Michael, and Anne Whitehead, eds. *Theories of Memory: A Reader*. Baltimore: Johns Hopkins UP, 2007. Print.

Roudometof, Victor. "Beyond Commemoration: The Politics of Collective Memory." *Journal of Political and Military Sociology* 31.2 (2003): 161–69. Print.

Royal, Susan. "*Schindler's List*: An Interview with Steven Spielberg." *Inside Film Magazine Online*. Web. 23 July 2011.

Ruddick, Sara. "The Rationality of Care." *Women, Militarism, and War*. Jean Bethke Elshtain and Sheila Tobias, eds. Lanham: Rowman and Littlefield, 1990. 229–54. Print.

Rukszto, Katarzyna. "The Other Heritage Minutes: Satirical Reactions to Canadian Nationalism." *Topia: Canadian Journal of Cultural Studies* 14 (Fall 2005): 73–91. Print.

———. "National Encounters: Narrating Canada and the Plurality of Difference." *International Journal of Canadian Studies* 1 (Fall 1997): 149–62. Print.

Rushton, Steve. "Tweedledum and Tweedeledee Resolved to Have a Battle." *Experience, Memory, Re-Enactment*. Anke Bangma, Steve Rushton, and Florian Wüst, eds. Rotterdam: Piet Zwart Institute, 2005. 5–12. Print.

Ryan, Jr., Allan A. *Quiet Neighbors: Prosecuting Nazi War Criminals in America*. London: Harcourt Brace Jovanovich, 1984. Print.

Said, Edward W. *Orientalism*. New York: Vintage, 1978. Print.

Samuel, Raphael. *Theatres of Memory*. London: Verso, 1994. Print.

Samuel, Raphael, and Paul Thompson. *The Myths We Live By*. London: Routledge, 1990. Print.

Sandlos, Karyn. "Unifying Forces: Rhetorical Reflections on a Pro-Choice Image." *Transformations: Thinking Through Feminism*. Sara Ahmed, Jane Kilby, Celia Lury, Maureen McNeil, and Beverley Skeggs, eds. New York: Routledge, 2000. 77–91. Print.

Sandro, Paul. "Singled Out by History: *La Jetée* and the Aesthetics of Memory." *French Cultural Studies* 10.28 (1999): 107–27. Print.

Sarasin, Philipp. *Darwin und Foucault: Genealogie und Geschichte im Zeitalter der Biologie*. Frankfurt: Suhrkamp, 2009. Print.

Saunders, Max. "Life Writing, Cultural Memory, and Literary Studies." *Media and Cultural Memory: An International and Interdisciplinary Handbook.* Astrid Eril and Ansgar Nünning, eds. Berlin: Walter de Gruyter, 2008. 321–32. Print.
Saving Grace. Season 1–3. Prod. TNT Network, Fox Television, Holly Hunter, and Nancy Miller. Dist. 20th Century Fox Home Entertainment, 2007–10. DVD.
Saving Private Ryan. Dir. Steven Spielberg. Perf. Tom Hanks, Tom Sizemore, Edward Burns. DreamWorks SKG, 1998. DVD. DreamWorks Home Entertainment, 1999.
Sayner, Joanne. "Memories of Victimhood: Nazism and the Challenge of the Autobiographical." *Forum for Modern Language Studies* 43.3 (2007): 301–15. Print.
Schachter, Daniel. *Searching for Memory: The Brain, the Mind, and the Past.* New York: Basic, 1996. Print.
Schäfer-Wünsche, Elisabeth. "Work and Net-Work: Reflections on a Global Metaphor." *American Studies / Shifting Gears.* Birte Christ et al., eds. Heidelberg: Winter, 2010. 201–21. Print.
Schaffer, Kay, and Sidonie Smith. *Human Rights and Narrated Lives: The Ethics of Recognition.* New York: Palgrave Macmillan, 2004. Print.
Schreiner, Olive. "From *Women and Labour*: Woman and War." *Women On War: An International Anthology of Women's Writings from Antiquity to the Present.* Daniela Gioseffi, ed. New York: Feminist Press CUNY, 2003. 221–22. Print
Schwarz, Gudrun. "SS-Aufseherinnen in nationalsozialistischen Konzentrationslagern 1933–1945." *Dachauer Hefte* 10 (1994): 32–49. Print.
Schefer, Jean Louis. "On *La Jetée.*" Paul Smith, trans. 1990. chrismarker.org 28 April 2011. Web.
Schindler's List. Dir. Steven Spielberg. Perf. Liam Neeson, Ben Kingsley, Ralph Fiennes. Universal Pictures, 1993. DVD. Universal Studios Home Video, 2004.
Scofield, Gregory. *Singing Home the Bones.* Vancouver: Raincoast, 2005. Print.
Scott, Jill. *A Poetics of Forgiveness: Cultural Responses to Loss and Wrongdoing.* New York: Palgrave Macmillan, 2010. Print.
Scott, Joan W. "Rewriting History." *Behind the Lines: Gender and the Two World Wars.* Margaret Randolph Higonnet, Jane Jenson, Sonya Michel, and Margaret Collins Weitz, eds. New Haven: Yale UP, 1987. 21–30. Print.
Sebald, W.G. *Austerlitz.* Anthea Bell, trans. London: Hamish Hamilton, 2001. Print.
———. *The Emigrants.* Michael Hulse, trans. London: Harvill, 1997. Print.
———. *Vertigo.* Michael Hulse, trans. New York: New Directions, 1999. Print.
Sellars, Simon. "Retrospecto: *La Jetée.*" *Ballardian*, 7 October 2005. Web. 12 April 2011.

Sherbert, Garry, Annie Gerin, and Sheila Petty, eds. *Canadian Cultural Poesis: Essays on Canadian Culture*. Waterloo: Wilfrid Laurier UP, 2006.
Shindler, Richard. *Hollywood Goes to War: Films and American Society, 1939–1952*. London: RKP, 1979. Print.
Sielke, Sabine. "'The Brain—is wider than the Sky—' or: Re-Cognizing Emily Dickinson." *Emily Dickinson Journal* 17.1 (2008): 68–85. Print.
———. *Fashioning the Female Subject: The Intertextual Networking of Dickinson, Moore and Rich*. Ann Arbor: University of Michigan Press, 1997.
———. "Joy in Repetition: Acht Thesen zum Konzept Serialität und zum Prinzip der Serie." *Populäre Serialität: Narration–Evolution–Distinktion. Zum seriellen Erzählen seit dem 19. Jahrhundert*. Frank Kelleter, ed. Bielefeld: Transcript, 2012. 385–400.
———. "Transatlantische Serialität: Zur Transformation von Ästhetik, Wahrnehmung und Sinnstiftung im 20. Jahrhundert." *Dialoge zwischen Amerika und Europa: Transatlantische Perspektiven in Philosophie, Literatur, Kunst und Musik*. Astrid Böger, Georg Schiller und Nicole Schröder, eds. Kultur und Erkenntnis. Tübingen: Francke, 2007. 243–56. Print.
———. "Postfeminismus und kulturelle Amnesie: Zur Serialität feministischer Perspektiven oder: Sind *Sex and the City*, *Fear of Flying*, und *The Feminine Mystique* Episoden ein und derselben Seifenoper?" *Screening Gender—Gendered Screens: Geschlechterszenarien im gegenwärtigen US-amerikanischen Film und Fernsehen*. Erlanger Studien zur Anglistik und Amerikanistik. Heike Paul und Alexandra Ganser, eds. Münster: LIT, 2008. 33–58. Print.
Simon, Joe, and Jack Kirby. *Captain America Comics* 1 (1941), Timely Comics [Marvel Comics]. Print.
Simon, Roger, Sharon Rosenberg, and Claudia Eppert. *Between Hope and Despair: Pedagogy and the Remembrance of Historical Trauma*. Lanham: Rowan and Littlefield, 2000. Print.
Singer, Wolf. "Erinnern schwächt Gedächtnis." *Gehirn&Geist* 5 (2005): 56. Print.
Sisson, Larry. "The Art and Illusion of Spiritual Autobiography." *True Relations: Essays on Autobiography and the Postmodern*. G. Thomas Couser and Joseph Fichtelberg, eds. London: Greenwood, 1998. 97–108. Print.
Smith, G. Gregory. *Scottish Literature: Character and Influence*. London: Macmillan, 1919. Print.
Smith, Robert. *Derrida and Autobiography*. New York: Cambridge UP, 1995. Print.
Spiegelman, Art. *The Complete Maus*. London: Penguin, 2003. Print.
Sonneman, Toby. *Shared Sorrows: A Gypsy Family Remembers the Holocaust*. Hatfield: U of Hertfordshire P, 2002. Print.
Spence, Alan. *Its Colours They Are Fine*. London: Phoenix, 1999. Print.

Spivak, Gayatari Chakravorty. "Subaltern Studies: Deconstructing Historiography." *In Other Worlds: Essays in Cultural Politics*. New York: Routledge, 1987. 197–221. Print.

Stam, Robert. *Literature Through Film: Realism, Magic, and the Art of Adaptation*. Oxford: Blackwell, 2005. Print.

Stanley, Liz. *The Auto/Biographical I: The Theory and Practice of Feminist Auto/Biography*. Manchester: Manchester UP, 1992. Print.

Stanley, Liz. "Moments of Writing: Is There a Feminist Auto/biography?" *Gender and History* 2.1 (Spring 1990): 58–67.

Stein, Gertrude. *The Geographical History of America or the Relation of Human Nature to the Human Mind*. 1936. New York: Vintage, 1973. Print.

———. "If I Told Him: A Completed Portrait of Picasso." 1923. *A Stein Reader*. Ulla E. Dydo, ed. Evanston: Northwestern UP, 1993. 464–66. Print.

———. "Picasso." *Selected Writings of Gertrude Stein*. Carl van Vechten, ed. New York: Vintage, 1972. 333–35. Print.

———. "Portraits and Repetition." *Lectures in America*. 1935. Boston: Beacon, 1985. 165–206. Print.

Stewart, Michael. "Remembering Without Commemoration: The Mnemonics and Politics of Holocaust Memories among the European Roma." *Journal of the Royal Anthropological Institute* 10.3 (2004): 561–82. Print.

———. "The Other Genocide." *Multidisciplinary Approaches to Romany Studies*. Michael Stewart and Márton Rövid, eds. Budapest: Central European UP, 2010. 172–95. Print.

Stojka, Ceija. *Bilder und Texte: 1989–1995*. Wien: Graphische Kunstanstalt Otto Sares, 1995. Print.

———. *Reisende auf dieser Welt: Aus dem Leben einer Rom-Zigeunerin*. Wien: Picus, 1992. Print.

———. *Träume ich, dass ich lebe? Befreit aus Bergen-Belsen*. Wien: Picus, 2005. Print.

———. *Wir leben im Verborgenen: Erinnerungen einer Rom-Zigeunerin*. Wien: Picus, 1988. Print.

Stojka, Karl. *Gas*. Vienna: 1996. Print.

Storey, John. "The Articulation of Memory and Desire: From Vietnam to the War in the Persian Gulf." *Memory and Popular Film*. Paul Grainge, ed. Manchester: Manchester UP, 2003. 144–61. Print.

Sturken, Marita. *Tangled Memories: The Vietnam War, the AIDS Epidemic, and the Politics of Remembering*. Los Angeles: U of California P, 1997. Print.

———. *Tourists of History: Memory, Kitsch, and Consumerism from Oklahoma City to Ground Zero*. Durham: Duke University Press, 2007. Print.

Swales, Martin. "Intertextuality, Authenticity, Metonymy: On Reading W.G. Sebald." *The Anatomist of Melancholy: Essays in Memory of W.G. Sebald*. Rudiger Görner, ed. Munich: Iudicium, 2003. 81–88. Print.

Swanwick, Helena. *Women and War* (1916). New York: Garland, 1971. Print.
Szabo, Franz, ed. *Austrian Immigration to Canada: Selected Essays*. Ottawa: Carleton UP, 1996. Print.
Taylor, Kathy. *The New Narrative of Mexico: Sub-Versions of History in Mexican Fiction*. London: Associated UPs, 1994. Print.
Teo, Stephen. *Wong Kar-wai*. London: BFI World Directors, 2005. Print.
Terdiman, Richard. *Present Past: Modernity and the Memory Crisis*. Ithaca: Cornell UP, 1993. Print.
Trainor, James. "Omer Fast: Truth Bends and Decays as It Travels." *ArtAsiaPacific* 68 (2010): 124–29. Print.
Treen, Joe. "Justice for a Beatle." In Jon Wiener, *Gimme Some Truth: The John Lennon FBI Files*. Berkeley: U of California P, 2000. 204. Print.
Treme. Season 1. Prod. Eric Overmeyer and David Simon. HBO, 2010. DVD.
Tristram Shandy: A Cock and Bull Story. Dir. Michael Winterbottom. Perf. Steve Coogan, Rob Brydon. BBC Films, 2005. DVD. Lionsgate Home Entertainment, 2006.
Trudeau, Pierre. *Federalism and the French Canadians*. Toronto: Macmillan, 1968.
Trumpener, Katie. "The Time of the Gypsies: A 'People Without History' in the Narratives of the West." *Critical Inquiry* 18.4 (Summer 1992): 843–84. Print.
Turim, Maureen. *Flashbacks in Film: Memory and History*. London: Routledge, 1989. Print.
Turner, Frederick Jackson. "The Significance of the Frontier in American History." 1893. *Rereading Frederick Jackson Turner: "The Significance of the Frontier in American History" and Other Essays*. John Mack Faragher, ed. New York: Holt, 1994. 31–60. Print.
Twain, Mark. *The Autobiography of Mark Twain*. Part 1. Charles Neider, ed. New York: Harper Collins, 1959. Print.
Umanksy, Lauri. *Motherhood Reconceived: Feminism and the Legacies of the Sixties*. New York: New York UP, 1996. Print.
Van Baar, Huub. "From 'Time-Banditry' to the Challenge of Established Historiographies: Romani Contributions to Old and New Images of the Holocaust." *Multidisciplinary Approaches to Romany Studies*. Michael Stewart and Márton Rövid, eds. Budapest: Central European UP, 2010. 153–71. Print.
Van Baaren, Rick, et al. "Where Is the Love? The Social Aspects of Mimicry." *Philosophical Transactions of the Royal Society* B 364.1528 (2009): 2381–89. Print.
Van Delden, Maarten. *Carlos Fuentes, Mexico, and Modernity*. Nashville: Vanderbilt UP, 1998. Print.
Van Dijck, José. *Mediated Memories in the Digital Age*. Stanford: Stanford UP, 2007. Print.

Varela, Francisco J., Evan Thompson, and Eleanor Rosch. *The Embodied Mind: Cognitive Science and Human Experience*. Cambridge: MIT Press, 1991. Print.
Vertigo. Dir. Alfred Hitchcock. Perf. James Stewart, Kim Novak. Paramount Pictures, 1958. DVD. Universal Pictures, 1998.
W.G. Sebald: A Critical Companion. J.J. Long and Anne Whitehead, eds. Seattle: U of Washington P, 2004. Print.
Wachtel, Eleanor. "Ghosthunter." *The Emergence of Memory: Conversations with W.G. Sebald*. Lynne Sharon Schwartz, ed. New York: Seven Stories, 2007. 37–61. Print.
Walker, David. "*Treme*: The HBO Series." *Times-Picayune*. nola.com. 30 November 2012. Web.
Walker, Janet. "Rights and Return: Perils and Fantasies of Situated Testimony After Katrina." *Documentary Testimonies: Global Archives of Suffering*. Bhaskar Sarkar and Janet Walker, eds. New York: Routledge, 2010. 83–114. Print.
———. *Trauma Cinema: Documenting Incest and the Holocaust*. Berkeley: U of California P, 2005. Print.
Walker, Nancy. *Feminist Alternatives: Irony and Fantasy in the Contemporary Novel by Women*. Jackson: UP of Mississippi, 1990. Print.
Wallmannsberger, Josef. "The Medium Is the Memory: Ars Memoriae in Its Age of Technological Reproducibility." *Semiotics of the Media: State of the Art, Projects, and Perspectives*. Winfried Nöth, ed. Berlin: de Gruyter, 1997. 589–601. Print.
War and Remembrance. Dir. Dan Curtis. Perf. Robert Mitchum, Jane Seymour. Dan Curtis Productions, 1988. DVD. MPI Home Video, 2003.
Ward, John. *Alain Resnais, or the Theme of Time*. London: Secker and Warburg, 1968. Print.
Webb, Walter Prescott. *The Texas Rangers: A Century of Frontier Defense*. Austin: U of Texas P, 1995. Print.
Weissman, Gary. Fantasies of Witnessing: Postwar Efforts to Experience the Holocaust. Ithaca: Cornell UP, 2004. Print.
Welzer, Harald. "Kriege der Erinnerung." *Gehirn&Geist* 5 (2005): 40–46. Print.
West, Emily. "Collective Memories on the Airwaves: The Negotiation of Unity and Diversity in a Troubled Canadian Nationalism." *Canadian Cultural Poesis: Essays on Canadian Culture*. Garry Sherbert, Annie Gerin, and Sheila Petty, eds. Waterloo: Wilfrid Laurier UP, 2006. 67–84.
Whipps, Heather. "How the Hyoid Bone Changed History." *Live Science*, 3 February 2008. Web. 23 April 2011.
Whitaker, Reginald. *Double Standard: The Secret History of Canadian Immigration*. Toronto: Lester and Orpen Dennys, 1987. Print.
White, Kenneth, ed. *Atoms of Delight: An Anthology of Scottish Haiku*. Edinburgh: Polygon, 2000. Print.

Whitehead, Anne. *Memory*. New York: Routledge, 2009. Print.
Wiesenthal, Simon. "Some Significant Cases: Hermine Braunsteiner." Simon Wiesenthal Archive, n.d. Web. 20 January 2011.
Wilden, Tony. *The Imaginary Canadian*. Vancouver: Pulp, 1981. Print.
Williams, Raymond. *Marxism and Literature*. Oxford: Oxford UP, 1977. Print.
———. *Television: Technology and Cultural Form*. New York: Schocken, 1975. Print.
Wills, David. *Prosthesis*. Stanford: Stanford UP, 1995. Print.
Wilson, Janelle L. *Nostalgia: Sanctuary of Meaning*. Pennsylvania: Bucknell UP, 2005.
Wilson, V. Seymour. "The Tapestry Vision of Canadian Multiculturalism." *Canadian Journal of Political Science* 26, 4 (1993): 645–69. Print.
Wiltsher, Anne. "Most Dangerous Women": Feminist Peace Campaigners of the Great War. London: Pandora, 1985.
Winter, Jay. *Sites of Memory, Sites of Mourning*. London: Cambridge UP, 1995. Print.
The Wire. Season 1–5. Prod. Eric Overmeyer and David Simon. Dist. HBO, 2002–08. DVD.
Wolf, Werner. "Gesichter in der Erzählkunst: Zur Wahrnehmung von Physiognomien und Metawahrnehmung von Physiognomiebeschreibungen aus theoretischer und historischer Sicht am Beispiel englischsprachiger Texte des 19. und 20. Jahrhunderts". *Sprachkunst* 33.2 (2002): 301–25. Print.
Wright, Robin. *Virtual Sovereignty: Nationalism, Culture, and the Canadian Question*. Toronto: Canadian Scholars' Press, 2004. Print.
Yates, Frances. *The Art of Memory*. Chicago: U of Chicago P, 1966. Print.
Young, James Edward. *The Texture of Memory: Holocaust Memorials and Meaning*. New Haven: Yale UP, 1993. Print.
Zeki, Semir. *Inner Vision: An Exploration of Art and the Brain*. Oxford: Oxford UP, 1999. Print.
Zelizer, Barbie. "Reading the Past against the Grain: The Shape of Memory Studies." *Critical Studies in Mass Communication* 12 (1995): 204–39. Print.
———. *Remembering to Forget. Holocaust Memory through the Camera's Eye*. Chicago: U of Chicago P, 1998. Print.
Ziarek, Ewa. "Kristeva and Levinas: Mourning, Ethics, and the Feminine." *Ethics, Politics, and Difference in Julia Kristeva's Writings: A Collection of Essays*. Kelly Oliver, ed. New York: Routledge, 1993. 62–78. Print.
Zinn, Howard. *A People's History of the United States: 1492–Present*. 1999. New York: HarperCollins, 2003. Print.
Zunke, Christine. *Kritik der Hirnforschung: Neurophysiologie und Willensfreiheit*. Berlin: Akademie-Verlag, 2008. Print.

About the Contributors

Kathy Behrendt is Associate Professor of Philosophy at Wilfrid Laurier University. Her research interests are in the areas of personal identity theory, self-knowledge, philosophy of mind, memory, and death. She has published essays on various subjects, including Sebald, narrative views of the self, the Neo-Kantian and Reductionist debate, personal identity, and fear.

Anders Bergstrom is a Ph.D. candidate in English and Film Studies at Wilfrid Laurier University. He is currently working on a project investigating subjectivity and modernity in global art cinema. In 2011 he contributed an introduction to the second volume of *Faith and Spirituality in Masters of World Cinema*. Before embarking on his Ph.D., Anders taught high school in Thailand for two years.

John Dean is Assistant Professor of American literature at Texas A & M International University. His research interests are in nineteenth- and twentieth-century American literature, especially on postcolonial theory and travel writing. He has published essays on travel narratives from New Mexico and on nineteenth-century views of the American landscape.

Graeme Gilloch is a Reader in the Department of Sociology at Lancaster University. His research interests are in the sociology of culture, with a particular focus on the writings of the Frankfurt School, and he is presently writing a study of Siegfried Kracauer. He is author of *Walter Benjamin: Critical Constellations* (2002) and *Myth and Metropolis: Walter Benjamin and the City* (1996) with Polity Press.

Sarah Henstra is an Associate Professor of English at Ryerson University in Toronto. She is the author of *The Counter-Memorial Impulse in Twentieth Century English Fiction* (2009), which examines the deliberate failure of traditional commemorative models in novels where loss is treated as an occasion for social critique. Sarah has published articles on narrative and public memory across various media: digital archives, documentary films, talk shows, and graphic fiction. Her current research focuses on feminist mourning and remembrance.

Marlene Kadar is Professor of Humanities and of Gender and Women's Studies at York University. She is the Undergraduate Program Director of Humanities and has served as the Graduate Program Director of Interdisciplinary Studies and the Coordinator of Fine Arts Cultural Studies. She is the Editor of the Life Writing Series for Wilfrid Laurier University Press, and has co-edited numerous volumes on life writing, including, *Photographs, Histories, and Meanings* (Palgrave Macmillan, 2009) with Jeanne Perreault and Linda Warley; and *Tracing the Autobiographical* (WLUP, 2005) with Susanna Egan, Jeanne Perreault, and Linda Warley.

Kenneth Keir is a doctoral candidate at the University of Aberdeen. His dissertation reads the work of Neil M. Gunn in the light of Freudian and Jungian psychological theories. He has published on Neil Gunn's *The Serpent, Highland River*, and *The Silver Darlings*. He has been on the board of *Causeway/Cabhsair*.

Russell J.A. Kilbourn is Associate Professor in English and Film Studies at Wilfrid Laurier University, where he serves as Film Studies Coordinator. Dr. Kilbourn publishes on film, cultural studies, and comparative literature and on the German author W.G. Sebald. His book, *Cinema, Memory, Modernity: The Representation of Memory from the Art Film to Transnational Cinema*, appeared with Routledge in 2010.

Tanis MacDonald is Associate Professor of English at Wilfrid Laurier University, where she has served as Graduate Coordinator from 2008 to 2009 and from 2010 to 2012. She has research interests in Canadian poetry, elegy studies, and gender and feminist theories. She is author of *The Daughter's Way: Canadian Women's Paternal Elegies* (WLUP, 2012) and editor of *Speaking of Power: The Poetry of Di Brandt* (WLUP, 2006). She has published numerous books of poetry, including *Rue the Day* (Turnstone Press, 2008), *Fortune* (Turnstone Press, 2003), and *Holding Ground* (Seraphim, 2000).

John McCullough is Associate Professor of Cinema and Media Studies in the Department of Film, York University. He is the author of *24* (Wayne State University Press, 2014) and co-editor of *Locating Migrating Media* (Lexington Books, 2010) with Greg Elmer, Charles Davis, and Janine Marchessault, and, with Tom Taylor, *John Porter's Film Activity Book* (Pleasure Dome, 1998). His research interests are in popular North American film and television, particularly representations of class relations, labour, and space. He is co-editor of *Locating Migrating Media* (Lexington Books, 2010) with Greg Elmer, Charles Davis, and Janine Marchessault; and, with Tom Taylor, *John Porter's Film Activity Book* (Pleasure Dome, 1998).

Erin Peters is a Ph.D. candidate in early modern history and cultural memory at the University of Worcester. Her mnemohistorical research analyzes print sources from the early Restoration era for examples of cultural memory construction, manipulation, and transmission. Other areas of interest include nostalgia and trauma, conceptions of identity, remembering and forgetting, censorship and propaganda.

Sheelagh Russell-Brown is a lecturer in the Department of English, Saint Mary's University, and an instructor in the University Pathways Programme of the Canadian Language Learning College. She has research interests in Roma studies, modern Czech culture, and Victorian and neo-Victorian literature, and has presented papers and published on Gerard Manley Hopkins, Václav Havel, Samuel Beckett, Charles Dickens, and Charles Palliser.

Stefan Sereda won a Gold Medal for his dissertation, "Cinema in Scare Quotes: Postmodern Aesthetics and Economics in the American Art Cinema," at Wilfrid Laurier University, where he has taught courses on American cinema and indie film. He has published two essays in his secondary area of interest on African cinema and literature in *Viewing African Cinema in the 21st Century*, edited by Ralph Austen and Mahir Saul (2010), and in *ARIEL* (2008), and has contributed a number of entries to the *Directory of World Cinema*.

Sabine Sielke is Chair of North American Literature and Culture and Director of the North American Studies Program and the German-Canadian Centre at the University of Bonn. Her research interests are in nineteenth- and twentieth-century American literature and culture, with a focus on poetry and poetics, modernist and postmodernist cultures, literary and cultural theory, gender studies, and cultural studies. Author of *Reading Rape: The Rhetoric of Sexual Violence in American Literature and Culture, 1790–1990* (Princeton UP, 2002) and *Fashioning the Female Subject: The Intertextual Networking of Dickinson, Moore and Rich* (U of Michigan Press, 1997), she has co-edited numerous volumes, including *Beyond 9/11* with Christian Klöckner and Simone Knewitz (Lang, 2013), *Verschleierungstaktiken* with Anne-Rose Meyer (Lang, 2011), *Orient and Orientalisms in US-American Poetry and Poetics* with Christian Klöckner (Lang, 2009), and *The Body as Interface* with Elisabeth Schäfer-Wünsche (Winter, 2007).

Amresh Sinha teaches film and media theory at New York University, at the School of Visual Arts, Brooklyn College, and at the College of Staten Island, CUNY. He has co-edited *Millennial Cinema: Memory in Global Film* (Wallflower, 2012) with Terence McSweeney and has published numerous articles on Adorno, Benjamin, Blanchot, and Alexander Kluge as well as on globalization, the use and abuse of subtitles, and other subjects.

Eleanor Ty is Professor of English at Wilfrid Laurier University. Her research areas are in Asian American and Asian Canadian literature, as well as eighteenth-century British women novelists. Author of *Unfastened: Globality and Asian North American Narratives* (Minnesota, 2010) and *The Politics of the Visible in Asian North American Narratives* (U of Toronto P, 2004), she has co-edited *Asian Canadian Writing beyond Autoethnography* with Christl Verduyn (WLUP, 2008) and *Asian North American Identities beyond the Hyphen* (Indiana UP, 2004).

Kate Warren is a Ph.D. candidate in the Art Theory Program of the Faculty of Art, Design and Architecture, Monash University. She is also a freelance writer and curator based in Melbourne, and was previously Assistant Curator at the Australian Centre for the Moving Image.

Index

Abella, Irving, 135
Acton, Carol, 80
Agamben, Giorgio, 138
Agnew, Vanessa, 294, 303
Ahmed, Sarah, 88
Alexander, Khandi, 282
Allen, Woody, 32, 227, 231–33
All the President's Men, 225
American Graffiti, 32, 225, 227, 230, 231
Anzaldúa, Gloria, 120
Apocalypse Now, 19, 225
Arendt, Hannah, 126, 138; "We Refugees," 126
Aristotle, 106
Ashes of Time, 199
Assmann, Aleida, 15, 17–18; communicative memory and cultural memory, 17–18
Assmann, Jan, 15, 17–18; communicative memory and cultural memory, 17–18
"As Time Goes By," 213–14, 218, 219
Atom of Delight, The (Gunn), 161–72; memory in, 171–72; and modernism, postmodernism, 163–68; radical indeterminacy in, 163; and "second self," 30, 171–72; as spiritual autobiography, 168–71; use of third-person narration in, 164–65, 166, 168, 170–71, 172

Augé, Marc, 31, 211–22; *Casablanca* (book), 31, 212, 216; and "figures of oblivion," 215–16, 221; *In the Metro*, 211; *Oblivion*, 213, 214–15
Augustine, Saint, 12, 13, 164, 168, 170, 187; *Confessions*, 13, 164, 168
autobiography, 11, 16, 17, 30, 125–38, 161–72; and "alter-biographical form," 138; and "autobiographical contract," 164; extrinsic vs. intrinsic validation in, 166–68, 169, 171; feminist, 137–38; importance of Hermine Braunsteiner's story to, 131–32; and "limit-case," 136; in modernism, 161, 165–66, 168; in postmodernism, 161, 162, 163, 169; progress of into autobiographical fiction, 164, 165–66; repressed material in, 126, 130, 132, 133, 134–36; from Roma authors, 147, 148, 152–57; spiritual, 161, 168–71; status of memory in, 161–63
Axworthy, Thomas, 251

Bach, Johann Sebastian 289; *St. Matthew Passion*, 289
Baker, Timothy C., 162
Bakhtin, Mikhail, 200, 253; and "chronotope," 200; and "historical inversion," 253

Baldwin, Robert, 258–59
Barry Lyndon, 225
Barthes, Roland, 30, 185, 221, 223n3; *Camera Lucida*, 221; theories of the photograph, 30
Bartov, Omer, 126
Baudrillard, Jean, 21, 31, 225, 226–29, 231, 232, 233–34, 235, 243–44
Behrendt, Johannes, 149
Bell, Duncan, 163
Bellour, Raymond, 186
Benjamin, Walter, 5, 27, 30, 44 181–82, 186, 188–89, 213, 217, 219–20; "Little History of Photography," 217; "On Some Motifs in Baudelaire," 181, 187–88
Bensmaïa, Réda, 182, 183
Berger, Karen, 155
Bergman, Ingrid, 213, 215, 239
Bergson, Henri, 5, 6–8, 34n3, 93–94, 107, 181, 186, 197–98, 203; and "attentive" vs. "instinctual recognition" (habit memory), 6, 7, 10; and "cone of time," 7, 8; importance of to film studies, 7–8; *Matter and Memory* (*Matière et mémoire*), 8, 93, 181, 197–98
Berkman, Joyce, 74
Berlant, Lauren, 88
Bhabha, Homi, 44; seriality in works of, 44
Bierce, Ambrose, 108, 109, 110; "A Horseman in the Sky," 110
Blade Runner, 19
Blanchett, Cate, 238
Blum, Howard, 132
Blustein, Jeffrey, 58
Body Heat, 225–26
Bogart, Humphrey, 214, 217, 239
Bolter, Jay, 19, 290; and "double logic" of remediation, 19, 289

Borden, Mary, 89; "Song of the Mud," 89
Bordwell, David, 8, 34n4, 199; and intensified continuity style, 8
Borges, Jorge Luis, 197; Borgesian cinema, 197
Botea, Irina, 292
Bouchard, Lucien, 261
Bourne Ultimatum, The, 8–11
Bow, Clara, 232
Boym, Svetlana, 253, 258
Brand, Dionne, 93–106; *A Map to the Door of No Return*, 98, 99, 100, 102–3; *A Perfect Kind of Speech*, 93, 106; *Inventories*, 100; *Land to Light On*, 100; and Marxism, 94, 97, 104; *Ossuaries*, 93–106
Braunsteiner, Friedrich, 127
Braunsteiner, Hermine, 29, 125–38; arrest, extradition, conviction of, 127, 129, 131; arrival of in Canada, 131, 133; as concentration camp guard, 127, 128–29, 132, 134, 137; disappearance of records concerning, 130, 133, 134–36; historical/autobiographical value of life of, 131–32; marriage of, 130–31; release from prison, 127, 135
Braunsteiner, Maria Ann Knodn, 127
Braziel, Jana Evans, 138; and "alterbiography," 138, 141n31
Bridges, Beau, 240
Brittain, Vera, 73, 75–76, 80–81
Britzman, Deborah, 135, 137, 138
Bronfman, Charles R., 249, 257, 262
Brown, Wendy, 88
Brzosko-Medryk, Danuta, 129
Buckley, Jerome, 165, 166, 169
Burgoyne, Robert, 226, 233–34, 243
Burwitz, Gudrun Himmler, 127
Butch Cassidy and the Sundance Kid, 230, 231

Butler, Joseph, 54
Butler, Judith, 44; seriality in works of, 44
Byatt, A.S., 65

Cagney, Jimmy, 232
Callenbach, Ernest, 176
Cameron, Elspeth, 257, 265
Campbell, Sue, 53, 61, 65n3; and accuracy in memory, 53, 65n3
Campion, Jane, 42
Canada, 27, 130–31, 133, 134, 135, 137, 140n14, 249–66; American influence on, 251, 256; collective memory in, 250–51, 254, 256, 260–64, 265; English–French relations in, 258–59; as haven for war criminals, 131, 133, 134, 135; immigration to, 255, 256; national identity, tension in, 250, 252–53, 254–57, 262, 265, 266; policy of multiculturalism in, 251, 255; Quebec separatist (sovereignty) movement in, 251, 253, 255, 257, 261–62; regionalism in, 259–60
Canadian Broadcasting Corporation (CBC), 256
Canfield, J. Douglass, 119
Cannadine, David, 252
Carr, Emily, 259–60; as subject of *Heritage Minutes*, 259–60
Carroll, Noël, 230; and "cinema of allusion," 230–31
Carter, Elliott, 41
Caruth, Cathy, 11, 12, 90, 145; "From Trauma and Experience," 11
Casablanca (city, Morocco), 212, 217, 218, 223n10
Casablanca (book, Augé), 31, 212, 216
Casablanca (film), 31, 212–22, 222n3, 234, 239; "figures of oblivion" in, 216, 221; as melodrama, 213, 218–19; music and song in, 213–14, 218, 218, 220, 224n21; self-sacrifice in, 220–21, 224n19; use of flashback in, 217, 219, 224n17
Casey, Edward, 191
Casting, The, 298–300, 302; *tableaux vivants* in, 299–300
Cather, Willa, 64; *My Ántonia*, 64
Catt, Carrie Chapman, 84
Charyn, Jerome, 41; *The Secret Life of Emily Dickinson: A Novel*, 41
Che, 228, 234, 240
Cheung, Maggie, 197
Chinatown, 32, 225, 227, 230–31
Chungking Express, 199
Cicero, 3
cinema: and art films, 8, 198–200, 209; Freudian influence on, 13; hyperreality in, 225, 228, 231–34, 239, 244; indexical and iconic qualities of, 196, 208; intermediality in, 18–19, 230; and "memory films," 19, 31, 195–210; movement-image in, 7–8; photographic nature of, 196, 208; remediation in, 18–19; "time image" in, 7–8. *See also* film
cinema of simulation, 225–44; and blurring of distinction between fiction and documentary, 233–34, 240; defined, 227; history mediated in, 226, 244; and hyper-histories, 229, 234–44; popular memory in, 235–37; and propaganda, 236; prosthetic memory in, 232–33; as response to postmodernism, 227; use of documentary footage in, 228, 231–32, 235, 240
Citizen Kane, 207–8

Citizen's Forum on Canada's Future, 255, 257
Clooney, George, 237
Cloverfield, 235
CNN Concatenated, 295
Coates, Paul, 178
Cohen, Stephen F., 237
Coldplay, 280
Collingwood, R.G., 293–94; *The Idea of History*, 293–94
Collins, Richard, 256
commemoration, 4, 15, 16, 30, 147, 152; art and performance as 148, 155, 166; in First World War, 71, 79–80, 81; and national identity, 158; of terrorist attacks on World Trade Center (2001), 4, 16, 17. *See also* memorial and memorializing
Common Cause, 74
Cook, Pam, 23, 34n14
Cook, Ramsay, 254
Copland, Aaron, 41
Cotillard, Marion, 197
CRB Foundation, 249, 251
Creighton, Jane, 110, 121n9
"Cultural Memory in the Present" (book series), 22
Cunningham, Valentine, 41
Curtiz, Michael, 212, 223n3

Danielová, Růžena, 144–45, 155
Dark Knight, The, 198
Darwin, Charles, 27, 48; evolutionary theory co-evolving with film, 48, 49
Das, Santanu, 76
Days of Being Wild, 203
Death Proof, 235
de Gastyne, Marc, 186; *La Merveilleuse Vie de Jeanne d'Arc*, 186
De Gaulle, Genevieve, 137

Delacroix, Eugène, 288; *July 28: Liberty Leading the People*, 288
Delbo, Charlotte, 138
Deleuze, Gilles, 7–8, 12, 27, 45, 49, 197, 203, 206, 208, 209; *Cinema 1*, 7; *Cinema 2: The Time-Image*, 208; and fork(s) in time, 7; and movement-image, 7–8; and theory of cinema as conceptual practice, 197; and theory of repetition and difference, 44, 45; and time-image, 7–8
DeLillo, Don, 20; *White Noise*, 20
Deller, Jeremy, 292
Del Rio, Elena, 175
"Dem Bones," 105
Dening, Greg, 293
Derrida, Jacques, 17, 20, 24–25, 126, 180, 182, 190; *Archive Fever*, 17, 24; and idea of *toujours déjà*, 20
De Vito, Tony, 134
Diary of the Dead, 235
Díaz, Porfirio, 111
DiCaprio, Leonardo, 195, 198
Dickinson, Emily, 27, 40–41, 42; remediating of her works in music, visual media, 41; seriality in work of, 40–41; "Wild Nights—Wild Nights!," 41
Dickinson, Rod, 292
Dilthey, Wilhelm, 181; *Das Erlebnis und die Dichtung*, 181
Dirty Dozen, The, 237
"Don't Panic," 280
Dovzhenko, Alexander, 209
Draeger, Christoph, 292
DreamWorks, 268
Dubois, Philip, 183
Dworkin, Andrea, 132

Earle, Steve, 276
Eastwood, Clint, 287

Eco, Umberto, 44, 219, 222n3, 224n19; seriality in works of, 44
Eglinton, Earl of, 288
Elsaesser, Thomas, 294; "Subject Positions, Speaking Positions," 294
Emigrants, The, 57–61
Erikson, Kai, 74
Erll, Astrid, 4, 11, 16, 17–19; *Memory in Culture*, 4
Eternal Sunshine of the Spotless Mind, 11
Ezenberger, Ulrich, 155

Facebook, 262–63, 292
Far from Heaven, 228, 234; genre memory in, 234
Farkas, Helen, 132
Farrow, Mia, 232
Fassbender, Michael, 236
Fast, Omer, 33, 287–303, 304n1, 304n10; works of, 289–91, 294–96, 298–302
Fawcett, Millicent, 74
Feldberg, Gina, 139
Feyder, Jacques, 186
film: intermediality in, 230; premediation in, 21, 243; re-enactment in, 287; remediation in, 18, 19, 26, 30–32; representations of history in, 15–16, 33, 225–44; representations of memory in, 3, 4, 5, 7–11, 12, 15, 19, 21, 22, 26–27, 30–32, 33, 175–91, 195–210, 211–22, 225–44, 287–303. *See also* cinema
film: style and techniques related to memory, 217, 219, 290; flashbacks, 7, 9, 10, 21, 31, 182, 202, 207, 219, 224n17; and *la mode retro*, 226–27, 229–35, 243, 245n10
film studies, 7–8, 180; importance of Bergson's theories to, 7–8

First World War, 71–91, 101, 106, 165; feminist-pacifists in, 74, 88–90, 91; omission of women's experience in, 72–73; propaganda in, 72, 74–79, 80, 86, 87; suffrage movement in, 74, 83, 84; women's memorializing of, 28, 71–91. *See also* memorial activities, First World War
Flags of Our Fathers, 287
Fleming, Sir Sandford, 260; as subject of *Heritage Minutes*, 260
Florence, Mary Sargent, 28, 81; *Militarism versus Feminism*, 82
Foringer, Alonzo, 75, 76, 79
Forrest Gump, 227, 233, 234
Four Lights, 89
Fox, Terry, 264
Fox Television, 268
Freud, Sigmund, 5, 6, 13, 14, 24, 126, 137, 138, 169–70, 215, 218; influence of in cultural sphere, 13; and memory as key component of identity, 13; *Totem and Taboo*, 169
Frow, John, 94, 106, 108, 120n1; and cultural memory, 108; and importance of forgetting to memory, 94
Fuentes, Carlos, 29, 107–20; *The Old Gringo*, 107–20; and remediation of history, 29
Fussell, Paul, 165, 166
FX Network, 268

Gatlif, Tony, 145
Gay y Blasco, Paloma, 147
Geddes, Jennifer, 138
Genevoix, Simone, 186
Gifford, Douglas, 168
Gilliam, Terry, 30, 175–76, 182, 191n1
Gilmore, Leigh, 136
Gilroy, Paul, 95

Glendinning, Victoria, 138
Gluck, Gemma La Guardia, 137
Godville, 295–96; installation of, 296
Goethe, Johann Wolfgang von, 31, 219; *Die Wahlverwandtschaften*, 31, 219–20
Goffman, Erving, 128
Goldie, Peter, 62–63, 64–65; "Dramatic Irony, Narrative, and the External Perspective," 62; and external perspective, 62–64; and perspective shifting, 62–63, 64–65
Gong Li, 203
Good German, The, 32, 228, 237–41, 242–44; branding and marketing of, 234–35; confusion of fact and fiction in, 240; representations of Second World War in, 228, 229, 237–38, 239–41, 242–44; and rewriting of popular memory to expose historical truths, 229, 237–41, 242–44; use of documentary footage in, 228, 240
Grainge, Paul, 230; and genre memory, 230, 234
Graves, Matthew, 107
Graves, Robert, 78, 169, 170; *Goodbye to All That*, 78; *The White Goddess*, 169
Grayzel, Susan R., 80
Great Escape, The, 237
Greengrass, Paul, 9
Grese, Irma, 129
Grindhouse, 235
Grobbel, Michaela, 147, 148, 152, 153, 155
Grusin, Richard, 19–21, 22, 290; and "double logic" of remediation 289
Guerin, Frances, 284
Guevera, Che, 240
Gunn, John, 167

Gunn, Neil, 30, 161–72; *The Atom of Delight*, 30, 163–68, 169, 170, 172; *Highland River*, 166–67; *Morning Tide*, 167
Gypsy. *See* Roma

Halbwachs, Maurice, 14, 18, 105, 181; and collective memory, 14–15, 18, 105, 181
Hamlet, 184, 190
Hancock, Ian, 147, 149
Hanks, Tom, 233
Hart, Francis Russell, 164
Hart, John Mason, 114; *Revolutionary Mexico*, 114
Haynes, Todd, 228, 234, 240
Hearst, William Randolph, 108, 114
Hegel, Georg Wilhelm Friedrich, 181, 184, 187
Heidegger, Martin, 13; *The Concept of Time*, 13
Helmuth, Chalene, 108–9
Henreid, Paul, 239
Herbermann, Nanda, 137
heritage, 17, 251–52; distinct from history, 251–52
Heritage Minutes, 32, 249–66; "Baldwin and LaFontaine," 258–59; "Emily Carr," 259–60; historical accuracy of, 257, 265; idea of heritage in, 252–53, 264; and "Make Your Own Minute" program, 264; and "Mock Minutes," 261–62; as part of Canadian collective (cultural) memory project (*lieux de mémoire*), 32, 249, 250–51, 257, 260–65, 266; regionalism in, 32, 259–60; relationship between Quebec and rest of Canada in, 32, 258–59, 265; "Sir Sandford Fleming," 260; use of nationalistic nostalgia in, 253, 258–60, 264,

265; using past for purposes of present, 250–51, 252, 258–60, 265, 266, 266n1
Herrigel, Eugen, 170; *Zen in the Art of Archery*, 170
Higgonet, Margaret R., 75, 81, 89; "The Double Helix," 75; "The Great War and Female Elegy," 89
Hill, Lawrence, 101; *The Book of Negroes*, 101, 104
Himmler, Heinrich, 127, 149
Hirsch, Marianne, 13, 27, 34n9, 51–65, 101; and "post-memory," 13, 15, 16, 27, 101
Historica Foundation, 249, 260, 261, 263, 264
history: mediations of, 180, 288, 292; relation of to memory, 117, 175–91; representations of in film, 225–44; rewritten to appeal to popular taste, 235–37
Hitchcock, Alfred, 7–8, 34n4, 182, 190, 192n1, 196, 204, 209; Freudian influence on, 13
Hitler, Adolf, 125, 132, 133, 236
Hodgkin, Katherine, 254; *Contested Pasts*, 254
Hoffman, Martin, 62
Hogg, James, 171; *The Private Memoirs and Confessions of a Justified Sinner*, 171
Holocaust, 15–16, 29, 125–39, 146, 240, 241; ethical responses to, 138; experience of Roma and Sinti in, 143–58 (*see also Porrajmos*); feminist scholarship of, 137; and Holocaust industry, 15–16; and postmemory, 51, 52, 56, 57, 58; reflected in film, 15, 33, 235–37, 241–44, 290–92, 294; reflected in literature, life writing, 16, 29, 131–39; remediation of, 290; and resistance of memory, 125–39. *See also* Braunsteiner, Hermine
Home Box Office (HBO), 269, 276, 277, 278, 279
Hong Kong, 27, 199–200, 202, 204; cinema of, 199
Horowitz, Sara, 137
Hoskins, Andrew, 16–17, 21–22, 24, 25; and "digital network memory," 21–22
Huerta, General Victoriano, 111, 112
Hughes, Mrs. E.A., 78
Hunter, Holly, 268
Hurricane Katrina (2005), 269, 275, 282–83; memorializing of, 269, 275–76, 280, 281–84, 284n5
Hutcheon, Linda, 28, 109, 120n2, 253, 257, 262; *A Poetics of Postmodernism*, 109
Huyghe, Pierre, 292
Huyssen, Andreas, 33, 153; and counter-memory, 153–54; and hypertrophy of memory, 33, 292

identity, 23–24, 83, 88, 195, 196, 210: influence of digital technologies on, 4: national, 32, 110, 113, 118–19, 148, 158, 250, 251, 253, 254–57, 259, 261, 262, 265–66, 296; politics of, 14–15, 30, 45, 152; relation of memory to, 4, 5, 13, 27, 54; in Roma *Porrajmos*, 143–58
I'm Not There, 228, 234, 240
Inception, 195–98, 200, 203, 204, 208–10; and collective memory, 201, 207; genre conventions in, 198, 200, 202, 209; as memory film, 209–10; reduplication and repetition in, 197, 206–8; science fiction elements in, 200–201
Incredibles, The, 235

Inglourious Basterds, 32, 228, 231, 235–37, 239, 241–44; genre memory in, 231; political agenda in, 229; representations of Second World War in, 228, 241–44; and rewriting of history to appea to popular taste, 235–37, 242
In Search of Lost Time (Proust), 5–6; *Swann's Way*, 5–6
intermediality, 14, 18, 19, 24, 25, 40; in film, 230
International Congress of Women (1915), 83
In the Mood for Love, 197, 199, 203, 209
Irigaray, Luce, 44; seriality in works of, 44

Jacobs, Gilles, 177
James, Henry, 27, 40, 41–42; portraiture in works of, 42, 43, 50n5
Jameson, Frederic, 31, 225–30, 232, 244
JanMohamed, Abdul R., 112; "The Economy of Manichean Allegory," 112
Je t'aime je t'aime, 209
Jetée, La, 30, 175–91, 191n1, 195, 196–98, 202; commentary in, 183, 184; history and memory in, 179–84; memory and photography in, 185; memory and trauma in, 185–87; temporality in, 175, 176, 182, 184, 191; voluntary and involuntary memory in, 187–91
JFK, 227, 233, 234
John, Dr., 276
Joyce, James, 13
Jung, Carl, 171, 181
Jus Suffragii, 86
Justin, Eva, 151, 157

Kaczynski, David, 301

Kaczynski, Ted, 301
Kadar, Marlene, 145
Kafka, Franz, 184
Kalderash, 144, 152. *See also* Roma
Kamester, Margaret, 91
Kecht, Maria-Regina, 146
Khan, Nosheen, 80
Kidd, Kenneth, 90
Kidman, Nicole, 42
Kierkegaard, Søren, 206
Kilbourn, Russell, 6, 22, 196, 208, 227–28; and "madeleine object," 6
Kimura, Takuya, 202
King, Rosemary A., 113, 118
King, Thomas, 96; *Truth and Bright Water*, 96
Kirchner, Leon, 41
Klages, Ludwig, 181
"Knock on Wood," 220
Kogawa, Joy, 15; *Obasan*, 15
Koonz, Claudia, 133
Kracauer, Siegfried, 218, 223n15
Kraków (Poland), 289, 291, 292; ghetto, 290
Krause, Johanna, 137
Kruger, Diane, 236

Lacan, Jacques, 185
LaCapra, Dominick, 146
Lächert, Hildegard, 129
Lady from Shanghai, The, 207
LaFontaine, Louis-Hippolyte, 258–59
La Motte, Ellen N., 72, 89; "Backwash of War," 72
Landsberg, Alison, 13, 104, 232, 233, 296–97, 299; and prosthetic memory, 13, 15, 16, 104, 296–97
Langlois, Henri, 177
Lanzmann, Claude, 290
L'Arrivée d'un train à La Ciotat, 206
Last Picture Show, The, 225, 230, 231
Last Year at Marienbad, 196–97, 203, 207, 208

Latcho Drom, 145
Lau, Carina, 203
Laub, Dori, 89
Laurent, Mélanie, 235
Lawlor, Nuala, 259
Lawrence, Jacob, 102; "Shipping Out" ("War Series"), 102
Lear, Norman, 278; television sitcoms created by, 278
Leary, Denis, 268, 277
Lee, Sky, 97; *Disappearing Moon Café*, 97
Lefebvre, Henri, 270
Le Goff, Jacques, 179–80, 251
Leighton, Roland, 75–76, 80–81
Lejeune, Philippe, 164; and "autobiographical contract," 164
Lelyveld, Joseph, 132
Lemon, Alaina, 145, 148, 156
Leo, Melissa, 282
Leung, Tony, 195
Levinas, Emmanuel, 24, 187; and Levinasian ethics, 86
Lewis-Kraus, Gideon, 295
Lewy, Guenter, 146, 149
Leys, Ruth, 12
life writing (auto/biography). See autobiography
L'Image, 186
literature, 56–61, 63–65, 93–106, 107–20; function of memory in, 161–72; and historical fiction, 107, 108–9, 118; as mode of memory, 26–27; modernist, 13, 161; poetry, 40–41, 44, 93–94, 103, 104; and postmemory, 56–61, 63–65; of women's mourning, 71–73, 80–90, 91. See also autobiography
literature, Canadian, 94, 96; Chinese Canadian authors in, 96, 97; First Nations authors in, 96–97
literature, Scottish, 164, 171

Locke, John, 54
Long, Jonathan, 24
Lovara, 144, 152. See also Roma
Luce, William, 41; *The Belle of Amherst*, 41
Luhmann, Niklas, 27, 47–48; *Die Realität der Massenmedien*, 47
Lumière brothers, 206
Lupton, Catherine, 186
Lütticken, Sven, 287, 288

Macbeth, 184
MacKinnon, Catherine, 132
Maguire, Tobey, 238
Makulová, Margita, 145
Marcus, Laura, 162, 164; *Auto/Biographical Discourses*, 162
Margolian, Howard, 131, 135; *Unauthorized Entry*, 135
Marker, Chris, 30, 175, 176, 184, 185, 186, 187, 189, 196; *Immemory*, 186
Marshall, Catherine, 28, 72, 81, 85, 86, 88, 91; "Women and War," 85
Martin, Stewart, 16
Martin-Jones, David, 7–10
Marx, Karl, 93, 96, 99, 104; *The Eighteenth Brumaire of Louis Bonaparte*, 93, 96
Maus (Spiegelman), 52
McCalman, Iain, 289
mediation, 13, 16, 17, 18, 20, 22, 23–24, 25, 26, 29, 302; in autobiographical texts, 30, 162, 165; in film, 31, 187, 190, 225–28, 232, 240, 242, 302; of identity, 23–24; in literature, 94, 96, 97, 99, 101, 102, 103–5, 107–20; in television, 32–33; related to trauma, 267, 272, 293; through seriality, 27, 37–49
Meek, Allan, 125
Memento, 19

memorials and memorializing, 28, 32–33, 53, 95, 97, 101, 267–84; collective authorship of, 275–76, 278; defined, 270–71; distinguished from monuments, 267, 269–71; role of fantasy in, 268, 275, 284; at site of former World Trade Center, 272, 275. *See also* commemoration; memorials First World War

memorials, First World War, 71–91; and alternative representations of female bereavement, 81–91; and anticipatory mourning, 74; in Australia, 80; in Britain, 71–91; in Canada, 80; constraints on women's, 71–74, 79–91; feminist perspective on, 82–85, 91; and overcoming of national interests, 86–87; and patriotism, 74, 75, 78–81, 87; in U.S., 80; at Verdun (France), 101

memory: accuracy as component of, 53–54, 65n3; and amnesty, 135; artificial vs. "natural," 3–4, 13, 14, 23; in cultural and media studies vs. cognitive sciences, 37–49; ethical dimension of, 25, 53–54, 71, 90–91; false, 16, 17; and film, cinema, 19, 30, 31, 195–210, 212, 216–17, 228, 232–33 (*see also* memory films); and forgetting, 39, 41, 45–46, 47, 94, 107–8, 126, 211, 214–18; and history, 23, 26, 30, 117, 175–91; and identity, 4, 5, 13, 27, 54, 158, 195; industries of, infrastructure, 15, 53, 182; "intrinsic validation" of, 166–68; and literature, 26–27, 40–41, 44, 71–73, 80–90, 91, 93–94, 103, 104, 107, 108–9, 118, 161–72; material conditions of, 24; and melodrama, 218–19; and music, 213–14, 215, 219, 223n7; philosophy of, 52–53, 57, 201; and photography, 185, 186, 189; political readings of, 104–5; post-prosthetic, 237, 244; prosthetic, 13, 15, 16, 23, 104, 228–29, 231, 232, 233, 243; public vs. private, 53; repressed, 126, 143, 154, 186; resistance to, 125, 132–34, 135–38; serving present and future more than past, 23, 45–46, 49, 258, 261; silenced or suppressed, 153–54, 261; traces, 24, 46, 94, 126, 148, 176, 181, 182, 186, 188, 281; and trauma, 11, 185–87; voluntary vs. involuntary, 5–6, 30, 187–89

memory, collective, 14–15, 16, 18, 23, 53, 90, 105, 108–9, 117, 120, 163, 180, 181, 242, 249, 254, 301; communicative vs. cultural, 18; defined, 250; importance of fantasy to, 300; importance of re-enactment to, 287, 292–93, 300; literalized in *Inception*, 201, 207; role of television and video in, 32. *See also* memory, cultural

memory, cultural, 15, 17–18, 27, 32, 33, 43, 72, 102, 107, 108, 162, 163, 250–51, 260, 279, 288, 290; and film, 19, 297, 300, 301; and history, 117; and re-enactment, 292; relationship of seriality to, 43. *See also* memory, collective

memory, metaphors for, 3–4, 46–47, 49, 94, 201, 208; archive, 24–25, 52–53, 281; bones, 98; mental palace, 3; storage, 3, 4, 94, 95; system of inscription, 3

memory films, 19, 31, 195–210; history of, 196–98, 209–10; memory-*reflexive* vs. memory-*productive*,

19; repetition in, 198; techniques in, 201, 202, 204
memory-image, 10, 11, 198, 204, 207, 217, 219
memory studies, 3–33, 267; critical readings in, 27–33; interdisciplinary nature of, 5, 17, 25–26; major developments in, 4–33; memory effects, 25–26; memory theory, main strands of, 5; related to literature and film, 3–33; remediation and premediation in, 18–24; transdisciplinary research in, 38, 43
Memory Studies, 17, 25–26
Mendelssohn, Felix, 289
Mettbach-Höllenreiner family, 151, 158
Mexico, 27, 29, 107–20; Euro-American constructions of, 109–20; and remediation of Mexican history, 107–20
Micarelli, Lucia, 276
Michaux, Henri, 177
Middle Passage. *See* slavery
Mierzewska, Hanna, 129
Miles, Malcolm, 270
Milk, 234
Miller, Nancy, 268
Milton, Sybil, 133
Minority Report, 21
mnemic hallucination, 9
mnemotechniques, 189–90
modernism, 20, 40, 41, 44, 45, 48, 49, 72, 161, 163–68
Monet, Claude, 44; seriality in works of, 44
monuments, 267, 269; defined, 269–70; distinguished from memorials, 267, 269–71
Morrison, Jack, 128
Morrison, Toni, 15, 28, 95, 96, 143, 144; *Beloved*, 15, 28, 143; *Playing in the Dark*, 103
Morton, Desmond, 251
mourning: ethical dimension of, 86, 88, 90; and melancholia, 86; and witnessing, 72, 86, 87, 89
MTM productions, 278; television shows created by, 278
Muhle, Maria, 298
Muir, Edwin, 171; *Scott and Scotland*, 171
Murphy, Cillian, 198

Nabokov, Vladimir, 5
Narkiewicz-Jokli, Hanna, 132
nationalism, 254–55, 257, 264; Canadian, in *Heritage Minutes*, 258–59, 260, 261, 264, 265
Nazis, 127, 131, 133, 134–35, 137, 146, 148–49, 151, 157, 158, 232, 235, 236, 237, 240–41, 242; antifeminist principles of, 134; and Austrian amnesty (1957), 134–35; and occupation of Paris, Second World War, 211, 212, 217, 224n17
Nietzsche, Friedrich, 185, 206, 288
Nolan, Christopher, 31, 195, 198, 201
Nora, Pierre, 15, 180, 191, 251, 266n1, 281; and "sites of memory" (*lieux de mémoire*), 15, 251, 266n1
nostalgia, 17, 23, 26, 31, 186, 253; in film, 32, 225–27, 229–34, 238–39; and hyper-histories, 32, 228; nationalistic, 253, 258–60
nostalgia films, 225–27, 229–34; techniques used in, 230–32, 233, 234, 238–39; use of soundtrack in, 230, 238

Oates, Joyce Carol, 41; "EDickinson-RepliLuxe," 41

Odin, Roger, 183
Ogden, C.K., 28, 72, 81, 85, 86, 87, 89, 91; *Militarism versus Feminism*, 82, 91; "Women's Prerogative," 85
Oklahoma City bombing (1995), 32, 268; memorializing of, 268, 278, 280
Old Gringo, The (Fuentes), 107–20; and Euro-American constructions of Mexico, 109–20
Oliveira, Michael, 93
Oliver, Christian, 238
Oliver, Kelly, 87
Olney, James, 163
Osborne, Brian, 139
Ossuaries (Brand), 93–106; metaphors for memory in, 97, 98–99; as response to slavery, 95–96; as work about memory, 95, 96–98, 99–101, 102–6
Ouditt, Sharon, 72, 78, 81

Page, Ellen, 201
Page, Joy, 220
Pankhurst, Adela, 74
Pankhurst, Christabel, 74
Pankhurst, Emmeline, 74
Pankhurst, Sylvia, 73, 74
Paris (France), 211, 212, 217, 221; Catacombs, 101
Passerini, Luisa, 261
Paz, Octavio, 113; "Literatura de Fundación," 113; "Re/Visions: Mural Painting," 113
Pearson, Lester B., 255
Pence, Jeffrey, 6, 16; and "redemptive" potential of memory, 6
Penley, Constance, 184
Peters, Erin, 32
Philip, M. Nourbese, 101; *Zong!* 101, 104

photograms, cinematic, 182–83, 188, 189
photography, 13, 16, 21, 22, 30, 42, 43, 44, 51, 158, 252, 289, 290; and film, 196, 208, 230; in *La Jetée*, 176, 182–83, 186, 187, 188–89; and memory, 185, 186, 189; role of in postmemory, 56, 59, 60
Picasso, Pablo, 38
Pick, J.B., 164
Pickering, Paul A., 289
Pitt, Brad, 179
Planet Terror, 235
Plato, 13, 24, 147, 177, 206; and anamnesis, 206
Polanski, Roman, 231
Porrajmos (Roma and Sinti Holocaust), 143–58; assertion of identity in defiance of, 145; reasons for scarce Roma memorializing of, 146–47, 148–58; Roma blamed for own suffering in, 149–51; uniting Roma culture, 152. *See also* Roma
Portrait of a Lady, The (film), 42
postmemory, 13, 15, 16, 51–65, 101; accuracy and witnessing in, 52–54, 57–60, 61, 65; and appropriation objection, 55–56; and Butler objection, 54–55; dangers and limitations of, 52, 54–56, 62; defined, 51, 65; and empathy, 55–56, 60, 61–62
postmodernism, 161, 163–68, 227
Pratt, Mary Louise, 118
premediation, 17, 18–24, 243; in memory studies, 19–21, 22
Prince, 39
propaganda, First World War, 72, 74–79, 76, 77, 80, 86, 87; Christian imagery in, 75–76, 76, 78;

and patriotism, 75; representations of femininity in, 74–79, 76, 77
Proust, Marcel, 5–6, 163, 178, 182, 187, 188, 189, 190, 199, 215; *In Search of Lost Time*, 5–6, 199; and voluntary vs. involuntary memory, 5–6

Rabinowitz, Dorothy, 129
Radstone, Susannah, 254; *Contested Pasts*, 254
Rains, Claude, 220
Ramaci, Lisa, 301
Rao, Dileep, 201
Rau, Johannes, 127
Rauca, Helmut, 134, 135
RCMP, 134
Rechniewski, Elizabeth, 107
Red Cross (American), 75, 76
re-enactment, historical, 17, 33, 287–303; addressing trauma, 292–95, 300, 301; and analogy, 295, 296, 302; in the arts, 288–89; and challenge to memory, history, 292–94; collaborative nature of, 300–302; and cultural, collective memory, 288, 290, 292, 300–302; and engagement, 297, 299, 300; and equivalence, 295–96; in film and television, 287, 289; history of, 288–89; and mediation, re-mediation of memory, history, 33, 288, 289–93, 302; and realism, authenticity, 289, 298, 299, 302; in works of Omer Fast, 287–303
re-enactors, 291; and experience of analogy, 295, 296; and experience of equivalence, 295–96
remediation, 14, 17, 18–24, 26, 27, 37, 38; defined, 18; in film (cinema), 18, 19, 26, 30–32; of Holocaust, 290; in literature, 13, 18, 28–29, 94, 105, 107–20; related to trauma, 267; through seriality, 37–49; in television, video, 32–33, 267, 273, 275–84
rememory, 143–44, 153, 155, 157; defined, 143
Rescue Me, 268, 277, 278, 280–81; episodic structure in, 274–75; "Guts" (pilot episode), 280–81; and memorializing of attacks on World Trade Center (2001), 268–69, 273–75, 278, 280–81; as "quality television," 269; seriality in, 273–74
Resnais, Alain, 196, 203, 207, 209
Reyes, Adelaida, 155
Ricciardi, Alessia, 71
Richards, Janet Radcliffe, 82
Rick Mercer Report, The, 261
Ricoeur, Paul, 135
Riegler, Roxane, 153–54
Ritter, Dr., Robert, 149, 151, 157
Rodal, Alti, 131, 134; *Nazi War Criminals in Canada*, 134
Rodowick, David, 175
Roma people, 29–30, 143–58; and assertion of identity, 145–46, 148, 150, 153, 156, 158; autobiographical writing of, 147, 148, 152–57; classification of by Nazis, 148–49, 157; cultural taboos of, 151, 158; and "Gypsiness," 145; and importance of family continuity, 156–57; racial stigmatizing of, 150–51; and reasons for scarce memorializing of *Porrajmos*, 143–58; trauma suffered by, 145–46, 151, 152, 154, 156. *See also Porrajmos*
Rose, Steven, 14
Rosenberg, Otto, 147, 148, 150, 151, 152, 155–57; *Das Brennglas* (*A Gypsy in Auschwitz*), 155–57

Rosenberg, Sharon, 139
Rosenhaft, Eve, 157
Roudometof, Victor, 158
Rousseau, Jean-Jacques, 164; *Confessions*, 164
Royal Canadian Air Farce, The, 261
Royal Commission on Bilingualism and Biculturalism, 255
Ruddick, Sara, 83, 87; "rationality of care," 87
Ruffins, Kermit, 276
Rushton, Steve, 292–93
Russell-Brown, Sheelagh, 29–30
Ryan, Russell, 127, 130–31, 132, 139n3

Samuel, Raphael, 251–52, 253, 260; *Theatres of Memory*, 251
Sandlos, Karen, 75
Sans Soleil, 175, 193n22
Sarasin, Philipp, 48
Saunders, Max, 161–62; and "memory cultures," 161–62
Saving Grace, 268, 277, 278, 280; memorializing of Oklahoma City bombing (1995), 268, 278, 280; as "quality television," 269; redemption in, 268
Saving Private Ryan, 19, 237, 287
Sayner, Joanne, 126
Schefer, Jean-Louis, 182, 183, 184
Schiano, Victor, 134
Schindler's List, 19, 33, 289–90, 291, 292, 297, 304n6, 305n11
Schreiner, Olive, 83; *Women and Labour*, 83–84
Scofield, Gregory, 96; *Singing Home the Bones*, 96
Scott, Jill, 126, 132; *A Poetics of Forgiveness*, 132
Scott, Joan W., 73
Sebald, W.G., 5, 16, 27, 52, 65; *Austerlitz*, 57–61, 63; and controversial inclusion in postmemory genre, 16, 27, 52, 56–61, 63–65; *The Emigrants*, 57–61, 63–64
Second World War, 15, 31, 145, 212; "Gypsies" in, 146, 151; internment of Japanese Americans, Canadians during, 15; and Nazi occupation of Paris, 211, 212, 217, 224n17; as represented in *Inglourious Basterds*, 228, 229, 236–37, 241–44; as represented in *The Good German*, 228, 229, 237–38, 239–41, 242–44. *See also* Holocaust; *Porrajmos*
Second World War concentration camps: Auschwitz (Poland), 144–45, 146, 147, 150, 154, 155, 158, 290; Bergen-Belsen (Germany), 146, 150, 153, 154; Berlin-Marzahn (Germany), 150, 156, 157; Camp Uckermark (Ravensbrück, Germany), 128; Majdanek (Poland), 127, 129, 134; Mauthausen (Austria), 150; Płaszów (Poland), 290; Ravensbrück (Germany), 29, 127, 128, 129, 132, 133, 137, 150, 154; Sachsenhausen (Germany), 133
seriality, 37–49; defined, 38; in literary texts, 44; in modernism, 44; as operational mechanism of mass media, 47, 49; in photography, cinema, television, 39, 44, 45, 272–74; significance of to memory and remediation, 37–49; significance of to memory research, 44–49; and technologies of reproduction, 44, 48
Shaw, Dr. Anna Howard, 83
Shoah, 290
Simon, David, 269, 275, 276, 277

Simpsons, The, 42
Singer, Wolf, 46
Singer, Yvonne, 139
Sinha, Amresh, 5, 30
Sinti. *See* Roma
Sirk, Douglas, 234
Sisson, Larry, 168–70
slavery (Middle Passage), 94, 95–96, 97, 101, 102, 105, 106, 143; and Black diaspora, 94, 98, 100, 103, 105
Smith, G. Gregory, 171; and "Caledonian Antisyzygy," 171
Soderbergh, Steven, 32, 228, 237, 238–39, 240, 241
Sonneman, Toby, 146, 148, 150, 151, 152, 156–57, 158; *Shared Sorrows*, 148
Sony Pictures Television, 268
Spence, Alan, 164
Spiegelman, Art, 52, 57; *Maus*, 52
Spielberg, Steven, 21, 287, 304n6
Spielberg's List, 33, 289–91, 294–95, 302
Spivak, Gayatari Chakravorty, 83
Stanley, Liz, 137–38
Star Wars, 225
Stein, Gertrude, 27, 38–39, 40, 41, 42, 48, 49; "If I Told Him: A Completed Portrait of Picasso," 48; "Picasso," 38; "Portraits and Repetition," 39, 41, 44; and seriality (insistence), 38–39, 41, 44
Stevenson, Robert Louis, 171; *The Strange Case of Dr. Jekyll and Mr. Hyde*, 171
Stewart, James, 204
Stewart, Michael, 147
Stojka, Ceija, 147, 148, 152–55, 156, 157; autobiography of, 152–54, 155
Stojka, Karl, 145, 147

Storey, John, 15; and "memory industries," 15
Stowe, Madeleine, 179
Sturken, Marita, 17, 250, 293, 300, 301; *Tourists of History*, 293
Sturtevant, Elaine, 44; seriality in works of, 44
Swales, Martin, 16
Swanwick, Helena, 28, 81, 84

Talk Show, 300–302
Tarantino, Quentin, 32, 236, 237, 242
technologies: and "digital network memory," 21–22, 45; impact of new, 18, 20, 21–22, 42–43, 45; impact of on memory, 3–4, 18, 21–23, 24–25; of reproduction, 27, 44, 45, 48, 188; and social networking sites, 292
television, 267–84; and creation of memorial spaces, 267–84; episodic structure in, 274–75; and flow, 271; hyperreality in, 278; melodrama in, 275, 277; "quality," 269, 273, 278–79; role of in mediation and remediation, 267, 275–76, 277, 279–80; seriality in, 272–74; studies, 271, 272–73
Teo, Stephen, 199
Terdimann, Richard, 163; and "memory crisis," 163
This Hour Has 22 Minutes, 261
Thompson, Jack, 238
Thompson, John Herd, 265
TNT Network, 268
Total Recall, 19
Toussaint, Alain, 276
Towne, Robert, 231
Trainor, James, 302
trauma, 11–13, 16, 27, 30, 88, 90–91, 145, 267–84; importance

of witnessing and translation in, 267–68, 279, 281–83, 284; mediation and remediation of, 267–84, 293; memorializing of, 32–33, 267–84; and postmemory, 27, 51, 52, 55–56, 63, 65; relation of to memory, 11, 27, 185–87; role of fantasy in working through, 268, 275, 284; theory and studies, 11–13, 16, 28, 30, 74, 90, 267, 279

Treme, 268, 269, 275–76, 277, 279, 280, 281–84, 284n5; and memorializing of Hurricane Katrina (2005), 269, 275–76, 280, 281–84, 284n5; as "quality television," 269, 278; redemption in, 269, 280

Tristram Shandy: A Cock and Bull Story, 303

Trudeau, Pierre, 32, 251, 255, 256; and multiculturalism policy, 32, 251, 255, 256–57

Truman, Harry, 241

Turim, Maureen, 195, 202, 224n17; *Flashbacks in Film*, 195, 202

Turner, Frederick Jackson, 109; "The Significance of the Frontier in American History," 109

12 Monkeys, 175, 178–79, 182, 183–84, 187, 188, 190, 191, 191n1; history and memory in, 179–84; memory and photography in, 185; memory and trauma in, 185–87; voluntary and involuntary memory in, 187–91

20th Century Fox Home Entertainment, 268

2046, 195–200, 201–5, 208, 209–10; exploration of memory in, 201; genre conventions in, 198–200, 209; as memory film, 209–210; reduplication and repetition in, 197, 204–5; science fiction elements in, 200, 201, 203

Umansky, Lauri, 83

United States, 20, 27, 29; and collective memory of expansion, 108–9, 111, 120n8, 122n10; and U.S.–Mexican relations, 29, 111, 112–13, 120; U.S. State Department, 129

Uthco, T.R., and Ant Farm, 292

van Baar, Huub, 146, 152

van Delder, Maarten, 113, 114; *Carlos Fuentes, Mexico, and Modernity*, 113

Van Dijck, José, 11, 22, 25, 34n3; *Mediated Memories in the Digital Age*, 22

Vellacott, Jo, 91

Vertigo, 7–8, 9, 10, *10*, 34n4, 183, 190, 192n1, 196–97, 203, 204, 209

Villa, Pancho, 108

Vincent, Steven, 301

von Braun, Werner, 240

Wächter, Hartmut, 150

Walker, Janet, 281–82, 284; and "disremembering," 284

Walker, Nancy, 90

Waltz, Christoph, 235

Warhol, Andy, 44; seriality in works of, 44

Watkins, Peter, 292

Webb, Walter Prescott, 116, 122n10

Weissman, Gary, 54–55

Wenders, Wim, 208

Whitaker, Reg, 131

White, Kenneth, 164; *Atoms of Delight* (haiku anthology), 164

Wiesenthal, Simon, 137, 139n3

Wild Nights: Stories about the Last Days of Poe, Dickinson, Twain, James, and Hemingway, 41
Williams, Daryl, 282
Williams, Raymond, 99
Willis, Bruce, 178, 187
Wills, David, 104; *Prosthesis*, 104
Wilson, Dooley, 213
Wilson, Woodrow, 108, 111, 114
Winfrey, Oprah, 302
Winter, Jay, 90
Winterbottom, Michael, 303
Wire, The, 269, 275
witnessing, 17, 27, 72, 118, 184–85, 289, 291; in postmemory, 52–54, 57–60, 61, 65; in trauma studies, 267–68, 279, 281–83, 284
Wolf, Werner, 42
Women's Peace Party (U.S.), 83, 89
Wong, Faye, 204, 205
Wong Kar-Wai, 31, 195, 197, 199–200, 204, 205, 209

Woolf, Virginia, 13, 89; *Jacob's Room*, 89
Wordsworth, William, 5
World Trade Center, terrorist attacks on (2001), 95, 126, 268–69, 273, 275, 281, 293; impact of on culture, 4, 16, 17, 20; memorializing of, 32, 268, 272, 273–75, 277, 278, 280–81, 293; and premediation, 20; re-enactment used in mediation of, 293

Zapato, Emiliano, 108
Zatzman, Belarie, 139
Zelig, 32, 227, 231–33, 234
Zelizer, Barbie, 137, 251
Zhang Ziyi, 205
Ziarek, Ewa, 86; "Kristeva and Levinas," 86
Zodiac, 234
Zvenigora, 209

www.ingramcontent.com/pod-product-compliance
Lightning Source LLC
Chambersburg PA
CBHW072146070526
44585CB00015B/1021